"One of the most thorough works on the history and evolution of the Chinese language, Dong's *A History of the Chinese Language* is a must for anyone studying any form of the language. Covering a range of topics in historical and contemporary linguistics, Dong deftly explains even the most complex linguistic theory in readily accessible ways and has something for anyone from a seasoned linguist to a casual learner."

Dr. Justin Winslett, The University of Sheffield, UK

"This 2nd edition preserves the previous edition's success in condensing the vast landscape of the historical development of Chinese languages into a brief, but comprehensive single volume. Reflecting on recent scholarship and new developments in the field, it carefully synthesizes Chinese linguistic facts, non-controversial research accomplishments, and fundamental facts about the history of the Chinese language, woven together with captivating stories and legends. It lays a solid foundation for readers and equips them for further exploration of the field, while proving to be a fascinating, engaging, and absorbing read in itself."

Song Jiang, Associate Professor,
The University of Hawai'i at Mānoa, USA

# A History of the Chinese Language

*A History of the Chinese Language* provides a comprehensive introduction to the historical development of the Chinese language from its Proto-Sino-Tibetan roots in prehistoric times to Modern Standard Chinese. Taking a highly accessible and balanced approach, it presents a chronological survey of the various stages of the Chinese language, covering key aspects such as phonology, syntax, and semantics.

The second edition presents a revised and updated version that reflects recent scholarship in Chinese historical linguistics and new developments in related disciplines.

Features include:

- Coverage of the major historical stages in Chinese language development, such as Old Chinese, Middle Chinese, Early Modern Chinese, and Modern Standard Chinese.
- Treatment of core linguistic aspects of the Chinese language, including phonological changes, grammatical development, lexical evolution, vernacular writing, the Chinese writing system, and Chinese dialects.
- Inclusion of authentic Chinese texts throughout the book, presented within a rigorous framework of linguistic analysis to help students to build up critical and evaluative skills and acquire valuable cultural knowledge.
- Integration of materials from different disciplines, such as archaeology, genetics, history, and sociolinguistics, to highlight the cultural and social background of each period of the language.

Written by a highly experienced instructor, *A History of the Chinese Language* will be an essential resource for students of Chinese language and linguistics and for anyone interested in the history and culture of China.

**Hongyuan Dong** is Associate Professor of Chinese Language and Linguistics in the Department of East Asian Languages & Literatures at the George Washington University. He is the author of *Semantics of Chinese Questions: An Interface Approach* (Routledge 2019).

# A History of the Chinese Language

## Second Edition

**Hongyuan Dong**

Routledge
Taylor & Francis Group

LONDON AND NEW YORK

Second edition published 2021
by Routledge
2 Park Square, Milton Park, Abingdon, Oxon, OX14 4RN

and by Routledge
52 Vanderbilt Avenue, New York, NY 10017

*Routledge is an imprint of the Taylor & Francis Group, an informa business*

First edition published by Routledge 2014

*British Library Cataloguing-in-Publication Data*
A catalogue record for this book is available from the British Library

*Library of Congress Cataloging-in-Publication Data*
Names: Dong, Hongyuan, 1976– author.
Title: A history of the Chinese language / Hongyuan Dong.
Description: Second edition. | Abingdon, Oxon ; New York, NY :
    Routledge, 2021. | Includes bibliographical references and index.
Identifiers: LCCN 2020031039 (print) | LCCN 2020031040 (ebook) |
    ISBN 9780367209841 (hardback) | ISBN 9780367209858 (paperback) |
    ISBN 9780429264665 (ebook)
Subjects: LCSH: Chinese language—History. | China—Languages—History. |
    Language and culture—China. | Historical linguistics—China.
Classification: LCC PL1075 .D64 2021 (print) | LCC PL1075 (ebook) |
    DDC 495.1—dc23
LC record available at https://lccn.loc.gov/2020031039
LC ebook record available at https://lccn.loc.gov/2020031040

ISBN: 978-0-367-20984-1 (hbk)
ISBN: 978-0-367-20985-8 (pbk)
ISBN: 978-0-429-26466-5 (ebk)

Typeset in Times New Roman
by Apex CoVantage, LLC

# Contents

# Tables

# Figures

# Syntax labels

| | |
|---|---|
| CL | classifier or measure word |
| COMP | complement marker |
| DUR | durative aspect marker |
| EXP | experiential aspect marker |
| MOD | marker of modifier |
| NEG | negator |
| NOM | nominalizer |
| PAR | grammatical particle |
| PASS | passive marker |
| PERF | perfective aspect marker |
| POL | polite form |
| POSS | possessive case marker or particle |
| PROG | progressive aspect marker |
| QUES | question particle |
| SUBJ | subject marker |
| TOP | topic marker |

# Preface to the second edition

With the many new developments in the field of Chinese historical linguistics in the past six years, it is now time for an updated edition of this book. Based on suggestions from published reviews and feedback from readers and students, this second edition contains major revisions and new additions, some of which are as follows.

Chapter 2 includes some discussion of recent research on the primary branching and time depth of the Sino-Tibetan language family using Bayesian inference on basic vocabulary. Such methodological innovations can further strengthen conclusions reached from various disciplinary perspectives, such as via comparative analysis in historical linguistics, archaeological findings of ancient cultures, and human population genetics. Chapter 3 compares Li's (1971) reconstruction of Old Chinese with the new system from Baxter and Sagart (2014). Major differences between the two systems are discussed. New methods and main features of the Baxter-Sagart reconstruction are introduced so that readers can appreciate the new advances in the field and understand the notations in the Baxter-Sagart system. More comparisons between Old Chinese and Middle Chinese are also made. Chapter 4 is updated with important traditional Chinese phonological concepts. The phonological developments from Old Chinese to Middle Chinese are explained in more detail.

The range of debates on various issues has been introduced more systematically, including the base dialect of the *Qièyùn* in Chapter 4, the base dialect of the *Zhōngyuán Yīnyùn* in Chapter 5, whether Classical Chinese was based on spoken Old Chinese in Chapter 6, whether diglossia applies to Chinese in Chapter 7, the standard dialect of Mandarin of the Ming dynasty in Chapter 9, and so on.

In each chapter, more and better examples have been added to illustrate various issues. Explanations of examples have also been clarified wherever needed. Chinese characters have been provided for the reconstructed systems of Old Chinese, Middle Chinese, and Old Mandarin so that readers can better understand the connections between the systems. There are also many minor updates with new research in various chapters. Typos and errors have been corrected.

In the first edition, it was decided that a jargon-free conversational style of writing would benefit readers with no prior knowledge in linguistics or Chinese linguistics per se. However, the casual style may have subtracted from the accuracy of discussions of various topics that involve technical nuances that are important in a field like Chinese historical linguistics. Therefore, in this edition, the style of writing has been adjusted so that more accuracy can be achieved.

I hope this new edition is more informative and more academically rigorous and balanced while still maintaining its original approachable readability.

# 1 Overview

This chapter sets the parameters and scope of this book by introducing some basic notions and concepts in general linguistics and Chinese linguistics, followed by an overview of the main topics.

## 1.1 What is Chinese historical linguistics?

Many people discovered their interest in the Chinese language and culture when they learned about Chinese classics such as the *Analects*. The language that was used in ancient Chinese works on history, philosophy, literature, religion, science, and medicine differs greatly from Modern Standard Chinese. Thus, knowledge of Chinese historical linguistics is often the key to these ancient texts. On a related note, in Modern Standard Chinese, elements from Classical Chinese can be readily spotted everywhere, which makes it necessary for native speakers, researchers of the Chinese culture, and students of the modern language to be somewhat acquainted with the ancient language in order to read more advanced modern texts. Moreover, if we just focus on how a language itself has changed throughout history, that is an interesting topic as well. Language is a system of communication unique to human beings. Thus, we may wonder how language changes in general and how studies of a particular linguistic history can inform us about the common factors, such as physical and cognitive ones, involved in language change.

We can study changes in different aspects of a language, including its phonology, syntax, and lexicon. There are a certain number of basic sounds in each language. Historical phonology studies how such a system of sounds has changed. For example, there are 22 consonants in Modern Standard Chinese, but more than 1000 years ago, in the language that can be said to be the ancestor of Modern Standard Chinese, there were more than 30 consonants. How were they pronounced? How did they change into the 22 consonants in Modern Standard Chinese? Chapters 3–5 focus on such changes and reconstruct the sound systems at different times. Besides sound change, studies of syntactic change look into how the rules of grammar and forms of grammatical constructions have developed. For example, passive constructions such as "*John is scolded by the principal*" in English are formed with the word *bèi* 被 in Chinese. Thus, we want to know when this construction first appeared in historical texts and how it developed into its current form and usage.

Chapters 6–7 illustrate the key features of Classical Chinese grammar and how some of the typical syntactic constructions in Modern Standard Chinese developed by studying texts in early vernacular writing. Another aspect of language change lies in the meaning of words, which is dealt with briefly in Chapter 8. We use the term "Modern Standard Chinese" to refer to the official language of China, which is called *Pǔtōnghuà* 普通話 ("Common Speech").[1] Chapter 9 provides a more detailed historical account of how this national standard language was created. Its major features are also discussed. In contrast to a national language, there are many regional varieties of Chinese, called *fāngyán* 方言 ("regional speech"), which can be said to have descended from a common ancestral language. Chapter 10 offers a brief description of such varieties of Chinese. Therefore, this book deals with how the sounds, words, and syntax of Chinese changed and how the current varieties of Chinese are related to earlier stages of the language.

How do we know anything about earlier stages of a language? If we want to have a direct impression of how a certain language sounded 50 years ago, we can simply listen to a recording of that language if such a recording is available. But in historical linguistics, the time depth is always greater than a mere few decades. Therefore, studies of linguistic history have to rely on written records. The great thing about written records in Chinese is that we have extensive continuous texts of Chinese that go all the way back at least 3200 years to the oracle bone script in the Shang dynasty (16th–11th centuries BC). Such a vast corpus is invaluable to the study of the history of the Chinese language. But what about prehistoric times where no written record is available? Even though we do not have ancient texts from before the Shang dynasty, the language undoubtedly existed in an earlier spoken form. Using modern linguistic methods, in combination with research findings from archaeology and human population genetics, we can actually push our knowledge of the Chinese language further back to prehistoric times when the language was more similar to the ancestral languages of Tibetan and Burmese. Topics on such genetic relations in the Sino-Tibetan language family are discussed in Chapter 2.

Although historical linguistics relies on written records, the study of the development of writing systems is usually a research field in itself that is different from historical linguistics per se. However, since the Chinese writing system is such an interesting but controversial topic, in Chapter 11, we provide a sketch of the development of Chinese characters from the oracle bone script to the current simplified forms.

Although the subject matter of historical linguistics is language itself, it cannot be studied in isolation, because language is an important aspect of human society. A history of a certain language touches upon how the language was connected to other realms in society at different times in terms of the sociological, cultural, and political contexts of language use. Thus, knowledge in linguistic history itself helps us gain insight into aspects of a society. First and foremost, to study the different stages of the Chinese language is, in some sense, to study the history of China from a linguistic perspective. Also, for example, the use of historical written records begins with an inquiry into how and why these materials were created in the first place. Furthermore, the written records used for the study of the history of the Chinese language include poetry, fiction, Buddhist texts, ancient classics, and so on. These are important cultural products in themselves. Although, generally speaking, language changes mostly by itself or naturally without deliberate human efforts, linguistic reforms can be carried out by governments purposefully to change various aspects of a language. Such linguistic reforms are usually motivated by certain sociopolitical factors. Therefore, studies of linguistic history are often complemented by a comprehensive view of a society and its culture in general.

## 1.2  Terminological clarification

When the word *"language"* is used in daily conversation, it can refer to the spoken or the written form. But in linguistics, *"language"* primarily refers to the spoken form. Historical linguistics studies the development of spoken language. The development of writing systems is actually a research field that is beyond the scope of historical linguistics per se. In light of this distinction, we say that this book titled *A History of the Chinese Language* focuses on how the spoken form of Chinese changed. But what does *"Chinese"* refer to as a spoken language? This may seem to be a simple question, but the fact is actually quite complicated.

Let's begin by dealing with the term *"Chinese dialects."* Roughly speaking, the language used in the northern and southwestern parts of China is Mandarin Chinese. Within this vast area, the different dialects are more or less mutually intelligible. For example, a person from the Harbin city in the Heilongjiang province in northeast China can converse with a person from Beijing quite freely if they speak their own dialects. Although it would be a little more difficult for a native of Beijing to talk to someone from Chengdu in the Sichuan province in southwest China when they both use their own dialects, they can still maintain a certain degree of mutual intelligibility. Their communication may be quite difficult at first, but once the speakers get used to each other's accents, their mutual understanding progresses rapidly. However, in the southern and southeastern parts of China, it is often the case that speakers from different regions either have great difficulties understanding each other or cannot communicate with each other at all if they use their local dialects, for example, Cantonese, Shanghainese, Fukienese, Hakka, and so on. A native speaker of Shanghainese cannot communicate with someone who speaks Cantonese unless they both use Modern Standard Chinese. Sometimes even within the same linguistic group, such as in the Fujian area, people from different places may not be able to communicate with each other in their native tongues. Traditionally, both the mutually intelligible Mandarin dialects and those that are not mutually intelligible in southern and southeastern China are regarded as *fāngyán* 方言, which literally means *"regional speech."* The common translation of this term in English is *"dialect."* But this translation causes a certain degree of misunderstanding and terminological chaos.

According to Mair (1991: 4), the English word *"dialect"* refers to "one of two or more mutually intelligible varieties of a given language distinguished by vocabulary, idiom and pronunciation." For example, someone from London might speak differently from a Sydney native in terms of pronunciation and vocabulary. But they can have a conversation with no major problems. This is true of the different dialects within Mandarin Chinese but not true of the situation between Mandarin and Cantonese or between Cantonese and Shanghainese. Mair (1991) compares the situation between these different varieties of spoken Chinese that are not mutually intelligible to that between English, Dutch, Swedish, and the other Germanic languages. Clearly, the translation of *fāngyán* as "*dialect*" is misleading. Thus, Mair (1991) proposes a new term, "*topolect*," in which "*topo*" corresponds to "*fāng*" and "*lect*" to "*yán*." This is indeed a better terminological choice for what *fāngyán* refers to in Chinese.

There are, however, overlaps between the Chinese notion of *fāngyán* and the notion of "*dialect*," in that some *fāngyán* are bona fide dialects. The difference between the Chinese notion of *fāngyán* and the Western concept of "*dialect*" lies in the different frameworks of discourse. The notion of *fāngyán* contrasts with that of a common non-regional form of speech, without direct reference to mutual intelligibility, while the notion of "*dialect*" contrasts with that of "*language*," focusing on the criterion of mutual intelligibility while not referring to any geographical distribution directly.

The main groups of Chinese *fāngyán* are not mutually intelligible. Thus, strictly speaking, they are different languages instead of different dialects of a single Chinese language. However, the traditional translation of *fāngyán* is still "*dialect*," and it has been widely used or maybe, to put it more accurately, misused, according to Mair (1991). Indeed, we have a dilemma with various terminologies. In this book, we follow the traditional terminology to call these varieties of Chinese different "*Chinese dialects*." Note that an alternative term commonly used in linguistic research is "*Sinitic languages*" in place of the phrases "*Chinese topolects*" or "*Chinese dialects*." Sometimes the terms "*Sinitic languages*," "*Chinese dialects*," "*fāngyán*," and "*varieties of Chinese*" are used interchangeably in this book.

Now the term "*Chinese dialects*" is clarified, we can give a more detailed description to the major dialect groups of Chinese. Traditionally, Chinese dialects are categorized into these seven major groups: Mandarin (官話), Wu (吳語), Xiang (湘語), Gan (贛語), Min (閩語), Kejia (客家話), and Yue (粵語), as shown in the following table with information on the principal geographic distribution of these dialects together with their names in Chinese and in English.

Mandarin is the largest group in terms of both the area and number of speakers. Each of the other six groups is usually spoken in one or two provinces south of the Mandarin area. Some varieties of Chinese that may be familiar to many people include Beijing Mandarin; Shanghainese in the Wu dialect group; and Cantonese, spoken in Guangzhou and Hong Kong from the Yue dialect group. Moreover, Hokkien (福建話, 閩南話), which is a Southern Min dialect, and Hakka are both quite well-known varieties of Chinese, especially in Southeast Asia. Usually, speakers from different groups cannot communicate with each other. The fact that there are so many different regional varieties of Chinese calls for a common language that can be used as a cross-dialectal form of speech, which is Modern Standard

*Table 1.1* Major groups of Chinese dialects

| Dialects | English | Principal Geographic Distribution |
|---|---|---|
| **Guānhuà**<br>官話 | Mandarin | Northern and southwestern China<br>(chiefly north of the Yangtze River) |
| **Wú yǔ**<br>吳語 | Wu dialects | Shanghai, Zhejiang, southern Jiangsu |
| **Xiāng yǔ**<br>湘語 | Xiang dialects | Hunan |
| **Gàn yǔ**<br>贛語 | Gan dialects | Jiangxi |
| **Kèjiā huà**<br>客家話 | Kejia dialects;<br>Hakka dialects | Fujian, Guangdong, Guangxi, Taiwan |
| **Mǐn yǔ**<br>閩語 | Min dialects | Fujian, Guangdong, Taiwan, Hainan |
| **Yuè yǔ**<br>粵語 | Yue dialects | Guangdong, Guangxi, Hong Kong |

Chinese, or *Pǔtōnghuà* ("Common Speech"), based on the Mandarin dialect spoken in Beijing.[2] Currently, Modern Standard Chinese is taught in all schools in China, and it is the language used for publications, radio and TV broadcasts, and all other formal communications. Because Modern Standard Chinese is based on Beijing Mandarin, and all the different Mandarin dialects are mutually intelligible, speakers of a southern variety of Chinese may actually be able to somewhat understand most Mandarin dialects, since the standard national language is nowadays used by most people from all different regions of dialects.

In addition to the varieties of spoken Chinese, or the *fāngyán*, which are the native tongues of the *Hàn* 漢 people, there are 55 other ethnic groups in China. Some of these peoples speak languages that are very different from Chinese, such as Mongolian, Zhuang, Tibetan, Uyghur, and so on, while some others, such as the Hui and the Manchu, adopted a variety of Chinese a long time ago. Similar to how speakers of a Chinese dialect learn to speak the national language, speakers of non-*Hàn* languages usually also learn to speak Modern Standard Chinese in school, often alongside classes in their own native languages.

Therefore, the overall linguistic situation in China is that there are regional varieties of Chinese, non-*Hàn* languages, and an official language for all speakers, including both *Hàn* Chinese and the other 55 ethnicities, to communicate with each other. If we go back in time, we would expect to find a similar situation with the existence of different dialects, languages, and a common cross-dialectal form of speech, which was often considered a *koiné*. Thus, when we say *"the Chinese language"* in this book, it is primarily used to refer to Modern Standard Chinese and its earlier stages in history. At the same time, since all modern Chinese dialects, including Beijing Mandarin as the basis of Modern Standard Chinese, descended from a common earlier language, we also discuss the connections of modern dialects with older stages of Chinese.

To sum up the discussion in this section, in a book on the history of the Chinese language, the main theme is the historical development of the spoken language Modern Standard Chinese from its earliest known stage to its current form, while modern dialects are also described in terms of their developments from a common ancestral language.

## 1.3   Periodization of the Chinese language

Different aspects of the language change at different paces. Usually, phonological criteria have been used by many linguists as the basis for the periodization of the Chinese language. The following table shows the major periods of the Chinese language and their relevant timespans, based on Wang (1958) and Xiang (1993).

Not shown in the table is the prehistoric time prior to Old Chinese. This period is when Chinese transitioned from Proto-Sino-Tibetan to its Sinitic form, which is the ancestral language of Old Chinese and all later stages of the language. Although there are hardly any written records from this prehistoric time, sporadic evidence in Old Chinese, in combination with detailed comparisons with related languages such as Tibetan, can help us to deduce some features that might have been present in the stage prior to Old Chinese.

The first textually attested period of Chinese is called Old Chinese, spoken mostly in the first millennium BC. During the Zhou dynasty, which extended from the Yellow River region in the north to the Yangtze River in the south, there were different dialects in the various states of Zhou in terms of vocabulary and pronunciation. Thus, correspondingly, the dialect of the Eastern Zhou dynasty capital, in present-day Luoyang of Henan province, was used as a cross-dialectal form of communication and as a standard for reading ancient classics.

Language change is gradual. Within each period of the language in Table 1.2, cumulative changes make the states of the language noticeably different toward the two ends of each period. Therefore, we can still divide each of the longer periods into further stages. Zhengzhang (2003) divides Old Chinese into three stages. The first stage, Early Old Chinese, is the language spoken during the Shang dynasty and early Zhou dynasty. Knowledge of the sounds of this stage is mostly based on the phonetic information encoded in early forms of Chinese characters, including the oracle bone script of the late Shang dynasty and bronze script inscribed on bronzeware from the Zhou dynasty. The middle stage is the following stage that extended to the Qin dynasty. This is actually what most people refer to as Old Chinese proper in terms of the sound system, since the written records on which Old Chinese studies are based are mostly from this period. From the Qin dynasty to the end of the Han dynasty is the third stage, called Late Old Chinese. In addition to the sounds of Old Chinese, knowledge of the grammar and vocabulary of Old Chinese is based on written records during the second half of the millennium, mostly the prose writings in the Chinese classics and major works in the Han dynasty.

The Qin dynasty is the first empire that unified China after a long period of disunity. *Qín Shǐ Huáng* 秦始皇 (259–210 BC), the first emperor of the Qin dynasty, carried out systematic standardizing measures, including the unification of the

*Table 1.2* Periodization of the Chinese language

| Periodization | Timespan and Relevant Historical Periods | |
|---|---|---|
| Old Chinese<br>*Shànggǔ Hànyǔ*<br>上古漢語 | 12th century BC–3rd century AD | |
| | Late Shang | (12th–11th centuries BC) |
| | Western Zhou | (11th century–771 BC) |
| | Spring and Autumn period | (770–476 BC) |
| | Warring States period | (475–221 BC) |
| | Qin | (221–207 BC) |
| | Western and Eastern Han | (206 BC – AD 220) |
| Middle Chinese<br>*Zhōnggǔ Hànyǔ*<br>中古漢語 | 4th–12th centuries AD | |
| | Three Kingdoms period | (AD 220–265) |
| | Western and Eastern Jin | (AD 265–420) |
| | Northern and Southern dynasties | (AD 420–589) |
| | Sui | (AD 581–618) |
| | Tang | (AD 618–907) |
| | Five Dynasties period | (AD 907–960) |
| | Northern and Southern Song | (AD 960–1279) |
| Early Modern Chinese<br>*Jìndài Hànyǔ*<br>近代漢語 | 13th–early 20th centuries AD | |
| | Yuan | (AD 1271–1368) |
| | Ming | (AD 1368–1644) |
| | Qing | (AD 1644–1911) |
| Modern Chinese<br>*Xiàndài Hànyǔ*<br>現代漢語 | Early 20th century AD–now | |

Chinese script. His troops also reached far into regions south of the Yangtze River, bringing Chinese-speaking people and their language as far as present-day Guangdong and Guangxi.

The subsequent Han dynasty was a period of major economic and political prosperity when the ethnic identity of the people was solidified, hence the origin of the name of the *Hàn* people and then the name of the Chinese language, *Hànyǔ* 漢語, meaning "*the language of the Hàn.*" It is during the estern Han that Confucianism was established as the official ideology of the empire. The significance of this for the study of the language lies in the fact that Confucian classics were studied almost religiously by Confucian scholars for thousands of years up to the early 20th century. An important part of a traditional Confucian education was the study of language and writing, called *xiǎoxué* 小學 ("small learning"), which was considered the foundation of *dàxué* 大學 ("great learning"), that is, the study of the ancient classics per se. Confucian scholars were among the first to have noted the differences between their own spoken language and the language recorded in the Confucian classics. Their commentaries and explanations of such linguistic differences are valuable written records for the changes of the language. This traditional linguistic education developed into a sophisticated form of philology in the Qing dynasty, when major discoveries of Old Chinese and later stages were made.

In addition to Confucian texts, translations of Buddhist canons are also important written records for the development of the language since the Eastern Han dynasty, when Buddhism was first introduced into China. Buddhist texts contain more vernacular elements that recorded the spoken language more directly than Confucian texts. Moreover, the original Buddhist texts were written in languages with phonetic writing systems, such as Sanskrit. Therefore, comparing these original languages with the Chinese translations may help us to figure out what the Chinese terms sounded like during the time of the translation.

Between the Eastern Han dynasty and the Sui dynasty (AD 581–618), there was a long period of political division, when constant wars in the northern part of the country displaced many Chinese-speaking people to the south, while peoples who originally spoke other languages ruled the north. Written records show that the sound system of the language during this period of domestic turmoil was already drastically different from the Old Chinese a thousand years earlier, and Middle Chinese, a literary pronunciation standard of the late Northern and Southern dynasties, was reconstructed on the basis of a rhyme dictionary called the *Qièyùn* 切韻 from the late 6th to early 7th centuries AD. Within the grammar and vocabulary system, we can trace the origins of many elements in various modern Chinese dialects up to this period as well.

The Imperial Examination system was established in the Sui dynasty in AD 605 as a model of selecting qualified Confucian scholars to serve as administrative functionaries. The system continued to be modified and utilized as the single most important civil servant examination in subsequent dynasties up until the early 20th century. This system gave rise to a series of literary language standards recorded in rhyme dictionaries, similar to the *Qièyùn*, compiled to set the correct pronunciations for Chinese characters used in the composition of essays and poetry, which were usually part of the examination. Such rhyme dictionaries are valuable sources of the sound systems of different periods of Chinese.

The Tang dynasty is known in Chinese history as a major empire with great cultural and historical significance. In terms of literature, Tang poetry has always been upheld as the highest achievement of the literary genre. Great poets such as *Lǐ Bái* 李白 (AD 701–762) and *Dù Fǔ* 杜甫 (AD 712–770) even nowadays are household names in all Chinese-speaking areas, and all Chinese speakers can recite some Tang poems from memory. Actually, Tang poetry contains important clues to how the literary language sounded during that time. The study of Middle Chinese is thus intertwined with Tang poetry and poetics.

After the Tang dynasty, there was a relatively short period of political disunity. But soon the country was once again unified by the Northern Song dynasty. By this time, the main phonological features of the earlier part of Middle Chinese as represented by the *Qièyùn* had undergone considerable changes, and Middle Chinese was in the process of transitioning into Early Modern Chinese. A special type of written material called rhyme tables, or *yùntú* 韻圖, from the late Tang to the Song dynasty, based on the sound system of the *Qièyùn* dictionary, are important sources of the sounds of Late Middle Chinese (Pulleyblank 1970, 1971). There are some debates about where the Song dynasty should belong in the periodization of Chinese. Jiang (2005: 5) points out that at least in terms of grammar and vocabulary, what we can call Early Modern Chinese had been established by the beginning of the Song dynasty. In terms of the sounds, Norman (1988) proposed that the language of the Song should be considered an earlier form of Old Mandarin, that is, the beginning of Early Modern Chinese, mostly during the Yuan dynasty.

A rhyme book called the *Phonology of the Central Plains,* or *Zhōngyuán Yīnyùn* 中原音韻, written in 1324 in the Yuan dynasty, is the major source of Old Mandarin. Major changes had taken place by the Yuan dynasty in terms of both the consonants and vowels compared to Middle Chinese. The main phonological properties of Modern Standard Chinese can be directly traced back to the system of the *Zhōngyuán Yīnyùn.* The subsequent stages include the Ming and Qing dynasties, when important changes toward Modern Standard Chinese, especially in the consonants, took place. Generally speaking, by the middle of the Qing dynasty, Beijing Mandarin was already sufficiently similar to Modern Standard Chinese in all aspects, including the sounds, vocabulary, and grammar. Some of the most well-known novels and other types of fiction writings in Chinese literature are from the Ming and Qing dynasties, written in a Mandarin dialect, which is quite similar to Modern Standard Chinese.[3]

Starting from the late Qing dynasty toward the end of the 19th century, progressive scholars looked to the West for models of modernization, among which building a national language became a priority. In 1911, the Qing dynasty was overturned, ending more than 2000 years of rule of successive imperial dynasties in Chinese history, bringing China into modern times. In the Republic of China, the standard of the national language continued to be debated, until finally, in 1926, in the New National Pronunciation, or the *Xīn Guóyīn* 新國音, it was agreed that the Beijing dialect was to be the basis of the new national language. In 1949, the People's Republic of China was founded, and almost immediately the new government embarked on work in linguistic reforms, which led to the official definition in 1956 of the new national language called *Pǔtōnghuà,* followed by the establishment in 1958 of a Romanization system called *pīnyīn* 拼音, to be used primarily as a way to annotate the pronunciations of Chinese characters. After a few decades of promotion, now the majority of people from different dialect regions in China can understand and speak *Pǔtōnghuà.* At the same time, various Chinese dialects are affected by *Pǔtōnghuà* to different degrees, when younger generations are taught *Pǔtōnghuà* in school, in a time of modern technology and media which have a homogenizing effect by bringing *Pǔtōnghuà* to every corner of the country. In recent years, there has been a rise in the awareness of regional cultures and identities that are deeply rooted in the use of different local varieties of Chinese. Thus, more and more people are becoming interested in their own dialects, which in turn brings renewed momentum to the research in Chinese dialects.

This chapter offers a very brief sketch of the history of the Chinese language from prehistoric times to its current uses. The remaining part of the book provides more detailed discussions of each stage of the Chinese language.

## Notes

1  It is often paraphrased as *pǔbiàn* 普遍 ("common, universal") and *tōngxíng* 通行 ("generally understood, widely-used").
2  The Mandarin spoken in Taiwan, called *Guóyǔ* 國語 ("*National Language*"), shares the same origin as *Pǔtōnghuà*, although there are noticeable differences in pronunciation, grammar, and vocabulary. Thus, *Guóyǔ* should not be confused with Taiwanese, the former being a standard language based on Mandarin and the latter being a Southern Min dialect (閩南話).
3  Literary Chinese (文言文) was still used up to the earlier 20th century for most formal writings.

# 2   Prehistory

Languages have their relatives and family trees, just as humans do. Therefore, in this chapter, we explore what languages are the closest relatives of the Chinese language and what languages are long-time neighbors of Chinese.

## 2.1   Establishing linguistic genetic relationships

Languages that are either related or interacted with each other as neighbors can all become similar in that some words sound alike among them, for example, as shown in Table 2.1, with words from Sanskrit, Greek, and Latin. The data are taken from Xu (1991) and Campbell (1999).

But, of course, words in different languages can be similar due to a variety of reasons. First, the words that sound alike may just be by chance. The now-obsolete, literary word *dàn* 旦 in Chinese has the same meaning as the word "*dawn*" in English. But such similarities are not systematic, since we can only find a few such pairs across different languages. Second, words can be similar because they mimic natural sounds. Cats "*miāo*" in Chinese, and they *meow* in English. These onomatopoeic words can be similar in many otherwise unrelated languages. Third, words can be borrowed from one language into another with corresponding phonological adaptations. It is probably not difficult to guess what the Chinese word "*màikèfēng*" means, since it is the word "*microphone*" borrowed from English.

What we are more interested in here is when languages share many words due to a common origin. Generally speaking, what sounds are used to represent what meaning in a language is, for the most part, arbitrary (de Saussure 1983). When

*Table 2.1* Indo-European cognate words

| Sanskrit | Greek | Latin | English |
|----------|-------|-------|---------|
| pitar- | pater | pater | father |
| dva- | dyo- | duo- | two |
| pad- | pod- | ped- | foot |
| aksah | haksos | axis | axis |

people say "*water*" in English, the Chinese use "*shui.*" They are totally different because the association between sounds and meaning is arbitrary. However, when we hear that Germans say "*Wasser*" to mean "*water,*" it is very likely that "*Wasser*" and "*water*" might have come from the same word, also because of the arbitrary association between sounds and meaning, which would make an explanation of these two similar-sounding words in German and English in terms of coincidence quite difficult to accept, especially when we can find a large number of such pairs of similar words from the two languages. In this case, the relationship between the two languages is very likely genetic, which is on a par with such a relationship in a biological sense. Languages that descended from the same ancestral language often share an extensive and systematic list of common words, and the sounds in one language correspond to those in another in a more or less regular fashion. By contrast, similarities due to coincidence or sound imitation are neither extensive nor regular. But loan words can be fairly extensive if a large number of words are borrowed between two languages, thus making the correspondences of sounds between these languages quite systematic. There are oftentimes historical records of one language borrowing words from another. Then such cases can be easily distinguished from those where two or more languages share the same origin. Therefore, the first step in establishing a genetic relationship between two languages is to compile a list of true cognate words, such as those in Table 2.1. Here by "*true cognate words,*" we mean that these words are not borrowed from each other. The words listed here from Sanskrit, Greek, Latin, and English have been independently confirmed by previous research to be true cognates. Especially when we compare the Sanskrit words with the other three languages, the similarity is striking, given the limited interactions between ancient India and Europe.

Once we have such a list, it is necessary to look at sound correspondences rather than word shape similarities. For example, in Table 2.1, in the first word, the sound *p-* in Sanskrit corresponds to *p-* in Greek, *p-* in Latin, and *f-* in English. Thus, a "*p-p-p-f*" correspondence among these languages is obtained. Actually, we can find the same sound correspondence in the third word, meaning "*foot,*" as well. Now let's look at the second word; the *d-* in Sanskrit corresponds to *d-* in Greek, *d-* in Latin, and *t-* in English. Thus, a "*d-d-d-t*" correspondence is established. The same correspondence can be found in the third word as well. The list of cognates here is very short, but if we have a larger dataset, we may find more instances of the two correspondences discovered here. When such sound correspondences are established regularly under the same phonological conditions, we may move to reconstructing the proto-sound for each of these correspondences. For example, for the "*p-p-p-f*" correspondence, one hypothesis is that in the ancestral language, the original sound would have been *\*p-*, and that sound developed into *f-* in English. Here the star "*\**" that precedes a sound indicates that it is a hypothetical proto-sound. Ultimately, all of the individual sounds in the proto-language would be reconstructed. Note that the methodology to reconstruct a proto-language is a highly complex technical process. The short example here is for illustrative purposes only. The technical details are introduced in Chapter 4. In the case of the Indo-European family of languages, the reconstructed ancestral language is called

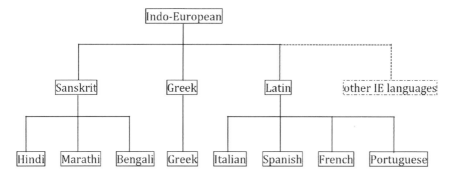

*Figure 2.1* A schematic family tree of Sanskrit, Greek, and Latin

Proto-Indo-European. One of the main objectives in reconstructing a proto-language is to explain how the ancestral language developed into different modern languages. We pick up the discussion of the reconstruction method in Chapter 4 when we talk about the reconstruction of the sound system of Middle Chinese.

Our little example here with the data in Table 2.1 shows how a genetic relationship can be established and the proto-language can be reconstructed step by step. Proto-Indo-European has been reconstructed successfully in great detail. Actually, modern English is genetically related to the other three ancient languages a little more indirectly, which requires a lengthier description of the development of the Indo-European languages. Therefore, let's focus on the ancient languages for now. Figure 2.1 shows the genetic relationship between Sanskrit, Greek, and Latin in a structure that looks like a family tree.

Figure 2.1 is only a very schematic representation of the Indo-European language family, which comprises over 400 languages and dialects. As shown in Figure 2.1, the Indo-European tree includes major branches, such as Sanskrit, Greek, and Latin, each of which can further split into more daughter languages, for example, Hindi, Bengali, and Marathi as descendants of Sanskrit. This representation is called the family tree model and is the main theoretical model for understanding genetic relationships among languages.

## 2.2   The Sino-Tibetan languages

The concept of a "*language family*" was established in the early 19th century based upon the Indo-European model, and afterwards linguists started to look at other languages and tried to classify them into different families. So what languages are genetically related to Chinese? We may look at those languages that are geographically neighbors of Chinese.

To the north, northeast, and northwest of Chinese, we find languages such as Mongolian, Manchu, Japanese, Korean, and Uyghur. These languages belong to the Altaic family, although some people believe that Japanese and Korean are isolates, meaning that they are not related to any other language or to each other. A quick look at Japanese and Korean words may reveal a high degree of similarity between these two languages and Chinese in terms of vocabulary. To the south of Chinese, we find languages like Vietnamese in the Austroasiatic family. There are also a large number of words in Vietnamese that are similar to those in Chinese. Table 2.2 shows examples of numerals from two varieties of Chinese (Mandarin and Cantonese) and from Japanese, Korean, and Vietnamese.

There are two sets of pronunciations in the columns for Japanese, Korean, and Vietnamese. The first pronunciation for each word looks similar to Mandarin and Cantonese. However, the second pronunciation does not look like Chinese at all. Therefore, it is very likely that the second pronunciation is the native pronunciation in these languages, while the first one was an early loanword pronunciation. Historical records show that Classical Chinese and Chinese characters were borrowed into Japan, Korea, and Vietnam during the Middle Chinese period. The pronunciations of Chinese characters were also imported into these languages with corresponding phonological adaptations. Therefore, based on the established facts of borrowing and the existence of two pronunciation systems, we may conclude that there is no genetic relationship between Chinese and such neighboring languages as Japanese, Korean, and Vietnamese.

Although the loanwords listed in Table 2.2 were borrowed from Chinese into the other languages, and some of these words are basic vocabulary items, in more modern times around the early part of the 20th century, especially during the New Culture Movement, when Chinese intellectuals looked to modernize China, a large number of words related to Western civilization, science, and technology were borrowed into Chinese from Japanese after new concepts were first translated from major European languages into Japanese using *kanji* characters in the second half of the 19th century as a result of the Meiji Restoration that started in 1868. For example, Chinese words such as *kēxué* 科學 ("science"), *mínzhǔ* 民主 ("democracy"), *shèhuì* 社會 ("society"), *jīngjì* 經濟 ("economy"), and *diànhuà* 電話 ("telephone") are all borrowed from Japanese in modern times. But these more recent loanwords are not basic vocabulary items, and in some sense, we may say that they are higher-level cultural words. One fundamental difference between true cognates and loanwords is that the latter tend to be such higher-level cultural words.

*Table 2.2* Numerals in Chinese, Japanese, Korean, and Vietnamese

| English | Mandarin (*Pīnyīn*) | Cantonese (*Jyutping*) | Japanese | Korean | Vietnamese |
|---------|---------------------|------------------------|----------|--------|------------|
| One | yī | jat[1] | ichi / hito(tsu) | il / hana | nhất / một |
| Two | èr | ji[6] | ni / futa(tsu) | i / dul | nhị / hai |
| Three | sān | saam[1] | san / mit(tsu) | sam / set | tam / ba |
| Four | sì | sei[3] | shi / yon, yot(tsu) | sa / net | tứ / bốn |
| Five | wǔ | ng[5] | go / itsu(tsu) | o / daseot | ngũ / năm |

For the remaining major Altaic languages mentioned previously, there are also a smaller number of loanwords between Chinese, Mongolian, and Manchu. For example, the Chinese word *zhàn* 站 ("a station; a stop"), used to refer to a bus stop, subway stop, or train station, was originally borrowed from Mongolian. A number of colloquialisms in Beijing Mandarin and northeastern Mandarin were borrowed from Manchu during the Qing dynasty, for example, *mǎmǎhūhū* 馬馬虎虎 ("in a careless way"). There are a number of Chinese loanwords in Mongolian and Manchu as well due to close cultural contacts in history. Apart from loanwords, there is no list of true cognate words that can be found between Chinese and Altaic to establish a genetic relationship.

Also relevant here is the language family called Austronesian, including the Formosan languages in Taiwan and languages spoken across the vast area between Taiwan and Indonesia, such as the Filipino and Indonesian languages. If there are connections between Chinese and Austronesian, such connections have to be quite remote. It is possible for the Austronesian people to have originated in southeastern mainland China before crossing the Taiwan Strait onto the island and then migrating further to other areas between Taiwan and Indonesia (Wang 1998; Brindley 2015). There is recent archeological and genetic evidence of early humans migrating from the mainland to Taiwan. Li (2015) discusses the significance of ancient skeleton remains dated 8060–8320 BP, discovered recently in 2011 on Liangdao, an islet of the Mazu archipelago just off the coast of Fujian. According to Li (2015), the genetics of the Liangdao man may be more closely related to the modern Formosan natives than to modern populations from South China and Southeast Asia. Thus, there is some evidence here for the mainland origin of the Austronesian languages. In fact, linguists have long been entertaining the possibility of a super language family, or a macro phylum, that would include both Chinese and one or more of its neighbors. Sagart (1993) proposes a genetic relationship between Chinese and Austronesian based on phonological correspondences, vocabulary similarities, and morphological connections. If the Austronesians indeed originated in mainland China, it would not be impossible for them to have migrated from northern China to the southeastern coastal areas before crossing the strait to Taiwan. But the conclusion in this area is still preliminary. Even if there is a genetic relationship between Chinese and Austronesian, it has to be a remote one that lies well beyond the kind of close genetic relationship that we are focusing on in this chapter.

In some parts of southern and southwestern China and in Southeast Asia, we find languages like Zhuang, Dong, Thai, and so on, which belong to the Kra-Dai family.[1] The subgroup of Kra-Dai that includes the Zhuang, Dong, and Thai languages is called Kam-Tai,[2] or Zhuang-Dong in Chinese. In southwestern and western China and the Himalayan regions, we find languages such as Tibetan, Burmese, Qiang, and rGyalrong, which are called Tibeto-Burman. There are also the Miao and Yao languages that are spoken in Hunan, Hubei, Guangxi, and southwestern China. These languages belong to the Hmong-Mien family, or Miao-Yao in Chinese. There are many similar words, including some basic vocabulary items, between Chinese and the Kam-Tai, Tibeto-Burman, and Hmong-Mien languages.

Unlike the similar words between Chinese, Japanese, Korean, and Vietnamese, which are known to be loanwords and tend to include many higher-level cultural words, we do not have readily available records to prove whether the similar words between Chinese and the Kam-Tai, Tibeto-Burman, and Hmong-Mien languages are loanwords or true cognate words, especially considering that some basic words are shared. If such similar words are loans, possibly borrowed in a very early time that was not systematically recorded, then there should be no genetic relation between Chinese and these languages. If these shared words turn out to be true cognates, then a genetic relationship can be established.

The concept of a Sino-Tibetan language family became popular during the 1930s at the University of California Berkeley due to the research by the Sino-Tibetan Philology Project. According to Li (1973), which is based on a paper written by him in 1937, the Sino-Tibetan family includes Chinese, Kam-Tai, Hmong-Mien, and Tibeto-Burman. Benedict (1972), which was actually written in 1942, argued that the Hmong-Mien languages and the Kam-Tai languages are not part of the Sino-Tibetan family, because the shared words between Hmong-Mien, Kam-Tai, and Chinese are very likely early borrowings. Nowadays some scholars would still hold that Li's (1973) classification of Sino-Tibetan that includes the four distinct groups of languages is basically correct, although Benedict's (1972) system including only Chinese and Tibeto-Burman is more of the consensus among researchers. In order to figure out which of these two theories is correct, we need to introduce the notion of "*basic vocabulary*" more formally here, although it has been mentioned a few times previously.

Swadesh (1971) proposed a list of 100 words which were meant to be universal and stable in that these words can be found in every language and they are less likely to be borrowed or replaced, since they refer to fundamental and essential aspects of life and culture. For example, words like "*I, you, one, two, man, woman, fish, dog, ear, eye, see, hear*" are among these basic words. The 100-word list was compiled from the earlier 200-word list also proposed by Swadesh. The 100-word list should be the even more basic ones among the 200 words. Generally speaking, higher-level cultural vocabulary items are easily borrowed due to cultural contacts, while words on the 100-word list or the 200-word list are less prone to being borrowed. Even though these basic vocabulary items do change over time, the change takes a much longer time than higher-level cultural words.

Since many of the shared words among Chinese and Tibeto-Burman, Kam-Tai, and Hmong-Mien are such basic vocabulary items, it has long been quite difficult to prove whether these words are loanwords or true cognates. In order to do so, we need to look at the basic vocabulary more closely. Chen (1996) studies how the people who speak the Dai language, a Kam-Tai language in southwestern China, and Chinese-speaking people interact with each other and borrow words from each other's language. Chen spent several years documenting the details of linguistic contacts between these two languages, including loanwords. Based on his observations, Chen (1996) argues that loanwords are possible even in basic vocabulary when there are prolonged close cultural contacts such as between the

Dai-speaking people and the local Chinese, but such borrowing is conditioned on a hierarchy of basic vocabulary. To illustrate this hierarchy, let's look at Chen's (1993) three groups of words among the 100 basic words. Group A is the most basic, including words like "*fly, dog, yellow, hand, sun, I, rain*," and so on. Group B includes "*white, nose, egg, ear, you, bird, new, know*," and so on. Group C includes "*not, two, drink, gray, name, man, woman, what, small, swim*," and so on. Based on such a hierarchy, Chen (1993) calculates shared basic vocabulary among the Chinese, Tibeto-Burman, and Kam-Tai languages and finds that when two languages share a number of basic words due to deep cultural contacts, these shared words tend to be among the less basic ones, meaning that between these two languages, there would be more similar words in Group C than in Group B and Group A; on the other hand, if two languages share basic words due to a common origin, these shared words tend to be among the more basic vocabulary items, meaning that in such a scenario, there would be more similar words from Group A than from Group B or Group C. For example, the percentage of shared basic vocabulary items between Old Chinese and Modern Standard Chinese is the highest in Group A words, followed by Group B and Group C. Since it has been independently established that Old Chinese and Modern Standard Chinese are genetically related, the generalization on the relation between the nature of shared words and the hierarchy of basic vocabulary that we have just sketched seems to be on the right track. In Chen's (1993) data, the percentage of shared basic vocabulary between Tibetan and Burmese is highest in Group A words, but lower in Group B and Group C, thus being compatible with their genetic relatedness. By contrast, the percentage of shared basic vocabulary between Chinese and Kam-Tai shows the inverse trend, that is, highest in Group C, followed by Group B and then Group A. This seems to suggest that the shared words between Chinese and Kam-Tai are loanwords due to close cultural contacts from a very early time period.

One major issue with Chen's (1993) three groups among the basic vocabulary is that the grouping seems arbitrary and not independently motivated. Therefore, Chen (1996) resorts to a hierarchy between the widely agreed-upon first 100 basic words and the other 100 words of the 200 basic words. The same trend is observed between the different languages by Chen (1996) using this new hierarchy of basic vocabulary. Thus, if his theory is correct, the statistical results suggest that Chinese and Kam-Tai are not genetically related. The common basic words between them are results of deep cultural contacts and sharing. Chen's (1996) study equally suggests that Chinese and Tibeto-Burman are genetically related and their shared words are due to a common origin.

Let's recall the two main theories on the classification of Sino-Tibetan: (1) Chinese and Tibeto-Burman are the only branches within Sino-Tibetan; (2) Chinese, Tibeto-Burman, Kam-Tai, and Hmong-Mien are all included in Sino-Tibetan. Chen's (1996) study suggests that Kam-Tai should not be a branch in Sino-Tibetan, thus lending support to the theory of only including Chinese and Tibeto-Burman in this language family. In terms of Hmong-Mien, a closer examination of its basic vocabulary also excludes it from Sino-Tibetan, as argued by

*Table 2.3* Sino-Tibetan cognate words[3]

| Words | Modern Standard Chinese | Old Chinese | Written Tibetan | Written Burmese |
|---|---|---|---|---|
| Eye | mù 目 | *C.m(r)[u]k | mig | myak |
| Six | liù 六 | *k.ruk | drug | khrok |
| Insect | fú 蜉 | *[b](r)u | 'bu | pûi |
| Poison | dú 毒 | *[d]ˤuk | dug | tok |

Benedict (1972). Now that we have a clearer idea of the main branches of the Sino-Tibetan language family, we further take a look at some cognates, as shown in Table 2.3, between Chinese, Written Tibetan, and Written Burmese. Chinese characters and pronunciations of the words are given first in Modern Standard Chinese, followed by Baxter and Sagart's (2014) reconstructed pronunciations of Old Chinese for further comparisons.

It is pointed out previously in this chapter that mere similarity of word shape is not enough to establish a genetic relationship between two languages. More convincing is regular sound correspondence. In Table 2.3, the final consonant in the first word meaning "*eye*" is -*k* in Old Chinese, -*g* in Written Tibetan, and -*k* in Written Burmese. Thus, we have a "*k-g-k* sound correspondence. This same correspondence can easily be seen in the second word, "*six*," and the fourth word, "*poison*." Additionally, the vowel in the second word, "*six*," is "*u*" in Old Chinese, "*u*" in Written Tibetan, and "*o*" in Written Burmese. Thus, we have a "*u-u-o*" correspondence. It is also shown in the fourth word, "*poison*." In Table 2.3, there are some other notations in Baxter and Sagart's (2014) reconstruction that need to be explained. We discuss their notations in more detail in Chapter 3. Figure 2.2 shows a very schematic representation of the Sino-Tibetan family tree.

The primary distinction is between Chinese, or the Sinitic branch, and Tibeto-Burman. The Chinese branch can further split into the major Chinese dialects. The Tibeto-Burman branch includes Tibetan, Burmese, and so on. There are two further issues associated with the Sino-Tibetan tree as shown in Figure 2.2. The first issue is regarding the structure of the Sinitic node. Currently, we simply put all seven major Chinese dialects equally in the Sinitic branch. However, different Chinese dialects split from the main Sinitic tree at different times, and therefore there should be further levels of branching within the Sinitic tree. We discuss this topic in Chapter 10 on Chinese dialectology. Second, although most linguists agree with the primary branching into Sinitic and Tibeto-Burman, there are alternative theories that would have a different primary branching, where Sinitic would be included as part of these primary branches, for example, van Driem (1999: 49). We discuss this issue next in conjunction with the topic of the Sino-Tibetan homeland and the time of divergence among the Sino-Tibetan languages.

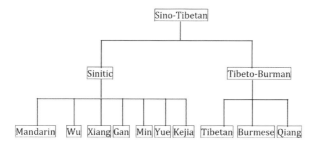

*Figure 2.2* A schematic family tree of Sino-Tibetan languages

## 2.3 How old is the Sino-Tibetan language family?

Now we have established the concept of a Sino-Tibetan language family, which includes the Chinese dialects, Tibetan, Burmese, and so on. There are three further questions to ask: (1) What is the primary branching in the Sino-Tibetan family of languages, as has just been mentioned? (2) Where is the homeland, or *Urheimat*, of the original Sino-Tibetan family? (3) When did the language begin to diverge into different daughter languages? To answer these questions, linguistic methods based on basic vocabulary, in combination with archeological and genetic evidence, can be utilized to reconstruct a scenario of migration from an ancient homeland to its current geographical distribution (Wang 1998). Here I first outline two main theories concerning the origin and divergence of the Sino-Tibetan family, based on the summary by Zhang et al. (2019), and then discuss some of the interdisciplinary methods and evidence that are used to answer these questions.

Most scholars nowadays tend to agree with the proposal that the primary branches of Sino-Tibetan are Sinitic and Tibeto-Burman; the homeland is located in the north of the current area of Sino-Tibetan languages, more specifically in the upper and middle Yellow River region; and the divergence into different daughter languages began 4000–6000 BP, when the Tibeto-Burman group migrated west and south to Tibet and Burma (Myanmar), while the Sinitic group migrated east and south to the mainland of East Asia.

An alternative theory by van Driem (1999) proposes that the primary branching is between a Western branch that includes languages in Nepal, Bhutan, northeastern India, and Bangladesh and an Eastern group further consisting of a Northern branch and a Southern branch. Sinitic is contained in the Northern branch at a tertiary level of branching, instead of being one of the primary branches. Thus, the whole language family is named Tibeto-Burman accordingly. The homeland of Tibeto-Burman is in the southwestern Chinese province of Sichuan. The group began to diverge more than 9000 years ago when the ancestors of the Western Tibeto-Burman migrated from Sichuan to an area around northeastern India, while subsequently in the 7th millennium BC, a group of Tibeto-Burman people moved from Sichuan northward to the Yellow River area in northwest China. These Northern Tibeto-Burmans were the ancestors of the Tibetan and Sinitic groups. The Southern Tibeto-Burmans that remained in Sichuan and the surrounding areas were ancestors of speakers of languages such as Burmese and Qiang.

The linguistic methods to determine the time depth and branching of a language family rely on basic vocabulary, for example, the list of 100 basic words, as introduced previously. These basic words are said to change or be replaced in any language at a rather slow rate compared to higher-level cultural words. Swadesh was inspired by the method of carbon-14 dating used to determine the age of fossils of animals or plants. Carbon-14 is a radioactive isotope of carbon that has a half-life of about 5700 years. If we assume that the 100 basic words in languages also change at a constant rate, which can be independently obtained by studying languages with a known divergence time, and that no contacts occurred between two daughter languages after the split, then by studying the percentage of shared cognate words in two languages, we can calculate the time when the ancestral language split into two languages. But this early method has been proven to be inaccurate. The rate at which basic vocabulary changes varies across different languages and across different semantic groups of words.

More recently, mathematical methods developed in phylogenetics in biology have been applied to the study of linguistic prehistory. Wang (1994) discusses a method based on percentage of shared cognates. The assumption is that the longer ago a language diverged into separate daughter languages, the lower the number of shared cognates tends to be. For example, the percentage of shared cognates between the Xiamen dialect in the Min group and Beijing Mandarin is 56% (Xu 1991: 422; Wang 1994: 1448), while the percentage is 79% between the Changsha dialect in the Xiang group and Beijing Mandarin. Such data can be converted to measures of distances among the dialects, which can then be visualized in a tree with branches of differing lengths. For example, the distance between Xiamen Min and Beijing Mandarin should be greater than that between Changsha Xiang and Beijing Mandarin. These two distance numbers can be drawn as different lengths of branches that connect the two dialects in each pair. Wang (1998) further shows how the method can be used to study how old the Sino-Tibetan family is.

First, Wang (1998) collects data on distances among the following three groups of languages: major Chinese dialects; major Sino-Tibetan languages; and representative Indo-European languages, including Singhalese, Tajik, Portuguese, and such Germanic languages as English, Danish, and German. Then trees are drawn according to the distance matrices for each group. These trees are then compared. It is shown that the time depth of the Chinese dialects is comparable to that of the Germanic languages. This corresponds well to the fact that the Chinese language started to diverge about 2000 years ago, roughly at the same time that the Germanic languages started to split. These divergence times are independently confirmed via written records. Therefore, the Germanic tree and the Sinitic tree can be used as yardsticks to measure a tree of an unknown time depth. Specifically, the Germanic languages form a subtree of the whole Indo-European tree. Since the time depth of the Germanic subtree is about 2000 years, we can now compare the length of the Germanic subtree to that of the Indo-European. It shows that the length of the Indo-European tree is about 3.5 times that of the Germanic subtree. Now we can tentatively conclude that the Indo-European language family is about 7000 years old. Wang (1998) points out that there are actually two major theories for when the Proto-Indo-European language started to split: 6000 BP and 8500 BP. Therefore, the 7000 BP here is situated right between these two numbers. This shows that the method may be a valid one that can yield reasonable results.

A comparison between the tree for the Chinese dialects and the whole Sino-Tibetan tree shows that the latter is about three times as deep as the former. Therefore, it seems to suggest that the Sino-Tibetan language family is 6000 years old, slightly younger than the Indo-European family. This number can be further corroborated by archaeological and genetic evidence. Wang (1998: 532) cites three maps from Chang (1986: 235) showing prehistoric cultures in East Asia at 9000 BP, 7000 BP, and 6000/5000 BP. The map at 9000 BP shows three clusters of cultures in the upper and middle Yellow River region, in the lower Yangtze River region, and in southern China, respectively. These cultures showed no clear evidence of interactions. The map for 7000 BP contains three major cultures that span the whole region of northern China, two cultures in the lower Yangtze River, and a vast culture that spans the southernmost coastal area of China. At this stage, there was still no major interactions between these cultures. The third map for 6000/5000 BP presents a picture of a network of cultures from north to south that had a significant degree of interactions.

Wang (1998) concludes that population movements brought about similarities between these cultures, and alongside such migrations, people brought their own languages to different areas. Therefore, a former linguistic community would split up into different linguistic communities; formerly different linguistic communities would also come into close contact with each other so that they could borrow words from each other. A possible scenario that can be reconstructed from the previously mentioned maps of prehistoric cultures is that the Sino-Tibetan people originally inhabited the upper and middle Yellow River region, and some of them migrated down the river to the east and then to the south, getting into contact with other cultures. This scenario is supported by linguistic evidence.

In the first millennium BC, that is, the Old Chinese period, there were various non-Sinitic peoples in the lower Yangtze River region and southern China. According to historical records, these peoples were called the *Bǎiyuè* 百越, that is, Hundred Yue, or ancient Yue. They had very different cultural practices from the northern *Huáxià* 華夏 culture, that is, what was to develop into the Chinese culture. As for the language that the ancient Yue peoples spoke, it might be related to the Austroasiatic, Kam-Tai, and Hmong-Mien languages (Brindley 2015: 45–61). If the ancestors of these languages were indeed those that were spoken by the ancient Yue, we may find very early loanwords as a result of cultural contacts.

Let's look at some examples of such loanwords now. There are two main words that can be used to refer to rivers in Chinese: *jiāng* 江 and *hé* 河. They are used more or less interchangeably to mean "*river*" in Modern Standard Chinese, although *jiāng* is usually a major river, because *jiāng* cannot be described by prefixing the word *xiǎo* 小 ("small"), but *hé* can be prefixed with either *dà* 大 ("big") or *xiǎo* 小 ("small"). Originally, *jiāng* was a proper name referring to the Yangtze River, and *hé* was a proper name for the Yellow River. In ancient times, the Chinese people inhabited the Yellow River region in the north, while a group of the Yue people lived along the lower Yangtze River. Therefore, these two words were how these different peoples referred to the rivers of their homelands. Later these two words would eventually be generalized to refer to rivers in Chinese. The word *hé* (Old Chinese: *\*[C.g]ˤaj*)[4] might be a native Chinese word that is related to the Written Tibetan word "*rgal-ba*" for "to pass or ford a river" (Schuessler 2007; Coblin 1986). The phonological connection between the first syllable of the Written Tibetan word, "*rgal*," and the reconstructed Old Chinese word is quite clear. On the other hand, Norman (1988: 18) relates the word *jiāng* to Austroasiatic languages such as Vietnamese. The reconstructed pronunciation of *jiāng* in Old Chinese is *\*kˤroŋ*; the reconstructed pronunciation of the word "*river*" in Vietnamese is *\*kroŋ*. Here the phonological similarity is even more evident. The Yangtze River may have been referred to by the ancient Yue people as "the river," and the northern Sinitic people adopted the Yue word to refer to the Yangtze River when they came into contact with the ancient Yue.

Norman (1988: 17) also gives an example of a loanword from the ancestral language of the Hmong-Mien language. There are two words for "*dog*" in Chinese: *quǎn* 犬 and *gǒu* 狗. The first one, *quǎn*, cannot be used as an independent word in most Chinese dialects now anymore, except for in some Min dialects. There are clear Sino-Tibetan cognates of this word, showing that it might be the original Chinese word for "*dog*." But in most modern Chinese dialects, the word for "*dog*" is related to the word *gǒu*. The reconstructed form of the word "*dog*" in Proto-Miao-Yao, that is, Proto-Hmong-Mien, is *\*klu² B* (Purnell 1970);[5] while the Old Chinese reconstruction is *\*Cə.kˤroʔ*. The phonological connection between the Proto-Miao-Yao form and the main syllable of the reconstructed Old Chinese form, *kˤroʔ*, is quite straightforward here as well. Therefore, it could be evidence of early contacts between the Sinitic people in the north and the Hmong-Mien people in the south.

Chen (1993) presents data for the contacts between the Sinitic people and the Kam-Tai people. There has been archaeological evidence for the early cultivation of rice in southern China. The word for "*rice plant*" in Classical Chinese is *hé* 禾, written with a different character from the word *hé* 河 for "*river*" mentioned previously. The reconstructed pronunciation of *hé* 禾 in Old Chinese is *\*[ɢ]ˤoj*. Chen (1993) lists the following pronunciations from Kam-Tai: *hau⁴* (Wuming Zhuang), *kha²* (Thai).[6] The phonological connection here may be less obvious, but these words are nonetheless related. Thus, it is possible that the word for "*rice plant*" was borrowed into Chinese when the Sinitic people came into contact with the ancient Yue people in the south and learned how to cultivate rice from them.

Therefore, the evidence from linguistics and archaeology supports a migration scenario where a group of Sino-Tibetan people migrated from their homeland in the upper and middle Yellow River area in the western part of northern China along the river first to the eastern part of northern China and then southward to the

Yangtze River area, coming into contact with the ancient Yue people, who spoke languages that may be related to the Austroasiatic, Hmong-Mien, and Kam-Tai languages. There was also a separate migration from the Sino-Tibetan homeland further west and then south to Tibet and the Himalayan region. Linguists have established over 300 cognate words between Chinese and Tibeto-Burman languages to firmly establish a common origin for these languages. Now we might look to human population genetics for evidence of this side of the story.

As Wang (1998) points out, genetics and languages often go separate ways. For example, during the Qing dynasty, the Manchu people adopted Mandarin Chinese as their native language. Currently, most of the Manchu people in China can only speak Chinese, while the Manchu language is spoken by the Xibe people in Xinjiang and also by Manchu people in a few villages in northeastern China. Similarly to how the Manchu people adopted Chinese as their native language, there are many other examples where genetically different ethnic groups in China speak Chinese as their native language. However, recent research in human population genetics can use a more reliable genetic marker to trace human migration. Su et al. (2000) argue that "as delineating migrations becomes one of the major themes in human evolution studies, Y chromosome markers began to show their power in tracing human prehistory." Their studies analyze the genetic structures of 31 Sino-Tibetan populations represented by 607 individuals residing in East, Southeast, and South Asia. Su et al. (2000) conclude that the Sino-Tibetan homeland is the upper and middle Yellow River basin, and about 5000–6000 years ago, the Proto-Sino-Tibetan language began to split into the Sinitic branch and the Tibeto-Burman branch. The Tibeto-Burman group migrated westward and then southward to the Himalayas. The Sinitic group expanded to the east and south.

As pointed out previously, there are two main theories regarding the primary branching of the Sino-Tibetan tree, the original homeland of the Sino-Tibetan people, and the time when the proto-language began to diverge. The evidence presented so far supports the northern origin, with a divergence time as early as 6000 BP. But we have not presented any evidence against the alternative theory of the Sino-Tibetan language family originating in southwestern China more than 9000 years ago, with a primary branching between a western group and an eastern group (van Driem 1999). To decide between these two theories, Zhang et al. (2019) apply statistical analyses based on Bayesian probability to a vast amount of data consisting of 949 lexical root-meanings from 109 Sino-Tibetan languages from China, Southeast Asia, and South Asia. The Bayesian phylogenetic method shares many basic assumptions with Wang (1994) and Wang (1998), as discussed previously.

First, the 949 lexical root-meanings are derived from the Swadesh 100 basic words. For a basic vocabulary item on the list, there may be different words in different languages, not all of which are cognates. In the study by Wang (1994), cognates need to be identified first, and then the percentage of shared cognates is calculated. However, to avoid the uncertainty associated with determining which words are cognates, we may look at root-meanings. Chang et al. (2015: 201–202) provide the following example. The English word "*feather*" and the Latin word "*penna*" share the same meaning of "*feather*" and the same Proto-Indo-European root *pet* ("to fly"), although they are not cognates because they did not descend from the same form. Thus, the English *"feather"* and the Latin *"penna"* form a root-meaning pair for the basic word meaning *"feather."* There are often other such pairs for the same basic word meaning. For example, Friulian *"plume"* and Spanish *"pluma"* form a root-meaning pair for *"feather"* as well. Therefore, similar data can be collected from the Sino-Tibetan languages and coded for whether they share the same root-meanings.

Second, prior knowledge of known events in the development of a language family is used in the statistical analysis. Similarly to how Wang (1998) uses the divergence time of 2000 BP among the Chinese dialects to assess the time depth of the whole Sino-Tibetan tree, here in the Bayesian analysis, prior knowledge is used to determine the most probable branching and time depth of a language family based on the root-meaning data. Chang et al. (2015) discuss the details of the Bayesian method, but for now, what we want to show is that new studies may lend support to the discussion of the Sino-Tibetan language family.

According to Zhang et al. (2019), the most probable primary branching within the Sino-Tibetan family is between the Sinitic branch and the Tibeto-Burman branch approximately 7800–4200 BP, with a mean of 5871 BP. They further link the primary branches of the Sino-Tibetan tree to two Neolithic cultures and ancient agriculture. The Yangshao culture, or *Yǎngsháo wénhuà* 仰韶文化, dated 7000 BP–5000 BP in the upper and middle Yellow River region, corresponds to the time depth of the Sino-Tibetan family, while a later culture to the west of Yangshao, called the Majiayao culture, or *Mǎjiāyáo wénhuà* 馬家窯文化, dated 5300 BP–4000 BP in the upper Yellow River area corresponds to the initial Tibeto-Burman divergence time at 4665 BP. Zhang et al. (2019) also argue that the theory of Sino-Tibetan language dispersal can be further validated by the geographical distribution of millet agriculture after 6000 BP.[7] The conclusions by Zhang et al. (2019) are therefore contra the alternative theory of the Sino-Tibetan family originating in the southwestern area of China more than 9000 years ago, with a primary branching between a western group and an eastern group.

## 2.4   Linguistic properties of Proto-Sino-Tibetan

Now one more question is in order. What was this Proto-Sino-Tibetan language like? The reconstruction of Proto-Sino-Tibetan has not yet been carried out to the extent of Proto-Indo-European. We do not have a full picture of the sounds, words, and grammar of Proto-Sino-Tibetan yet, but we can look at some features of Chinese and Tibetan in the hope of glimpsing what the original ancestral language may have been like. The branch of linguistics that classifies languages into different types based on their formal features, rather than genetic relationship, is called typology. Although typologically similar languages often do not belong to the same language family, languages which descended from the same ancestral language may preserve the original typological features of the proto-language to different extents. Thus, if we find that there are many typological differences between Modern Standard Chinese and Modern Standard Tibetan, then the proto-language may very well have a selection of these features.

One of the most common criteria of typological classification is basic word order of the subject, the object and the verb. For example, in the English sentence "*John loves Jane*," "*John*" is the subject, "*loves*" is the verb, and "*Jane*" is the object. Therefore, this sentence has the subject-verb-object, or SVO, word order. A typical sentence in English would be in the SVO form. Thus, we say that English is an SVO language. In terms of basic word order, Modern Standard Chinese is normally considered an SVO language, while Tibetan is SOV. With such a contrast, it may be the case that Proto-Sino-Tibetan was either SVO or SOV, and in some modern languages, the word order has changed. Actually, there is evidence that the SOV word order was more common in Classical Chinese, which is discussed in Chapter 6. Thus, it is very likely that Proto-Sino-Tibetan was SOV.

Another feature of Modern Standard Chinese is that there is no morphological change; that is, a verb or a noun will always have the same form, while grammatical functions and relations are indicated by separate morphemes. In contrast, Tibetan has a complex morphological system. As it turns out, Classical Chinese had more word shape changes compared to Modern Standard Chinese, although the nature of the Chinese writing system makes such morphological properties of Classical Chinese less obvious. We provide evidence for Classical Chinese morphology in Chapter 6 as well. Thus, it is likely that the Proto-Sino-Tibetan language may have had a complex system of morphological devices.

In terms of the phonological system, we may consider two features, that is, tones and consonant clusters. Modern Standard Chinese has four tones. Modern Standard Tibetan based on Lhasa has four tones,[8] while Amdo Tibetan spoken in the Qinghai province region does not have tones. Therefore, there are both tonal and non-tonal languages in the Sino-Tibetan family. If tones are an inherent feature of a language, meaning that a tonal language would always have tones, then it contradicts the theory of a Sino-Tibetan language family. We provide evidence in Chapter 3 that Old Chinese very likely did not have tones either and that in general, tones can develop within a language that did not have tones. Thus, Amdo Tibetan may have been more representative of the Proto-Sino-Tibetan in not having tones. The second phonological feature is consonant clusters at the beginning of a syllable. For example, in Tibetan, we find words that begin with more than one consonant, such as in "*zgo*" ("door") and "*pki*" ("carry") from Daofu Tibetan (Hu 1980). However, consonant clusters of any type are not allowed in Modern Standard Chinese. Only one consonant can occur at the beginning of a modern Chinese syllable. Given the diverse composition of consonant clusters in Tibetan and in many other Sino-Tibetan languages, it is less likely for these consonant clusters to have developed later, because simplification of consonant clusters is universally more common. We provide evidence in Chapter 3 that there were consonant clusters in Old Chinese. Proto-Sino-Tibetan probably also had consonant clusters.

Thus, by looking at all these different parameters that can be incorporated into the reconstruction of Proto-Sino-Tibetan, we may conclude with some confidence here that Modern Standard Chinese has changed drastically in terms of its grammar, morphology, and phonology compared to its Sino-Tibetan relatives. But if we go back 2000 years to Old Chinese, the language at that time might have been a little more similar to the original Sino-Tibetan language. Chapter 3 provides a comprehensive introduction to the sounds of Old Chinese, while the grammar and morphology of Old Chinese are dealt with in Chapter 6 on Classical Chinese.

## Notes

1　The older name for this language family is Tai-Kadai, but following a recent proposal by Ostapirat (2000), we use the more correct term Kra-Dai here.
2　This classification is based on Edmondson and Solnit (1988). For a more recent but different classification system, see Ostapirat (2005).
3　Written Tibetan and Written Burmese pronunciations are taken from Norman (1988: 13). The Old Chinese pronunciations are from the new Baxter-Sagart system. See Chapter 3 for details on the notation in the Baxter-Sagart system.
4　This is also the new Baxter-Sagart system.
5　In Purnell's (1970) reconstruction here, the letter B represents a tonal category; the main vowel $u^2$ represents some type of [ u ] sound.
6　The superscript numbers, that is, 2 and 4 here, are tones.
7　Additionally, Sagart et al. (2019) use data on cognate words and the Bayesian phylogenetic methods to study the Sino-Tibetan family and arrive at comparable conclusions to Zhang et al. (2019), although in the study by Sagart et al. (2019), the time depth of the Sino-Tibetan family is 7200 BP, which is considerably earlier than the 6000 BP that other studies suggest. But their conclusions are otherwise consistent with the northern origin of the Sino-Tibetan family.
8　The tonal system of Lhasa Tibetan is variably described as having either two tones, that is, high vs. low, or four tones, that is, high-level, high-falling, low-level, low-falling.

# 3 Old Chinese

## The elegant speech

The phrase "*zǐ yuē shī yún* (子曰詩云)" is commonly used in Chinese to refer to classical learning in general, but its literal meaning is "*thus spake Confucius; so says the Classic of Poetry.*" Confucius has been considered the most important educator and philosopher in Chinese history. Although we can read about his teachings recorded in Classical Chinese texts, we still wonder what spoken language Confucius used and what the poems in the *Classic of Poetry* sounded like in ancient times. We know the content of "*zǐ yuē shī yún*," but can we know the sounds of "*zǐ yuē shī yún*"?

## 3.1 Evidence of sound change

To ask the question about the sounds of the language spoken by Confucius approximately 2500 years ago, we have to know that sounds have changed in the first place. The fact that linguistic sounds change is obvious for speakers whose language has been written down in a phonetic writing system such as the English alphabet. Take the first line of the Old English saga *Beowulf*, for example: "*Hwæt wē Gār-Dena in geār-dagum . . .*"[1] Although the letters look familiar enough, we cannot readily pronounce the words unless we have some knowledge of Old English phonology. The spelling shows that the Old English language may have sounded quite different more than 1000 years ago. In comparison, the Chinese writing system, which uses symbols called "*characters*," actually tends to hide sound change, since the characters do not represent sounds *directly*. Although there is often phonetic information encoded in the composition of a type of characters called phono-semantic compounds, that is, *xíngshēngzì* 形聲字 (literally "form-and-sound character"), there are some reasons why sound change is not easily detected in Chinese.

For one thing, quite a number of characters such as pictograms do not contain any phonetic information. For example, the character 人, meaning "*person*," is a pictogram and has not changed much in terms of its shape for over 2000 years. The Modern Standard Chinese pronunciation of this character is *rén*. But in the written graph, there is no component that would correspond to the sounds "*r*," "*e*," "*n*" or the tone. In Old Chinese, the pronunciation of 人 was *\*ni[ŋ]* in the reconstruction system by Baxter and Sagart (2014). Even though the shape of the written symbol actually has changed a little, such changes have nothing to do with sounds. In this case, at different times in the history of the Chinese language, people just associated different pronunciations with the same written graph 人. This leads to the second reason, which is that for all Chinese characters, including the phono-semantic compounds, the association of sounds with the written symbols is much freer than in phonetic writing systems. The same character can be read in any pronunciation system, even in English. You could pronounce the graph 人 as "*person.*" Therefore, when a modern Chinese speaker reads the *Analects*, they read all the characters using modern pronunciations, while in contrast, a modern reader can appreciate Cicero's oratorial eloquence in Latin after just a few hours of studying how to pronounce the letters. Therefore, the Chinese writing system, in some respect, may be an obstacle to the study of sound change. If we had a phonetic alphabet of the Chinese language in Old Chinese and Middle Chinese, a study of these written symbols could reveal a great deal about the sounds of the Chinese language at these stages. But since Chinese has always been written down in characters,[2] we have to either use other materials that could show how the language was spoken or try to see if any phonetic information in Chinese characters can be utilized systematically to study the sounds of Old Chinese.

Before we move on to the next topic, a caveat is in order here to caution against the "*Ideographic Myth*" that has been debunked by DeFrancis (1984). A common misconception of the Chinese writing system is that the written symbols are ideographic, that is, representing ideas without any involvement of sounds. As illustrated previously, there are pictograms in Chinese characters such as the one for the word "*person,*" that is, 人, but each one of such non-phonetic symbols is associated with a sound, and the majority of Chinese characters are of the phono-semantic type which encodes phonetic information. Therefore, it is not correct to consider the Chinese writing system a silent one, contrasting sharply with a phonetic writing system such as the Latin alphabet. If indeed Chinese characters were silent, it would be almost impossible to deduce the phonological properties of Old Chinese at all. We show in this chapter that Chinese characters are one of the key sources for the reconstruction of Old Chinese. For a detailed discussion of various issues related to the Chinese writing system, please refer to Chapter 11 of this book.

Now let's digress briefly to the reign of the Emperor Wu of Han during the 2nd and 1st centuries BC in the Han dynasty, when Confucianism was elevated to the status of the ruling ideology of the empire. This led to extensive and continuous studies of Confucian classics for the next 2000 years, ultimately preserving and producing a wealth of written records on the language from Old Chinese up to more recent times. Another factor for the dominance of Confucianism in Chinese culture is that in the Sui dynasty, around the turn of the 7th century AD, with the establishment of the Imperial Examination system, all scholars would have to know the Confucian classics very well by heart in order to pass the examination and secure a place in the imperial government. The rhyme dictionary called the *Qièyùn* 切韻 from the Sui dynasty would become the literary standard sanctioned by the central government for the imperial examination in the next few centuries. This examination system, which developed into ever more complicated forms until it was abolished in the early 20th century,[3] further strengthened the status of Confucian classics. The original Classical Chinese works are the textual basis for the study of Old Chinese, while subsequent works, including commentaries made by later scholars on these classics and rhyme dictionaries like the *Qièyùn*, can be used to study the development of the Chinese language since Old Chinese. In this chapter, we focus on the written sources of Old Chinese.

One of the two most important sources for the reconstruction of Old Chinese phonology is the *Classic of Poetry*, or the *Shījīng* 詩經, from the 10th–7th centuries BC.[4] The *Shījīng* is a collection of poems in the Western Zhou dynasty and the Spring and Autumn period. There are 305 poems that belong with one of the three genres: folk songs (*fēng* 風), court hymns (*yǎ* 雅), and eulogies (*sòng* 頌). Although these are normally called or translated as "*poetry*," they were originally songs that could be sung to music. It is believed that both early court musicians and Confucius edited the collection in terms of the language. The importance of these poems can be seen in Confucius' famous diction that "if you do not learn the Odes, you will not be fit to converse with."[5] Consequently the *Shījīng* assumed a central role in classical education in later dynasties.

When reading the poems using Modern Standard Chinese pronunciations, we encounter many problems with rhyming. Take the following verse from the *Shījīng*, as shown in Table 3.1, as an example. Note that in the *Shījīng*, we often find that a character appears in multiple lines, but these reoccurring characters are usually functional words, as opposed to words with concrete meanings, and therefore we have to exclude them from the rhymes; for example, the word *zhī* 之 in the verse here, and then the characters next to the word *zhī*, that is, 芼 and 樂, are in the rhyme positions. But the vowels in Modern Standard Chinese pronunciations of these two characters, that is, *mào* and *lè*, are so different that it would take quite a bit of imagination to make them rhyme.

The rhyming problem in reading the *Shījīng* is not a recent one. As early as in the Northern and Southern dynasties, when people read the *Shījīng*, in many cases, the poems sounded out of rhyme, with no clue as to what the original rhymes would be. One view of this phenomenon was that the characters that did not rhyme in the contemporary pronunciation were probably copied wrong in the process of transmission. Therefore, to make these poems rhyme, one could change the character to another one with a sound that could make the poem rhyme. An alternative view is that although some poems did not rhyme well, it could be that in the time

*Table 3.1* A sample verse from the *Shījīng*

| Chinese Characters | Modern Standard Chinese | English Translation (by James Legge) |
|---|---|---|
| 參差荇菜， | cēncī xìng cài | Here long, there short, is the duckweed; |
| 左右芼之。 | zuǒ yòu mào zhī | On the left, on the right, we cook and present it. |
| 窈窕淑女， | yǎotiǎo shū nǚ | The modest, retiring, virtuous, young lady: |
| 鍾鼓樂之。 | zhōng gǔ lè zhī | With bells and drums let us show our delight in her. |

of the *Shījīng*, rhyming was not strict, and therefore the characters did not need to be changed because they were not meant to rhyme precisely in the first place. A third view, called *xiéyīn* 叶音, is that the pronunciations could be temporarily changed for rhyming purposes. For example, if we change the *lè* to *lào* in the verse in Table 3.1, then they would rhyme again. The influential Confucian scholar *Zhū Xī* 朱熹 (AD 1130–1200) in the Southern Song dynasty was a proponent of this theory. For all of these views on the rhyming issue in the *Shījīng*, they either fail to realize that sounds change over time or fail to correctly understand what sound change means. Not until the Ming dynasty did Chinese scholars finally articulate in clear terms the concept of sound change. *Chén Dì* 陳第 (AD 1541–1617) stated that "there is a temporal distinction between the past and the present, and a geographical distinction between the south and the north. It is thus inevitable that characters and sounds change accordingly."[6] He demonstrated that the rhyming practice in the *Shījīng* was systematic and the pronunciations of characters in ancient times were different from modern times. *Chén Dì*'s theory pioneered the philological study in the Qing dynasty, that is, the *xiǎoxué* 小學 (literally "small learning"), which greatly advanced our understanding of the historical development of the Chinese language.

## 3.2    Syllable structure of Chinese

Before discussing how we can use the rhyming scheme in the *Shījīng* for the study of Old Chinese, some basic phonological knowledge of the structure of Chinese syllables is needed. First, there are two traditional concepts called *shuāngshēng* 雙聲 (literally "double initials") and *diéyùn* 疊韻 (literally "double rhymes"), which have been used to describe phonological connections between characters. *Shuāngshēng* is similar to a type of alliteration in English. For example:

Chinese example：忐忑 *tǎntè* ("nervous"); English example: *teeny tiny*

If two characters start with the same sound, then they are in the *shuāngshēng* relation. The word 忐忑 *tǎntè* for "nervous" has two syllables, and they start with the same consonant, "*t*." The first two characters in the poem in Table 3.1, that is, *cēncī*, form another instance of *shuāngshēng*.

*Diéyùn* is when two characters rhyme. For example:

Chinese example: 窈窕 *yǎo tiǎo* ("elegant"); English example: *prime time*

The word "*yǎotiǎo*" consists of two morphemes that have the same rhyme "*ao*" in modern pronunciation. Thus, this pair of traditional terminology analyzes a Chinese syllable in terms of its initial sound and rhyme.[7] Note that in the word "*yǎotiǎo*," the sounds represented by the letters "*y*" and "*i*" are not considered in determining the rhymes. In modern terminology, the sounds represented by the letters "*y*" and "*i*" here are called medials. Then the medial together with the rhyme form a unit called the final. For example, in "*tiǎo*," the initial is "*t*," the medial is "*i*," the rhyme is "*ao*," and furthermore "*iao*" is the final.

Another feature of Chinese is its tones. For example, in English, when one says "*yes?*" as in doubt or "*yes!*" as in confirmation, the word "*yes*" itself is considered unchanged in its basic meaning, although the intonations associated with these two utterances are different, with the former being a rising tone and the latter being a falling tone. Such pitch differences in intonation do not change basic word meanings in English. But in Chinese, each syllable is associated with a specific pitch pattern, comparable to the intonation mentioned here. The same syllable in Chinese can mean different things when associated with different pitch patterns or tones. By analogy, if "*yes*" were a Chinese syllable, "*yes?*" and "*yes!*" could be two words with different unrelated meanings. In Modern Standard Chinese, there are four tones. They are commonly referred to as the 1st, 2nd, 3rd, and 4th tones. Table 3.2 shows examples of four words that can be distinguished by their tones only.

The same syllable, "*ma*," can be uttered with four different pitch shapes. The 1st tone is a high flat tone; the 2nd tone is a mid rising tone; the 3rd tone is a low dipping tone; the 4th tone is a high falling tone. The diacritics above the syllable "*ma*" indicate the four tones. A more accurate way of representing tones is to use numerals on a scale of 1–5, as shown in the third row of Table 3.2. These numerals correspond to the contours in Figure 3.1.

The vertical line on the right represents the levels of pitch distinctions needed to make all the tonal distinctions in a given language, with 1 being the lowest and 5 the highest. The 1st tone is represented by 55, which means the starting pitch is 5, and it should be maintained all throughout. The 2nd tone is 35, the 3rd tone is

*Table 3.2* Four tones in Modern Standard Chinese

| Tones | 1st Tone | 2nd Tone | 3rd Tone | 4th Tone |
|---|---|---|---|---|
| Pinyin | mā | má | mǎ | mà |
| Numerals | 55 | 35 | 214 | 51 |
| Characters | 媽 | 麻 | 馬 | 罵 |
| Meaning | mother | hemp, flax | horse | scold |

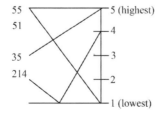

*Figure 3.1* Pitch contours of Modern Standard Chinese tones

214, and the 4th tone is 51. This system can be used to describe any tonal system, including all the tones in Chinese dialects. Moreover, when it is necessary, we can use such numerals to describe the shape of Chinese tones in different stages of the history of the language.

*Shěn Yuē* 沈約 (AD 441–513) of the Northern and Southern dynasties was the first person to describe tones in Chinese. Traditionally, there were four tones in Middle Chinese, including *píngshēng* 平聲 ("the level tone"), *shǎngshēng* 上聲 ("the rising tone"), *qùshēng* 去聲 ("the departing tone"), and *rùshēng* 入聲 ("the entering tone"). But these four tones are not the same as the four tones in Modern Standard Chinese, although they are historically related. We describe how the tones changed throughout the history of the language as we go. It is useful to establish here the notion of tones and the basic four-tone system in Middle Chinese, that is, *píng*, *shǎng*, *qù*, and *rù*, since they are the most important tonal categories that are used as references to tonal changes in Chinese.

There is also a system of notation for tonal categories by using a half circle on the four corners of a character or a syllable. For example, ₒ平, ᶜ上, 去ᵒ, 入ᵒ, which have the *píng*, *shǎng*, *qù*, and *rù* tones, respectively, in Middle Chinese. The *píng* tone is indicated via the small circle on the lower left corner of the character, the *shǎng* tone corresponds to the small circle on the upper left corner, the *qù* tone is labeled with a flipped half circle on the upper right corner, and the *rù* tone is noted by the flipped half circle on the lower right corner. If a tonal category splits into an upper *yīn* register and a lower *yáng* register, the *yáng* tone is indicated by an underline. For example, the four tones in Modern Standard Chinese are also called *yīnpíng* 陰平, *yángpíng* 陽平, *shǎngshēng* 上聲, and *qùshēng* 去聲 in terms of their historical origins. We may indicate these tonal categories by using the same half circles. For example, the four syllables in Table 3.2 can be labeled as ₒma, ₒma, ᶜma, maᵒ, in the order from the 1st tone to the 4th tone. This notation is very useful when comparing tonal categories between different stages of the language or among different dialects.

We have introduced four components of a Chinese syllable: initial, medial, rhyme, and tone. Thus, in terms of sound changes, all of these components can change. Table 3.3 shows how these components are structured in a syllable.

The initial, or *shēngmǔ* 聲母, is usually a consonant, but sometimes when the syllable does not have an initial consonant, a zero initial can be posited to keep the structural analysis uniform. The part of the syllable minus the initial is called the final, or *yùnmǔ* 韻母, which in turn comprises the medial called *jièyīn* 介音 and the rhyme called *yùn* 韻.[8] The rhyme itself is further composed of the main

*Table 3.3* Syllable structure of Chinese

| Tone | | | |
|---|---|---|---|
| (Initial) | Final | | |
| | (Medial) | Rhyme | |
| | | Main Vowel | (Coda) |

vowel called *yùnfù* 韻腹 (literally "belly of the rhyme") and a coda called *yùnwěi* 韻尾 (literally "tail of the rhyme"). In this connection, the medial can also be described as the *yùntóu* 韻頭 ("head of the rhyme"). In Modern Standard Chinese, the medial is one of the following three sounds: *i*, *u*, and *ü* in the *pīnyīn* notation, or equivalently in International Phonetic Alphabet (IPA, see Appendix II) notation as [ i, u, y ]. Codas include -*i*, -*o*, -*n*, and -*ng* represented in *pīnyīn*, or equivalently [ i, u, n, ŋ ] in IPA. The tone is superimposed on the syllable.[9] Table 3.4 shows various representative syllable types in Chinese with an analysis of their initials, medials, and rhymes. The tones are all omitted from these syllables. All the letters are *pīnyīn* letters.

As can be seen from the table, the only component that cannot be omitted is the main vowel. The brackets in Table 3.3 indicate such optionality.

The terminology introduced so far is the primary framework used in Chinese linguistics, but in general linguistics, phonological systems are described primarily in terms of consonants and vowels. For example, the English syllable "*pet*" has a CVC structure, meaning that it consists of a consonant followed by a vowel and then by another consonant. In the reconstruction of a proto-language, it is the consonants and vowels that are reconstructed. We could do the same with Chinese. But traditionally and practically, it is more convenient in Chinese linguistics to use terms such as *initial*, *medial*, *rhyme*, *main vowel*, *coda*, and *tone* rather than *consonant* and *vowel*. The concepts of "*initial*" and "*consonant*" are actually quite different. In Modern Standard Chinese, there are 22 consonants, including a velar nasal sound [ ŋ ] like the "*ng*" in the English word "*sing*." This consonant cannot appear at the beginning of a Modern Standard Chinese syllable and thus is not an initial, although it is a consonant. On the other hand, if we consider the zero initial, it is not a consonant. Thus, not all consonants are initials, and not all initials are consonants. The concepts of "*final*" and "*vowel*" are even more different. A final can comprise a vowel plus a consonant, for example, "*en*" and "*ong*," or two

*Table 3.4* Sample analysis of syllable structure of Modern Standard Chinese

| *Syllable* | Shēngmǔ *Initial* | Yùntóu *Medial* | Yùnfù *Main Vowel* | Yùnwěi *Coda* |
|---|---|---|---|---|
| tiao | t | i | a | o |
| tai | t | | a | i |
| tuan | t | u | a | n |
| yan | | y | a | n |
| an | | | a | n |
| a | | | a | |
| tang | t | | a | ng |
| ta | t | | a | |
| ya | | y | a | |

vowels, for example, "*eï*" and "*ao*." Despite such terminological differences in the theoretical frameworks, the two systems can be converted back and forth. For example, after the system of consonants and vowels is established, we can derive the initials and finals. Conversely, if the initials and finals are the primary objects of study, we can also extract the consonants and vowels from the system of initials and finals. In this book, we focus on the traditional methods based on notions such as *initial*, *final*, *rhyme*, and *tone* primarily.

## 3.3   Rhyme groups of Old Chinese

For the reconstruction of all stages of the Chinese language, the phonological system recorded in the Middle Chinese rhyme dictionary *Qièyùn* 切韻, and its expanded version called the *Guǎngyùn* 廣韻 is a standard reference system. Since most of the poems in the *Shījīng* have rhymes, we can simply compare the rhymes of Middle Chinese to the rhyming practice in the *Shījīng* to see which characters rhymed in Old Chinese and then regroup the rhymes of Middle Chinese into rhyme groups, or *yùnbù* 韻部, in Old Chinese. After the rhyme groups of Old Chinese have been established, their phonetic values can be reconstructed based on the reconstructed system of Middle Chinese and other relevant materials and evidence. Chapter 4 discusses Middle Chinese phonology and may be read before this chapter if one prefers. Alternatively, one can focus on this current chapter but consult Chapter 4 whenever needed.

Rhyming in the *Shījīng* is fairly systematic. Thus, let's assume that whenever two characters appear in rhyme positions of a poem, they should have the same rhyme in Old Chinese, regardless of whether they still rhyme in modern pronunciation. This assumption is to be modified. Here, if we study all 305 poems and link the characters that appear in rhyme positions, we can put these characters into a finite number of groups representing distinct rhymes of Old Chinese. Let's look at the following poem from the *Shījīng*, in Table 3.5.

In this poem, called *Jiānjiā* 蒹葭 ("Reeds"), there are three stanzas. Each stanza comprises eight lines, of which seven lines have four characters each, and the eighth line has five characters.

In the first stanza, the characters at the end of lines 2, 4, 6, 8 are 霜, 方, 長, and 央, and they all belong with the rhyme class called 陽 in Middle Chinese, as recorded in the *Guǎngyùn*. The character 蒼 at the end of line 1 belongs with the Middle Chinese 唐 rhyme. According to a note in the *Guǎngyùn*, characters from the 陽 class can rhyme with those from the 唐 class. Thus, it seems reasonable to assume here in the first stanza that lines 1, 2, 4, 6, 8 all rhymed in Old Chinese, and correspondingly the characters 蒼, 霜, 方, 長, and 央 belong with one rhyme group in Old Chinese. As a further confirmation, all five characters are pronounced with the same rhyme, "*ang*," in Modern Standard Chinese. This suggests that despite sound changes, the rhyming scheme here in the first stanza is preserved very well in Modern Standard Chinese.

The rhyming situation in the second stanza is quite complicated. Let's look at the third stanza before returning to the second. Since the even-numbered lines,

Table 3.5 The linking method for rhyme groups in Old Chinese

| Verses | Rhyme Groups | English Translation (by James Legge) |
| --- | --- | --- |
| jiānjiā cāng**cāng**, báilù wéi **shuāng** <br> 蒹葭蒼**蒼**，白露為**霜**。 <br> suǒ wèi yī rén, zài shuǐ yì **fāng** <br> 所謂伊人，在水一**方**。 <br> sù huí cóng zhī, dào zǔ qiě **cháng**. <br> 溯洄從之，道阻且**長**。 <br> sù yóu cóng zhī, wǎn zài shuǐ zhōng **yāng** <br> 溯游從之，宛在水中**央**。 | Rhyme Group A: <br> 蒼霜方長央 | The reeds and rushes are deeply green, <br> And the white dew is turned into hoarfrost. <br> The man of whom I think, <br> Is somewhere about the water. <br><br> I go up the stream in quest of him, <br> But the way is difficult and long. <br> I go down the stream in quest of him, <br> And lo! he is right in the midst of the water. |
| jiānjiā qī**qī**, báilù wèi **xī** <br> 蒹葭淒**淒**，白露未**晞**。 <br> suǒ wèi yī rén, zài shuǐ zhī **méi** <br> 所謂伊人，在水之**湄**。 <br> sù huí cóng zhī, dào zǔ qiě **jī** <br> 溯洄從之，道阻且**躋**。 <br> sù yóu cóng zhī, wǎn zài shuǐ zhōng **chí** <br> 溯游從之，宛在水中**坻**。 | Rhyme Group B: <br> 淒晞湄躋坻 | The reeds and rushes are luxuriant, <br> And the white dew is not yet dry. <br> The man of whom I think, <br> Is on the margin of the water. <br><br> I go up the stream in quest of him, <br> But the way is difficult and steep. <br> I go down the stream in quest of him, <br> And lo! he is on the islet in the midst of the water. |
| jiānjiā cǎi**cǎi**, báilù wèi **yǐ** <br> 蒹葭采**采**，白露未**已**。 <br> suǒ wèi yī rén, zài shuǐ zhī **sì** <br> 所謂伊人，在水之**涘**。 <br> sù huí cóng zhī, dào zǔ qiě **yòu** <br> 溯洄從之，道阻且**右**。 <br> sù yóu cóng zhī, wǎn zài shuǐ zhōng **zhǐ** <br> 溯游從之，宛在水中**沚**。 | Rhyme Group C: <br> 采已涘右沚 | The reeds and rushes are abundant, <br> And the white dew is not yet ceased. <br> The man of whom I think, <br> Is on the bank of the river. <br><br> I go up the stream in quest of him, <br> But the way is difficult and turns to the right. <br> I go down the stream in quest of him, <br> And lo! he is on the island in the midst of the water. |

plus the first line, rhyme in the first stanza, we may look at the same positions in the third stanza to look for any clues of rhyming. But the characters at the end of lines 1, 2, 4, 6, and 8 belong with three different rhyme classes in Middle Chinese, and none of their modern pronunciations rhyme at all. Although the main vowels of the characters at the end of lines 2, 4, 8 are spelled the same in their modern pronunciations, the letter "*i*" nonetheless represents three different sounds. The IPA for the vowel in "*yǐ*" is [ i ], that is, the same as the pronunciation of the letter "*e*" in English. The vowel in "*sǐ*" sounds more like a prolonged "*z*" such as in "*zzzz*," and the vowel in "*zhǐ*" is similar to the "*s*" sound in the word "*measure*" but prolonged as well. Yet if we look more closely, we find that the characters at the end of lines 2, 4, and 8 are actually from the same Middle Chinese rhyme class 之. Therefore, at least there is reason to assume that lines 2, 4, 8 may have rhymed in Old Chinese. If we further assume that the rhyme pattern in the third stanza is the same as the first stanza, then lines 1, 2, 4, 6, 8 should have rhymed in Old Chinese. Correspondingly, a new rhyme group is derived, that is, 采已涘右沚.

Now let's look at the second stanza. The characters at the end of lines 1, 2, 4, 6, and 8 belong with three different rhyme classes in Middle Chinese. Although the modern pronunciations suggest that lines 1, 2, 6 rhyme, the characters 淒躋 from lines 1 and 6 belong with the Middle Chinese rhyme class 齊, and the character 晞 on line 2 is from a different rhyme called 微 in Middle Chinese. The remaining two characters 湄坻 on lines 4 and 8 are from the Middle Chinese rhyme 脂. Therefore, no clear pattern of rhyming emerges if we just use Middle Chinese rhymes as a reference. However, since both the first and third stanzas may have followed the same rhyming scheme on lines 1, 2, 4, 6, and 8, we may assume that the same lines in the second stanza also rhymed in Old Chinese, although sound changes had broken the rhyming scheme by Middle Chinese. Therefore, we may derive another rhyme group of Old Chinese, that is, 淒晞湄躋坻.

So far, three rhyme groups are derived. Let's temporarily call them Rhyme Group A: 蒼霜方長央, Rhyme Group B: 淒晞湄躋坻, and Rhyme Group C: 采已涘右沚. Some of these characters may occur in other poems in rhyme positions. Thus, each of these groups can be expanded by adding more characters as we study more poems. Sometimes these groups may be modified based on more nuanced observations of rhyming. For example, the character 晞 from Rhyme Group B is now generally regarded as belonging with a rhyme group called 微, a distinct rhyme from the group called 脂 that includes the other four characters 淒湄躋坻 in Group B here, because the characters from these two groups tend to not rhyme in the *Shījīng*, among other supporting evidence (Wang 1937: 528–534).

As the example here shows, to determine which lines should rhyme in Old Chinese is a very complicated procedure fraught with uncertainties. The rhyming principles of the *Shījīng* are not explicitly stated anywhere. This is in contrast with the Tang dynasty regulated verses, the rhyming rules of which were extensively recorded and discussed in ancient texts. Therefore, oftentimes scholars may make different judgments as to which lines should rhyme in the *Shījīng*, and this in turn would lead to different analyses of rhyme groups.

Now to sum up the discussions on rhyming in the *Shījīng*, in general, Middle Chinese rhymes from the *Guǎngyùn* can be used as a reference when looking for the rhyming patterns in the *Shījīng*, although modern pronunciations may sometimes be helpful as well. The *Shījīng* rhymes may correspond to one or more rhymes in Middle Chinese. Therefore, the rhymes in Middle Chinese may be projected back to Old Chinese via merging the groups or splitting a group variously. Since the rhyming characters in the 305 poems of the *Shījīng* form a finite set, it is possible to exhaustively study them and obtain a number of rhyme groups. For example, Wang (1958) proposed 29 rhyme groups based on analyses of the *Shījīng*, while Li (1971) arrived at 31 groups.

Despite its usefulness, the *Shījīng* still has many limitations. For one thing, we can only link the characters that appear in rhyme positions, but there are many other characters that never occur in rhyme positions in the 305 poems. The goal of researching the rhymes of Old Chinese is to categorize each character in at least one rhyme group. Therefore, in addition to the *Shījīng*, we need other methods to further expand or modify the groups. The Qing dynasty philologist *Duàn Yùcái* 段玉裁 (AD 1735–1815) discovered that Chinese characters that share a common phonetic component, called *xiéshēngzì* 諧聲字,[10] would often be used in rhyme positions in the *Shījīng*. This suggests that a series of *xiéshēngzì*, or simply a phonetic series, would be in the same rhyme group in Old Chinese. Table 3.6 shows two examples of phonetic series.

The first phonetic series contains the characters 方房紡放, where the first one, that is, 方, is the shared phonetic component in the other three characters: 方 is the inside component on the bottom of 房, the component on the right of 紡, and the component on the left of 放. The character 方 itself is not a phono-semantic compound[11] but can be included in the analysis of phonetic series, since by definition, its pronunciation is similar to those that contain 方 itself as a phonetic component. Now let's look at the pronunciations of all four characters in Modern Standard Chinese indicated by the *pīnyīn* on top. They all have the same rhyme, "*ang*," although their tones are different. Thus, it may be the case that these four characters were in the same rhyme group in Old Chinese, and they are still in the same rhyme group in Modern Standard Chinese, although the exact phonetic value of the rhyme in Old Chinese may or may not be the same as "*ang*."

The second phonetic series in Table 3.6 contains the characters 央泱英映, where the first one, that is, 央, is the shared phonetic component in the other three characters: 央 is the component on the right in the second and the fourth characters

*Table 3.6* Examples of phonetic series

| fāng | fáng | fǎng | fàng |
|------|------|------|------|
| 方 | 房 | 紡 | 放 |
| yāng | yāng | yīng | yìng |
| 央 | 泱 | 英 | 映 |

決映; it is the component on the bottom of the third character 英. The character 央 itself is not a phono-semantic compound.[12] The rhymes of the first two characters are both "*ang*," while the rhymes of the third and fourth characters are "*ing*." Their Modern Standard Chinese pronunciations do not have the same rhyme anymore, but if we use the first phonetic series as an analogy, then the four characters in the second phonetic series may have had the same rhyme in Old Chinese, despite their modern pronunciations.

According to the generalization due to *Duàn Yùcái*, characters in a phonetic series should belong with the same rhyme group in Old Chinese. This can be further confirmed by the fact that characters from the same phonetic series sometimes would occur in rhyme positions in the *Shījīng*. The rhyming relation is often still preserved in Modern Standard Chinese, as shown in the first phonetic series in Table 3.6. But as the second phonetic series in Table 3.6 shows, in many cases, sound changes made the rhymes of characters in a phonetic series differ considerably from each other. Such cases are actually more interesting, because they provide more clues to sound change.

Therefore, by applying *Duàn Yùcái*'s generalization, the two phonetic series in Table 3.6 correspond to two rhyme groups in Old Chinese, and let's call them Rhyme Group D: 方房紡放 and Rhyme Group E: 央決英映. Since the rhyme groups derived from phonetic series and from the *Shījīng* are consistent, we may actually compare them in order to combine the rhyme groups whenever possible, especially when we find a common character in different rhyme groups. For example, the characters 方 and 央 in Rhyme Groups D and E also occur in Rhyme Group A 蒼霜方長央. Therefore, we can link all three groups, A, D, and E, into a larger group: 方房紡放央決英映蒼霜長. This means that all of these characters should have the same rhyme in Old Chinese, although they may or may not still rhyme in Modern Standard Chinese. This larger group is generally named 陽, which is the name of the Middle Chinese rhyme that can be considered a descendant of the ancient rhyme group. Each rhyme group in Old Chinese is similarly named with a Middle Chinese rhyme from the *Guǎngyùn*. But note that in the method using the *Shījīng* and phonetic series, we only have different categories of sounds but not their phonetic values. The traditional Chinese philologists mostly focused on the classification of Chinese characters in terms of their Old Chinese sounds. The reconstruction of the phonetic values of the rhyme groups is mostly based on that of Middle Chinese, which we deal with in Chapter 4.

## 3.4   Initials of Old Chinese

As mentioned previously, one limitation to using the *Shījīng* is that not all characters appear in rhyme positions in the poems. Another limitation is that the *Shījīng* does not contain information on the initials of the characters because rhyming only refers to the main vowel and the coda of a syllable. To study the initials of Old Chinese, we may have to rely on phonetic series again. Let's take another look at the characters in Table 3.6, focusing on the initials now. We see that in the first phonetic series, that is, 方房紡放, all four characters share the same initial, "*f.*"

In the second series, that is, 央決英映, the characters all start with a vowel, and therefore they all have the zero initial. Note here that the letter "*y*" in the syllable "*yāng*" represents the medial [ i ], and the letter "*a*" is the main vowel, while the letters "*yi*" in the syllable "*ying*" represent just one sound, that is, the main vowel [ i ]. These spellings do not correspond to any initials. Such preliminary observations suggest that the initials of characters in a phonetic series may have been quite similar in Old Chinese as well. Let's look at more examples, as shown in Table 3.7.

In the first series, that is, 丁頂汀亭, the character 丁 is the shared phonetic component. The initials of the four characters are either "*d*" or "*t*" in *pīnyīn*. The *pīnyīn* letter "*d*" in Modern Standard Chinese, despite the spelling, does not represent a voiced alveolar stop [ d ] as in the word "*day*" in English, but rather, the *pīnyīn* letter "*d*" is a voiceless unaspirated alveolar stop [ t ], similar to the "*t*" in the English word "*style*" or the "*t*" in Spanish "*tu*." The *pīnyīn* letter "*t*" is a voiceless aspirated alveolar stop [ tʰ ], similar to the "*t*" in the English word "*time*."[13] Both sounds, [ t ] and [ tʰ ], are produced when the tip of the tongue is pressed against the upper teeth or the gum. These sounds are referred to as either dentals or alveolars depending on the actual area of contact. Therefore, we say that the initials [ t ] and [ tʰ ] of the character 丁頂汀亭 are pronounced in the same region of the mouth.

Now let's look at the second series in Table 3.7, that is, 中仲沖忡. The initials are either "*zh*" or "*ch*" in *pīnyīn*. The spelling "*zh*" represents an unaspirated retroflex sound, which is similar to the "*j*" in the English word "*join*," but the tip of the tongue needs to be rolled further up above the alveolar ridge. The spelling "*ch*" in *pīnyīn* is an aspirated retroflex sound, similar to the "*ch*" in the English word "*chase*," but the tip of the tongue is rolled up further above the alveolar ridge too. Therefore, the initial consonants "*zh*" and "*ch*" are pronounced in the same region of the mouth as well.

It is shown in both phonetic series in Table 3.7 that even though the initial sounds of the characters in a phonetic series are not necessarily exactly the same, these initials are pronounced in the same region of the vocal tract. Karlgren (1923) proposed that the initials of characters in a phonetic series should have a single point of articulation (Norman 1988: 44–45). Then, if there are discrepancies in modern pronunciation, a hypothesis on Old Chinese initials can be made. Thus, to study Old Chinese initials, we have to rely on the application of the principle just mentioned here to characters and phonetic series. Now, with such a methodological principle in mind, let's discuss some major properties of Old Chinese initials.

The first one is concerning the labial initials in Old Chinese, initially discussed by *Qián Dàxīn* 錢大昕 (AD 1728–1804) of the Qing dynasty. Based on close

*Table 3.7* Initials in phonetic series

| dīng | dǐng | tīng | tíng |
|------|------|------|------|
| 丁 | 頂 | 汀 | 亭 |
| zhōng | zhòng | chōng | chōng |
| 中 | 仲 | 沖 | 忡 |

readings of ancient texts and commentaries, *Qián Dàxīn* noticed discrepancies between the pronunciations of the *Shījīng* era and his own time. For example, some early texts mention that the character 佛 should be pronounced similarly to 弼. Let's use modern pronunciations to illustrate the problem. The first character 佛 is *fú*; the second character 弼 is *bì*. If their pronunciations were similar in ancient times, then they should have similar initials.

The sound "*f*" in *fú* is a labiodental fricative, uttered with the lower lip against the upper teeth forcing the air out with audible friction. The *pīnyīn* letter "*b*" in *bì* is a voiceless unaspirated bilabial stop, which is similar to the voiceless "*p*" in the English word "*spy*." The sound [ pʰ ], represented in *pīnyīn* as "*p*," is an aspirated bilabial stop similar to the sound "*p*" in the English word "*pie*." We have seen a similar distinction between the unaspirated [ t ] and the aspirated [ tʰ ] previously, and here it is the same distinction of aspiration between the unaspirated [ p ] as in "*spy*" and the aspirated [ pʰ ] as in "*pie*." But both are bilabial consonants, pronounced with the lips touching.

Therefore, the initials of 佛 and 弼 are different, with the former being labiodental and the latter being bilabial. There are many other examples in ancient texts and commentaries where characters are said to have similar pronunciations but their modern initials are labiodental and bilabial. Based on such textual evidence, *Qián Dàxīn*'s conclusion was "*gǔ wú qīngchúnyīn*" (古無輕脣音), meaning "there were no labiodental sounds in ancient times," that is, in the Old Chinese period. The traditional term *qīngchúnyīn* 輕脣音 (literally "light lip sound") may be translated as "*labiodental sounds*" in modern terminology, while the traditional term for bilabial sounds is *zhòngchúnyīn* 重脣音 (literally "heavy lip sound").

*Qián Dàxīn*'s discovery can also be illustrated via phonetic series, as shown in Table 3.8.

In the first phonetic series 非菲輩裴, the character 非 is the common phonetic component. The initials of the first two characters are the labiodental "*f*" or [ f ] in IPA, while the initials of the other two characters are the bilabial "*b*" and "*p*" in *pīnyīn* or [ p ] and [ pʰ ], respectively, in IPA. Similarly in the second series 甫輔補浦, where 甫 is the shared phonetic component, the initials of the first two characters are both labiodental, but the initials of the remaining two characters are both bilabial stops. If we follow the methodological principle that the initials of characters in a phonetic series should share the same place of articulation in Old Chinese, then the initials here should all be either labiodental or bilabial in Old Chinese.

*Table 3.8* Labial initials in phonetic series

| fēi | fēi | bèi | péi |
|-----|-----|-----|-----|
| 非 | 菲 | 輩 | 裴 |
| fǔ | fǔ | bǔ | pǔ |
| 甫 | 輔 | 補 | 浦 |

But which type of sound should be the original one? Should it be the labiodental type or the bilabial type? Modern Chinese dialects may provide some clue.
Although Modern Standard Chinese, based on Beijing Mandarin, does have the
initial "*f*," in the Southern Min dialect spoken in Xiamen, there is still no labiodental "*f*," and some Beijing Mandarin words that have the initial "*f*" are actually pronounced with a bilabial stop in Xiamen. For example, the word *fáng* 房
("side room, house") is pronounced as [ paŋ²⁴ ] in the colloquial pronunciation in
Xiamen.[14] The fact that some dialects do not have labiodental initials seems to
suggest that the labiodental sounds are due to a later development. Therefore, our
hypothesis is that in Old Chinese, there were only bilabial initials, such as [ p ]
and [ pʰ ]. Later, the initials of some words that had bilabial sounds became [ f ].
We may represent this sound change as *$*p > f$ (under certain phonological conditions). Although the dialect data just mentioned here do not definitively show that
the bilabial sounds were the original, there are other types of supporting evidence
we may use. For example, the sound change $*p > f$ is a recurrent pattern in many
unrelated languages, but the reverse change $*f > p$ is not. We discuss such recurrent
sound change patterns in more detail in Chapter 4.

Now let's turn to the second major discovery of Old Chinese phonology concerning alveolar or dental initials, also due to *Qián Dàxīn*. Descriptions of sounds
in early texts often point toward the similarity of Old Chinese words that now have
alveolar and retroflex initials. One text says that the character 沖 should be pronounced similarly to 動. In modern pronunciation, 沖 is *chōng*, with a retroflex initial, and 動 is *dòng*, with an alveolar initial. Based on such evidence, *Qián Dàxīn*'s
conclusion was that "*gǔ wú shéshàngyīn*" (古無舌上音), translating into "there were
no retroflex initials in ancient times." The traditional category of sounds called
*shéshàngyīn* 舌上音 (literally "above-the-tongue sound") corresponds to modern
retroflex initials. The traditional class of sounds called *shétóuyīn* 舌頭音 (literally
"tip-of-the-tongue sound") is interpreted as alveolar consonants in modern terms.
Thus, in *Qián Dàxīn*'s view, the *shéshàngyīn* ("retroflex sounds") developed from
the original *shétóuyīn* ("alveolar sounds"). This can also be shown in phonetic
series as in Table 3.9.

In the first series, 者都著褚, the character 者 is the common phonetic component. The initials of these characters include the unaspirated retroflex "*zh*" or IPA
[ tʂ ], the aspirated "*ch*" or [ tʂʰ ], and the alveolar stop "*d*" in *pīnyīn* or [ t ] in IPA.
It is the same with the second series in the table, that is, 登證澄橙. Also according
to our understanding of the relations among the initials of characters in a phonetic
series, each of the two series of characters in Table 3.9 should share a single place

*Table 3.9* Alveolar and retroflex initials in phonetic series

| zhě | dū | zhù | chǔ |
|-----|-----|-----|-----|
| 者 | 都 | 著 | 褚 |
| dēng | zhèng | chéng | chéng |
| 登 | 證 | 澄 | 橙 |

of articulation for their initials in Old Chinese. But their initials have clearly different places of articulation in modern pronunciations. A hypothesis may be that in Old Chinese, the initials could have been either alveolar or retroflex, although the data so far do not point to a definite answer. Again, modern dialects may provide some supporting evidence. In some dialects from the Min and the Xiang areas, some characters with retroflex initials in Beijing Mandarin, such as those shown in Table 3.9, are actually pronounced with an alveolar initial. For example, 者 *zhě* is pronounced as [ ta²¹ ] in the Xiang dialect spoken in Shuangfeng, Hunan. Such variations in dialect pronunciations support the hypothesis here. More comprehensive considerations of all available evidence, including phonetic series, dialect variations, commentaries in ancient texts, comparative linguistic analyses, and so on will still be needed to conclude whether originally in Old Chinese there were only alveolar initials or retroflex initials. But for now, let's go with *Qián Dàxīn*'s view that the alveolar consonants were the original initials. Thus, in many Chinese dialects, some words with the original alveolar initials changed to their corresponding retroflex versions, for example, $*t > t\!s$, while such consonants are retained to different extents in some other dialects.

The two discoveries by *Qián Dàxīn* are among the most important features of Old Chinese initials. Both can be seen from the phonetic series examples in Table 3.8 and Table 3.9. The discussion in this section has shown that phonetic series indeed contain important clues to Old Chinese initials and rhymes. Let's summarize the two principles of using phonetic series. First, the initials of characters in a phonetic series should have the same place of articulation in Old Chinese. Second, the characters in a phonetic series should be in the same rhyme group in Old Chinese. These two principles do not refer to modern pronunciations. Sometimes the phonetic relations are still intact in modern pronunciations, while sometimes they may have changed. When the phonetic relations are still maintained in modern pronunciations, it is worth noting here that the exact phonetic values may have changed in a uniform direction. The sounds in Old Chinese may be different from those in modern pronunciations, but the phonetic relations may still be the same. Phonetic series are the primary source for analyses of Old Chinese initials. In the next section, we discuss how phonetic series can be used to argue for the existence of consonant clusters in Old Chinese.

## 3.5   Consonant clusters

Modern dialects of Chinese generally do not allow more than one initial consonant. Therefore, consonant clusters such as *spl-* in the English word "*splash*" and *bl-* in "*blue*" do not exist in modern varieties of Chinese. However, commentaries on pronunciations in ancient texts seem to suggest that there were consonant clusters in Old Chinese. In the earliest Chinese dictionary called *Ěryǎ* 爾雅 ("The Literary Expositor"), composed during the Old Chinese era, it is said that 不律 *búlǜ* is how one says 筆 *bǐ*.[15] Suppose we say 不律 *búlǜ* fast enough; the two syllables may sound as if they are fused into one, starting with a consonant cluster *bl-* in *pīnyīn* notation. However, it is not entirely clear what such a text really refers to. It could simply be an early example of *fǎnqiè* 反切, a traditional method of indicating the pronunciation of a character by using two other characters that have the same initial and the same final, respectively. In such *fǎnqiè* annotations, one way to figure out how to pronounce the actual word is to read the two characters in the *fǎnqiè* quickly. See Chapter 4 for a more detailed description of how *fǎnqiè* works. Thus, here, the example from the *Ěryǎ* may not conclusively prove the existence of consonant clusters such as *bl-* in Old Chinese (Sun 2002; Shi 2002).

Actually, if we look at the characters 律 *lǜ* and 筆 *bǐ*, they both have the phonetic component 聿, thus being in the same phonetic series. According to the two principles mentioned previously, these two characters should have initials at the same place of articulation. But the initial "*l*" is an alveolar sound, and the "*b*" is a bilabial stop. They do not share the same place of articulation anymore. We can find many such examples, as shown in Table 3.10.

In the first phonetic series 禀凜廩檁 in Table 3.10, the character 禀 is the common phonetic component. The initials of these characters include "*b*" and "*l*" in *pīnyīn* notation. In the second series 各客洛絡, the common phonetic component is 各, and the initials include "*g*," "*k*," and "*l*" in *pīnyīn* notation. Their places of articulation are all different, not conforming to how we understand the relation among initials in phonetic series. Thus, the hypothesis is that the initials in each series could have been very similar in Old Chinese, but sound change has made them differ. However, it is not possible to posit a single initial consonant as the Old Chinese initial here. If we posit that the alveolar lateral consonant "*l*" is the original sound, then we have to explain why "*l*" changed into "*b*," "*g*," "*k*," and so on. Such changes without any clear phonological conditions are highly unusual. On the other hand, if we posit that the original sound is the "*b*," "*g*," "*k*," and so on, then an explanation is needed for their convergence into "*l*," which, again, is highly unusual without any clear phonological conditions. Therefore, to make the initials of the characters in each series similar enough, we may resort to consonant clusters such as *bl-*, *gl-*, *kl-*. Then if the *-l-* is dropped, the initials would become *b-*, *g-*, *k-*; if the first sound in each cluster is dropped, then they all merge to "*l*." Such an explanation via consonant clusters seems quite plausible given the evidence we have so far.

Further evidence may be cited from modern Chinese dialects. We can find monosyllabic words that have alternative forms with two different syllables. For example, in the dialect spoken in the Shanxi province and the adjoining parts of Hebei and Inner Mongolia, there is a special type of words formed by putting the sound "*l*" between the initial and the final. In the dialect spoken in Hohhot,

*Table 3.10* Consonant clusters and phonetic series

| bǐng | lǐn | lǐn | lǐn |
|------|-----|-----|-----|
| 禀 | 凜 | 廩 | 檁 |
| gè | kè | luò | luò |
| 各 | 客 | 洛 | 絡 |

the capital city of Inner Mongolia, the word 擺 *băi* ("sway") can be pronounced as *bulăi*, and the Modern Standard Chinese word 巷 *xiàng* ("alleyway") can be pronounced as either *hàng* or *helàng*. In the disyllabic versions of these words, the first syllable is unstressed without a tone, and the main vowel in the first syllable is usually quite weak as well. Thus, these disyllabic versions sound as if they are monosyllabic with a consonant cluster. For example, the form *bulăi* is pronounced almost the same as *blăi* and *helàng* almost the same as *hlàng*. There is no obvious semantic difference between these two forms. They are purely phonological variants. The data here show that modern Chinese dialects may have words with a minor syllable that can be reduced and result in a consonant cluster. Although such evidence cannot directly prove the existence of consonant clusters in Old Chinese, it nonetheless points to the possibility of consonant clusters in Chinese and provides some auditory clues as to what such complex initials may have sounded like in Old Chinese.

Thus, by combining data from ancient texts, phonetic series, and modern dialects, we may reasonably argue that at some point in Old Chinese, there were initial consonant clusters. Although such a theory has not been universally accepted, it is clear that the Proto-Sino-Tibetan language had complex initial consonant clusters. As mentioned in Chapter 2, there are many highly complex consonant clusters in Classical Tibetan and also in some archaic dialects of modern spoken Tibetan. If consonant clusters existed in the proto-language, they could still possibly be retained to some extent in Old Chinese.

## 3.6   Methodology of Old Chinese reconstruction

So far, we have discussed how to use the *Shījīng* and phonetic series of Chinese characters to study the rhymes and initials in Old Chinese. Such methods only indicate how many different initials and rhymes there were in Old Chinese but not their concrete phonetic values. To reconstruct the sounds of Old Chinese, we mostly rely on the phonological system of Middle Chinese. The written records of Middle Chinese are much more extensive. To some extent, most modern Chinese dialects are descendants of Middle Chinese. Therefore, we can use the pronunciations of modern dialects and the written records together to reconstruct the phonetic values of Middle Chinese initials and finals. Then, by comparing the phonetic values of Middle Chinese sounds and the categories of Old Chinese rhymes and initials, the phonological system of Old Chinese can be deduced from that of Middle Chinese, and the development of sounds from Old Chinese to Middle Chinese is also accounted for via positing various phonological conditions.

For example, the reconstructed system of Middle Chinese contains just one set of labial initials, that is, the bilabial series such as [ p, pʰ, b, m ], but not the labiodentals such as [ f ]. According to *Qián Dàxīn*'s discovery, there were no labiodental initials in Old Chinese. Then we simply posit the same set of bilabial initials [ p, pʰ, b, m ] in Old Chinese.

There is a series of alveolar stops in Middle Chinese, that is, [ t, tʰ, d, n ], and a retroflex series [ ʈ, ʈʰ, ɖ, ɳ ]. According to *Qián Dàxīn*'s other discovery mentioned previously, there were no retroflex initials in Old Chinese. Thus, we posit just the alveolar stops in Old Chinese but not the retroflex ones. In order to explain why some Old Chinese alveolar initials became retroflex in Middle Chinese, Li (1971) proposed a medial -*r*-. Thus, words that begin with an alveolar followed by the medial -*r*- in Old Chinese would have a retroflex initial in Middle Chinese, due to the assimilatory effect of the medial -*r*- on the preceding consonant. For example, *\*tr*- would develop into ʈ-, which can be notated as *\*tr*- > ʈ-. By analogy, the retroflex affricates in Middle Chinese, such as [ tʂ ], would be derived from Old Chinese alveolar affricates with the medial -*r*-, for example, *\*tsr*- > tʂ-.

The rhymes of Old Chinese can be similarly reconstructed. For example, the Old Chinese rhyme group 陽, mentioned in Section 3.3 previously, corresponds to the 陽 [ aŋ ], 唐 [ ɑŋ ], 庚 [ ɐŋ ] rhymes in Middle Chinese. Since they all have some kind of [ a ] sound as the main vowel, we may simply posit [ aŋ ] for the Old Chinese rhyme group 陽. Then various medials may affect the Old Chinese vowel [ a ] differently, resulting in three vowels in Middle Chinese. More specifically, the medial -*r*- would cause the main vowel to become [ ɐ ], as in *\*kraŋ* > *kɐŋ* 庚. The medial -*j*- would retain the main vowel, as in *\*kjaŋ* > *kjaŋ* 姜, while in the absence of any medial, the main vowel would retract to the back [ ɑ ], as in *\*kaŋ* > *kɑŋ* 岡.

Here we only provide a sketch of the methodology for the reconstruction of Old Chinese. In Chapter 4, we further illustrate the developments from Old Chinese to Middle Chinese once the phonological system of Middle Chinese is reconstructed.

## 3.7 Tones in Old Chinese

Besides rhymes and initials, there is one more aspect of the sound system of Old Chinese that needs to be studied, that is, tones. Similar to how reconstruction of Old Chinese depends on Middle Chinese, as sketched previously, we may first look at the four tones in Middle Chinese, that is, the *píng*, *shǎng*, *qù*, and *rù* tones. In the regulated verse in the Tang dynasty, the rhyming words are from the same tonal category. Therefore, if the first rhyme position in a Tang poem has a *píng*-tone character, then the other rhyme positions should also use characters with the *píng* tone. Such poetic rules are clearly documented and described. But we do not have any written description of the rhyming rules for the *Shījīng* poems. If, however, it turns out that the rhyming characters in the *Shījīng* are mostly from the same Middle Chinese tonal categories, then we may argue that the same tonal categories existed in Old Chinese, although the actual tonal contour shapes may be different. Therefore, what is the actual rhyming practice in the *Shījīng* in terms of the tones?

It is very common for the poems in the *Shījīng* to have rhyming characters from the same tonal category in terms of the four tones in Middle Chinese. For example, in Table 3.5, the first stanza uses the following characters in the rhyme positions: 蒼霜方長央, and they all have the *píng* tone in Middle Chinese, although according to the modern pronunciation, 長 has a different tone from the other four characters. The rhyming characters in the second stanza are *píng*-tone characters in Middle Chinese as well, although two of them, that is, 湄坻, have a different tone from the other three in Modern Standard Chinese. In the third stanza, except for line 8, which uses 右, a *qù*-tone character, to rhyme, all the other lines have characters in the *shǎng* tone in the rhyme positions. The rhyme character on line 4, that is, 浼, originally had a *shǎng* tone in Middle Chinese, but in Modern Standard Chinese, its tone is the same as the tone of 右. Therefore, in the third stanza, one character with the *qù* tone of Middle Chinese rhymes with the other four characters from the *shǎng* tone category of Middle Chinese. It seems that there is indeed a strong tendency for rhyming characters in the *Shījīng* to have the same tone in the four-tone system in Middle Chinese.

According to statistics from Shi (1985) and Chen (1995), 82.2% of the 1679 rhyming units in the *Shījīng* use characters from the same Middle Chinese tonal category, compared to 17.8% of them that use characters with different tones. If we focus on the majority of these, that is, 82.2% of the rhyming units, then it may be argued that there were tones in Old Chinese, and the categories are mostly the same as in Middle Chinese. However, we cannot simply ignore the 17.2% of the rhyming units that have characters from different tonal categories. The cross-category rhyming units seem to suggest that either there were no tones in Old Chinese or the tones were different from the Middle Chinese ones.

*Duàn Yùcái*, a Qing dynasty philologist, noticed that *qù*-tone characters could rhyme with characters with the *píng*, *shǎng*, or *rù* tones and proposed that there was no *qù* tone in Old Chinese. Wang (1958) further argued that the *qù* tone in Middle Chinese developed from the *rù* tone with a long vowel in Old Chinese. Thus, for these scholars, there were tones in Old Chinese, but they were different from Middle Chinese.

On the other hand, the Ming dynasty scholar *Chén Dì*, who first clearly stated that sounds do change, as mentioned previously in this chapter, also maintained that "the ancients did not have the distinction among the four tones."[16] Is it really possible that Old Chinese did not have tones? Before answering this question, we need to ask whether tones are an inherent property of a language that has tones. If tones are inherent, then a tonal language always has tones, although the actual phonological properties of these tones can change over time. In this scenario, Old Chinese should have tones, because modern varieties of Chinese do. If tones are not inherent, then it suggests that a language can develop tones under certain linguistic conditions. In this scenario, Old Chinese probably did not have tones. Furthermore, many Sino-Tibetan languages today do not have tones, while some others do. For example, there is no tonal distinction in Amdo Tibetan, but Lhasa Tibetan has tones. Amdo Tibetan and Lhasa Tibetan share a single ancestral language. Logically speaking, there are two possibilities: either Lhasa Tibetan developed tones, or Amdo Tibetan lost tones. Since Classical Tibetan does not have tones, it is likely that Lhasa Tibetan developed tones.

Therefore, the most relevant question here is whether there is convincing evidence that tones can be a later development, and the answer is yes. The data are from the development of tones in Vietnamese and its relation to the other Mon-Khmer languages in the Austroasiatic family. In terms of cognate words, Vietnamese is clearly related to the other Mon-Khmer languages such as Mon, Mnong, Khmu, and Riang. But Vietnamese has four major tonal categories, which are usually marked as A, B, C, and D, while the other languages are mostly not tonal. If tones are inherent, then the existence of tones in Vietnamese is a major obstacle to establishing a genetic relationship between Vietnamese and the other Mon-Khmer languages. The dilemma here is similar to that between Amdo Tibetan, which does not have tones, and Lhasa Tibetan, which does have tones.

Haudricourt (1954) proposed that tones in Vietnamese were a later development. First, he called attention to Maspero's (1912) original observation that in certain cognates, Vietnamese words from tone category C often correspond to words ending with an -*h* or an -*s* in the other languages. For example, the word for "*root*" is "*rẽ*" in Vietnamese, "*rüh*" in Mon, and "*ries*" in Mnong (Haudricourt 1954: 80). Based on such evidence, a hypothesis can be that originally there was an -*s* at the end of the word, and then the -*s* became -*h* and was further lost altogether at an even later time. The coda consonant -*h* is a laryngeal configuration that can cause the vocal cords to slacken, thus resulting in a lowering of the pitch of the preceding vowel, which is equivalent to a falling tone. At this stage, when both the coda consonant -*h* and its phonetic effect on the vowel were present, the pitch contour was secondary in distinguishing meaning, but with the loss of the coda, the pitch property became a primary distinctive feature as a compensatory development in response to the loss of the coda consonant.

Haudricourt (1954: 80–81) further showed that for Vietnamese words of tone category B, the tone often corresponds to a glottal stop in the other Mon-Khmer languages. For example, the word for "*leaf*" is "*lá*" in Vietnamese, "*hlaʔ*" In Khmu, and "*laʔ*" In Riang. The hypothesis here is that in the Vietnamese word "*lá*," originally there was also a glottal stop coda -*ʔ*, which involves a laryngeal configuration of increased tension in the vocal folds, resulting in a rising pitch contour of the preceding vowel. This coda was later lost, and as a result, the pitch property of the syllable became a distinctive feature to compensate for the loss of the consonant.

The emergence of tones as a compensatory development with the loss of coda consonants is called tonogenesis and has been reported widely in other languages as well. Specifically in Vietnamese, tone B developed from syllables with a glottal stop coda, and tone C developed from a syllable with an -*s* coda via an intermediate stage of -*h*. These two consonant codas involve laryngeal configurations that affect the pitch properties of the preceding vowels differently (Thurgood 2002). Thus, the tonogenesis process is phonetically motivated instead of being strictly a language-specific development. In light of this general tonal development pattern, our question here is whether the same can be said of the tones in Chinese.

Maspero (1912) and Haudricourt (1954) showed that Middle Chinese loanwords in Old Vietnamese[17] often have fixed corresponding tonal categories. Chinese words with the *shǎng* tone were borrowed into Vietnamese with the tone B; Chinese words with the *qù* tone were borrowed into Vietnamese with the tone C. Thus, the tonal contours of the Middle Chinese *shǎng* tone may have been quite similar to Old Vietnamese tone B in having the rising contour, while Middle Chinese *qù* tone may have been similar to Old Vietnamese tone C in having a falling contour. Additionally, the Chinese *píng* tone corresponds to the Vietnamese tone A, and the Chinese *rù* tone corresponds to the tone D in Vietnamese.

In theory, we may posit that there were no tones in Old Chinese and that a syllable with a glottal stop coda, that is, -*ʔ*, would develop into a syllable with the *shǎng* tone in Middle Chinese, while a syllable with an -*s* coda would develop into the *qù* tone in Middle Chinese. This view reminds us of *Chén Dì*'s claim that there were no tones in Old Chinese. However, do we have concrete evidence for the existence of such syllabic codas in Old Chinese? Mei (1970) argued for the existence of a glottal stop coda in the *shǎng* tone syllables. For example, the description of the Middle Chinese rising tone, that is, the *shǎng* tone, in Buddhist texts is that the tone is high, short, and level. Mei (1970: 97) points out that "in five dialects of the southeastern coastal area, the rising tone has a final glottal stop." Therefore, the high, short syllables in Middle Chinese may be associated with a final stop consonant, while such a consonant, that is, the glottal stop, may have been retained in certain modern dialects. Mei (1980) further provides evidence for the existence of the -*s* coda in the *qù* tone syllables via comparisons with Tibetan cognate words. It is shown that *qù*-tone words in Middle Chinese often correspond to syllables with a final -*s* coda in Tibetan. See Chapter 6 for a more detailed description of such correspondences between Chinese and Tibetan.

Li (1971) also leaned toward the view that there were no tones in Old Chinese. In his reconstruction of Old Chinese, the letter -*x* is used to mark characters that belong with the *shǎng* tone category in Middle Chinese, and an -*h* is used for the *qù* tone characters. This notation with the extra -*x* or -*h* is probably better regarded as a convenient way of distinguishing the *shǎng* and *qù* tones rather than indicating real different consonants.

However, in more recent systems of reconstructions of Old Chinese, for example, Zhengzhang (2003) and Baxter and Sagart (2014), syllables with the *shǎng* tone are clearly reconstructed with a final glottal stop, and syllables with the *qù* tone are reconstructed as having a final -*s* coda. For example, we can use the names of the four tones to illustrate this because 平 *píng* itself has an even tone, 上 *shǎng* itself has a rising tone, 去 *qù* itself has a departing tone, and 入 *rù* itself has an entering tone. The reconstructed pronunciations of these four characters in Zhengzhang's (2003) reconstruction are 平 *beŋ*, 上 *djaŋʔ*, 去 *kʰas*, 入 *njub*. The *píng* tone does not have an obstruent stop coda, the *shǎng* tone has a glottal stop coda, and the *qù* tone has an -*s* coda, while the *rù* tone has a stop coda that corresponds to the Middle Chinese -*p*, -*t*, or -*k*.

In summary, there is strong evidence that there were no tones in Proto-Sino-Tibetan and Old Chinese. The Middle Chinese tones were originally associated with different types of syllables in Old Chinese. With the loss of some of the syllable coda consonants, pitch properties of the syllables became the primary distinctive features, giving rise to tones in Middle Chinese.

## 3.8    A reconstructed system of Old Chinese

Now it is time to take a look at the reconstructed sounds of initials and vowels in Old Chinese. We introduce Li's (1971) system first, because it is the standard reference for later reconstructions. Then a brief comparison is made between Li's (1971) reconstruction and the new system from Baxter and Sagart (2014), highlighting some of the new methodological developments. The descriptions of Li's (1971) system are based on the version from Li (1980: 21) here. Table 3.11 shows the reconstructed initials.

Table 3.11  Old Chinese initials[18]

| Phonetic Features | Plosive & Affricate | | | Nasal | | Lateral | | Fricative | Flap |
|---|---|---|---|---|---|---|---|---|---|
| | *Voiceless Unaspirated* | *Voiceless Aspirated* | *Voiced* | *Voiceless* | *Voiced* | *Voiceless* | *Voiced* | | |
| Labials | 幫 p | 滂 pʰ | 並 b | 忽 m̥ | 明 m | | | | |
| Alveolar | 端 t | 透 (帖) tʰ | 定 d | 歎 n̥ | 泥 n | 寵 l̥ | 來 l | 心 s | 以 r |
| | 精 ts | 清 tsʰ | 從 dz | | | | | | |
| Velars | 見 k | 溪 kʰ | 羣 g | 許 ŋ̥ | 疑 ŋ | | | | |
| | kʷ | kʰʷ | gʷ | ŋ̥ʷ | ŋʷ | | | | |
| Laryngeal | 影 ʔ | | | | | | | 曉(歇) h | |
| | ʔʷ | | | | | | | hʷ | |

This system is characterized by the following features. First, there is a three-way contrast in the plosive and affricate initials among the voiceless unaspirated, the voiceless aspirated, and the voiced, for example, [ p, pʰ, b ]. Second, there are labialized versions of [ k, kʰ, g, ŋ, ŋ̊, ʔ, h ] written with a superscript *w*, meaning that the lips should be rounded when pronouncing these sounds. Li (1971) used these labialized initials to account for the development into Middle Chinese syllables with the medial -*w*- or -*u*-, for example, 光 *$k^w$aŋ* > *kwaŋ*. The arrow > shows the development from Old Chinese to Middle Chinese. All examples follow this pattern in this chapter. Third, each of the nasal initials has a voiceless version, based on evidence from phonetic series. For example, the Middle Chinese pronunciation of the character 物 is *mjuət*, while 忽 is *xuət*. The common phonetic component is 勿. Therefore, these two characters are in the same phonetic series, and their initials should have a single point of articulation in Old Chinese, although their Middle Chinese initials are the voiced bilabial nasal *m*- and the voiceless velar fricative *x*-, respectively. A hypothesis is that the Middle Chinese initial *x*- in 忽 was originally a voiceless nasal *m̥*-, thus conforming to the phonetic series principles. The developments of these two words from Old Chinese to Middle Chinese are: 物 *$mjət$* > *mjuət*, 忽 *$m̥ət$* > *xuət*. Similarly, a voiceless version can be reconstructed for the other nasal initials as well. One clarification is that in Li's (1971) original notation, the voiceless nasals are indicated by attaching *h*- to the nasals, for example, *hm*- instead of *m̥*-. In addition to making typesetting less complicated, one other reason for his original notation is that it is possible that in earlier stages, the voiceless nasals may have been prefixed with a voiceless consonant. Here in this chapter all these voiceless nasals are instead indicated by standard IPA symbols with a tiny circle underneath each nasal.

The *r* sound, according to Li's (1980: 14) description, is similar to the flapped "*d*" in American English "*ladder*," or the "*t*" in American English "*later*." Consonant clusters can be formed in several different ways, including (1) by prefixing an initial consonant with *s*-, such as *st*ʰ-, (2) by adding the medial -*l*- or -*r*-, for example, *kl*-, *pr*-, or (3) by both prefixing and adding a medial, for example, *skʰr*-.

Table 3.12 shows the reconstructed rhymes in Li's (1971) system. The sounds in Table 3.12 are based on the version from Li (1980). There are three types of syllables, the ones with voiced stop codas correspond to Middle Chinese open syllables called *yīnshēngyùn* 陰聲韻, the ones with voiceless stop codas are called *rùshēngyùn* 入聲韻, and the ones with nasal codas are called *yángshēngyùn* 陽聲韻. Note that the phonetic nature of the voiced stop codas is not determined, since Li (1980: 33) pointed out that there is no concrete evidence that these were necessarily voiced stops. The main function of these voiced stop codas is to match their corresponding voiceless stop codas.

There are 22 rhyme groups in Li's (1971) reconstruction. With the exception of the rhymes 緝 -*əp* and 葉 -*ap*, in general, the rhymes with voiceless stop codas are incorporated into the corresponding rhymes with voiced stop codas. For example, the rhyme group 之 includes both -*əg* and -*ək*. However, to make the system more useful to compare to Middle Chinese, the rhymes with voiceless stop codas, for example, 職 -*ək*, are listed here in their own column with the names of those

*Table 3.12* Old Chinese rhymes

| Rhymes with stop codas | | Nasal Rhymes |
| --- | --- | --- |
| With Voiced Stop Codas, or -r as Coda | With Voiceless Stop Codas | |
| 之 -əg | 職 -ək | 蒸 -əŋ |
| 幽 -əgʷ | 覺 -əkʷ | 中 -əŋʷ |
| (-əb) | 緝 -əp | 侵 -əm |
| 微 -əd | 物 -ət | 文 -ən |
| 祭 -ad | 月 -at | 元 -an |
| 歌 -ar | | |
| (-ab) | 葉 -ap | 談 -am |
| 魚 -ag | 鐸 -ak | 陽 -aŋ |
| 宵 -agʷ | 樂 -akʷ | |
| 脂 -id | 質 -it | 真 -in |
| 佳 -ig | 錫 -ik | 耕 -iŋ |
| 侯 -ug | 屋 -uk | 束 -uŋ |

rhymes in characters as well. Also note that the 歌 *-ar* rhyme has a sonorant *-r* coda instead of a stop coda, but we place this rhyme in the column with voiced stop codas here because of their similar developments from Old Chinese to Middle Chinese. Thus, there are actually 31 different rhymes in this reconstruction. The two rhymes in brackets, that is, *-əb* and *-ab*, are possible earlier rhymes that merged with other rhymes in the time of the *Shījīng*.

The rhymes with voiced stop codas correspond to Middle Chinese rhymes without a consonant coda, that is, open syllables, or *yīnshēngyùn* 陰聲韻. The rhymes with voiceless stop codas develop into syllables with the entering tone in Middle Chinese, that is, *rùshēngyùn* 入聲韻. However, in phonetic series, these two types of syllables would often share the same phonetic component, for example, 囿 *$g^wjək$ > juk* and 有 *$g^wjəgx$ > jǒu*. Note here the *-x* is the notation for the *shǎng* tone but not necessarily a separate consonant coda. These two characters are in a phonetic series because 有 is the phonetic component of 囿. But in their Middle Chinese pronunciations, one is a *rù*-tone syllable, with the rhyme *-uk*, while the other is an open syllable *jǒu*. Thus, to conform to the phonetic series principles as much as possible, the open syllable was reconstructed as having a corresponding voiced stop coda, that is, *-g*, in Old Chinese. The word 囿 is from the 職 *-ək* rhyme, and the word 有 is from the 之 *-əg* rhyme in Table 3.12. These two types of syllables are sometimes used in rhyme positions in the *Shījīng* as well. Thus, it seems to suggest that for two words to rhyme in the *Shījīng*, the main vowels should be the same, but the codas may be different. This is also why in Li's (1971) reconstruction, *-əg* and *-ək* are considered to be in the same rhyme group. As mentioned previously, we originally assume that the rhyming characters in the *Shījīng* should have the same rhyme, that is, the main vowel and the coda, as is standard in Tang poetics. However, the poems in the *Shījīng* were primarily songs, and rhyming in singing may be different, especially in folksongs.

Using similar evidence from phonetic series and rhyming examples in the *Shījīng*, we may reconstruct the 歌 -*ar* rhyme that pairs with the 元 -*an*. Both rhymes have the same vowel. The codas are both alveolar sonorant consonants. An example using phonetic series is: 觶 \**tjarh* > *tɕjě* and 禪 \**djanh* > *dʑjen*. Note here the -*h* in the Old Chinese notation is to indicate the *qù* tone but is not necessarily a separate consonant coda.

The rhymes with a labialized coda, for example, 幽 -*əgʷ*, 覺 -*əkʷ*, 中 -*əŋʷ*, 宵 -*agʷ*, 藥 -*akʷ*, would develop into Middle Chinese rhymes with rounded main vowels or codas such as -*o* and -*u*. For example: 目 \**mjəkʷ* > *mjuk*, 冬 \**təŋʷ* > *tuoŋ*, 毛 \**magʷ* > *mau*.

We have shown that there is strong evidence for Old Chinese to lack tones. It does not seem to be necessary to reconstruct the tonal contours for Old Chinese. However, as mentioned in the discussion of tonogenesis, before tones emerged, the laryngeal features of the consonant codas should already have effects on the pitch of the main vowel. In this sense, Zhengzhang (2003) tentatively proposes that different syllables in Old Chinese had concurrent pitch contours: a short 3 contour for syllables ending with -*p*, -*t*, or -*k* in Li's system,[19] which would eventually develop into the *rù* tone; a 31 contour for syllables ending with -*h* or -*s*, which would eventually develop into the *qù* tone; a 35 contour for syllables ending with a glottal stop -*ʔ*, which would eventually develop into the *shǎng* tone; a 33 contour for other types of syllables, which would eventually develop into the *píng* tone. These tonal contours are consistent with the tonogenesis process and how these four tones were described in Middle Chinese. The *rù* tone is a short one, the *qù* tone is a falling tone, and the *shǎng* tone has a rising shape, while the *píng* tone is flat or even. Note further that these pitch contours in Old Chinese were not tones yet, since they were secondary phonetic properties associated with different types of syllables instead of being independent distinctive features. Only after the loss of the -*h* and -*ʔ* codas would the pitch properties begin to be tones, that is, a primary distinctive feature in the phonological system.

Li's (1971) reconstruction is one of the early systems. There have been many new modifications ever since. The most recent system is by Baxter and Sagart (2014), which has gradually become the new standard reference of Old Chinese reconstruction. Although the full scope of Baxter and Sagart's (2014) methodology and their new reconstruction cannot be adequately introduced here, we nonetheless make some comparisons between Li's (1971) system and the new Baxter-Sagart reconstruction by highlighting major methodological innovations and important new phonological features of Old Chinese that have been proposed.

There are two main differences between the reconstructed initials in the two systems. First, in order to better account for certain examples of phonetic series that involve words with Middle Chinese guttural initials, that is, *hóuyīn* 喉音 (literally "throat sound"), three uvular stops [ q, qʰ, ɢ ] and three corresponding labialized versions [ qʷ, qʷʰ, ɢʷ ] are proposed based on a proposal by Pan (1997). For example, 囿 (Middle Chinese: *juk*) and 賄 (Middle Chinese: *xuǎi*) are in the same phonetic series by sharing the phonetic component 有. Thus, their Old Chinese initials should have the same place of articulation. In Li's (1971) reconstructions, their Old Chinese forms are *$g^wjək$ and *$h^wəgx$. But $g^w$- is velar, and $h^w$- is glottal, or laryngeal. Their places of articulation are not the same. In the Baxter-Sagart system, their Old Chinese forms are *[ɢ]$^w$ək-s and *$q^{whʕ}əʔ$. There are some other special symbols here, such as the brackets and the superscripted pharyngeal ʕ. We discuss them subsequently. But here the voiced uvular stop ɢ and the labialized voiceless aspirated uvular stop $q^{wh}$ share the same place of articulation. Such uvular stops are probably also closer to the traditional Chinese term for these sounds, that is, guttural sounds. Apart from these uvular stops, the other initials are mostly the same as in Li's (1971) system.

Second, each of the initials in the Baxter-Sagart reconstruction has a pharyngealized version, such as the pharyngealized *$l^ʕ$-, as opposed to the usual *l*-. In terms of its phonetics, a pharyngealized consonant is produced by retracting the tongue root to the back of the throat while keeping the same place and manner of articulation as in the usual version of the consonant. An approximation to the pharyngealized *$l^ʕ$* here can be found in the English "dark *l*" such as in "*cool*," in which the back of the tongue is raised against the velum, that is, the soft palate. If, instead of the tongue raising, it retracts back toward the throat while "*l*" is uttered, a pharyngealized version of "*l*" is produced. This type of guttural or "*emphatic*" consonants are more common in Arabic. The reason for proposing pharyngealization across the board for all initial consonants in Old Chinese is to account for the development of two types of syllables in Middle Chinese. Type B syllables, also called division-III syllables in traditional terminology, are often considered to contain the medial -*j*-, or the vowel -*i*-, while type B syllables do not. This contrast is mostly maintained in the same way in Li's (1971) Old Chinese system. For example: 綱 *$kaŋ$ > *kaŋ* vs. 疆 *$kjaŋ$ > *kjaŋ*. Based on Norman's (1994) proposal, Baxter and Sagart (2014) explain the distinction between the two types of syllables via pharyngealization, for example, 綱 *$k^ʕaŋ$ > *kaŋ* vs. 疆 *$kaŋ$ > *kjaŋ*. The pharyngealized consonants, for example, $k^ʕ$- here, have retracted tongue root that resists palatalization, while the non-pharyngealized consonants, for example, *k*- here, may move further to the front more easily, resulting in palatalization, that is, *k*- > *kj*-. Although at first, the pharyngealized versions of consonants look quite unfamiliar, they can account for the development of the same rhyme in Old Chinese into Middle Chinese type A and type B syllables quite well. We may simply understand the pharyngealization as associated with retracted tongue root, which blocks palatalization. Roughly speaking, palatalization refers to the change of the place of articulation of a consonant to palatal when it is followed by [ i ] or [ j ]. See Chapter 4 for details.

In terms of the rhymes, the main difference is in how many basic vowels there are in the two systems. Li's (1971) reconstruction is famous for its parsimony of having only four vowel phonemes: *i, u, ə, a*, partially due to the complex consonants that are reconstructed which would affect the main vowels and cause them to develop in different directions. In the new Baxter-Sagart system, there are six basic vowels: *i, u, ə, a, e, o*. By contrast, in Middle Chinese, there are many more vowels. For example, in Karlgren's system, there are 16 vowels (Norman 1988: 38–39), or 11 vowels if we ignore the distinction of vowel length. The six-vowel system of Old Chinese may better account for the development into the rich inventory of vowels in Middle Chinese.

As discussed previously, the rhyming practice in the *Shījīng* only requires the main vowel to be identical, and the coda consonants can be different. In most previous reconstructions, each rhyme group shares the same main vowel. However, in the Baxter-Sagart reconstruction, there may be multiple vowels in the same rhyme group, especially when data from phonetic series would suggest more than one vowel. For example, the 元 -*an* rhyme in Li's (1971) system now has three different vowels, "*e*," "*o*," and "*a*," in the Baxter-Sagart system. As Ho (2016: 176–184) points out, such different vowels within the same rhyme group may be problematic considering Chinese poetic traditions and, more generally, rhyming in folksongs in Chinese and many other languages. Zhengzhang (2003) argued that at least some of the information from phonetic series may be rather related to an earlier stage of Chinese prior to the *Shījīng*. Therefore, according to Ho (2016), because Old Chinese rhymes are largely derived via studying the rhymes in the *Shījīng*, more weight should be given to evidence from the *Shījīng* rather than phonetic series.

Some other differences between the rhymes in the two systems include the following. The Baxter-Sagart system does not have tones, and instead consonant codas such as -*ʔ* and -*s* are used in syllables that would develop into Middle Chinese *shǎng*-tone and *qù*-tone syllables. Moreover, the Baxter-Sagart system contains many open syllables, while Li's (1971) system only contains closed syllables, because in Li's (1971) reconstruction, every rhyme has a consonant coda. It is very rare for languages to completely lack open syllables. In many other reconstructions, the rhymes that have the -*b*, -*d*, -*g* stop codas in Li's (1971) system are open syllables without the stop codas.

Some other major methodological innovations in the Baxter-Sagart system include use of data on archaic Chinese dialects and early Chinese loanwords in Vietic, Hmong-Mien, and Kra-Dai languages and comparative analysis with other Sino-Tibetan languages. They have also reconstructed the morphology of Old Chinese more extensively than before. Affixes such as the prefixes *\*s-*, *\*t-*, *\*m-*; the infix *\*-r-*; and the suffix *\*-s* have various morphological functions and can sometimes be stacked, for example, *\*m-s-*. The syllable structure may include a minor syllable preceding the main syllable, for example, 種 *\*k.toŋʔ*, and 舌 *\*mə.lat*. Here, the consonant before the syllable boundary indicated by the dot, or the consonant plus the weak vowel *ə*, would be the minor syllable.

Now that we have compared two reconstructed systems of Old Chinese initials, medials, and rhymes, we can illustrate the reconstructions using the first four lines from the *Shījīng* poem in Table 3.5. Modern Standard Chinese pronunciations are provided first as a reference, followed by the two reconstructed versions. Note again that the letters -*x* and -*h* in Li's (1971) system are only tone category symbols but not necessarily separate consonants. Furthermore, in Baxter and Sagart's (2014) notation, square brackets "[ ]" indicate uncertainty. Thus, [*k*] means that it is very likely to be "*k*," but evidence is inconclusive. Parentheses show that the element may or may not be there. For example, *ɢʷ(r)aj* means that the word could be either *ɢʷraj* or *ɢʷaj*. A dot is a syllable boundary, for example, *s.tur?*. The hyphen, for example, *s-*, indicates a morpheme boundary. The notation <r> means that the *-r-* is an infix. The uppercase letter C represents an unspecified consonant. The word 葭 is not reconstructed in Baxter and Sagart's (2014) system, so the form here is derived from other reconstructed forms with similar phonological properties.

**Chinese characters:**

> 蒹葭蒼蒼，白露爲霜。
> 所謂伊人，在水一方。

**Modern Standard Chinese:**

> jiānjiā cāngcāng / bái lù wéi shuāng //
> suǒ wèi yī rén / zài shuǐ yì fāng //

**Li's (1971) reconstruction:**

> kiam krag tsʰaŋ tsʰaŋ / brak lagh gʷjar srjaŋ //
> srjagx gʷjədh ʔjid njin / dzəgx hrjidx ʔjit pjaŋ //

**Baxter and Sagart's (2014) reconstruction:**

> [k]ˤem kˤra [tsʰ]ˤaŋ [tsʰ]ˤaŋ / bˤrak p.rˤak-s *ɢʷ(r)aj [s]raŋ //
> s-qʰ<r>aʔ [ɢ]ʷə[t]-s ʔij ni[ŋ] / [dz]ˤəʔ s.turʔ ʔi[t] C-paŋ //

An important clarification is to be made here. Reconstructed sounds are theoretical constructs that represent a synthesis of available data and hypotheses to account for phonological developments. They are not meant to be how a certain language was actually spoken thousands of years ago. Especially as shown in the Baxter-Sagart system, there are many uncertainties, and some of the sounds are not existent in any modern Chinese dialects. Despite the hypothetical nature of linguistic reconstructions, they can nonetheless be the basis for our understanding of older stages of a language.

This chapter introduces the main data, methods, and findings relating to Old Chinese phonology. The two most important written sources are the *Shījīng* and characters in phonetic series. One remaining question concerns the nature of the spoken language on which these written records are based. It is clear that there were different dialects in the Old Chinese period, and a common spoken language may have existed in the Zhou dynasty. According to a passage from the *Analects*, Confucius used the *yǎyán* 雅言 ("elegant speech").[20] This elegant speech is also interpreted as the "*correct speech*," because it was the standard dialect, that is, the dialect of the capital of the Zhou dynasty. The earlier capital of the Zhou dynasty was in what is present-day Xi'an, and the later capital was present-day Luoyang. Therefore, in Confucius' time, the "*correct speech*" may very well be based on the dialect of the capital city Luoyang. Thus, Old Chinese as the elegant speech can be regarded as the common spoken language from the late Shang dynasty until the end of the Han dynasty in the 3rd century AD. The subsequent centuries would be the transitional period from Old Chinese to Middle Chinese, to which we turn in the next chapter.

## Notes

1   The Modern English translation is "Listen! We the Spear-Danes in the days of yore . . ." At the least, we can see that the words for "*what*," "*we*," and "*day*" are quite similar to Modern English, while the others are more different. The word "*gār*" might have been replaced in Modern English.

2   There were phonetic transcriptions of Chinese characters, such as those in the *ḥP'ags-pa* script in the Yuan dynasty. See Chapter 5 of this book for more discussion of the *ḥP'ags-pa* script. But the main writing system for Chinese has always been character based.

3   The imperial examination was suspended for more than 30 years during the Yuan dynasty.

4   It is also variously translated as *Book of Songs*, or *Book of Odes*.

5   This is James Legge's translation of 不學詩，無以言 from the chapter 季氏 of the *Analects*.

6   This is my translation of 蓋時有古今，地有南北；字有更革，音有轉移，亦執所必至.

7   Some scholars distinguish the word "*rhyme*" from the word "*rime*." The word "*rime*" is a noun that refers to part of a syllable in Chinese, while "*rhyme*" is used primarily as a verb. In this book, only the word "*rhyme*" is used as either a noun or a verb, depending on the context.

8   The status of the medial is controversial, since it has relations with both the preceding initial and the following main vowel. The traditional view is that the medial forms a unit with the main vowel and the coda. This unit is called the final, as opposed to the initial. However, there are various alternative theories, one of which is that the medial is actually a glide and can be added to the initial consonant as secondary articulation (Duanmu 2007). For example, instead of analyzing the syllable "*duo*" as an initial consonant [ t ] plus a final [ uo ], it could be alternatively analyzed as a complex initial [ tʷ ] plus a main vowel [ o ]. In this book, we use the traditional theory of including the medial as part of the final.

9   But, strictly speaking, the tone-bearing unit is the rhyme, instead of the whole syllable. Jacques (2006) cites Howie (1974), saying "another important feature is the tone, that bears on the rime."

10   Here the notion of *xiéshēngzì* is essentially and practically the same as that of *xíngshēngzì*, that is, the phono-semantic compound characters introduced earlier in this chapter.

11   The character 方 is a pictogram, according to the *Shuō Wén Jiě Zì* 說文解字. See Chapter 11 for more on the different types of Chinese characters.

12   According to the *Shuō Wén Jiě Zì* 說文解字, the character 央 is originally an ideogrammic compound character.

13   Aspiration refers to the puff of air that follows the release of a consonant, usually a stop. Although the two instances of the letter "*t*" in English words such as "*time*" and "*style*" are considered the same phonologically, that is, the same phoneme / t /, their actual physical properties are different. When the "*t*" follows "*s*," it is usually not aspirated and thus is noted as [ t ]. When it is at the beginning of a word, it is pronounced as an aspirated sound, noted as [ tʰ ]. Although aspiration of stops is not used to distinguish

minimal pairs of words in English, it is a distinctive feature in Chinese. For example, [ ta⁵⁵ ] and [ tʰa⁵⁵ ] are different words.

14 The dialect pronunciation is taken from *Hànyǔ fāngyīn zì huì* 汉语方音字汇 [ *A collection of dialect pronunciations of Chinese characters* ], edited by the Department of Chinese Language and Literature, Peking University (北京大学中国语言文学系语言学教研室编). Beijing, China: Wénzì Gǎigé Chūbǎnshè 文字改革出版社 [ Script Reform Press ], 1962.

15 The original text is 不律，謂之筆 from the chapter 釋器 of the 爾雅.

16 This is my translation of 四聲之辨，古人未有.

17 This is the stage of the Vietnamese language before the 10th century, which corresponds roughly to Middle Chinese. In Haudricourt's (1954) terminology, this is called *l'ancien viètnamien*, or "Ancient Vietnamese."

18 Li (1980: 21) did not provide the names of these initials by using characters. It is probably due to the complex correspondences between Old Chinese and Middle Chinese initials. However, here we provide the characters for each initial. Most of the characters are standard names from Middle Chinese. Thus, these names in characters can help with the comparisons between the two systems. The initial [ tʰ ] corresponds to the Middle Chinese initial 透, but the character 透 itself probably had [ l ] as its initial in Old Chinese. Therefore, we provide the common name 透 itself followed by a character, that is, 帖 here, which had [ tʰ ] in Old Chinese. This character 帖 is in parentheses. Similarly, for [ h ] and [ hʷ ], we have 曉(歇), because 曉 probably had [ ŋ ] in Old Chinese, while 歇 did have [ h ] in Old Chinese. The characters for voiceless nasals, that is, 忽 for [ m̥ ], 歠 for [ n̥ ], and 許 for [ ŋ̊, ŋ̊ʷ ], are selected more or less randomly from the reconstructed words in Li's (1980) system. The character 竉 for [ l ] is based on Zhengzhang (2003: 85).

19 In Zhengzhang's (2003) reconstruction, the *rù*-tone syllables have voiced codas such as *-b, -d, -g*, rather than the voiceless codas *-p, -t, -k* in Li's (1971) system.

20 The chapter titled 述而 *Shù Ér* from the *Analects* says "子所雅言，詩、書、執禮，皆雅言也" ("The Master's frequent themes of discourse were: the Odes, the History, and the maintenance of the Rules of Propriety. On all these he frequently discoursed." Trans. James Legge). The second occurrence of the phrase 雅言 can be interpreted alternatively as "the elegant speech."

# 4 Middle Chinese

## The poetic language

Old Chinese is the standard, or the elegant speech, associated with ancient classics. Similarly, Middle Chinese is the linguistic standard in Tang poetry. This chapter introduces the written records of Middle Chinese, the comparative method, the reconstructed system of Middle Chinese, and its comparison to Old Chinese.

## 4.1 The rhyme dictionary *Qièyùn*

One of the major written records of Middle Chinese is the rhyme dictionary *Qièyùn* 切韻 dated to AD 601 by *Lù Fǎyán* 陸法言. However, the original version of AD 601 has been largely lost. Thus, most of the research on Middle Chinese is based on the expanded version called the *Guǎngyùn* 廣韻, completed in AD 1011 in the Northern Song dynasty. During the early 20th century AD, fragments of the *Qièyùn* were discovered in the Library Cave at Dunhuang. Additionally, a modified version called *Kānmiù Bǔquē Qièyùn* 刊謬補缺切韻 ("Corrected and supplemented *Qièyùn*"), authored by *Wáng Rénxù* 王仁昫 in AD 706 in the Tang dynasty, was discovered in 1947. A comparison between the *Guǎngyùn* and different versions of the *Qièyùn* shows that the phonological systems are basically the same. Thus, the *Qièyùn* and the *Guǎngyùn* are generally referred to interchangeably for the purpose of Middle Chinese phonology.

The preface to the *Qièyùn* has been preserved in the *Guǎngyùn*, and we may obtain very useful information about this dictionary by reading the preface. It is mentioned that at the beginning of the *Kāihuáng* 開皇 era (AD 581–600) of the reign of Emperor Wen of Sui, there was a small gathering hosted by *Lù Fǎyán*, where discussions about correct pronunciations came up. They noted that the dialects at that time had considerable phonological differences, and a standard or correct pronunciation system was need by scholars and their students. Therefore, they compared the pronunciations from the south and the north and decided on the correct pronunciations, often with reference to older rhyme dictionaries, thus producing the first manuscript of the *Qièyùn*.

Here, some preliminary remarks can be made based on the preface. The gathering took place toward the end of the Northern and Southern dynasties (AD 420–589) and at the beginning of the Sui dynasty (AD 581–618). The purpose was to set a standard for literary pronunciations. However, it is not clear what the base dialect of this standard is. There are different views on this issue. Karlgren (1954) proposed that the *Qièyùn* was based on the *Cháng'ān* dialect. For one thing, the gathering was probably in *Cháng'ān*, near present-day Xi'an. The Sui dynasty capital was based in the same area from AD 581–605 but moved to Luoyang from AD 605–618. *Cháng'ān* again became the capital during the Tang dynasty (AD 618–907). Zhou (1966) held the view that the *Qièyùn* standard was a mixed system, with elements from both southern and northern dialects, such as the *Jīnlíng* dialect in the south and *Yèxià* in the north. It is indeed mentioned in the preface that the scholars at the gathering considered pronunciations from different dialects. However, the contribution of these two varieties of Chinese may not have been equal. As Norman (1988: 25) pointed out, *Jīnlíng*, the present-day Nanjing, was the cultural center of the southern dynasties, and two of the most influential discussants at the gathering were from the south. Thus, Norman (1988: 25) argued that the phonology of the *Qièyùn* was largely that of *Jīnlíng*. Pan (2000) suggests that before the Sui dynasty, the base dialect of the common spoken language had always been that of Luoyang and its surrounding areas in present-day Henan province. Even during the Northern and Southern dynasties period, the imperial court and government officials of *Jīnlíng* in the southern dynasties spoke the Luoyang dialect brought to the lower Yangtze River area from the north. There is no consensus among researchers as to what the base dialect of the *Qièyùn* is, but it is clear that the *Qièyùn* was not meant to be a vernacular standard as an actual spoken language, and thus it probably does not correspond faithfully to any particular dialect of that time. As of now, Zhou's (1966) may still be the most widely accepted view on the phonological nature of the *Qièyùn*; that is, it was the cross-dialectal literary standard of the late Northern and Southern dynasties period. Maybe it is partially due to the fact that the *Qièyùn* was a cross-dialectal system with elements from both the southern and the northern dialects that it became very popular soon after it was completed in AD 601. It is the standard of Tang poetry, and the Song dynasty officially approved it in the form of the *Guǎngyùn*. Note that in addition to dialectal elements, the *Qièyùn* may have been rather conservative, in that it preserved some older pronunciations from previous rhyme dictionaries. The pronunciations of characters are indicated in the *Qièyùn* and the *Guǎngyùn* via a method called the *fǎnqiè* 反切.

## 4.2  The *fǎnqiè* method

In the *fǎnqiè* 反切 method, two characters are used to indicate the pronunciation of another character. The following example is taken from the *Guǎngyùn*.

冬：都宗切

We may illustrate how it works by using modern pronunciations. The first character 冬 *dōng* is the one that needs a pronunciation annotation. The second character 都 *dū* has the same initial as 冬 *dōng*, while the character 宗 *zōng* shares the same final and tone with 冬 *dōng*. If we single out the initial of 都 and the final plus tone of 宗, then we get *d-* plus *-ōng*, which, put together, is the pronunciation of 冬 *dōng*.

The structure is usually this: the character to be annotated A is given a *fǎnqiè* consisting of a character B, of which the initial is to be used, and a character C, of which the final and tone are used. The word *qiè* 切 indicates that this is the *fǎnqiè* method.[1] We use a colon here to separate the character to be annotated from the *fǎnqiè* itself. But punctuation marks were not used in traditional Chinese texts. The colon is only a convenient way here to show the structure. It is not part of the original *fǎnqiè* scheme.

The whole method probably seems quite redundant to modern readers. Why don't we just indicate the pronunciation of 冬 with the *pīnyīn* spelling *dōng*? As we mentioned in Chapter 3, the Chinese writing system is not a phonetic one. There was no Chinese alphabet to be used in ancient times. Moreover, for speakers of Chinese, each character would be pronounced as a whole syllable and is not analyzed in terms of individual sounds such as consonants or vowels. However, traditional Chinese scholars did notice that some characters share the same initial sound and some characters rhyme, as shown in the traditional concepts of *shuāngshēng* 雙聲 ("alliteration") and *diéyùn* 疊韻 ("rhyming"), discussed in Chapter 3 as well. Such a phonological analysis may be associated with the construction of the *fǎnqiè* method, which is actually a remarkable phonetic technique based on the nature of Chinese characters.

In the example 冬: 都宗切 here, Modern Standard Chinese pronunciations are used to illustrate how it works. But *fǎnqiè* from the *Gǎngyùn* should be based solely on Middle Chinese phonology. Although sound change has not affected the phonological connections among the characters in the example 冬: 都宗切, that is often not the case. The following *fǎnqiè* is also taken from the *Guǎngyùn*.

東：德紅切

The character that needs a pronunciation annotation is 東 *dōng*. The modern pronunciations of the two characters in the *fǎnqiè* are: *dé* for 德 and *hóng* for 紅. If we put them together, we get the pronunciation *dóng*, which is not the correct pronunciation of 東 *dōng*, because the tones are different. In their Middle Chinese pronunciations, there should be no problem with the tones. Although this example here still works fine in terms of its initial and final, there are many cases where modern pronunciations do not yield the correct initials, medials, rhymes, or a combination of them. However, the pronunciations should be correct for the time when the *fǎnqiè* was created.

Although the *fǎnqiè* method is a very accurate way of indicating sounds in Chinese, there are a number of disadvantages. First, in order to make it work, one has to know how to pronounce the two characters used in the *fǎnqiè*. Otherwise, we have to look up one or both of the two characters, where we may still encounter *fǎnqiè* with unfamiliar new characters. The whole process can go in circles if the *fǎnqiè* characters are not carefully selected by using common characters to avoid a loop in the system. Second, since no fixed character is used in the *fǎnqiè*, there are many possible ways of indicating the same sound. The system is at least very inefficient. Despite these imperfections, the large number of *fǎnqiè* annotations in the *Guǎngyùn* provide a wealth of information for the studies of Middle Chinese phonology.

## 4.3 Structure of the *Guǎngyùn*

In Middle Chinese poetics, especially in the Tang regulated verse, rhyming requires the characters to have the same tone, in addition to the same main vowel and coda. For example, a character with the pronunciation *dōng* can rhyme with *gōng*, but not with *gòng*. Since the *Guǎngyùn* was primarily used for composing poems, the rhymes of different tones had to be separated. Therefore, the major division of the *Guǎngyùn*, that is, *juàn* 卷 ("volume"), is based on the four tones in Middle Chinese: *píngshēng* 平聲 ("the level tone"), *shǎngshēng* 上聲 ("the rising tone"), *qùshēng* 去聲 ("the departing tone"), and *rùshēng* 入聲 ("the entering tone"). There are five volumes in the *Guǎngyùn*. Since there are more characters in the *píng* tone category, the first two volumes are dedicated to *píng*-tone characters. The third volume contains characters in the *shǎng* tone category, the fourth volume is for *qù*-tone characters, and the fifth volume is for the *rù* tone.

Each volume is divided into a number of *yùn* 韻 ("rhymes"), usually listed in the front of each volume in a table of contents. The first character in each rhyme, called *yùnmù* 韻目 ("the eye of the rhyme"), is used as the name of the whole rhyme. Within each rhyme, there are a number of homophonous groups of characters, that is, strictly homophonous in terms of their initials, finals, and tones, because rhymes of different tones are separated. Each homophonous group is preceded by a circle called *niǔ* 紐 "knob." The first character in each homophonous group is provided with a *fǎnqiè*, followed by a number indicating how many homophonous characters there are all together in this group. Figure 4.1 shows a page from the *Guǎngyùn*.

The reading direction of traditional Chinese texts is from right to left and from top to bottom. To read the page in Figure 4.1, we go from the upper right corner down and then move left to the next column, starting from the top again. The five columns on the right of the page are part of the table of contents. Then, starting from the sixth column from the right is the real content of the dictionary. The numbers 1, 2, 3, and so on are not part of the dictionary. They are added here in the illustration so that we can refer to different sections of the page.

Let's start from the number 1, which reads 側詵 *cèshēn* from right to left. This is the pronunciation in *fǎnqiè* for the name of the rhyme represented by the character below it marked with the number 2 here, that is, 臻 *zhēn*. Then the part labeled with the number 3, 第十九 ("No. 19"), is an ordinal number indicating where this rhyme appears in the dictionary. In this case, it is the 19th rhyme in this volume. The first character there in the 19th rhyme, that is, 臻, is used as the name for the whole rhyme. The lower section in the first column from the right is the 20th rhyme, described in exactly the same way as the 19th rhyme.

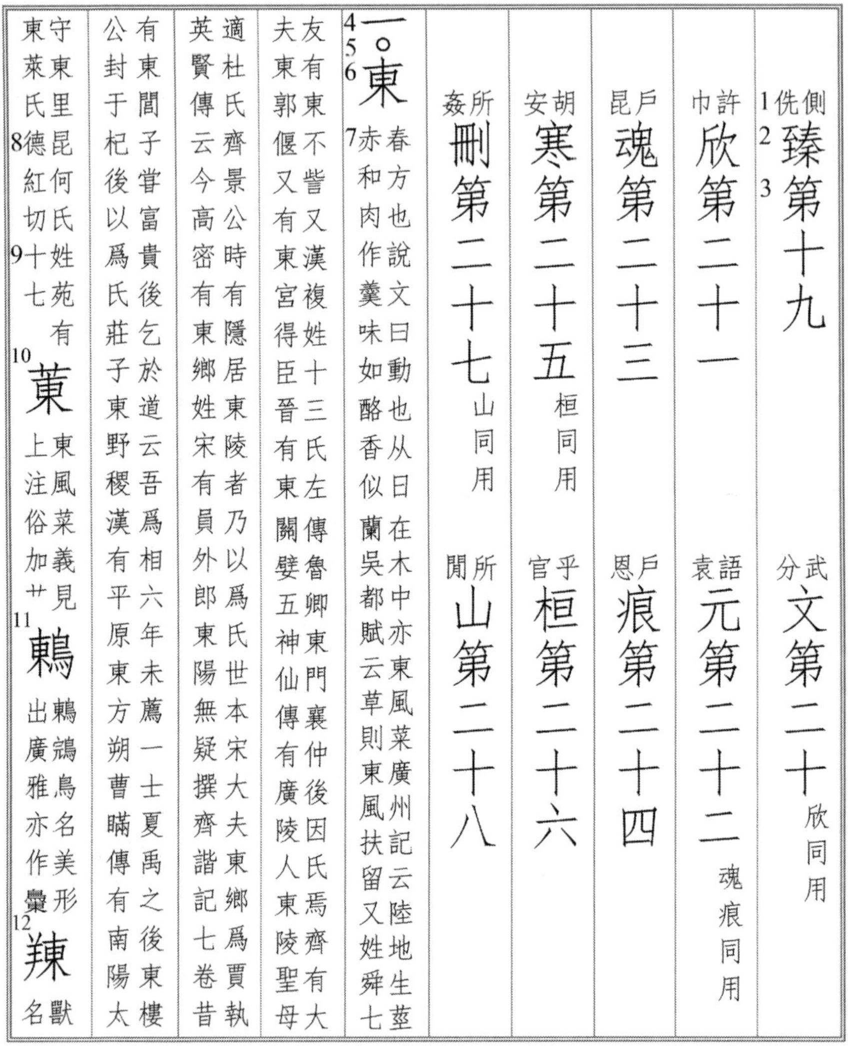

東守東萊氏昆德何氏姓苑有　菓　上東注俗菜加艹見　鶇　出鶇鴿雅名美形　辣　名獸

東里昆紅切十七苑有

公封于杞後以為氏莊子東野稷漢有平原東方朔曹瞞傳有南陽太
有東閭子嘗富貴後乞於道云吾為相六年未薦一士夏禹之後東樓

英賢傳云今高密有東鄉姓宋朝有員外郎東陽無疑撰齊諧記七卷昔
適杜氏齊景公時有隱居東陵者乃以為氏世本宋大夫東鄉為人

夫友有東郭又有東宮複姓十三氏左傳魯卿東門襄仲後因氏焉又有東關嬖五神仙傳有廣陵人東陵聖母

一。東
赤和肉作羹味如酪香似蘭吳都賦云東風扶留又姓舜七
春方也說文曰動也從日在木中亦東風菜廣州記云陸地生莖

所姦　刪第二十七　山同用
聞所　山第二十八

胡安　寒第二十五　桓同用
官平　桓第二十六

昆戶　魂第二十三
恩戶　痕第二十四

巾許　欣第二十一
袁語　元第二十二　魂痕同用

側　臻第十九
分武　文第二十　欣同用

*Figure 4.1* A sample page from the *Guǎngyùn*

Now let's look at the part with the number 4 on the top of the sixth column from the right. This character 一 *yī* is the cardinal number "one." It indicates that this is the first rhyme in the volume. Number 5 is a tiny circle that separates homophonous groups in the rhyme. Number 6 is the first character in the first homophonous group, that is, the *yùnmù* of this whole rhyme. Here it is the character 東 *dōng*, meaning "east." Below it is the explanation of the meaning of this character, illustrated with textual quotes from various sources. Note that there are two vertical lines of characters in the explanatory notes. Reading direction is from top of the line on the right down to the bottom and then, jumping to the top of the second vertical line, the reading continues from there down to the bottom. Then we move to the next column and do the same thing to read the two vertical lines.

At the position of number 8, the pronunciation of the first character 東 in this homophonous group is given by the *fǎnqiè* 德紅切, which has been used as an example previously to show how *fǎnqiè* works. At number 9, the characters 十七 ("seventeen") indicate the total number of homophonous characters in this group, including the first one 東. Thus, the characters at the positions of numbers 10, 11, and 12, that is, 菄, 鶇, 辣, are homophonous with 東. The modern pronunciations of all these characters are *dōng*. *Fǎnqiè* is only provided for the first character 東, because all the other 16 characters have exactly the same pronunciation, including the tone.

Although the *Guǎngyùn* is the primary written record of Middle Chinese, the phonological system is hidden among the *fǎnqiè* examples. There is actually a related source for Middle Chinese, called "*rhyme tables*," which represents sophisticated analyses of the phonological system of the *Guǎngyùn*.

## 4.4   Rhyme tables

In the Song dynasty, a specialized type of phonological analysis based on rhyme tables, or *yùntú* 韻圖, flourished. These rhyme tables resemble a modern Chinese combination table of initials, finals, and tones.

In Table 4.1, the header row on top is the various initials in Modern Standard Chinese. There are 22 initials in Modern Standard Chinese, but we only list 8 here and omit the rest with dots to just illustrate what a combination table is. The first column on the left is the final "*ong*" in the 1st, 2nd, 3rd, and 4th tones, respectively. Therefore, each cell in the table represents a possible combination. For example, the initial *d-* can be combined with the final *-ong* with the 1st tone to form the syllable "*dōng*," which is written by different characters such as 東, 菄, 鶇, 辣, and so on. The circles in the table indicate that those combinations are not part of the syllable inventory of Modern Standard Chinese. For example, the combination of the initial *d-* with the final *-ong* in the 2nd tone, that is, *dóng*, does not represent an actual word or morpheme in Modern Standard Chinese.

*Table 4.1* Combination table of initials, finals, and tones

|      | b | p | m | f | d | t | n | l | . . . . . . |
|------|---|---|---|---|---|---|---|---|-------------|
| ōng  | O | O | O | O | dōng | tōng | O | lōng | . . . . . . |
| óng  | O | O | O | O | O | tóng | nóng | lóng | . . . . . |
| ǒng  | O | O | O | O | dǒng | tǒng | O | lǒng | . . . . . . |
| òng  | O | O | O | O | dòng | tòng | nòng | lòng | . . . . . . |

Thus, in such a combination table, all the initials are listed on the top row, the finals vertically on the left, and the actual syllables in each of the cells in the middle, with circles to indicate non-actual syllable combinations. If one final is listed in each table, as done here, there are as many tables as there are finals to show all the actual combinations. Table 4.1 shows just one of these tables.

A rhyme table is structurally quite similar. But there are two major differences. First, since there was no phonetic annotation system at the time of the rhyme tables, all sounds have to be represented by characters. Second, there is an extra dimension called *děng* 等 ("division, grade") in the rhyme tables. Figure 4.2 is the first table from a book of rhyme tables called the *Yùnjìng* 韻鏡 ("Mirror of Rhymes").

Again here, we use numbers to label the different areas of the rhyme table for ease of reference, although the numbers themselves are not part of the original rhyme tables. The rightmost column that runs the whole length of the page describes what type of syllables these are. Then the top row, labeled with the number 1, with three lines of Chinese characters in each cell, contains the initials referred to by their descriptive names. For example, the first initial, that is, on the right, in the upper right corner is described as 脣音清 *chúnyīn qīng* (literally "lip-sound clear"), which may be interpreted as a voiceless labial sound, such as [ p ] or [ f ]. In the *Yùnjìng*, there are 36 initials, described first by where the sounds are produced in the vocal tract, for example, lip, tongue, and so on, and then by

| | 1 / 2 齒音舌 清清 濁濁 | 音 喉 清 濁濁清清 | 音 齒 次 濁清濁清清 | 音 牙 清 次 濁濁清清 | 音 舌 清 次 濁濁清清 | 音 脣 清 次 濁濁清清 | 內轉第一開 |
|---|---|---|---|---|---|---|---|
| 東 5 | ○籠 | ○洪烘翁 | ○摲叢忽薉 | 峺○空公 | ○同通東 | 蒙蓬○○ | |
| 6 | ○○ | ○○○○ | ○○崇○○ | ○○○○ | ○○○○ | ○○○○ | |
| 7 | 戎隆 | 肜雄○○ | ○○○充終 | 狋窮穹弓 | ○蟲忡中 | 瞢馮豐風 | |
| 8 | ○○ | 融○○○ | ○嵩○○○ | ○○○○ | ○○○○ | ○○○○ | |
| 董 | ○瓏 | ○懵嗊蓊 | ○啟○○緫 | ○○孔○ | 繷動桶董 | 蠓莽○琫 | |
| | ○○ | ○○○○ | ○○○○○ | ○○○○ | ○○○○ | ○○○○ | |
| | ○○ | ○○○○ | ○○○○○ | ○○○○ | ○○○○ | ○○○○ | |
| | ○○ | ○○○○ | ○○○○○ | ○○○○ | ○○○○ | ○○○○ | |
| 送 | ○弄 | ○閧烘甕 | ○送敕認糉 | ○○控貢 | 齈洞痛凍 | 夢捧○○ | |
| | ○○ | ○○○○ | ○○糉○○ | ○○○○ | ○○○○ | ○○○○ | |
| | ○○ | ○○趙○ | ○○○銃衆 | ○○焢○ | ○仲○中 | 幪鳳賵諷 | |
| | ○○ | ○○○○ | ○○○趙○ | ○○○○ | ○○○○ | ○○○○ | |
| 屋 | ○祿 | ○穀熇屋 | ○速族瘯鏃 | ○○哭穀 | ○獨禿縠 | 木暴扑卜 | |
| | ○○ | ○○○○ | ○縮○珿縬 | ○○○○ | ○○○○ | ○○○○ | |
| | 肉六 | 囿○畜郁 | 塾叔○儵粥 | 砡䐄麹菊 | 朒逐畜竹 | 目伏蝮福 | |
| | ○○ | 育○○○ | ○蕭歗鼀蹙 | ○○○○ | ○○○○ | ○○○○ | |

*Figure 4.2* A sample page from the *Yùnjìng*

their perceived auditory properties, for example, clear, muddy, and so on. These two dimensions of descriptions can be roughly interpreted as place and manner of articulation in modern terminology.

The first column from the left, indicated by the number 2, contains the four rhymes 東 *dōng*, 董 *dǒng*, 送 *sòng*, and 屋 *wū*, that is, the first rhymes from the *píng, shǎng, qù,* and *rù* volumes of the *Guǎngyùn*. The four characters here are used for their rhymes only, very similar to the vertical column on the left in Table 4.1. The initials of these four characters do not matter and can be different.

The circles in the cells of the table represent non-actual combinations. Each of the characters in the combination cells represents a real syllable in Middle Chinese. These characters are taken from the homophonous groups in the *Guǎngyùn*. For example, the first homophonous group in the 東 rhyme includes characters such as 東菄鶇涷 and so on. Their pronunciations are all *dōng* in Modern Standard Chinese. The first character of this homophonous group, that is, 東, is put in the corresponding combination position in the rhyme table here, as indicated by the number 3. The second homophonous group in the 東 rhyme in the *Guǎngyùn* includes characters like 同仝童僮 and so on. Their pronunciations are all *tóng* in Modern Standard Chinese. The first character 同 of this homophonous group is placed in the corresponding combination position in the rhyme table, indicated by the number 4. Since the homophonous group under 東 is also the first homophonous group in this rhyme in the *Guǎngyùn*, 東 is both the name of the rhyme and also the representative character of the first homophonous group. Thus, it appears twice in this table, but their functions are quite different. The 東 at position number 3 represents a whole syllable, including the initial, the rhyme, and the tone, while the 東 in large font on the left only represents the rhyme and tone but not the initial.

Let's look at the cell with 東 and 同 again. There are actually four lines of characters and circles in that cell. Both 東 and 同 are placed on the first line. There are only circles on the second line, three characters on the third line, and only circles again on the fourth line. In the other cells, some have characters on each of the four lines, and some have very few characters. These four lines are called *děng* 等 ("division, grade"). The first line, indicated by the number 5, is the first *děng*, or *division I*; the second line, indicated by the number 6, is the second *děng*, or *division II*; the third line, as labeled with the number 7, is the third *děng*, or *division III*, and the fourth line, labeled with the number 8, is the fourth *děng*, or *division IV*. The concept of *děng* is a totally new one here, which does not have any correspondence in the combination table in Table 4.1. If each row represents the same rhyme, then how can the characters of different divisions in the same row be distinguished? One widely accepted view on the nature of *děng* is that the division III syllables have a *-j-* medial. We discuss this in more detail later in this chapter.

Rhyme tables, originally written by Chinese Buddhist monks who studied Sanskrit, can be traced back to late Tang dynasty in the 9th and 10th centuries, although rhyme tables became more popular in early Song dynasty (11th century). The *Yùnjìng*, as shown in Figure 4.2, was probably written in the 10th century but first published in the Song dynasty in AD 1161. It is the earliest rhyme table that has been passed down to modern days. These rhyme tables are very valuable written records of the sounds of Middle Chinese. They represent a great step forward to a real phonetic analysis of the language. The previous rhyme dictionaries do not tell us directly what the phonological system is like, that is, how many initials there were in Middle Chinese and how they could be combined with the medials and rhymes. Furthermore, rhyme dictionaries are difficult to use for the study of phonology of Middle Chinese, because information needs to be collected from different places in the dictionaries and then analyzed. But rhyme tables show the whole system of the *Guǎngyùn* in a few dozen tables. Thus, rhyme tables may be used as a guide to the study of the *Guǎngyùn* to discover the Middle Chinese phonological system. There are a few complications, though. For one thing, the system of the *Qièyùn*, or the *Guǎngyùn*, represents the literary pronunciation of the late Northern and Southern dynasties in the 6th century, while the *Yùnjìng* was first composed in the 10th century, a few hundred years after the *Qièyùn*. How different was the Luoyang dialect in the 6th century from the *Cháng'ān* dialect in the 10th century? It is reasonable to assume that the authors of the rhyme tables in the Song dynasty could not reliably understand all the detailed phonological distinctions in the *Qièyùn*.

So far, we have introduced the two main sources for Middle Chinese: rhyme dictionaries such as the *Guǎngyùn* and rhyme tables such as the *Yùnjìng*. The next step is to find a method to systematically summarize the information in such written materials.

## 4.5    The linking method for analyzing the *Guǎngyùn*

Similarly to how Old Chinese is reconstructed, there are two steps to reconstruct Middle Chinese. First, characters need to be placed into a finite number of categories of initials and of rhymes. Then, the phonetic values can be reconstructed. In this section, we discuss the traditional linking method used on the *fǎnqiè* in the *Guǎngyùn* and show how this method can yield a number of categories of sounds.

Since the *Guǎngyùn* lists characters according to their rhymes, the different rhyme categories are therefore easily obtained by looking at the table of contents. For example:

The rhymes of the *píng* tone volume are:     東    冬 and so on
The rhymes of the *shǎng* tone volume are:    董    腫 and so on
The rhymes of the *qù* tone volume are:       送    宋 and so on
The rhymes of the *rù* tone volume are:       屋    沃 and so on

Looking at the listed rhymes vertically, we find that 東董送 only differ in their tones, but they have exactly the same rhyme, that is, the main vowel plus the coda. This can be partially deduced from how the dictionary separates the same rhyme into different tonal volumes. The 屋 rhyme in the *rù* tone volume has the same main vowel as the 東董送 rhymes but has a different syllable coda. Thus, 東董送 is in the same rhyme category, and it pairs with the 屋 rhyme. We use the first character 東 to name the rhyme category that includes 東董送. As mentioned in

Chapter 3, there are three types of rhymes in Middle Chinese: *yīnshēngyùn* 陰聲韻 ("open rhymes"), *yángshēngyùn* 陽聲韻 ("nasal rhymes"), and *rùshēngyùn* 入聲韻 ("rhymes with stop codas"). Usually, a nasal rhyme, that is, *yángshēngyùn*, pairs with a *rùshēngyùn* when their consonant codas are pronounced in the same area in the vocal tract or, put in modern terminology, when the codas share the same place of articulation. For example, the 東 rhyme has the velar nasal coda -*ŋ*, while the 屋 rhyme has the velar stop coda -*k*.

In the *Guǎngyùn*, there are 206 rhymes listed, including 57 *píng*-tone rhymes, 55 *shǎng*-tone rhymes, 60 *qù*-tone rhymes, and 34 *rù*-tone rhymes. If we ignore the distinction among the *píng*, *shǎng*, and *qù* tones and only count the different rhymes in terms of the main vowel and coda, as has just been shown with 東董送, there are actually 61 categories of open and nasal rhymes. The *rù*-tone rhymes need to be counted separately because they do not have the same coda consonants. Thus, counting both the 34 *rù*-tone rhymes and the other 61 rhymes, we get a total of 95 rhyme categories.

But the most useful information in the *Guǎngyùn* is to be sought in the *fǎnqiè* by using the traditional linking method. Let's recall the structure of a *fǎnqiè*, which can be represented as A: B C 切. A is the character to be annotated. B is the character used for its initial. C is the character used for its final and tone. Thus, the characters A and B should have the same initial; the characters A and C should have the same final and tone. Then the characters A and B are in the same initial category, and the characters A and C are in the same category of finals. By studying all of the *fǎnqiè* examples in the *Guǎngyùn*, we may link all of the characters into a finite number of categories of initials and finals. Suppose we have the following two *fǎnqiè* examples:

A: B C 切
D: E C 切

Then we can deduce that the characters A and C have the same final and that D and C have the same final. Since the character C is the common link, all three characters, A, C, and D, are in the same final category. Let's use the following two real examples from the *Guǎngyùn* to illustrate how the linking method works.

東: 德紅切
同: 徒紅切

From these two examples of *fǎnqiè*, we first obtain the following two groups of characters that share the same final within each group.

Group 1: 東紅
Group 2: 同紅

Since the second character in each group, that is, 紅, is the common link, we may further place 東紅同 into the same category of finals.

Here we have introduced a distinction between a category of finals and one of rhymes. This is because within the same rhyme in the *Guǎngyùn*, there are further subgroupings. Let's use the *píng*-tone rhyme 東 to illustrate this point. After applying the linking method to all of the *fǎnqiè* examples in this 東 rhyme, we obtain the following two subgroups:

Subgroup 1: 東紅公 and so on
Subgroup 2: 中弓戎融宫終 and so on

There is no shared character between these two subgroups to link them up. Since all of the characters in Subgroup 1 and Subgroup 2 are in the same 東 rhyme, according to the definition of a rhyme dictionary, they should have exactly the same main vowel and coda. But they are divided into different subgroups. There should be a way in which they differ.

Interestingly, if we look back at the rhyme table shown in Figure 4.2, we find that 東 from Subgroup 1 is on the first line in a cell, as indicated by the number 3, while 中 from Subgroup 2 is on the third line right below 東. In terms of the overall pattern of distribution among the characters in the row for the 東 rhyme, it seems that the characters are either on the first line or the third line, with a few exceptions. Recall that the four lines are called four different divisions, that is, *děng*. Thus, ignoring the few exceptions for now, we can say that the characters in the 東 rhyme belong with either division I or division III. Similar patterns of distribution can be observed for the other rows in the rhyme table. All of the characters on the row of the *shǎng*-tone rhyme 董 are in division I. On the row for the *qù*-tone rhyme 送, most of the characters belong with either division I or division III. It is the same with the *rù*-tone rhyme 屋. Thus, there is a more or less regular pattern of distribution: the characters from the 東董送屋 rhymes belong with either division I or division III, and the distribution matches the subgroups derived from the linking method on the *fǎnqiè*. As mentioned briefly previously, research shows that division III should have the -*j*- sound as its medial. Thus, Subgroup 1 represents a final without the -*j*- medial, while Subgroup 2 represents one with the -*j*- medial, although both finals share the same main vowel and the same coda. In Karlgren's reconstruction as modified by Li (1971), the Middle Chinese form of Subgroup 1 is -*uŋ*, and Subgroup 2 is -*juŋ*. In addition to -*j*-, there are other types of medials as well. We provide evidence as to how such a conclusion is reached later in this chapter.

Thus, there is a distinction between the rhymes listed in the *Guǎngyùn* and the actual number of finals. After applying the linking method to the 1190 *fǎnqiè* examples in the *Guǎngyùn*, Tang (2013: 95–97) identifies 293 different subgroups, including 83 groups in the *píng*-tone rhymes, 76 groups in the *shǎng*-tone rhymes, 83 groups in the *qù*-tone rhymes, and 51 for the *rù*-tone rhymes. If we ignore the tonal differences among rhymes with the *píng*, *shǎng*, and *qù* tones and count the *rù*-tone rhymes separately, we obtain 91 categories of open and nasal finals plus 51 *rù*-tone finals, all together 142 categories of finals. This is a larger number than the 95 categories of rhymes consisting of 34 *rù*-tone rhymes and 61 other rhymes, because there are subgroups within many rhymes, similar to what has just been shown in the example previously with the 東 rhyme.

In terms of the categories of initials, the same linking method can be used as well. Suppose we have the following two examples of *fǎnqiè*:

A: B C 切
D: B E 切

Then the characters A and B have the same initial; D and B have the same initial. Since the character B is the common link, we can place all three characters, A, B, and D, in the same category of initials. Let's use the following two real examples from the *Guǎngyùn* to illustrate how the linking method works.

冬: 都宗切
當: 都郎切

From these two examples of *fǎnqiè*, we first obtain the following two groups of characters that share the same initial within each group.

Group 1: 冬都
Group 2: 當都

Since the second character in each group, that is, 都, is the common link, we may further place 冬都當 into the same category of initials.

Therefore, by linking the characters that have the same initials in all of the *fǎnqiè* examples in the *Guǎngyùn*, a certain number of categories of initials can be obtained. Tang (2013: 76–77) identifies 51 categories of initials. However, these 51 categories are not 51 distinctive initials. As mentioned previously, within a rhyme in the *Guǎngyùn*, there are often subgroups corresponding to the different divisions on the rhyme tables. Therefore, in line with such a distinction, the characters used for their initials in the *fǎnqiè* tend to separate into subgroups as well. The characters in the *fǎnqiè* with a division III final tend to be different from those in the other divisions. According to Chen (1995), between the following two related categories of initials, the one group including 居舉九 is often used as initials with division III finals, while the other group including 見公過 goes with the other divisions. But the two groups do not represent actual different initials, and therefore these characters can be placed into one same category of initials, that is, 居舉九見公過. Similarly, other categories of initials can be further combined. Tang (2013: 78) reduces the 51 categories into 35 actual different initials. Generally, the number of initials in the *Guǎngyùn* is around 35, with differences only in a few of these initials in various reconstructed systems. For example, in Karlgren's reconstruction modified by Li (1971), there are 37 initials, of which 34 are based upon the same categories as in Tang's (2013: 78) 35 initials, although the actual reconstructed phonetic values of these 34 initials are not all the same in these two systems.

*Table 4.2* The 36 initials of the *Yùnjìng*

| Modern Interpretation | Categorization | Names of Initials |
|---|---|---|
| Labials | Lip 脣 | 幫滂並明 |
| | | 非敷奉微 |
| Coronals | Tongue 舌 | 端透定泥 |
| | | 知徹澄娘 |
| Velars | Back-tooth 牙 | 見溪羣疑 |
| Sibilants | Tooth 齒 | 精清從心邪 |
| | | 照穿牀審禪 |
| Gutturals | Throat 喉 | 影曉匣喻 |
| Sonorants | Half tongue 半舌 | 來 |
| | Half tooth 半齒 | 日 |

A related system called the 36 initials from the *Yùnjìng*, as mentioned previously in the discussion of the rhyme table in Figure 4.2, represents the initials of the Song dynasty and therefore can be compared with the *Qièyùn* initials to figure out what sound changes may have taken place in the few hundred years in between. Table 4.2 shows the 36 initials, each represented by a character.

The characters in the table are used for their initials only, and their finals are not relevant. The traditional categorization mostly refers to how the sounds are produced in various areas of the vocal tract, as is apparent from the category names such as "*lip*," "*tooth*," and so on. Among the lip sounds, there are two subcategories, usually interpreted to be bilabial and labiodental. Subcategories also exist in some of the other sounds. There are many subtle differences between these 36 initials and the 35 or 37 initials in the *Guǎngyùn*. But we do not discuss such differences at length here.

Thus, by using the linking method, we can obtain a number of categories of initials and finals of the *Guǎngyùn*. Although rhyme tables have done exactly this by listing the categories of initials, rhymes, and finals in the tables, the composition of rhyme tables was mostly in the Song dynasty, and we cannot assume that the phonological analysis in rhyme tables is the same as that of the *Guǎngyùn*. Actually, we can compare the categories of sounds in rhyme tables with those in the *Guǎngyùn* and figure out what differences there may be. The next step is to reconstruct the actual phonetic values of categories of sounds.

## 4.6   The comparative reconstruction method

Bernhard Karlgren (1889–1978) was the first scholar who applied modern methodology to reconstruct the actual phonetic values of Middle Chinese. The original materials that Karlgren used include the *Guǎngyùn* and rhyme tables[2] from which the categories of sounds may be obtained. Karlgren primarily focused on the categories of sounds from the rhyme tables and used modern Chinese dialect pronunciations of characters in these categories to deduce the original sounds in Middle Chinese. Additionally, Karlgren also used Japanese, Korean, and Vietnamese pronunciations of Chinese characters, because Classical Chinese was borrowed into these countries during the Middle Chinese period together with the pronunciations of the characters in Middle Chinese. According to Xu (1991), the *Go'on* 吳音 pronunciations of Chinese characters in Japanese were borrowed during the 5th and 6th centuries AD from the *Jiànkāng* 建康 (present-day Nanjing) area of the Southern dynasties, while the *Kan'on* 漢音 pronunciations of Chinese characters in Japanese were based on Middle Chinese pronunciations of the 7th century AD from the capital city *Cháng'ān* in the northwest. The Korean pronunciations of Chinese characters are related to the sounds of Middle Chinese around the 7th century. Vietnamese pronunciations of Chinese characters are related to Middle Chinese pronunciations during the 8th and 9th centuries. These pronunciation systems in Japanese, Korean, and Vietnamese can definitely help us understand the sounds of Middle Chinese. However, because Middle Chinese was essentially a foreign language borrowed into these societies and phonological adaptations may have been made accordingly, we need to be more judicious in using data from these pronunciation systems. Therefore, the most important sources for reconstructing Middle Chinese are various modern Chinese dialects. It has been pointed out previously in this book that the Chinese dialects are sometimes called different "*Sinitic languages*," because these different varieties of Chinese are not necessarily mutually intelligible. In historical linguistics, methods have been developed to reconstruct the proto-language based on modern languages that have descended from a common origin. Thus, such methodology can be applied to reconstructing Middle Chinese as well. Let's take a detailed look at the comparative method in historical linguistics first.

To establish a genetic relationship between two languages, a list of true cognate words is the primary dataset that is the basis for further work. Here is a concrete example of comparative reconstruction using cognate words from Romance languages such as French, Spanish, and Italian, which descended from Vulgar Latin. Table 4.3 shows a cognate set with four words from these three languages. The data in Table 4.3 are taken from Campbell (1999: 125).

The first step is to go through each word sound by sound to establish all the correspondences. For example, looking at the first sound in the word for "*path*," we

*Table 4.3* An example of the comparative reconstruction method

| Word | French | Spanish | Italian |
|------|--------|---------|---------|
| **PATH** | chemin | camino | cammino |
| **SHIRT** | chemise | camisa | camicia |
| **HAIR** | cheveu | cabello | capello |
| **HORSE** | cheval | caballo | cavallo |

find that the sound "*ch*" in French corresponds to the sound "*c*" in Spanish and Italian. The "*ch*" combination here in French is pronounced as the "*ch*" in the English word "*chef*." It is one sound, although in writing there are two letters. This sound is a palatal fricative, represented by [ ʃ ] in IPA. The "*c*" in Spanish and Italian is pronounced as [ k ] in IPA. Let's write this sound correspondence as *ʃ-k-k* in the order of French-Spanish-Italian. Then we go to the second sound and obtain the correspondence *e-a-a*. Skipping to the word "*shirt*," we find that the first two correspondences are the same as in the word for "*path*," that is, *ʃ-k-k* and *e-a-a*. Now, in terms of the first three sounds in the word "*hair*," there are three correspondences: *ʃ-k-k*, *e-a-a*, and *v-b-p*. The first two are the same as in the previous two words, and the correspondence *v-b-p* is new. Skipping again to the word for "*horse*," we get the following three correspondences *ʃ-k-k*, *e-a-a*, *v-b-v*. The first two sounds are repetitions again, and the third one is a new one. One simplification in the demonstration here is regarding the "*b*" sound in Spanish, which is pronounced as a bilabial fricative [ β ] when it occurs between two vowels. However since the sounds [ b ] and [ β ] are considered variants of the same phoneme in Spanish, we write "*b*" in the correspondences here to make the comparisons easier.

The whole process of finding correspondences would continue throughout all the words in the cognate set in a sound-by-sound fashion. Since our purpose here is only illustrative, and the correspondences other than those just mentioned previously are more complicated, let's just focus on the four correspondences that have been obtained, listed as follows:

Correspondence 1:  *ʃ-k-k*
Correspondence 2:  *e-a-a*
Correspondence 3:  *v-b-p*
Correspondence 4:  *v-b-v*

Multiple occurrences of the same correspondence, such as *ʃ-k-k*, which occurs four times in this cognate set, suggest that such a correspondence is regular. Although *v-b-p* and *v-b-v* only occur once each in our cognate set here, it is due to the limited number of words in the dataset.

The second step is to reconstruct the original sound. If there are variations in the correspondences, we need to figure out the possibilities of reconstruction. For example, in Correspondence 1: *ʃ-k-k*, there are two sounds, *ʃ* and *k*. One possibility is that the original sound was *$k$ and it changed to *ʃ* in French. The star "*" in front of a reconstructed sound indicates that it is a hypothetical form rather than being the actual sound in the ancestral language. We can use the notation "A > B" to mean that A developed into B or "B < A" to mean that B came from A. Therefore, the sound change in Correspondence 1 may be expressed in the form of *$k$ > *ʃ*, which occurred in French. But theoretically speaking, it is also possible that the original sound was *ʃ* and it became *k* in Spanish and Italian. If there is no evidence in favor of either hypothesis, "*majority wins*" can be used as a justification to choose the sound that appears in the majority of current languages as the proto form. Thus, let's posit *$k$ as the original sound, since it occurs in more languages.

But the principle of "*majority wins*" should be used as a last-resort type of reason, since, for one thing, it can be easily overwritten by considerations of naturalness in sound change, meaning that certain sound change patterns are more likely to occur. Take the sound changes *$k > ʃ$ and *$ʃ > k$, for example. We actually find that *$k > ʃ$ is quite common across many different languages. For example, the word "*church*" in English and the word "*Kirche*" in German are cognates. It turns out that the original $k$ sound became a palatal affricate [ tʃ ] in English, that is, the "*ch*" as in the word "*church*." In terms of articulatory phonetics, it is easy for certain sounds to become palatal when they precede a high front vowel. Such an assimilatory change, called "*palatalization*," occurs frequently in different languages, because there is a phonetic reason for it to take place. Thus, such sound changes are considered natural. Although the vowel in the word "*church*" in English is not a high front vowel, its Old English form *circe* does have the high front vowel "*ī*" that follows the first consonant. By contrast, however, it is very rare to find cases such as *$ʃ > k$, where a palatal consonant $ʃ$ turned into a velar consonant $k$. Therefore, between the two sound changes *$k > ʃ$ vs. *$ʃ > k$, justification in terms of naturalness or directionality favors *$k > ʃ$, since it is an instance of the recurrent pattern called "*palatalization*."

For Correspondence 2: *e-a-a*, there is no strong evidence to determine which is the original sound, but since "*a*" is the majority, we can temporarily reconstruct *$a$. Additionally, the original Latin form "*caminus*" ("path") and "*camisia* ("shirt") can be consulted here. Apparently, the first vowel in these words is "*a*," and thus this is another type of evidence that can be used here to further justify the reconstruction of *$a$ as the proto-form.

Let's move on to Correspondence 4: *v-b-v*, because it is less complicated than Correspondence 3. We may have a better idea after the reconstruction of Correspondence 4 is made. Two possibilities can be considered, *$b$ or *$v$, as the proto-form for Correspondence 4. In this case, "*majority wins*" would predict *$v$. But naturalness would prefer *$b$, meaning that it is more common for a stop consonant such as $b$ to become a fricative such as $v$ between two vowels. In terms of articulatory phonetics, vowels are continuant sounds, while stop consonants are not. To facilitate the articulation of successive sounds, a non-continuant sound surrounded by two continuant ones may become a continuant sound, and this process is called "*fricativization*," which is another recurrent sound change pattern attested in many different languages. In the word for "*horse*" in French, the two vowels "*e*" and "*a*" surround "*v*." Thus, the phonological condition for fricativization is met. The same goes with Italian. Similarly, as mentioned earlier, the actual pronunciation of the letter "*b*" in Spanish in these words is a bilabial fricative. Thus, it seems that fricativization also took place in Spanish, although in a somewhat different fashion. By contrast, the reverse change *$v > b$ is very rare.

For Correspondence 3: *v-b-p*, the reconstruction possibilities include *$v$, *$b$, *$p$. Similar to Correspondence 4, it is more natural for $b$ or $p$ to become $v$ rather than the other direction. But between *$b$ and *$p$, which one should be the original form? If we observe the position of this sound in each word, we find that it is also between two vowels. Vowels are normally voiced. Thus, a voiceless sound such as *p* tends to become voiced between two voiced sounds. This is called "*intervocalic voicing.*" It is a common sound change found in many languages as well. Therefore, *\*p > b* would be more natural here. Intervocalic voicing of *\*p > b* took place in Spanish, and *\*p > b > v* took place in French, if the fricativization *\*b > v* in Correspondence 4 is taken into consideration.

Now let's look at the Latin word for "*hair,*" which is "*capillum,*" with a "*p*" in the corresponding position. The Latin word for "*horse*" is "*caballus,*" with a "*b*" in the corresponding position. Thus, such written records confirm our reconstructions of *\*p* for Correspondence 3 and *\*b* for Correspondence 4.

When studying sound changes, we look at individual sounds instead of whole words, because once a single sound changed under certain phonological conditions, it would generally change in all words that contain it as long as the conditions are met. Here, the phonological conditions often refer to other sounds adjacent to the sound under consideration, for example, the high front vowel that follows a consonant in palatalization and the two vowels surrounding a stop consonant in fricativization and intervocalic voicing. The principle of naturalness or directionality, when considering *\*A > B* vs. *\*B > A*, may be very useful for reconstructing the proto-sounds if one of the two sound changes fits a well-established recurrent pattern across different languages.

In some sense, sound changes are regular in that they apply in a law-like fashion. One of the most famous sound change laws is Grimm's Law concerning a set of sound changes in Proto-Germanic that separated the Germanic languages from the other Indo-European languages. Table 4.4 shows a sample cognate set with three groups of words from English, Latin, and Sanskrit. The data in Table 4.4 are taken from Campbell (1999).

*Table 4.4* Cognate set for Grimm's Law

| English (Germanic) | Latin (Group I and II) and Sanskrit (Group III) |
| --- | --- |
| **Group I** | |
| *father* | *pater* |
| *three* | *trēs* |
| *hound* | *canis* |
| **Group II** | |
| *slip* | *lūbricus* |
| *two* | *duo* |
| *kin* | *genus* |
| **Group III** | |
| *brother* | *bhrắtar* |
| *do* | *dhā-* |
| *goose* | *haṁs-á* |

Let's focus on the first consonant of each word, except for the word "*slip*," where the sound "*p*" occurs at the end in the English word, which corresponds to the Latin cognate word with the "*b*" in the middle. Table 4.5 are the relevant correspondences.

The sound "*h*" in Group I in English actually came from an earlier velar fricative [ x ], which is the "*ch*" sound in the German pronunciation of the name of the composer "*Bach*." The sound "*h*" in Group III in Sanskrit came from an earlier "*gh*," which is an aspirated *g* sound. What sounds can be reconstructed as the original ones?

In Group I, the three English consonants *f/th/h* are fricatives, and the non-Germantic consonants *p/t/k* are stops. If *$p$, *$t$, and *$k$ were the originals, then we have three similar sound changes, that is, *$p > f$, *$t > th$ (as in "*thin*"), *$k > x > h$, and these are instances of fricativization, a recurrent sound change pattern, as discussed previously. Thus, we may reasonably take *$p$, *$t$, and *$k$ as the proto-forms.

For Group II, there are at least two possibilities for reconstruction: *$p$/*$t$/*$k$ vs. *$b$/*$d$/*$g$. Since we already reconstructed *$p$/*$t$/*$k$ for Group I, the two groups of sounds would not be distinguished if we reconstruct *$p$/*$t$/*$k$ for Group II as well. Therefore, let's see if there is strong evidence for reconstructing *$b$/*$d$/*$g$, which are all voiced sounds. If they were the original sounds, then they developed into the corresponding voiceless stops in Germanic, that is, *$b > p$, *$d > t$, *$g > k$. Such sound changes are called "*devoicing*," which is actually another recurrent pattern. Thus, we may reasonably reconstruct *$b$, *$d$, and *$g$ as the proto-forms here.

For group III, *$bh$, *$dh$, *$gh$ should be reconstructed as the proto-sounds. For one thing, aspirated stops are generally rarer than their unaspirated versions. Thus, it is more plausible for a less common sound to become a more common one, for example, *$bh > b$, rather than *$b > bh$. Moreover, the aspirated stops are stronger

*Table 4.5* Correspondences for Grimm's Law

| English (Germanic) | Non-Germanic |
| --- | --- |
| **Group I** | |
| f | p |
| th (as in "*thin*") | t |
| h (< x) | k |
| **Group II** | |
| p | b |
| t | d |
| k | g |
| **Group III** | |
| b | bh |
| d | dh |
| g | h (< gh) |

sounds, and going from *\*bh > b* can be described as a process of weakening, which is also quite common in different languages. Thus, we may again reasonably reconstruct *\*bh, \*dh,* and *\*gh* as the original sounds, and therefore *\*bh > b, \*dh > d, \*gh > g* took place in Germanic.

Jacob Grimm (1785–1863) first discovered such changes from Proto-Indo-European to Proto-Germanic, hence the name of this sound change law. Figure 4.3 shows these three sound changes in a more systematic way.

Although the name "*Grimm's Law*" contains the word "*law*," it is not to be mistaken for a physical law which applies universally. Grimm's Law only applies to Proto-Germanic, and it does not mean that the same changes should happen in other languages. However, on the other hand, since Grimm's Law touches upon three recurrent sound change patterns, that is, fricativization, devoicing, and weakening, knowledge of Grimm's Law may nonetheless guide us in our research in the reconstruction of proto-sounds in other languages. In other words, the patterns in Grimm's Law may be used as references for "*naturalness*" or "*directionality*." Suppose we are faced with two possible reconstruction options, either *\*p > f* or *\*f > p*. Unless there is clear evidence for *\*f > p,* it is definitely more reasonable to posit *\*p > f,* since it is an instance of fricativization. Now recall *Qián Dàxīn's* two discoveries regarding Old Chinese initials. One of them is that there were no labiodental sounds in ancient times. Our discussion in Chapter 3 is not conclusive, because no clear evidence is produced to favor either *\*p* or *\*f* as the reconstructed sound for Old Chinese. Now in terms of naturalness, *\*p* is certainly a better reconstruction, because *\*p > f* is a recurrent sound change pattern.

One more clarification on the notion of "*naturalness*" is that it refers to sound change patterns but not individual sounds. In terms of "*naturalness*," different directions of sound changes are considered, for example, *\*p > f* vs. *\*f > p*. The change from *p* to *f* is recurrent and has a phonetically based explanation. Thus, it is more natural in this sense. Because of the consideration of sound changes in opposite directions, the principle of "*naturalness*" is also called "*directionality*."

The comparative method has been developed based on Indo-European languages, but it is a robust scientific method that has been used in reconstructing

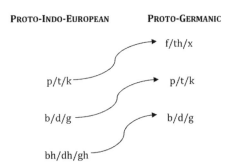

PROTO-INDO-EUROPEAN       PROTO-GERMANIC

                                       f/th/x

        p/t/k                          p/t/k

        b/d/g                          b/d/g

        bh/dh/gh

*Figure 4.3* Grimm's Law

other proto-languages. Assuming that most modern Chinese dialects are descendants of Middle Chinese, the comparative method can be readily applied to reconstruction of Middle Chinese. In Karlgren's methodology, the categories of sounds based on rhyme tables, together with information from the *Guǎngyùn*, are the starting point of the reconstruction. Then the pronunciations of these characters in modern Chinese dialects and in the Sino-Japanese, Sino-Korean, and Sino-Vietnamese systems are collected and treated as datasets of cognate words. The comparative method is used to reconstruct the original sounds for these categories of initials, rhymes, and finals in Middle Chinese. For example, in rhyme tables from the Song dynasty, there are four dental initials called 端透定泥, as shown in Table 4.2. These categories of initials include the following characters, meaning that in each of the categories, all of the characters share the same initial.

1  端：都丁多當得德冬 and so on
2  透：他吐土託湯天通台 and so on
3  定：徒杜特度唐同陀堂田地 and so on
4  泥：奴乃那諸內 and so on

Table 4.6 shows the pronunciations of some of these characters from modern Chinese dialects.

We focus on the initial consonant in each word, since these characters are selected for the phonetic values of their initials. The following correspondences can be established:

| 1 | 端 | *t-t-t* | *\*t* |
| 2 | 透 | *tʰ-tʰ-tʰ* | *\*tʰ* |
| 3 | 定 | *t-d-t* | *\*d* |
|   |   | *tʰ-d-tʰ* | *\*d* |
| 4 | 泥 | *n-n-n* | *\*n* |

*Table 4.6* A reconstruction example of Middle Chinese initials[3]

|  | *Beijing* | *Suzhou* | *Guangzhou* |
|---|---|---|---|
| 端 **class** | | | |
| 德 | tɤ | tɤʔ | tɐk |
| 冬 | tuŋ | toŋ | tʊŋ |
| 透 **class** | | | |
| 他 | tʰa | tʰɒ | tʰa |
| 土 | tʰu | tʰəu | tʰou |
| 定 **class** | | | |
| 地 | ti | di | tei |
| 徒 | tʰu | dou | tʰou |
| 泥 **class** | | | |
| 奴 | nu | nəu | nou |
| 內 | nei | nᴇ | nɔi |

For the correspondence in 1, there is no variation across the selected dialects. Therefore, we can just posit *$t$ as the original sound. Similarly, for the correspondences in 2 and 4, the consonants *$t^h$ and *$n$ are reconstructed as the original sounds. There are two different correspondences in 3. For the first one, that is, *t-d-t*, reconstruction possibilities include *$t$ or *$d$. Simply in terms of naturalness, *$d$ can be reconstructed, since *$d > t$ would be an instance of devoicing, just like in Grimm's Law, while *$t > d$ would not be possible, since the consonant is at the initial position of the syllable but not between two vowels, in which case intervocalic voicing is a possibility. For the second correspondence in 3, that is, *t^h-d-t^h*, theoretically it could be either *$t^h$ or *$d$, and again in terms of directionality or naturalness, *$d > t^h$ would be another instance of devoicing, and the phonological condition for intervocalic voicing in *$t^h > d$ is not met. Thus, *$d$ is selected as the original sound. However, there is an even stronger reason for reconstructing *$d$ because we have established the four categories of initials by using Middle Chinese written records. It has been determined that the correspondences in 1–4 are from four different initials, and therefore their phonetic values should be distinct. Since *$t$ and *$t^h$ have been reconstructed for correspondences 1 and 2, it would not be possible for *$t$ or *$t^h$ to be reconstructed for the correspondences in 3. Therefore, the only option is *$d$. Moreover, even though there are two correspondences in 3, they should have the same reconstructed form, since they belong to the same category of initials. Since our reasoning in terms of naturalness is also sound, the conclusions initially reached via "*naturalness*" are consistent with the definition of categories of sounds. Therefore, the reconstructed phonetic values for these four initials in Middle Chinese are: 端 *$t$-, 透 *$t^h$-, 定 *$d$-, 泥 *$n$-. Here, the dash that follows each letter means that these are the initial sounds. All categories of sounds in Middle Chinese can be similarly reconstructed. Next, let's see how the method can be used to reconstruct the rhymes and medials.

## 4.7  The notion of *děng* ("division, grade")

It is shown previously that there are two subgroups in the 東 rhyme: 東紅公 vs. 中弓戎融宮終. Such a distinction is also manifested in the *Yùnjìng* where characters like 東紅公 are arranged on the 1st *děng*, that is, division I, and 中弓戎 融宮終 are on the 3rd *děng*, that is, division III. With Karlgren's methodology, it is possible to reconstruct the sounds of these two subgroups and see where the distinction lies. Table 4.7 shows the pronunciations of 東公 of the 1st *děng*, and 中弓 of the 3rd *děng* in three modern Chinese dialects.[4]

Because these characters are selected for the phonetic values of their rhymes and medials, their initials are different and are irrelevant here. We ignore the initial consonants, and then the following correspondences between these dialects can be obtained.

| | | |
|---|---|---|
| 1 | *u-ɔ-ʊ̆* | *$u$ |
| 2 | *ŋ-ŋ-ŋ* | *$ŋ$ |
| 3 | *zero-i-zero* | *$i$ |

*Table 4.7* A reconstruction example of Middle Chinese rhymes and medials

| Divisions | Words | Beijing | Xiamen (lit.) | Guangzhou |
|---|---|---|---|---|
| **Division I** | 東 | tuŋ | tɔŋ | tʊŋ |
| | 公 | kuŋ | kɔŋ | kʊŋ |
| **Division III** | 中 | tʂuŋ | tioŋ | tʃʊŋ |
| | 弓 | kuŋ | kioŋ | kʊŋ |

For the correspondence in 1, both [ u ] and [ ʊ ] are high vowels, but [ ʊ ] is a lax version of [ u ]. By "*majority wins*," *u can be selected temporarily as the original sound for lack of enough evidence to the contrary. For the correspondence in 2, *ŋ is reconstructed because there is no variation. In 3, there is a medial [ i ] in the literary pronunciations of these words in Xiamen, but there is no medial sound in Beijing and Guangzhou, as indicated by the "*zero.*" In general, if a certain sound was lost in some daughter languages but not the others, there are often "*zeros*" in the correspondence set. On the other hand, it is theoretically possible for certain daughter languages to develop a new sound where there was nothing in the proto-language. But unless we have definitive evidence for the emergence of a new sound from nothing, such a sound change is disfavored. For one thing, if we assume here that the original sound in 3 is the "*zero*" and a new medial "*i*" developed, it would be difficult to explain why it should be specifically the sound "*i*" but not any other random sound. By contrast, no such justification is needed if an original sound was simply deleted or lost. Another reason for disfavoring the "*zero*" as the original is because in that case, there would not be any difference between the characters from the two divisions. Thus, combining all the evidence together, *i should be reconstructed. Therefore, the 東 rhyme has two subgroups: the division I version is [ uŋ ], and the division III version is [ iuŋ ].

Karlgren proposed that the main property of division III is that there is a -*j*-medial, as can be observed in our reconstruction example here, with only a minor adjustment of -*i*- to -*j*-. Here, the glide -*j*- is similar to the first sound in the English word "*yes.*" Additionally, the main vowels on the four divisions are generally different. More details on this vowel distinction are provided later when Middle Chinese reconstructions are discussed.

Note that the method introduced here, pioneered by Karlgren, differs from the typical applications of the comparative method. In general, modern pronunciations are used to reconstruct a proto-language, especially when there is no written record of that older language. The phonetic values of words in Old English do not need to be reconstructed, because of the nature of the alphabetical writing system, but in Chinese, although there are extensive written records, Chinese characters do not directly indicate phonetic values; the categories of initials, rhymes, and finals therefore need to be reconstructed. Moreover, the starting point of the comparative method is modern pronunciations, and the procedure is to discover the sounds in the proto-language. However, in the reconstruction of Middle Chinese, the categories of sounds from written records are the starting point. Modern pronunciations are only used to fill in the phonetic values of these established categories of sounds.

## 4.8   A reconstructed system of Middle Chinese

Karlgren was the first scholar to have reconstructed the whole phonological system of Middle Chinese in his *Études sur la phonologie chinoise* ("Studies on Chinese phonology") published between 1915 and 1926. Subsequently, other scholars built upon his reconstructions with modifications in various aspects. One of the more recent reconstructions is Pan (2000). However, because Karlgren's system is the standard reference, and most of his reconstructions are still valid today, we choose to present Karlgren's reconstruction in its slightly modified form by Li (1971). Table 4.8 lists the initials in Middle Chinese. Note that Li's (1971) reconstructions are also presented in Li (1980), and the system of initials listed here is based on Li (1980: 7).

In addition to the initial *j-*, Li (1971) also included a very similar *ji-*, but most scholars would only accept one such initial, which is usually *j-*. Thus, in Table 4.8, only *j-* is retained, but *ji* is deleted, while all the other initials are the same as in Li (1971).

The most striking feature of the initials in Table 4.8 is the set of voiced obstruents, that is, [ b, d, g, ɖ, dʐ, dz, z, dʑ, ʑ, ɣ ],[5] because there are no voiced obstruent initials in Modern Standard Chinese. Therefore, at some point after Middle Chinese, these voiced consonants would become voiceless. Another feature of Middle Chinese initials is the series of retroflex stops, that is, [ ʈ, ʈʰ, ɖ, ɳ ]. The non-nasal ones would later become retroflex affricates. Although there is a series of palatal affricates and fricatives in Table 4.8, that is, [ tɕ, tɕʰ, dʑ, ɳʑ, ɕ, ʑ ], they are actually not sources of Modern Standard Chinese palatal consonants. The ones here in Middle Chinese would later merge with the retroflex affricates and fricatives. Additionally, the labiodental initial *f-* in modern Chinese had not developed from the bilabial stops by this time during the Middle Chinese period.

In Chapter 3, we have already described how Old Chinese sounds can be reconstructed based on the Middle Chinese reconstruction. Now with the complete

*Table 4.8* Middle Chinese initials

| Bilabial stops | 幫 p | 滂 pʰ | 並 b | 明 m | | |
|---|---|---|---|---|---|---|
| Alveolar stops and lateral | 端 t | 透 tʰ | 定 d | 泥 n | | 來 l |
| Retroflex stops | 知 ʈ | 徹 ʈʰ | 澄 ɖ | 娘 ɳ | | |
| Alveolar affricates and fricatives | 精 ts | 清 tsʰ | 從 dz | | 心 s | 邪 z |
| Retroflex affricates and fricatives | 莊 tʂ | 初 tʂʰ | 崇 dʐ | | 生 ʂ | |
| Palatal affricates and fricatives | 章 tɕ | 昌 tɕʰ | 船 dʑ | 日 ɳʑ | 書 ɕ | 禪 ʑ |
| Velars stops and fricatives | 見 k | 溪 kʰ | 羣 g | 疑 ŋ | 曉 x | 匣 ɣ |
| Glottal stop and palatal glide | 影 ʔ | 以 j | | | | |

inventory of initials in Middle Chinese given, let's figure out how the initials here correspond to those in Old Chinese. First, there are some sounds that could be more or less directly projected back from Middle Chinese to Old Chinese, for example, the bilabial, alveolar, and velar stops. Note that according to *Qián Dàxīn*, there were no labiodental sounds in ancient times, and we have provided evidence that there indeed were no sounds such as *f-* in Old Chinese. In fact, the labiodental *f-* had not developed in Early Middle Chinese yet.

Moreover, the other discovery by *Qián Dàxīn* that there were no retroflex sounds in ancient times would require the retroflex obstruents in Table 4.8, that is, the ret-roflex stops, affricates, and fricatives, to be deleted from Old Chinese. The devel-opment of retroflex initials from Old Chinese to Middle Chinese can be accounted for by positing the medial *-r-*. The retroflex stops developed out of the Old Chinese alveolar stops plus the medial *-r-*, in four assimilatory changes, such as *\*tr-* > *ʈ-*, *\*tʰr-* > *ʈʰ-*, *\*dr-* > *ɖ-*, *\*nr-* > *ɳ-*. For example, the word 知 (*zhī*, "to know") in Old Chinese is *\*trig*. It became *ʈjĕ* in Middle Chinese. Thus, we can represent this change as *\*trig* > *ʈjĕ*, with the first starred form being Old Chinese and the second form being Middle Chinese. Similarly, we have 超 (*chāo*, "surpass") *\*tʰrjagʷ* > *ʈʰjɛu*, 澄 (*chéng*, "clear") *\*drjəŋ* > *djəŋ*, 赧 (*nǎn*, "blush") *\*nranx* > *ɳan*. Without the medial *-r-*, the alveolar stops in Old Chinese would still be alveolar stops in Middle Chinese. As for the retroflex affricates and fricatives in Middle Chinese, they can be explained by positing the following sound changes: *\*tsr-* > *ʈʂ-*, *\*tsʰr-* > *ʈʂʰ-*, *\*dzr-* > *dʐ-*, *\*sr-* > *ʂ-*. Some examples are: 莊 (*zhuāng*, "luxuriant") *\*tsrjaŋ* > *ʈʂjaŋ*, 察 (*chá*, "examine") *\*tsʰriat* > *ʈʂʰat*, 崇 (*chóng*, "lofty") *\*dzrjəŋʷ* > *dzjuŋ*, and 刪 (*shān*, "delete") *\*sran* > *ʂan*.

Furthermore, there is evidence in phonetic series that the Middle Chinese pala-tal affricates and fricatives did not exist in Old Chinese either. For instance, the character 終 (Middle Chinese: *tɕjuŋ*) contains 冬 (Middle Chinese: *tuoŋ*) as its phonetic component, but their initials, that is, palatal *tɕ-* and alveolar *t-*, differ in terms of place of articulation. It is more likely that the original initials are both alveolar, considering palatalization as a more natural type of sound change. Thus, Old Chinese forms of these two characters are: 終 *\*tjəŋʷ* and 冬 *\*təŋʷ*. The medial *-j-* would lead to the palatalization of the alveolar *t-* to the palatal *tɕ-*. More examples include: 章 (*zhāng*, "chapter") *\*tjaŋ* > *tɕjaŋ*, 春 (*chūn*, "spring") *\*tʰjən* > *tɕʰjuĕn*, 順 (*shùn*, "smooth") *\*djənh* > *dzjuĕn*, and 熱 (*rè*, "hot") *\*njat* > *ɳʑjɛt*. Some palatal sounds may have developed from velar stops followed by the medial *-j-* and often also preceded by *s-*, such as 支 (*zhī*, "support") *\*skjig* > *tɕjĕ* and 兒 (*ér*, "son") *\*ŋjig* > *ɳʑjĕ*.

Thus, Middle Chinese initials can be projected back to Old Chinese based on the categories of initials obtained from phonetic series, and then sound changes and their phonological conditions may be posited.

Now let's take a look at the reconstructed finals in Middle Chinese. First, Table 4.9, based on Li (1980: 8), shows the finals without any consonant codas, including all the *yīnshēngyùn* 陰聲韻 from the *Guǎngyùn*.

There are a couple of new phonological concepts in Table 4.9. In the column on the left, seven characters are listed, that is, 果, 假, 遇, 蟹, 止, 效, 流, each of

*Table 4.9* Middle Chinese finals without consonant codas[6]

|  | Division I | Division II | Division III | Division IV |
|---|---|---|---|---|
| 果 | 歌 ɑ<br>戈 uɑ |  | 戈 jɑ<br>戈 juɑ |  |
| 假 |  | 麻 a<br>麻 wa | 麻 ja |  |
| 遇 | 模 uo |  | 魚 jwo<br>虞 ju |  |
| 蟹 | 哈 ăi<br>灰 uăi<br>泰 ɑi<br>泰 wɑi | 皆 ăi<br>皆 wăi<br>夬 ai<br>夬 wai<br>佳 aï<br>佳 waï | 祭 jɛi, jiɛi<br>祭 jwɛi, jwiɛi<br>廢 jɐi<br>廢 jwɐi | 齊 iei<br>齊 iwei |
| 止 |  |  | 支 jě, jiě<br>支 jwě, jwiě<br>脂 ji, i<br>脂 jwi, wi<br>之 ï<br>微 jěi<br>微 jwěi |  |
| 效 | 豪 ɑu | 肴 au | 宵 jɛu, jiɛu | 蕭 ieu |
| 流 | 侯 ɔu |  | 尤 jɔu<br>幽 jiɔu |  |

which corresponds to one or more rhymes in the *Guǎngyùn*. These characters represent the concept of *yùnshè* 韻攝 ("rhyme group")[7] to further group rhymes with similar main vowels and also generally the same coda. For example, the 果 group includes the *Guǎngyùn* rhymes 歌 and 戈, and they have the same main vowel [ ɑ ]. The 蟹 group includes the *Guǎngyùn* rhymes 齊佳皆灰哈祭泰夬廢. Their main vowels are different but similar enough. They all have the coda [ i ].[8] The number of distinct rhymes in the *Guǎngyùn* is large compared to Old Chinese and Modern Standard Chinese. The concept of *yùnshè* 韻攝 can help us simplify the rhyme system in the *Guǎngyùn* to just 16 different groups. Here in Table 4.9, there are seven groups with no consonant codas, and the remaining nine groups with consonant codas are shown in Table 4.10.

The second new concept is *kāi-hé* 開合 ("open and closed"),[9] which is further distinguished between the *kāikǒu* 開口 ("open-mouth") and *hékǒu* 合口 ("closed-mouth").[10] In Table 4.9, some cells contain two finals, such as the division I rhymes in the 果 group, where both of the finals [ ɑ ] and [ uɑ ] contain the same main vowel [ ɑ ], but [ uɑ ] has the medial -*u*-. Similarly, we find the contrast between [ a ] and [ wa ] in the 麻 rhyme. In traditional Chinese terminology, finals with labial medials -*u*- or -*w*-, such as in [ uɑ ] or [ wa ], and finals with -*u* as the main vowel are called *hékǒu* 合口 ("closed-mouth") and otherwise are called *kāikǒu* 開口 ("open-mouth"). This is because when the medial -*u*- or -*w*- is present, the syllable starts with the mouth more closed than without the medial -*u*- or -*w*-. The same can be said of finals with -*u* as the main vowel.

By now we have introduced all of the major concepts of Middle Chinese phonological distinctions, that is, (1) *yùnshè* 韻攝 ("rhyme group"), (2) *kāi-hé* 開合 ("open and closed"), (3) *děng* 等 ("division"), (4) tonal category, (5) rhyme, (6) initial. A Middle Chinese syllable may be described by specifications in terms of these six distinctions. For example, the word 韡 (*xuē*, "boot") is specified with 果合三平戈曉, which can explained as follows.

果: the 果 group in terms of 韻攝 *yùnshè*
合: closed-mouth in terms of 開合 *kāi-hé*
三: division III in terms of 等 *děng*
平: *píngshēng* ("even tone") in terms of tonal categories
戈: the 戈 rhyme in term of rhymes
曉: the 曉 initial in term of initials

The Middle Chinese reconstructed form for any word may be put together by following such a series of distinctions. The word 韡 is thus [ xjuɑ ] with an even tone. Such a system with six categories of distinctions not only helps us to figure out the reconstructed form of a certain word but also facilitates diachronic and synchronic comparisons. The phonetic details in reconstructions may be different according to different scholars, but these six categories are the same. Thus, we may refer to them when comparing different stages of the Chinese language, for example, between Modern Standard Chinese and Middle Chinese, or when comparing synchronic differences among Chinese dialects.

Now let's take a closer look at Table 4.9. The breve accent on top of a vowel symbol indicates that it is a shorter version of that vowel. For example, ĕ is a shorter version of *e*. There are four medials in this system, including -*w*-, -*u*-, -*j*-, -*i*-, and their combinations, such as -*jw*-, -*ju*-, -*iw*-. The medial -*i*- is only associated with the division IV finals in Li's (1971) system, but most other reconstructions, for example, Pulleyblank (1984: 198), do not have any such -*i*- medial for Early Middle Chinese division VI finals, based, among other things, on evidence from Chinese loanwords in Old Vietnamese. Thus, let's focus on the medial -*j*- associated with division III finals and the *hékǒu* 合口 version of these division III syllables, such as -*jw*- and -*ju*-. One major change from Middle Chinese to Modern Standard Chinese is that the -*jw*- and -*ju*- medials would later fuse into [ y ] to bring about four types of finals called *sìhū* 四呼 ("four vocalizations"). See Chapter 9 for more on the *sìhū*.

The medial -*j*- can only distinguish division III finals from the other three divisions. But what would be the distinction among all four divisions? We may look at groups that have finals in four divisions, for example, the 效 group. Division I has the low back vowel [ ɑ ], division II the low front [ a ], division III the mid-low front [ ɛ ], and division VI the mid-high front [ e ]. Thus, the distinction among the four divisions lies in their main vowels, which change from back to front as the division distinction changes from division I to division IV. The vowels also move from low to a higher position at the same time.

All of the rhymes in this table are *yīnshēngyùn*, that is, rhymes without consonant codas. They correspond to Old Chinese rhymes with a voiced stop coda, as shown in the first column in Table 3.12. When the voiced stop codas dropped or changed into a vowel such as *-i* or *-u*, these rhymes would develop into the *yīnshēngyùn* rhymes in Middle Chinese here. Some examples are: 飛 (*fēi*, "to fly") *pjəd > pjwĕi and 厚 (*hòu*, "thick") *gugx > ɣə̆u. The *-r* coda in Old Chinese rhyme 歌 *-ar* was generally deleted as well, for example, 多 (*duō*, "many") *tar > ta. More specifically, Li (1980: 36) posited sound change rules such as *-r > -ø, that is, completely deleted; *-d > -i; *-g > -i, -u, -ø; and *-gw > -u, -i.

Now let's take a look at the finals with nasal and stop codas in Middle Chinese, as shown in Table 4.10, which is based on Li (1980: 8–9).

The patterns in Table 4.10 are quite systematic. First there are three types of nasal codas, that is, *-m* in the 咸深 groups, *-n* in the 山臻 groups, and *-ŋ* in the 宕梗曾通江 groups, and each of these nasal codas has its matching stop coda, that is, *-p* in the 咸深 groups, *-t* in the 山臻 groups, and *-k* in the 宕梗曾通江 groups.[11] Thus, we have two types of syllables here in Table 4.10. The nasal rhymes, called *yángshēngyùn* 陽聲韻, and the rhymes with stop codas, called *rùshēngyùn* 入聲韻, developed from those same types in Old Chinese, respectively.

It is obvious from Table 4.9 and Table 4.10 that there is a plethora of finals and basic vowels in Middle Chinese compared to Old Chinese in Table 3.12. In Li's (1971) Middle Chinese, there are 11 basic vowels [ ɑ, a, æ, e, i, u, o, ɔ, ɛ, ɐ, ə ], plus 4 shorter versions [ ɑ̆, ă, ĕ, ɔ̆ ] and thus 15 vowels in its inventory. In Karlgren's original reconstruction, there is also a shorter [ e ] sound that functions as a glide, written as [ ė ]. Counting this [ ė ] as a vowel, then, in Karlgren's Middle Chinese, there are 16 vowels (Norman 1988: 38–39). In addition to these vowels, there are also four medials, *-j-, -i-, -w-, -u-* in both systems. In contrast, Li's (1971) Old Chinese only has four basic vowels, including [ a, i, u, ə ]. The development from the four-vowel system in Old Chinese to the much more complex system in Middle Chinese depends on the consonants both before and after the main vowel. The division III finals in Middle Chinese would also have the medial *-j-* in Old Chinese, for example, 涼 (*liáng*, "cool in temperature, cold") *gljaŋ > ljaŋ. In terms of the rounded medials in Middle Chinese, such as *-w-*, the labialized initials in Old Chinese in general may develop into Middle Chinese *hékǒu* finals, for example, 國 (*guó*, "country, state") *kʷək > kwək. In addition to labialized initials, there are also labialized consonant codas in Li's (1971) system, such as *-ŋʷ*. The lip-rounding feature, that is, *-w* in these labialized coda consonants, can cause the main vowel to become rounded as well. The Old Chinese rhymes with these rounded stop codas include 幽 *-əgʷ*, 覺 *-əkʷ*, 中 *-əŋʷ*, 宵 *-agʷ*, 藥 *-akʷ*. Some of the words in these rhymes developed into Middle Chinese rhymes with rounded vowels. For example, 中 (*zhōng*, "middle") *trjəŋʷ > tjuŋ, 豐 (*fēng*, "abundant") *pʰjəŋʷ > pʰjuŋ, 告 (*gào*, "tell") *kəkʷ > kuok, 沃 (*wò*, "fertile, rich") *ʔakʷ > ʔuok,

Table 4.10 Middle Chinese finals with consonant codas

| | Finals with nasal codas | | | | Finals with stop codas | | | |
|---|---|---|---|---|---|---|---|---|
| | Division I | Division II | Division III | Division IV | Division I | Division II | Division III | Division IV |
| 咸 | 談 ɑm<br>覃 ʌm | 銜 am<br>咸 ăm | 鹽 jem, jiem<br>嚴 jɐm<br>凡 jwem | 添 iem | 盍 ɑp<br>合 ʌp | 狎 ap<br>洽 ăp | 葉 jep, jiep<br>業 jɐp<br>乏 jwep | 帖 iep |
| 深 | | | 侵 jəm, jiəm | | | | 緝 jəp, jiəp | |
| 山 | 寒 ɑn<br>桓 uɑn | 刪 an<br>刪 wan<br>山 ăn<br>山 wăn | 仙 jen, jien<br>仙 jwen, jwien<br>元 jɐn<br>元 jwɐn | 先 ien<br>先 iwen | 曷 ɑt<br>末 uɑt | 鎋 at<br>鎋 wat<br>黠 ăt<br>黠 wăt | 薛 jet, jiet<br>薛 jwet, jwiet<br>月 jɐt<br>月 jwɐt | 屑 iet<br>屑 iwet |
| 臻 | 痕 ən<br>魂 uən | 臻 jæn | 真 jĕn, jiĕn<br>諄 juĕn, juiĕn<br>欣 jən<br>文 juən | | 沒 ət<br>沒 uət | 櫛 jæt | 質 jĕt, jiĕt<br>術 juĕt, juiĕt<br>迄 jət<br>物 juət | |
| 宕 | 唐 ɑŋ<br>唐 wɑŋ | | 陽 jaŋ<br>陽 jwaŋ | | 鐸 ɑk<br>鐸 wɑk | | 藥 jak<br>藥 jwak | |
| 梗 | | 庚 aŋ<br>庚 waŋ<br>耕 æŋ<br>耕 wæŋ | 庚 jaŋ<br>庚 jwaŋ<br>清 jæŋ<br>清 jwæŋ | 青 ieŋ<br>青 iweŋ | | 陌 ɐk<br>陌 wɐk<br>麥 æk<br>麥 wæk | 陌 jɐk<br>陌 jwɐk<br>昔 jæk<br>昔 jwæk | 錫 iek<br>錫 iwek |
| 曾 | 登 əŋ<br>登 wəŋ | | 蒸 jəŋ | | 德 ək<br>德 wək | | 職 jək<br>職 jwək | |
| 通 | 東 uŋ<br>冬 uoŋ | | 東 juŋ<br>鍾 jwoŋ | | 屋 uk<br>沃 uok | | 屋 juk<br>燭 jwok | |
| 江 | | 江 ɔŋ | | | | 覺 ɔk | | |

and 毛 (*máo*, "hair") \**mag^w* > *mau*. Additionally, the medial *-r-* sound may also affect the main vowel, for example, 麥 (*mài*, "wheat") \**mrək* > *mæk*.

Thus, the phonetic values of initials and finals have been presented. The next question is regarding the tones. Although it is not possible to reconstruct the tonal contours by applying the same comparative method, there were contemporary written descriptions of Middle Chinese tones, which would be very useful for figuring out roughly what the tonal contours could have been. If a tone was described as being high and even, it may very well be 55 or 44. Mei (1970) provides a very detailed analysis of Buddhist texts that describe the tonal contours or shapes in Middle Chinese. Pan (2000) and Zhengzhang (2003) also discuss the interpretations of various descriptions of Middle Chinese tones recorded in texts from the Tang and Song dynasties. Zhengzhang (2003: 74) listed the following tonal values for the early stage of Middle Chinese. The *píng* tone can be described as flat and even, neither high nor low. Its tonal value is 33. The *shǎng* tone is a rising tone, which can be rendered as 35. The *qù* tone is high and falling, which can be represented as 41. The *rù* tone is generally very short, thus being just 3. The underline in the *shǎng* and *rù* tones indicates that the tones are short.

In Chapter 3, we show that evidence supports the view that there were no tones in Old Chinese. Thus, the four tones in Middle Chinese correspond to different types of syllables in Old Chinese. The *rù* tone corresponds to syllables with *-p*, *-t*, or *-k* codas. The *qù*-tone syllables would have had an *-h* or *-s* as coda, while the *shǎng*-tone syllables would have had a glottal stop *-ʔ* as coda. The *píng* tone would correspond to all the other types of syllables. With the disappearance of the original final *-s* via an intermediate stage of *-h*, the *qù* tone became a separate tonal category. As for the *shǎng* tone, Zhengzhang (1987) argued that the glottal stop coda *-ʔ* may have lingered longer than the *qù*-tone coda *-h*. Zhengzhang's (2003: 74) descriptions of Middle Chinese tones still retain the glottal stop for the *shǎng* tone, noted as ʔ35, in the *Qièyùn* system.

One additional note on Middle Chinese tones is that in Karlgren's original reconstruction, the *shǎng* tone is marked with a colon, for example, 上 *zjaŋ:* , and the *qù* tone is represented by a dash, for example, 去 *kʰjwo-*. The *píng* tone is not marked, while the *rù* tone is self-evident by their stop codas *-p*, *-t*, or *-k*.

Now it is time to appreciate Tang poetry in the reconstructed forms of Middle Chinese. The following lines are from the poem 月下獨酌 *Yuè xià dú zhuó* ("Drinking alone under the moon") by the Tang dynasty poet *Lǐ Bái* 李白 (AD 701–762), arguably the most famous poet in Chinese literature. The modern pronunciations and Middle Chinese reconstructed forms are provided, along with the original Chinese version in characters, which can be translated liberally as: "Amongst the flowers is a jug of wine, and I'm drinking alone with no company. Let me raise my goblet to invite the bright moon. Now with my shadow, there is a party of three."

**Chinese characters:**

花間一壺酒，獨酌無相親。
舉杯邀明月，對影成三人。

**Modern Standard Chinese:**

huā jiān yì hú jiǔ / dú zhuó wú xiāng qīn //
jǔ bēi yāo míng yuè / duì yǐng chéng sān rén //

**Middle Chinese:**

xwa³³ kăn³³ ʔjĕt³ ɣuo³³ tsjə̆u³⁵ / duk³ tɕjak³ mju³³ sjaŋ³³ tsʰjĕn³³ //
kjwo³⁵ puăi³³ kieu³³ mjɐŋ³³ ŋjwɐt³ / tuăi⁴¹ ʔjɐŋ³⁵ zjɛŋ³³ sɑm³³ ȵʑjĕn³³ //

*Lǐ Bái* probably did not chant his poems using the exact sounds presented here, because the reconstruction is a hypothetical system as a theoretical account of available data. But given the abundance of linguistic evidence for the reconstructed forms, the language used by *Lǐ Bái* may have contained many of the phonological properties presented in this chapter.

The language of the *Qièyùn* era was the earlier stage of Middle Chinese in the late Northern and Southern dynasties in the 6th century AD. After a few hundred years of development from the Sui and Tang dynasties to the Song dynasty, the language of the Yuan dynasty became quite different from the *Qièyùn* era and moved closer to the modern Mandarin dialects.

## Notes

1  In the *Qièyùn*, the method is indicated via the word 反 *fǎn* instead of the word 切 *qiè* used in the *Guǎngyùn*.
2  Karlgren used rhyme tables from the *Qièyùn zhǐzhǎngtú* 切韻指掌圖, which actually dates to a later time than the *Yùnjìng*. Therefore, most scholars would depend on the *Yùnjìng* more than the *Qièyùn zhǐzhǎngtú*.
3  Most of the dialect pronunciations are taken from *Hànyǔ fāngyīn zìhuì* 汉语方音字汇 [*A Collection of Dialect Pronunciations of Chinese Characters*], first published in 1962 by the Department of Chinese Language and Literature, Peking University.
4  The pronunciations from Xiamen are literary pronunciations instead of their colloquial pronunciations. In many southern Chinese dialects, there are two types of pronunciations for Chinese characters. The colloquial pronunciations normally reflect their native phonology, while the literary pronunciations were borrowed from the common spoken language at different times.
5  In Li's (1971) reconstruction, 船 is *dz-*, while 禪 is *z-*. But according to Baxter (1992: 52–54), the reconstructed sounds should be reversed, that is, 船 is *z-*, while 禪 is *dz-*.
6  The division III finals in this table include those that are arranged on the division IV in rhyme tables but should be division III, according to the *Guǎngyùn*. The traditional term for this phenomenon is *chóngniǔ* 重紐 ("doublets").
7  Note that although the term 韻攝 *yùnshè* is translated as "rhyme group" here, it is not to be confused with the Old Chinese rhyme groups called 韻部 *yùnbù*.
8  The rhyme 佳 has the *-ï* coda, but in Li's (1971) system, it is phonetically the same as *-i*. The notation with *-ï* is only to distinguish two very similar rhymes in the *Guǎngyùn*.
9  The concept of 開合 *kāi-hé* is often referred to as 呼 *hū* ("vocalization"), as in the 四呼 *sìhū* ("four vocalizations") in Modern Standard Chinese. See Chapter 9 for details on the 四呼 *sìhū*.
10  The traditional Chinese terms 開口 *kāikǒu* and 合口 *hékǒu* should not be confused with the modern phonological concepts of "open syllables" and "closed syllables." The

traditional Chinese terms refer to the onset of a syllable, while the modern terminology refers to the coda of a syllable. For example, a Chinese word with the final *-ap* is considered 開口 *kāikǒu*, but in modern terms, syllables containing the consonant coda *-p* are closed. Similarly, a Chinese word with the final *-ua* is considered 合口 *hékǒu*, but in modern terminology, such syllables are open.

11 The finals with *-p*, *-t*, or *-k* codas are associated with the *rù* tone exclusively. Therefore, the *rù* tone is not necessarily solely a tonal property, since it is tied to a specific type of syllable.

# 5  Old Mandarin of Yuan dynasty dramas

Following the Middle Chinese period is *Jìndài Hànyǔ* 近代漢語, that is, Early Modern Chinese, from the Yuan dynasty to the Qing dynasty, and then, starting in the early 20th century, standards of the modern national language were created to bring about Modern Standard Chinese. But in terms of the linguistic developments in Mandarin of northern China, Norman (1988: 23) divided the period starting from the Song dynasty until modern times into three stages. Old Mandarin can be traced back to the Song dynasty in its early form, and it includes the subsequent Yuan dynasty and the beginning years of the Ming dynasty.[1] Middle Mandarin includes the Ming and early Qing. Modern Mandarin started from the 19th century in the mid-Qing dynasty. In this chapter, we focus on the phonology of Mandarin in the Yuan dynasty.

## 5.1  The rhyme book *Zhōngyuán Yīnyùn*

If Middle Chinese can be characterized as a literary language associated with poetry of the Tang dynasty, then Old Mandarin was the language used in the new poetic genre called *qǔ* 曲 in the Yuan dynasty. One major difference between these two poetic genres is that the *qǔ* in the north used the actual spoken Mandarin dialect of the time, while Tang poetry rhyming in the *Qièyùn* standards was based on a cross-dialectal system of reading pronunciation. The *qǔ* genre was used in performances of dramas in the Yuan dynasty. The language used in such performances was certainly much closer to the actual spoken language of the audience. Thus, the written records associated with Yuan dramas would be very useful for reconstructing sounds of Old Mandarin.

The main source for Old Mandarin is the rhyme book *Zhōngyuán Yīnyùn* 中原音韻 ("*The Phonology of the Central Plains*"), written by *Zhōu Déqīng* 周德清 in 1324. The purpose of this book is to facilitate the composition of the *qǔ*. Zhōu Déqīng compiled the book by using actual rhyming examples from the works in the *qǔ* genre by famous writers such as *Guān Hànqīng* 關漢卿, *Mǎ Zhìyuǎn* 馬致遠, and so on. But what is the actual dialect recorded in this book? There are two main views on this issue.

First, as the title of the rhyme book suggests, it is the phonology of the Central Plains, which mostly refers to the area of what is present-day Henan province.

In Old Chinese and Middle Chinese, the Luoyang dialect in the Henan province had been one of the most influential dialects for thousands of years. Therefore, it is quite reasonable to argue that the base dialect of the *Zhōngyuán Yīnyùn* is that of Henan. According to Li (1983), the area where the Henan dialect was spoken in the Yuan dynasty was much larger than just the Henan province. Even in the Yuan capital *Dàdū* 大都, that is, present-day Beijing, the main dialect was also the Henan dialect, which was brought there as a result of large waves of immigration from the Central Plains to *Dàdū*. Therefore, even though two of the major authors of the *qǔ*, that is, *Guān Hànqīng* and *Mǎ Zhìyuǎn*, lived in the *Dàdū* area, the dialect used in their works might still be the Henan dialect. Thus, in this view, the base dialect of the *Zhōngyuán Yīnyùn* is that of Henan.

On the other hand, according to Ning (1985: 186), the dialect of the *Zhōngyuán Yīnyùn* should be that of *Dàdū*. He cites comments made by *Zhōu Déqīng* about the language used in the book and argues that it should be the *Dàdū* dialect. However, if the dialect of *Dàdū* was the same as that of Henan, as Li (1983) argues, then there is no real difference between these two views. If, however, the *Dàdū* dialect was different from that of the Central Plains, then the debate on this issue cannot be settled yet. It is worth noting that no matter what the *Dàdū* dialect was like some 700 years ago, we should not make a simple connection between that dialect and the modern Beijing dialect, partially because of the Manchu influence on the Beijing dialect during the Qing dynasty.

Now let's take a look at a page from the *Zhōngyuán Yīnyùn*, as shown in Figure 5.1. Numbers are added so that references can be made to different parts of the page.

The *Zhōngyuán Yīnyùn* lists 5876 characters, commonly used in representative works of the *qǔ*, and arranges them in 19 rhyme groups. In Figure 5.1, at the position of the number "1" is where the name of the rhyme group is listed. This is the first rhyme group, called 東鍾. Most of the characters in the names of the rhyme groups in the *Zhōngyuán Yīnyùn* are combinations of names of the *Guǎngyùn* rhymes, as a result of simplification of the Middle Chinese phonological system and hence loss of distinctions in many cases. Within each rhyme in the *Zhōngyuán Yīnyùn*, the characters are grouped under different tones. There are three major tonal categories: *píngshēng* (平聲), *shǎngshēng* (上聲), and *qùshēng* (去聲). Here the number "2" is where the major tonal categories are mentioned. In this case, it is the *píngshēng* category. Under the *píngshēng* category, there are two subcategories labeled with 陰 *yīn*, shown at number 3 in Figure 5.1, and 陽 *yáng*, shown at number 4. Therefore, in terms of the number of tones, there are four tones in the *Zhōngyuán Yīnyùn*, that is, *píngshēng yīn*, *píngshēng yáng*, *shǎngshēng*, and *qùshēng*.

For characters of the *rù* tone in Middle Chinese, they are listed as separate groups under three of the four tones, that is, *píngshēng yáng*, *shǎngshēng*, and *qùshēng*. This means the *rù*-tone words that had the stop codas -*p*, -*t*, -*k* can now rhyme with open syllables. For example, in the 齊微 rhyme in the *Zhōngyuán Yīnyùn*, there is a section called 入聲作平聲 *rùshēng zuò píngshēng* ("*rù tone used as píng tone*"), where the word 十 (*shí*, "ten," Middle Chinese: *dzjəp*) can be used to rhyme with 迷 (*mí*, "myth," Middle Chinese: *miei*). There is debate on whether

繃　蕄　功　匆　宗　充　東　　　　　　中
○　○　攻　葱　椶　衝　冬　　3　2　1　原
烹　凶　公　聰　駿　春　○　　陰　平　東　音
　　兇　蚣　驄　○　忡　鍾　　　　聲　鍾　韻
　　詗　弓　囪　風　椿　鐘　　　　　　　變正
　　洶　躬　突烟　楓　稺　中　5　　　　　雅語
　　兄　恭　○　豐　翀　忠　　6　　　　之之
4　○　宮　蹤　封　种　衷　　　　　　　端本
陽　翁　龔　縱　葑　○　終
　　轟　供　樅　峯　邕　○
　　癰　肱　○　鋒　噰　通
　　廱　觥　穹　烽　雍　蓪
　　辟　○　芎　丰　○　○　　　　　高
　　雍　烘　傾　蜂　空　松　　　　　安
　　泓　叿　○　○　悾　嵩　　　　　挺
　　○　聲入　工　鬆　○　○　　　　齋
　　崩　轟　　　惚　　　沖　　　　　周
　　　　　　　　○　　　　　　　　德
　　　　　　　　　　　　　　　　　清
　　　　　　　　　　　　　　　　　輯

*Figure 5.1* A sample page from the *Zhōngyuán Yīnyùn*

the *rù* tone actually disappeared by the time of the *Zhōngyuán Yīnyùn*. One view is that the *rù* tone was still distinct from the other tones, although it may be used to rhyme with the other tones in the composition of the *qǔ*. Lu (1946) proposed two subcategories of *rù* tones for the *Zhōngyuán Yīnyùn*: *yīnrù* and *yángrù*. However, Ning (1985: 166) argues that judging from *Zhōu Déqīng*'s own comments, there should be no *rù* tone in the *Zhōngyuán Yīnyùn*, although the *rù* tone was preserved in other dialects of that era. Another reason the *rù*-tone words are listed separately may be in reference to the *Guǎngyùn* system, which contemporary scholars were familiar with.

Let's continue with the description of the structure of the rhyme book shown in Figure 5.1. Within each tonal section of a rhyme, homophonous groups are listed, for example, 東冬, indicated by the number 5 in Figure 5.1. Different homophonous groups are separated by a circle, such as the one at the number 6. If we look at the page a little more closely, we find that there are only characters but no definitions or *fǎnqiè* pronunciations. This is an important aspect of the *Zhōngyuán Yīnyùn* that is different from the *Guǎngyùn*, a dictionary with both *fǎnqiè* and explanations of the meanings of characters. The *Zhōngyuán Yīnyùn* was rather a reference guide as to which characters could rhyme in the *qǔ* of the north, assuming that composers or authors had already known the pronunciations and meanings of the characters. The first character in each homophonous group is normally a very familiar and relatively easy character so that readers could pronounce it and use it as a way to figure out the pronunciations of all the other characters in the same homophonous group.

## 5.2   Categories of initials and finals in Old Mandarin

How do we use the *Zhōngyuán Yīnyùn* to study the categories of initials and finals in Old Mandarin? Since there is no *fǎnqiè*, the linking method used for Middle Chinese does not work here. But since Middle Chinese is the pivotal reference system in the study of Chinese historical phonology, we can compare Middle Chinese categories of sounds with groups of characters in the *Zhōngyuán Yīnyùn* to figure out which Middle Chinese categories merged or split in Old Mandarin, and this is similar to how Old Chinese rhymes were derived by comparing the rhymes in the *Shījīng* with Middle Chinese.

First, let's see how initials can be compared. Luo (1932) proposed a method based on homophonous characters with references to Middle Chinese initials, especially the 36 initials in Late Middle Chinese in Song dynasty, as shown in Table 4.2. If characters in a homophonous group in the *Zhōngyuán Yīnyùn* had more than two initials in Middle Chinese, then these initials should have merged in the Yuan dynasty. For example, the six characters in the second homophonous group in Figure 5.1, that is, 鍾鐘中忠衷終, had two different initials in Middle Chinese: 鍾鐘終 had the initial 章 *tɕ*-, and 中忠衷 had the initial 知 *ţ*-. Therefore, it can be deduced that these two initials merged in the *Zhōngyuán Yīnyùn*, because now they are homophones. Another more complicated example provided by Luo (1932) concerns the contrast between the Middle Chinese voiced and voiceless initials. There is a homophonous group in the *Zhōngyuán Yīnyùn* that includes these *qù*-tone characters 洞動棟凍崠, of which 洞動 had a voiced initial 定 *d*- and 棟凍崠 had a voiceless initial 端 *t*- in Middle Chinese. Because they are all homophones now, the two Middle Chinese initials *d*- and *t*- in these characters should not contrast here in Old Mandarin. However, the situation is a little different in the *píng* tone, where characters that originally had a voiced initial would belong with the *píngshēng yáng* tonal category, while those that originally had a voiceless initial would be in the *píngshēng yīn* tonal category. One explanation that can account for both facts is that the contrast between the voiced initials and the voiceless initials was lost in Old Mandarin. In the *qù* tone, the loss of the voicing distinction results in the merger of previously different syllables into homophones, while in the *píng* tone, the voicing distinction is also lost, but the *píng* tone itself split into two subcategories corresponding to the previous distinction of voicing, in a process called "*tonal split*," which is described further subsequently in this chapter.

The categories of rhymes in the *Zhōngyuán Yīnyùn* can be straightforwardly listed, since there are 19 rhyme groups in the book. Furthermore, it is clear which Middle Chinese rhymes are the sources for the rhymes in the *Zhōngyuán Yīnyùn*, as can be seen in the naming scheme, for example, 東鍾. Thus, comparisons between characters in the 東鍾 rhyme listed here and the characters in the 東 and 鍾 rhymes in Middle Chinese can yield further useful information. In terms of the categories of finals, they can be obtained by comparing homophonous groups after the categories of initials have been established. Chen (1995) provides the following example. In the rhyme 東鍾 in Figure 5.1, there are two homophonous groups, 空悾 and 穹芎傾. They all have the initial 溪 *kʰ*- in the *Zhōngyuán Yīnyùn*, as has been established via the method mentioned previously. Since they are different homophonous groups within the same rhyme category 東鍾, the only way for them to be different is in their medials. It turns out that there are two different finals within the 東鍾 rhyme. The homophonous group 空悾 has the *-uŋ* final, while the group 穹芎傾 has the *-iuŋ* final.

## 5.3   Reconstruction of Old Mandarin initials and finals

Once the categories of initials, rhymes, and finals are established, the next step is to posit the phonetic values of these categories. To do this, several different methods may be combined. First, we can use the reconstruction of Middle Chinese as a starting point and figure out the changes that took place between the two systems. Modern Mandarin dialects can also be used as a reference point. Additionally, there was a new phonetic script in the Yuan dynasty called the *ḥP'ags-pa* script, or 八思巴文 *Bāsībā-wén*, which was designed by a Tibetan monk for Kublai Khan in 1269 as a unified script for different languages in the Yuan dynasty, including Chinese. The *Měnggǔ Zìyùn* 蒙古字韻 ("*Rhymes of Chinese in the Mongolian Script*") was a rhyme dictionary that used the *ḥP'ags-pa* script to annotate the pronunciations of Chinese characters. The phonological system of the *Měnggǔ Zìyùn* in the phonetic script is an important reference in reconstructing Old Mandarin (Shen 2020: 241–246).

Table 5.1 shows the 21 initials of Old Mandarin reconstructed by Ning (1985: 8).

One of the most obvious differences between this system and that of Middle Chinese is that the voiced obstruents in Middle Chinese, that is, the voiced stops, affricates, and fricatives such as [ b, d, g, dz, z ], all disappeared. As a rule of

*Table 5.1* Initials of Old Mandarin[2]

| Bilabial | Labiodental | Alveolar | | Retroflex | Velar | Zero |
|---|---|---|---|---|---|---|
| 幫 p | 非 f | 端 t | 精 ts | 照 tʂ | 見 k | 影 ø |
| 滂 pʰ | | 透 tʰ | 清 tsʰ | 穿 tʂʰ | 溪 kʰ | |
| 明 m | | 泥 n | 心 s | 審 ʂ | 曉 x | |
| | 微 ʋ | 來 l | | 日 ɽ | 疑 (敖) ŋ | |

thumb, voiced stops and affricates like [ b, d, g, dz ] and so on became aspirated sounds, such as [ pʰ, tʰ, kʰ, tsʰ ] in the *píng* tone, and unaspirated, that is, simply [ p, t, k, ts ] in the other tones. This sound change is a type of devoicing, and its phonological condition in Chinese is based on the tones. Some examples are 徒 (*tú*, "walk"), which had a voiced *d-* initial and a *píng* tone in Middle Chinese, and 杜 (*dù*, "stop"), which in Middle Chinese also had the initial *d-* but a *shǎng* tone. The initials of these two words in Old Mandarin are the aspirated voiceless *tʰ-* and the unaspirated voiceless *t-*. Their reconstructed forms in both stages of the language are: 徒 Middle Chinese *duo*³³ > Old Mandarin *tʰu*⁴⁵; 杜 Middle Chinese *duo*³⁵ > Old Mandarin *tu*⁵¹. Note here that the tone of the word 杜 changed from *shǎng* in Middle Chinese to *qù* in Old Mandarin. This tonal merger is described subsequently in this chapter.

The second major change is that there are two sets of affricates and fricatives in this system, that is, the retroflex sounds such as [ tʂ ] and the alveolars such as [ ts ], while in Middle Chinese of the *Qièyùn* time, there were three sets, including palatals such as [ tɕ ], retroflex affricates and fricatives such as [ tʂ ], and alveolar sounds such as [ ts ]. The *Qièyùn* system represents Early Middle Chinese, while the rhyme tables represent Late Middle Chinese. The 36 initials from rhyme tables, as shown in Table 4.2, contain only two sets of affricates and fricatives, showing that the retroflex and palatal affricates and fricatives in Early Middle Chinese merged into a set of retroflex consonants in Late Middle Chinese, that is, *tɕ > tʂ* in the Song dynasty (Xiang 1993). Thus, the three sets of affricates and fricatives were reduced to two sets. Another related change is that the retroflex stops such as [ ʈ ] in Middle Chinese, which were still present in the 36 initials of the Song dynasty rhyme tables, eventually merged into the retroflex series as well, that is, *ʈ > tʂ*, in the Yuan dynasty. To summarize these changes, the Middle Chinese alveolar affricates and fricatives developed into the same series in Old Mandarin, for example, *ts > ts*. The palatal affricates and fricatives and then the retroflex stops merged into the retroflex series of affricates and fricatives, for example, *tɕ > tʂ* and *ʈ > tʂ*.

The third important change involves the bilabial stops in Middle Chinese. There were no labiodental initials in the Middle Chinese of the *Qièyùn* era. But in the 36 initials of the rhyme tables, there were two sets of labial sounds. Besides the original set of bilabials such as [ p, pʰ, b, m ], there was a corresponding set of initials represented by 非敷奉微. According to Xiang (1993), the reconstructions of these new sounds are all labiodental, including [ f, fʰ, v, ɱ ]. The sound [ fʰ ] is similar to [ f ] but with stronger aspiration. The sound [ ɱ ] is similar to [ m ] but uttered with the upper teeth touching the lower lip. Thus, from Early Middle Chinese to Late Middle Chinese, a set of labiodental sounds split off from the bilabials. The phonological condition for this development is that the bilabial initials in words with a division III 合口 *hékǒu* final would become labiodental, for example, 放 (*fàng*, "to place, to put") *pjwaŋ > faŋ*.

After the new set of labiodental sounds developed, they were further simplified in Old Mandarin. The initials [ f, fʰ, v ] merged into [ f ] first, and then [ ɱ ] filled in the blank left by the former [ v ] and developed into a voiced labiodental approximant represented with the symbol [ ʋ ]. To sum up these discussions, the following sound changes took place from Middle Chinese to Old Mandarin. First, in the Song dynasty, some bilabials became labiodental, for example, *p > f*. In Old Mandarin, the four labiodentals further simplified: *fʰ > f, v > f, ɱ > v*. The change of *v > f* left a blank to be filled by *ɱ > v*.

Now let's take a look at the 46 finals reconstructed by Ning (1985: 9), as shown in Table 5.2.

*Table 5.2* Finals of Old Mandarin

| *Rhymes* | 開 *kāi* | 齊 *qí* | 合 *hé* | 撮 *cuō* |
|---|---|---|---|---|
| 支思 | ï | | | |
| 齊微 | | i | ui | |
| | | ei | | |
| 魚模 | | | u | iu |
| 尤侯 | əu | iəu | | |
| 車遮 | | iɛ | | iuɛ |
| 歌戈 | ɔ | iɔ | uɔ | |
| 家麻 | a | ia | ua | |
| 皆來 | ai | iai | uai | |
| 蕭豪 | ɑu | iau | | |
| | au | | | |
| 侵尋 | əm | iəm | | |
| 廉纖 | | iɛm | | |
| 監咸 | am | iam | | |
| 真文 | ən | iən | uən | iuən |
| 先天 | | iɛn | | iuɛn |
| 桓歡 | | | uɔn | |
| 寒山 | an | ian | uan | |
| 東鍾 | | | uŋ | iuŋ |
| 庚青 | əŋ | iəŋ | uəŋ | iuəŋ |
| 江陽 | aŋ | iaŋ | uaŋ | |

The primary pattern in Table 5.2 that arranges the finals in four columns resembles the *sìhū* 四呼 ("four vocalizations") distinction of Middle Mandarin in the late Ming and early Qing. The column labeled with 開 *kāi* contains finals without any sort of [ i ] or [ u ] sound as the medial or the main vowel. The column labeled with 齊 *qí* has finals with [ i ] as the medial or the main vowel. The 合 *hé* finals have [ u ] as the medial or the main vowel, while the 撮 *cuō* finals have [ iu ]. The different main vowels [ i ] and [ u ] mostly developed from similar vowels in Middle Chinese. In terms of the medials, their sources vary. In general, the medial -*i*- in the 齊 *qí* finals developed from the Middle Chinese division III finals, the medial -*u*- in the 合 *hé* finals developed from the Middle Chinese 合口 *hékǒu* finals that are not of division III, and the -*iu*- in the 撮 *cuō* finals is from the Middle Chinese division III 合口 *hékǒu* finals. The two components in the -*iu*- would eventually fuse into the rounded high front vowel [ y ] in Modern Standard Chinese. Therefore, the system of the four vocalizations is still not quite complete in the *Zhōngyuán Yīnyùn*. But since the four types of finals here are sufficiently similar to the *sìhū*, we label them with the corresponding terms, although the terminology of *sìhū* was a later invention.

One striking feature of Old Mandarin finals is how much more simplified it is compared to the highly complex system of Middle Chinese finals. It is mostly a result of multiple mergers. For example, the Middle Chinese rhymes 東冬鍾 contain four different finals, that is, -*uŋ*, -*juŋ*, -*woŋ*, -*iwoŋ*, but in Old Mandarin, they all merged into one category of rhyme that represents two finals, that is, -*uŋ* and -*iuŋ*. Similar changes took place in many other rhymes of the Middle Chinese system.

Another structural feature of the finals in Table 5.2 is that the three nasal codas -*m*, -*n*, -*ŋ* in Middle Chinese are still retained in Old Mandarin. In Modern Standard Chinese, there are only two nasal codas, that is, -*n* and -*ŋ*, as a result of the merger of the bilabial nasal coda -*m* into the alveolar nasal coda -*n*.

In terms of syllable types, Middle Chinese had three types of syllable: open syllables, nasal syllables, and syllables with -*p*, -*t*, or -*k* codas, which are associated with the *rù* tone. In Table 5.2, there are only open and nasal finals, while the -*p*, -*t*, -*k* codas disappeared and became open syllable. Meanwhile, with the loss of this type of syllables, the *rù* tone was lost as well. That is why the original *rù*-tone characters are distributed to the other three tones in the *Zhōngyuán Yīnyùn*. But note here that some scholars would argue that the *rù*-tone category still existed in Old Mandarin, probably in the form of a glottal stop coda -*ʔ*, as a result of the merger of the -*p*, -*t*, -*k* codas.

Furthermore as shown in Table 5.2, the apical vowels [ ɿ , ʅ ] emerged as an independent final. In Modern Standard Chinese, there is a special type of apical vowel [ ʅ ] in syllables such as *zhi*, *chi*, *shi*, and *ri*, although some linguists may prefer to analyze it as a syllabic consonant, similar to a prolonged version of the sound represented by the letter "*s*" in the English word "*measure*." In modern Chinese syllables like *zi*, *ci*, *si*, there is another apical vowel [ ɿ ], and some may prefer to describe it as a prolonged *z* sound similar to the "*z*" in "*zoo*." Note that although these two vowels are phonetically different, they are not strictly contrastive, because they only combine with their respective types of initials, that is, the retroflex and alveolar sibilants. Therefore, they may be considered variants of the same phoneme. In Old Mandarin, this phoneme is represented by the symbol [ ï ] as the phonetic value for the 支思 rhyme.

## 5.4  Tonal development

We have discussed the development of initials and finals from Middle Chinese to Old Mandarin. What about the tones? As is evident in the structure of the *Zhōngyuán Yīnyùn*, the Middle Chinese *píng* tone split into two different tones: *yīn* and *yáng* varieties of the former *píngshēng*. Chapter 3 points out that a language without tones can develop tones under the influence of consonant codas such as -ʔ and -s. It turns out that after tones developed, they can further split.

Tones are associated with the phonetic properties of pitch. The same syllable may be uttered with a higher pitch or a lower one, according to the voicing quality of the initial consonant. For example, when we say the syllable "*bah*," the pitch is naturally slightly lower than that of the syllable "*pah*," because the voicing of the initial consonant *b-* tends to lower the pitch of the following vowel. Suppose we have two Middle Chinese syllables of the *píng* tone, that is, *ba* and *pa*, both with a level tonal contour. Because of the influence from the voiced *b-*, the level tone associated with "*ba*" is slightly lower than the level tone of "*pa*," thus creating a distinction between an upper register and a lower register within the same tonal category. Based on tonal descriptions by a Japanese monk in the 9th century, Mei (1970) shows that a register distinction in each of the four Middle Chinese tonal categories had already developed by the late Tang dynasty, resulting in the contrast as shown in Table 5.3.

The tone of a word with a voiceless initial became the upper-register version, usually called the *yīn* tone, while the tone of a word with a voiced initial became the lower-register version, called the *yáng* tone. Since there are eight tones here, they are sometimes referred to by the numbers 1–8.

If we assume that the tones in Old Mandarin developed from the eight tones in Table 5.3, then the register distinction is only retained in the *píng* tone category in Old Mandarin, while the other tones may have merged.

Let's first describe the tonal split in the *píng* tone category. Consider the following examples. The reconstructed form of the character 兵 (*bīng*, "soldier") in Middle Chinese is *pjɐŋ*, and that of 平 (*píng*, "flat, even") is *bjɐŋ*. Both of them had

*Table 5.3* Tonal splits

| Initials | 平 *píng* | 上 *shǎng* | 去 *qù* | 入 *rù* |
|---|---|---|---|---|
| **Voiceless** | yīnpíng 陰平1 | yīnshǎng 陰上3 | yīnqù 陰去5 | yīnrù 陰入7 |
| **Voiced** | yángpíng 陽平2 | yángshǎng 陽上4 | yángqù 陽去6 | yángrù 陽入8 |

the *píng* tone. The only difference between them is that the first one had a voiceless initial *p-*, while the second one had a voiced initial *b-*. The voicing contrast between *p-* and *b-* resulted in a register distinction between an upper even tone in the word 兵, and a lower even tone in 平. At this stage, the register distinction is a by-product of the voicing contrast between *p-* and *b-*. However, in Old Mandarin, the voiced obstruents became voiceless, and as a compensatory phonological development, the register distinction became the primary distinctive feature, resulting in a split in the tone.

In terms of the merger among the non-*píng* tones, the *yīnqù* and *yángqù* tones merged in Old Mandarin. The *rù* tone, generally, is distributed to the other tones as follows: the *rù*-tone words in Middle Chinese with voiced obstruent initials became Old Mandarin *yángpíng* words, the *rù* tone that was associated with Middle Chinese voiceless initials became the Old Mandarin *shǎng* tone, while the *rù* tone with voiced sonorant initials such as *m-*, *n-*, *l-* became the *qù* tone.

Another major tonal merger in Old Mandarin is that Middle Chinese words of the *shǎng* tone with voiced obstruent initials such as *b-*, *dz-*, *ɣ-* merged into the *qù* tone in Old Mandarin. For example, the word 上 (*shàng*, "up") had the voiced initial *dz-* and the *shǎng* tone in Middle Chinese, but in the *Zhōngyuán Yīnyùn*, it is in the *qù* tone, while at the same time, its initial also devoiced into the voiceless retroflex fricative *ʂ-*. Another example is the word 道 (*dào*, "path") with the Middle Chinese initial *d-* and the *shǎng* tone. It is in the *qù* tone in the *Zhōngyuán Yīnyùn*, with a voiceless initial *t-*. The Middle Chinese words in the *yángshǎng* tone that did not have voiced obstruent initials merged into the *yīnshǎng* tone in Old Mandarin. Since only a part of *yángshǎng* merged with *qù*, while the remaining *yángshǎng* merged with *yīnshǎng* in Old Mandarin, these tonal changes are not obvious because now we have only one *shǎng* tone and one *qù* tone. Thus, when we look at the *qù*-tone words in Old Mandarin, and also in Modern Standard Chinese, we have to be aware that some of those words actually had the *shǎng* tone originally.

As for the tonal shapes of Old Mandarin, according to *Zhōu Déqīng*'s descriptions of the tones and how different tones were used in the composition of the *qǔ*, Ning (1985) posits the following tonal numerals for the four tones in the *Zhōngyuán Yīnyùn*: *píngshēng yīn* is a low even tone with the shape of 22; *píngshēng yáng* is a high rising tone with the shape of 45; *shǎngshēng* is a low dipping tone with the value of 215; *qù* tone is a high falling tone of 51.

Now with the complete reconstructed system of Old Mandarin provided, let's see a larger text in the reconstructed form. The following is a famous work of the *qǔ* titled 天淨沙·秋思 *Tiānjìngshā Qiūsī* ("*Autumn thoughts in the tune of Sunny Sky and Clear Sand*") by 馬致遠 *Mǎ Zhìyuǎn*, one of the four major authors that *Zhōu Déqīng* studied for the compilation of his rhyme book. The meaning of this poem can be translated with no intention to rhyme as: "There are withered vines on an old tree in which crows are perching at dusk. By the river with a little bridge, there was a house. In westerly winds on the ancient roadway on the back of a scrawny horse was a heart-broken person travelling to the edges of the world with the sun setting to the west."

**Chinese characters:**

枯藤老樹昏鴉，
小橋流水人家，
古道西風瘦馬。
夕陽西下，
斷腸人在天涯。

**Modern Standard Chinese:**

kū téng lǎo shù hūn yā /
xiǎo qiáo liú shuǐ rén jiā /
gǔ dào xī fēng shòu mǎ //
xī yáng xī xià /
duàn cháng rén zài tiānyá //

**Old Mandarin:**

kʰu²² tʰəŋ⁴⁵ lɑu²¹⁵ ʂiu⁵¹ xuən²² ia²² /
siau²¹⁵ kʰiau⁴⁵ liəu⁴⁵ ʂui²¹⁵ ɽiən⁴⁵ kia²² /
ku²¹⁵ tɑu⁵¹ si²² fuŋ²² ʂəu⁵¹ ma²¹⁵ //
si²² iaŋ⁴⁵ si²² xia⁵¹ /
tuɔn⁵¹ tʂʰaŋ⁴⁵ ɽiən⁴⁵ tsai⁵¹ tʰiɛn²² ia⁴⁵//

So far, we have given a detailed picture of the developments in the phonological system of the Chinese language from Old Chinese to Middle Chinese, and then to Old Mandarin. We pick up such discussions in Chapter 9 in terms of the phonological developments from Old Mandarin to Modern Standard Chinese, which is based on the modern Mandarin dialect of Beijing. The major dialects of Chinese are discussed in Chapter 10.

Our descriptions of older stages of the Chinese language have mostly focused on phonology. In the next three chapters, we turn to the development of grammar and vocabulary of the Chinese language as attested in Classical Chinese and vernacular writing.

## Notes

1 Note that the word Mandarin, or *Guānhuà* 官話, usually refers to the common spoken language in the Ming and Qing dynasties. It is a sort of *koiné* (Norman 1988: 48). The use of the word *Guānhuà* can be traced to the Yuan dynasty (Mair 1994: 728).
2 The initial [ ŋ ] corresponds to the Middle Chinese initial 疑, but the character 疑 itself has a zero initial in Old Mandarin. Therefore, we provide the common name 疑 itself followed by a character, that is, 敖 here, which has the initial [ ŋ ] in Old Mandarin. This character 敖 is in parentheses.

# 6    Classical Chinese grammar

This chapter provides an overview of the syntax and morphology of Classical Chinese, especially in terms of its relation to the other Sino-Tibetan languages.

## 6.1    What is Classical Chinese?

The term "*Old Chinese*" ("*Shànggǔ Hànyǔ,*" 上古漢語) is a modern term used in historical linguistics to refer to the period of Chinese as attested in early written records such as the *Shījīng* and characters in phonetic series. Roughly speaking, it can be described as the common spoken language in the first millennium BC. In contrast, Classical Chinese refers to the language recorded in texts from the end of Spring and Autumn period (5th–6th centuries BC) to the Han dynasty (206 BC–AD 220). The Han dynasty texts are generally regarded as Classical Chinese. The major part of the classical period is roughly the second half of the first millennium BC. Texts written in the first half of the first millennium BC, that is, prior to the classical era, had noticeable properties in the grammar that are different from Classical Chinese. Thus, pre-classical texts such as the *Shàngshū* 尚書 ("*Book of Documents*") are not the focus of our discussions here.

The received view is that Classical Chinese was based on the spoken language in the Old Chinese period, although the texts are generally in a much more succinct or elliptical form than the spoken language. After the Han dynasty, Classical Chinese continued to be used as the literary language, despite the fact that the vernacular language began to diverge slowly from Classical Chinese as a result of natural linguistic change in terms of sounds, grammar, and vocabulary. Literary Chinese refers to such later uses of Classical Chinese in the post-Han era. Literary Chinese continued to function as the standard written language in China until the early 20th century, when the written language began to be based on the modern vernacular. For writers after the classical period to write in Literary Chinese, they were actually not writing down their own spoken language but rather imitating an older stage of the language. This distinction is useful when we study grammatical and lexical changes in Chinese. The texts in the classical period may be more authentic in representing the early period of Chinese, while Literary Chinese texts in post-classical times, for example, in the Tang dynasty, do not accurately reflect the grammar and vocabulary of the base language of Classical Chinese. In this chapter and the next one, examples are carefully selected to make sure that they are reliable records of the grammar we are looking at. When we focus on Classical Chinese, in its strict sense, examples in Literary Chinese, for example, from the Tang dynasty, should not be cited. When we focus on the grammar of the actual spoken varieties of Chinese in the Tang dynasty, Literary Chinese texts generally cannot be used as the primary source.

Thus, there had been a divergence between the written language and the spoken language for more than 1500 years in China. In most of the imperial period of Chinese history, educated people wrote in Literary Chinese, while they used quite different spoken languages. This linguistic situation is a type of diglossia, literally meaning "*two languages.*" In many societies, the written language is based on an earlier stage of the language, which is quite different from the current spoken languages or dialects. For example, Written Tibetan, Written Burmese, and Standard Arabic are all such written languages, while the various Tibetan and Burmese dialects and the varieties of spoken Arabic are different from the written languages to varying degrees. Normally the written language is used for formal purposes such as education and government documents, while the vernacular is for daily communication needs.

Although we are making a distinction between Classical Chinese and Literary Chinese, in practical terms, they are often not strictly distinguished, such as in the Chinese terms 文言文 *wényán wén* (literally "*Written Language*"), 古文 *Gǔwén* ("*Ancient Texts*"), and 古代漢語 *Gǔdài Hànyǔ* ("*Ancient Chinese*"). Their definitions are not clearly defined, referring mostly to formal texts from both the classical period and various subsequent dynasties. Mair (1994: 708) argues that the written language in the classical era of China also differed considerably from the spoken language, because the written texts are significantly abbreviated and contain many "nonvernacular conventions used only in writing." Thus, even during the classical period, and probably as early as the late Shang dynasty in the oracle bone script, the written language and the spoken language were drastically different. Mair (1994: 708) further contends that this written literary language in pre-modern China was "unsayable," hence merely being a written form detached from the living language at any time period. In this view, even Classical Chinese texts should be used with caution when we study the grammar of Old Chinese, because the written texts were probably not based on the spoken form of Old Chinese. However, the notion that Classical Chinese was an exclusively written language may be an overstatement. Mair (1994: 709) cites arguments made by Tsu-Lin Mei and agrees that some texts, such as the *Analects*, do reflect the spoken language, because, among other things, there are fusion words that can only occur in fast speech.

Therefore, the debate is still ongoing. What we may temporarily conclude here is that Classical Chinese does have its own grammar, which must be based on some real grammatical system in a natural language, although we may not know exactly how Classical Chinese records deviate from such a real grammar or whether the grammar corresponds to Old Chinese or to an even earlier stage. Despite all these issues, Classical Chinese is the only systematic source for the grammar of early Chinese, and we have to rely on these records to uncover the grammatical features of Old Chinese, as long as we are aware of the uncertainties.

## 6.2   Morphology

Morphology studies the structure of words and word formation rules. The basic concept in morphology is, unsurprisingly, the morpheme, which can be defined as the smallest meaningful unit of language. For example, the English word "*happiness*" contains two meaningful components, that is, "*happy*" and "*-ness*," although the meaning of "*-ness*" is a little elusive. Neither of these two components can be further divided meaningfully. Thus, "*happy*" and "*-ness*" are both morphemes, which can be used in different ways to form other words, for example, "*happily*," "*happier*," "*boldness*," "*sweetness*," and so on. Some morphemes in English have one syllable, for example, "*-ness*," while many others have more than one, for example, "*happy*." In comparison, Classical Chinese morphemes are mostly monosyllabic, and furthermore a large portion of words are composed of just one morpheme in Classical Chinese. Therefore, in many cases, one syllable is equal to one morpheme, which is in turn equal to one word in Classical Chinese. However, Modern Standard Chinese words are often disyllabic, although morphemes are still predominantly monosyllabic. Consequently, when we translate a text from Classical Chinese to Modern Standard Chinese, the number of syllables often doubles. For example:[1]

(1) *Pīnyīn*:        *Xué   ér   shí   xí      zhī*              (*The Analects*)
    Characters:   學    而   時   習    之。
    Gloss:          study and often practice it
    Translation:  "Study and often practice what you learn."[2]

The sentence in (1) is Classical Chinese, with five syllables. It can be translated into Modern Standard Chinese as "*Xuéxí érqiě shícháng liànxí tā* 學習而且時常練習它," which contains nine syllables. Each of the first four monosyllabic words in the original Classical Chinese example is translated as a disyllabic word in Modern Standard Chinese, thus almost doubling the length of the text. In some sense, Classical Chinese is highly condensed both in words and meaning. Knowing this property of Classical Chinese can help us avoid misinterpretations. When we see something that looks like a modern word, they are most likely two different words in Classical Chinese. For example:

(2) *Yán   zhě   suǒ   yǐ   zài   yì,   dé   yì   ér   wàng   yán.* (*The Zhuāngzǐ*)
    言    者    所    以   在   意,   得   意   而   忘    言。
    word SUBJ NOM   with exist idea obtain idea and forget word
    "Words are employed to convey ideas; but when the ideas are apprehended, men forget the words." (Trans. James Legge)[3]

In the gloss in (2), there are grammatical words which are labeled by their functions. For example, "SUBJ" is a subject marker, that is, a grammatical word that indicates the preceding phrase is the subject of the sentence. The abbreviation "NOM" is short for "*nominalizer*," which is explained later in this chapter.

In Modern Standard Chinese, "*suǒyǐ*" (所以) is the word for "*therefore*"; "*zàiyì*" (在意) means "*to take notice of, to mind*"; and "*déyì*" (得意) can be paraphrased as "*proud of oneself.*" But in Classical Chinese, each of these words comprises two monosyllabic monomorphemic words, the meanings of which are very different from those in Modern Standard Chinese. In Classical Chinese, however, there are a small number of disyllabic morphemes that cannot be meaningfully further divided into smaller components. A good portion of these disyllabic morphemes fall into the category of words called *liánmiáncí* 聯綿詞 (literally "indivisible words"). The meaning of a disyllabic morpheme in *liánmiáncí* is expressed by both syllables, which are normally in the *shuāngshēng* ("alliteration") or *diéyùn* ("rhyming") relation. For example, *cēncī* 參差 ("uneven," attested in the *Shījīng*) is a *shuāngshēng* word; *wàngyáng* 望洋 ("looking up," attested in the *Zhuāngzi*) is a *diéyùn* word. Both words have one disyllabic morpheme instead of two monosyllabic morphemes.

Thus, Classical Chinese morphemes are mostly monosyllabic, although some morphemes in *liánmiáncí* are disyllabic. Morphemes can be combined in different ways to form words. We discuss three types of word formation in Classical Chinese: reduplication, compounding, and affixing.

Reduplication is a process of doubling the morpheme to make a new word. For example, in English there are words like "*bye*" and "*bye-bye*," "*night*" and "*night-night*." In Classical Chinese, there are words of this kind as well, for example, 巍 (*wēi*, "high") and 巍巍 (*wēiwēi*, "lofty"), attested in the *Analects*. There is also a type of onomatopoeic reduplication that mimics natural sounds, for example, *guānguān* 關關 from the *Shījīng*, mimicking the sound of an osprey bird.

Compounding is another morphological device that puts two words together to form a new one, for example, "*blackboard.*" In Classical Chinese, there are compound words such as *jūnzǐ* 君子 ("person of virtue"), and *tiānxià* 天下 ("world"). Generally, the meaning of the whole word can be more or less deduced from the component words.

Some morphemes are free because they can stand alone as words, for example, the English word "*happy*," while bound morphemes cannot function alone and have to be attached to other words, for example, the English "*-ness.*" Affixes are such a type of bound morpheme. If an affix is attached before another word, it is called a prefix, for example, the "*en-*" in the English word "*entrust*"; if attached after another word, it is called a suffix, for example, the "*-ly*" in "*brotherly.*" If the affix is placed inside a word, it is called an infix.

There are clearly affixes in Classical Chinese, but because Chinese characters often do not reflect such affixes, it is not apparent what affixes there were unless a separate character is used for a certain affix. For example, in pre-classical written records, the word *yǒu* (有) is often prefixed to names of tribes. For example, *Huángdì* 黃帝, a legendary emperor of prehistoric China, is also called the "*Yǒu*

*Xióng Shì* (有熊氏)." This prefix was later extended to be used with names of states and dynasties. Another prefix attested rather late in the classical era is *ā-* (阿), which can be attached to kinship terms to convey a sense of familiarity. In texts as early as the Han dynasty, the word *ā-mǔ* (阿母) is attested in the *Shǐ Jì* 史記 ("*Records of the Grand Historian*") to refer to a "*wet nurse*." The prefix *ā-* (阿) is attached to the syllable "*mǔ* (母)," the word for "*mother*." As for suffixes, -*rán* (然) is usually attached to an adjective, or a state verb, to turn it into an adverbial, for example, *pèi-rán* 沛然 "(of rain) abruptly, copiously" from the *Mencius*.

For affixes that are not written with separate characters, we may still find evidence for the existence of affixes by studying the phonological properties of certain words. There is a morphological process called "*derivation by tone change*" in Classical Chinese. A change in the tone can turn the relevant word into a related word of a different part of speech. The most common type is to turn a verb into a noun. Many such distinctions are still maintained in Modern Standard Chinese. Table 6.1 gives a few such examples.

The word *liáng* 量 is a verb meaning "*to measure*," while *liàng* 量 is the corresponding noun "*quantity*." Although the same Chinese character is used to write these two words, the character itself has to be pronounced differently according to the meaning in context, for example, in compound words such as *cèliáng* 測量 ("to measure") and *zhòngliàng* 重量 ("weight"). The pronunciations of these words only differ by their tones. In terms of their original tonal categories in Middle Chinese, *liáng* had a *píng* tone, while *liàng* had a *qù* tone. Thus, by changing a non-*qù* tone to a *qù* tone, the word changes from a verb to its corresponding noun. The second example is similar. Although the initials of these two words are different in Modern Standard Chinese, they had the same initial in Middle Chinese. Both *chuán* 傳 ("to transmit") and *zhuàn* 傳 ("biography, record") had the [ ɖ ] initial. Therefore, originally, their pronunciations were different only by their tones. The verb *chuán* had a *píng* tone in Middle Chinese, while the noun *zhuàn* had a *qù* tone. Examples of this distinction in Modern Standard Chinese compounds include *chuándì* 傳遞 ("to pass") and *zìzhuàn* 自傳 ("autobiography"). The other two examples are similar.

Mei (1980) focuses on this type of "*derivation by tone change*," that is, changing a verb to a noun via a tonal distinction, and compares them with their Sino-Tibetan cognate words in Tibetan. Interestingly, there is a suffix in Written Tibetan in the form of -*s*, which can turn a verb into a noun, for example, *grang-ba* "to

*Table 6.1* Derivation by tone change

| Verb | Noun |
| --- | --- |
| 量 liáng "to measure" | 量 liàng "quantity" |
| 傳 chuán "to transmit" | 傳 zhuàn "biography; record" |
| 處 chǔ "to locate" | 處 chù "place" |
| 背 bēi "to carry on back" | 背 bèi "back" |

count" and *grangs* "a number." Let's recall the discussion on tonogenesis in Old Chinese from Chapter 3. Data suggest that in Old Chinese, there were no tones, and instead, the Middle Chinese *shǎng* tone corresponds to Old Chinese syllables with a glottal stop -ʔ coda, while the Middle Chinese *qù* tone corresponds to Old Chinese syllables with an -*s* coda. In the Baxter-Sagart reconstruction of Old Chinese, the two meanings associated with the character 量 have the following forms: \*[r]aŋ and \*[r]aŋ-s, which are clearly related to the Written Tibetan words mentioned here.

Mei's (1980) hypothesis is that in Old Chinese, there was a nominalizing suffix \*-*s* which would turn a verb into a noun. The suffix \*-*s* later became \*-*h* and was subsequently lost in Middle Chinese, creating the tonal contrast between the *qù* tone and the other tones. Based on Huang's (1996) discussion of the perfective suffix -*s* in Tibeto-Burman languages, Mei (2012) further argues that the Old Chinese \*-*s* probably had such a function as well, for example, in the contrast between 張 (*zhāng*, "to stretch") and 脹 (*zhàng*, "bloated, to be distended"), in which the word zhàng 脹 is the perfective form of the verb *zhāng* 張. In fact, some of the examples in Table 6.1 may have been related to this perfective suffix \*-*s*. For example, the original meaning of the noun *zhuàn* 傳 may be *"transmitted,"* that is, the perfective form of the verb *chuán* 傳 ("to transmit"). The perfective form can be reanalyzed as a noun, that is, *"what is transmitted, the transmitted."* Thus, Mei (2012) hypothesizes that in Proto-Sino-Tibetan, there was a suffix \*-*s* with two functions. The primary function is a past tense or perfective aspect marker, and its secondary function is a nominalizer. In Old Chinese, there are traces of such a distinction, that is, between the pair written with 傳 and the pair with 量, but a reanalysis would make the perfective \*-*s* merge with the nominalizer \*–*s*.

Mei (1989, 2012) and Sagart and Baxter (2012) show that in Old Chinese, there was a prefix \*s-, with multiple functions, one of which is a causative marker. Mei (2012) provides the following example: 滅 (*miè*, "to destroy"), with Old Chinese form \*[m]et, and 威 (*xuè*, "to cause to be destroyed"), with the form \*m̥et. Here, the Old Chinese \*m̥et is usually regarded to have developed from an earlier form of \*smet. Thus, the contrast between \*[m]et and \*s-met seems to suggest that the \*s- prefix turns a verb into a causative one.

Baxter and Sagart (2014) also argue that Old Chinese had a nasal prefix \*N-, which would usually turn a transitive verb into a stative intransitive one.[4] For example, 折 (*zhé*, "to bend, to break") is reconstructed as \*tet > tɕjet and 折 (*shé*, "to be bent, to be broken") as \*N-tet > dzjet.[5] In each word, the first form with a star is Old Chinese; the second form after the arrow is Middle Chinese. The nasal prefix would often result in a voicing contrast between the voiceless initial in the transitive word and the voiced initials in the prefixed version in the intransitive verb, that is, tɕ- vs. dz-. This phenomenon is often called 清濁別義 *qīngzhuó biéyì* ("*to distinguish meanings via clear and muddy sounds*"),[6] but it turns out that such a distinction is a result of the loss of an earlier prefix \*N-.

In addition to \*-*s*, \*s-, and \*N-, Baxter and Sagart (2014) also propose several other affixes in Old Chinese, including the prefixes \*m-, \*t-, and \*k- and an infix

\*<r>, each of which has multiple functions. Although there are still debates on the functions of some of these affixes, it is clear that the Proto-Sino-Tibetan language may have had an abundance of morphological devices, some of which were still present in Old Chinese, although the nature of the Chinese writing system may have disguised the existence of affixal morphology in Old Chinese. These affixes were mostly lost in subsequent phonological developments, but their phonological influences are still observable in Modern Standard Chinese, for example, in the distinctions in tones and initials.

Although on the surface, it may seem that there is very little morphology in Classical Chinese, be it reduplication, compounding, or affixing, compared to Indo-European languages, we are discovering more and more morphological properties of Old Chinese with the help of modern linguistic methodology.

## 6.3  Word classes

Syntax is mostly about sentence formation. First we have to know how many different classes of words there were in Classical Chinese, that is, parts of speech such as nouns, verbs, adjectives, and so on. Second, the rules to put words together can be studied, for example, where to put the nouns and verbs, and so on.

In languages with a highly developed morphology, it is relatively easy to identify classes of words such as nouns, verbs, adjectives, pronouns, conjunctions, and so on based on the kind of morphological processes that they are associated with. For example, in English, verbs can inflect for tense and person to have forms such as "*like, likes, liked.*" But in Chinese, it is easier to distinguish words that have concrete meanings from words that only have grammatical functions or, put in an equivalent way, to distinguish words that are like nouns from words that are like verbs. But it is difficult to further distinguish words within each of these two classes, partly due to the simpler morphological system in Chinese. Traditionally, Chinese scholars only distinguish the following two classes of words: *shízì* 實字 ("concrete words") and *xūzì* 虛字 ("empty words"). For example, the word "*kè*" (客) has a concrete meaning, that is, "*guest,*" while the word "*ér*" (而, "and") serves to connect verbs, thus having a specific grammatical function but not a tangible meaning. Therefore, when we refer to meanings of words, we are more precisely referring to the meanings of concrete words and the functions of "*empty words.*" Both classes of words were studied by traditional Chinese scholars who commented on classical works.

The first modern system of Classical Chinese grammar in China was developed by *Mǎ Jiànzhōng* 馬建忠 (1845–1900) in his book titled 馬氏文通 *Mǎ Shì Wén Tōng* ("Ma's Grammar") published in 1898, although in the Ming and Qing dynasties, there had been earlier studies of the grammar of Classical Chinese by missionaries and Western scholars.[7] Based on the paradigms in Latin grammar, *Mǎ Jiànzhōng* categorized Classical Chinese words into nine classes. The concrete words are categorized into nouns, adjectives, verbs, pronouns, and adverbs. The empty words include prepositions, conjunctions, helping words (助詞, *zhùcí*), and interjections. He also discussed the structures of sentences using concepts such as subject, object, predicate, predicative, and so on. Most subsequent grammar books on Literary Chinese would be built on *Mǎ Jiànzhōng*'s framework. Therefore, let's refer to these categories of words without going into the details of criteria of classification and discuss some of the features of word classes in Classical Chinese.

First, intuitively, or notionally, nouns in Classical Chinese are words that refer to objects and people, for example, *niú* 牛 ("cow") and *zǐ* 子 ("child"). But in many cases, nouns can be temporarily used as verbs, such as in (3).

(3) *Jūn     jūn     chén     chén     fù     fù     zǐ     zǐ*          (*The Analects*)
    君      君，   臣       臣，    父     父，  子     子。
    prince prince minister minister father father child child
    "(There is government, when) the prince is prince, and the minister is minister; when the father is father, and the son is son." (Trans. James Legge)

In this quote from the *Analects*, there are four sentences, each of which contains two words that are exactly the same. For example "*jūn jūn*" is a sentence with two instances of the word "*jūn*," originally meaning "*prince, ruler*." If the first "*jūn*" is the subject, then the second "*jūn*" must be the predicate. In this case, it should be temporarily used as a verb. The other three short sentences in (3) can be interpreted in a similar fashion. Now let's look at another example of nouns functioning as verbs.

(4) *Jūnzǐ              bú     qì*                               (*The Analects*)
    君子              不     器。
    person of virtue not   utensil/instrument/vessel
    "The accomplished scholar is not a utensil." (Trans. James Legge)

In this quote, the word "*qì*" is modified by the negation word "*bù*," which is typically used with a verb or an adjective. Thus, we can deduce that "*qì*" is used as a verb in example (4). The following is a similar example from the *Zhàn Guó Cè* 戰國策 ("Strategies of the Warring States"), a history book dated between the 3rd and 1st centuries BC.

(5) *Mèngcháng-jūn     kè     wǒ*                              (*Zhàn Guó Cè*)
    孟嘗君              客     我。
    Lord Mengchang guest me
    "Lord Mengchang treats me as his guest."[8]

In this quote, the word "*kè*" ("guest") is followed by another noun, which looks like the object in the sentence. Thus, the word "*kè*" should be interpreted as a verb. Here it can be paraphrased as "*treat . . . as a guest.*" This type of use of nouns is called "*putative.*" Admittedly, that nouns can be used as verbs in the right context is probably not a unique feature of Chinese, since in many languages, nouns can be turned into verbs very easily, for example, "*to man a ship*" in English. But it does seem that in Classical Chinese, there are many more *ad hoc* uses of nouns as verbs. The verbal meaning is not conventional or fixed. Therefore, readers have to use the context and their knowledge of grammar to deduce what the correct interpretation would be.

Adjectives in both Classical Chinese and Modern Standard Chinese can function as the predicate of a sentence without the copula verb. Therefore, they are also regarded as a special type of verb (Pulleyblank 1995: 24). Some scholars prefer the term "*stative verb*" to the term "*adjective.*" But we use "*adjective*" here as long as the reader is aware of the verbal properties of adjectives in Chinese. The following example shows that Classical Chinese adjectives, in addition to functioning as intransitive stative verbs, can often be turned into transitive verbs.

(6) *Dēng   Tài   shān   ér   xiǎo   tiānxià*          (*The Mencius*)
    登     泰    山     而    小     天下。
    ascend Tai   Mount and small  world
    "(Confucius) ascended the Mount Tai and considered the word small."

In this sentence, the word "*xiǎo*" is an adjective, followed by a noun that looks like the object. Similar to the case in (5), the adjective here should be interpreted as a verb, meaning "*consider . . . to be small,*" in the putative sense. Adjectives can also be used as causative verbs, for example:

(7) *Kǔ   qí   xīn   zhì*                              (*The Mencius*)
    苦    其    心    志。
    bitter his mind will
    "(It would first) make his mind suffer."

In (7), the word "*kǔ*" ("bitter") should be the verb, while "*qí xīn zhì*" would be the object. Here the adjective is interpreted in the pattern of "*cause . . . to be <adjective>.*" In the case of the adjective "*kǔ,*" it should be translated as "*cause . . . to be bitter.*" The whole sentence in (7) means "*make his mind bitter, or suffer.*"

Similarly, other intransitive verbs, that is, verbs like "*come, rise, sleep, run*" and so on, which cannot take an object, are often used in a causative sense when followed by an object. For example:

(8) *Jì   lái   zhī,   zé   ān   zhī*                    (*The Analects*)
    既    来    之，   则    安    之。
    PERF come them  then content them
    "When they have been so attracted, they must be made contented and tranquil." (Trans. James Legge)

In the quote in (8), the intransitive verb "*lái*" ("to come") should be paraphrased in the causative pattern as "*cause . . . to come,*" which is translated as "*attract*" here. In the second half of the quote, the adjective "*ān*" ("content") is also used in a causative sense. The gloss "PERF" means that it specifies a perfective aspect.

In summary, examples (3)–(8) show that nouns and adjectives can be used temporarily as verbs and that intransitive verbs, including stative verbs, that is, adjectives, can be used as causatives. Such uses are very common in Classical Chinese. This is one of the reasons scholars argue that Classical Chinese words should just be categorized into "*concrete words*" and "*empty words*" without further distinctions within either category. But such a radical view may be an overstatement of word categories in Classical Chinese. In order to analyze Classical Chinese syntax, a more refined system that includes more than just two classes of words is needed. Therefore, we continue to refer to words as, for example, verbs, adjectives, nouns, and so on in Classical Chinese, although there is a greater degree of flexibility among some classes as compared to other languages.

Now let's take a brief look at the pronoun system in Classical Chinese. For the first-person pronoun, the word *wǒ* 我 (Old Chinese: *$\eta^\varsigma aj\text{?}$, in the Baxter-Sagart system) can be found in written records as early as in the oracle bone script from the Shang dynasty prior to Old Chinese. In the subsequent Zhou dynasty, another related word, *wú* 吾 (Old Chinese: *$\eta^\varsigma a$), developed. In Classical Chinese, both 我 *wǒ* and 吾 *wú* are used but in different ways. 我 *wǒ* is used as either the subject or the object, while 吾 *wú* is often used as the subject and the possessive, that is, pronouns like "*my, our.*" Such a distinction may be a kind of case distinction, similar to the English "*me*" vs. "*my.*" The Old Chinese forms of 我 and 吾 are *$\eta^\varsigma aj\text{?}$ and *$\eta^\varsigma a$, which were possibly derived from the same root. The following two examples illustrate their functional contrast.

(9)   Cǐ   fēi   wú   jūn   yě                              (*The Mencius*)
      此   非   吾   君   也。
      This isn't my/our prince PAR
      "This person is not our prince."

(10)  Qí         shī   fá   wǒ                               (*Zuǒ Zhuàn*)
      齊         師   伐   我。
      State of Qi troops attack us
      "The troops of Qi attacked us."

In the gloss in (9), the label "PAR" stands for "*grammatical particle.*" The word "*yě* 也" is often used in a copula construction to express a sense of factuality. In this example, the word "*wú*" modifies the noun "*jūn,*" and the phrase "*wú jūn*" can be translated as "*my prince*" or "*our prince.*" For such possessive meanings, the word "*wǒ*" is not used, because it tends to appear in the object position to mean "*me*" or "*us,*" as shown in example (10). Thus, the division of labor between *wǒ* and *wú* is that the former is used as the object, while the latter is used as the possessive. Both can be used as the subject, although, as Norman (1988) pointed out, *wǒ* in the subject position tends to have a contrastive sense, that is, "*I (or we) but no one else.*" Generally, there is no grammatical distinction between singular and plural nouns or pronouns in Classical Chinese. If a distinction between the singular and the plural needs to be made, words that refer to a group of people, such as *chái* 儕, can be added to *wú* 吾 or *wǒ* 我. The word *wúchái* 吾儕 ("we") is more common than *wǒchái* 我儕 ("we"). After the Han dynasty, the morpheme for "*a group of people*" is usually *bèi* 輩 instead of the earlier *chái* 儕. Thus, *wǒbèi* 我輩 ("we, us") and *wúbèi* 吾輩 are both attested in texts from the post-classical era.

For second-person pronouns, there are two major forms: *rǔ* 汝 and *ěr* 爾. Different from the division of labor in the first-person pronouns, there is no clear distinction here with respect to different positions in the sentence, such as the subject, object, and so on. Usually in Classical Chinese, addressing someone by "爾" or "汝" is considered impolite. Therefore, various honorific expressions of addressing people more appropriately can be used. For example, *zǐ* 子 ("master") is originally a polite word that refers to a man, such as, *Kǒngzǐ* ("Confucius", "*Kǒng*" is his family name). The word *zǐ* can be used to address people in general in a polite fashion.

The third-person pronouns have a clear distinction between the possessive *qí* 其 ("his, her, its, their") and the object pronoun *zhī* 之 ("him, her, it, them"). We have seen an example of *qí* in (7) and an example of *zhī* in (8) previously. Here's another example of *qí*:

(11)  *Tīng  qí  yán  ér  guān  qí  xíng*        (*The Analects*)
      聽   其   言   而   觀   其   行。
      listen their word and observe their conduct
      "I listen to their words and observe their conduct."

As the examples so far have shown, not only do pronouns in Classical Chinese lack a distinction between singular and plural forms, but there is also no distinction of gender, either. No real third-person pronoun for the subject position is used, and instead *bǐ* 彼, the word for "*that*," may be substituted.

Next, regarding demonstrative pronouns in Classical Chinese, *bǐ* 彼 is "*that*" and *cǐ* 此 is "*this*," and a related form for "*this*" is *shì* 是, which developed into the copula verb "*to be*" in Modern Standard Chinese. More details on this grammatical change are discussed in Chapter 7. The difference between these two words for "*this*," that is, *cǐ* 此 vs. *shì* 是, is that *shì* is more general, while *cǐ* is more specific, referring to something or someone that is actually present (Norman 1988: 90). For interrogative pronouns, the most common ones include *shuí* 誰 for "*who*" and *hé* 何 for "*what, why, how, where*" depending on the context.

Now let's take a look at prepositions in Classical Chinese. Actually, the term "*preposition*" may not be accurate, since in both Classical Chinese and Modern Standard Chinese, a "preposition" can function either as a verb or a preposition *per se* according to their syntactic positions in a sentence. Thus, the term "*coverb*" is often used in place of "*preposition*" (Pulleyblank 1995: 47). Therefore, in Chinese, there is no real preposition like in English. We use the term "*preposition*" here, but be aware that these words may also be verbs.

Classical Chinese prepositions, or coverbs, include the instrumental *yǐ* (以, "with"), benefactive *wèi* (爲, "for"), comitative *yǔ* (與, "with"), locative *yú* (於, "at," Old Chinese: *[ʔ]a) and *yú* (于, "at," Old Chinese: *ɢʷ(r)a). Although the Modern Standard Chinese pronunciations 於 and 于 are exactly the same, their Old Chinese forms are quite different. According to Xiang (1993), these two prepositions have similar functions in Classical Chinese, but in earlier times before Old Chinese, for example, in the oracle bone script and bronze script, there was only 于. In early Old Chinese such as in the *Shījīng* and the *Shàngshū*, there are only a few examples of 於, while 于 is more common. Starting from Classical Chinese, 於 became more commonly used and eventually replaced 于.

Prepositions in Classical Chinese were originally verbs. For example, the instrumental *yǐ* 以 also functions as a verb to mean "*to grasp, to use, to lead*"; the first locative *yú* 于 means "*to do, to be*" as a verb, while the other *yú* 於 can mean "*to go.*" The verbal use of the benefactive *wèi* 爲 is either "*to help*" or "*to make,*" in which case it is pronounced as *wéi* in Modern Standard Chinese. The comitative *yǔ* 與 is also a verb meaning "*to give, to wait.*" Here's an example with the instrumental *yǐ*.

(12) *Shì   yǐ   wèi zhī  wén      yě*                          (*The Analects*)
    是　以　謂　之　文　也。
    this  with call  him cultured PAR
    "With this, people call him Wén."

In this example, the pronoun "*shì*" is the object of the preposition "*yǐ*." A literal translation of "*shì yǐ*" is "*with this*," but more naturally, it means "*because of this.*"

We have discussed major word classes in Classical Chinese. The next two sections deal with word order, sentence formation, and special grammatical constructions in Classical Chinese.

## 6.4   Basic word order

The basic word order in Classical Chinese is subject-verb-object. Let's abbreviate this simply as SVO. Example (10) cited previously is a perfect example. However, there are many cases where the object can be placed before the verb or a coverb, that is, a preposition. For example, in (12), the object of the preposition *yǐ* is pre-posed, as is often the case with the preposition *yǐ*. In this sense, the word *yǐ* is not exactly a preposition anymore but rather a postposition.

The most common type of pre-verbal object occurs in negative sentences, where the object, if it is a pronoun, is normally put before the verb, such as in (13).

(13) *Suì   bù   wǒ   yǔ*                                      (*The Analects*)
    歲　不　我　與。
    year  not  us   wait
    "The years do not wait for us." (Trans. James Legge)

Compared to the object "*wǒ*" in (5) and (6) in a post-verbal position in an affirmative sentence, the "*wǒ*" in (13) is pre-verbal in a negative sentence.

Another type of pre-verbal object is interrogative pronouns, such as *hé* 何 and *shuí* 誰. For example:

(14) *Xiānshēng  jiāng  hé  zhī*                    (*The Mencius*)
　　 先生　　　將　　何　之。
　　 master　　 will　 where go
　　 "Master, where are you going?" (Trans. James Legge)

(15) *Wú  shuí  qī*                                 (*The Analects*)
　　 吾　誰　欺 ?
　　 I　 who　impose-upon
　　 "Whom should I impose upon?" (Trans. James Legge)

Besides these two types of pre-verbal objects, there are special functional words, such as *zhī* 之 and *shì* 是, which can be used to extract the object and put it in front of the verb. Pre-verbal objects are quite common in pre-classical works such as the *Shījīng*. Although generally speaking, Chinese from the earliest records has always been predominantly SVO, the existence of pre-verbal objects in Classical Chinese and earlier times suggests that such an SOV word order might be a Proto-Sino-Tibetan feature, since both Tibetan and Burmese are SOV languages. The fact that the object of *yǐ* in Classical Chinese can often be pre-posed, thus making the word *yǐ* a postposition, is interesting, since according to Greenberg (1963: 45), "with overwhelmingly greater than chance frequency, languages with normal SOV order are postpositional."

Besides basic word order, prepositional phrases can either precede or follow the verb, but the tendencies with each preposition vary. Phrases with *yǐ* or *wèi* can appear on either side of the verb. For example, in (16), the prepositional phrase "*yǐ shí*" follows the verb-object "*shǐ mín*," while in (17), the prepositional phrase "*yǐ yán yǐ*" precedes the verb "*bì*."

(16) *Shǐ  mín  yǐ  shí*                             (*The Analects*)
　　 使　民　以　時。
　　 use　people with　time
　　 "Employ the people according to the seasons."

(17) *Yì  yán  yǐ  bì  zhī*                          (*The Analects*)
　　 一　言　以　蔽　之。
　　 one　word　with cover it
　　 "To summarize it with one phrase."

Worth noting here in example (17) is that the object "*yì yán*" of the preposition "*yǐ*" precedes the preposition "*yǐ*." If we consider the "*yǐ*" a coverb, then this OV word order is consistent with example (12), which might be a remnant feature of the earlier SOV word order. If we consider the word "*yǐ*" a postposition, as opposed to a preposition, it is also consistent with the overall SOV word order, according to Greenberg's (1963: 45) generalization.

Phrases with the comitative *yǔ* generally only occur in front of the verb, as in (18). In contrast, phrases with the preposition *yú* tend to follow the verb, as in (19).

(18)  *Yǔ    péngyǒu  jiāo    ér  bú  xìn    hū*          (*The Analects*)
     與    朋友    交    而 不 信    乎?
     With friends    interact and not sincere QUES
     "Have I been sincere or not when I interact with my friends?"

(19)  *Fūzǐ    zhì    yú shì bāng    yě*          (*The Analects*)
     夫子    至    於 是 邦    也。
     Confucius arrive at    this country PAR
     "When the master arrives at this country, . . ."

Furthermore, modifiers generally precede the nouns or verbs that they modify. In (20), the monosyllabic adjective "*qiáng*" can modify the noun "*guó*" directly, while in (21), two adjectives are used to modify the noun "*guān*" with the help of a structural marker of modifiers, that is, *zhī*, here indicated by the label "MOD."[9] This marker often intervenes between the modifier and the modified.

(20)  *Jìn    qiáng    guó yě*          (*Hán Shī Wài Zhuàn*)
     晉,    強    國 也。
     State of Jin powerful  state PAR
     "The State of Jin is a powerful state."

(21)  *Dà    xiǎo  zhī  guān*          (*Qián Fū Lùn*)
     大    小    之  官
     big    small  MOD  officials
     "government officials of higher and lower ranks"

Sometimes a modifier can appear after a noun that it modifies. In (22), the adjective "*lì*" follows the noun phrase "*zhuǎ yǎ*" with the help of the modifier marker "*zhī*." Such post-nominal adjectives can be found in pre-classical texts such as the *Shījīng* as well. Post-nominal modifiers are usually longer phrases formed with the word *zhě* 者, as shown in (23). The *zhě* is sometimes classified as a special type of pronoun, although its function is to turn a verb phrase into a nominal one, thus being a nominalizer. The nominalized phrase in (23) is "*kě shǐ bào Qín zhě*." It modifies the preceding noun "*rén*." In Literary Chinese, the marker of modifiers "*zhī*" is also used frequently between the noun and the post-nominal modifier phrase.

(22) *Yĭn        wú        zhuǎ yá    zhī    lì*                    (*The Xúnzĭ*)
     蚓          無          爪 牙      之      利。
     earthworm not-have claw tooth MOD sharp
     "The earthworm does not have sharp claws or teeth."

(23) *Qiú    rén    kě shĭ        bào    Qín        zhé*          (*Shĭ Jì*)
     求      人      可 使        報      秦          者。
     look-for person can be-envoy report State of Qin NOM
     "They looked for a person who could serve as an envoy to report to the Qin."

In general, modifiers of verbs, such as adverbs, manner, directions, and so on, also precede the verb in Classical Chinese.

## 6.5   Special grammatical constructions

This section discusses three types of nominalizations with the nominalizers *zhě* 者, *suǒ* 所, and *zhī* 之, equative sentences and passive constructions.

First let's look at nominalization, which is a process of turning a verbal structure into a nominal phrase. Since adjectives, or rather "*stative verbs,*" in Classical Chinese share similar properties with verbs, nominalization can be applied to adjectives as well. According to Xiang (1993), neither *zhě* 者 nor *suǒ* 所 can be found in the oracle bone script or the bronze script in the Shang and Western Zhou dynasties. These two nominalizers seem to be later developments in the Spring and Autumn period. The word *zhě* can be attached to a verbal structure or an adjective, and the nominalized structure as a whole refers to the subject of the verb or the adjective. For example, from "*zhī*" (知, "to know") and *zhī* (之, "it"), we can derive "*zhī zhī zhě*" (知之者), which can be paraphrased as "*those who know it.*" This use is similar to the agentive suffix -*er* in English, such as in "*knower,*" "*doer,*" "*writer,*" and so on. Besides verbs, *zhě* may nominalize an adjective, such as when it is attached to "*gāo*" (高, "tall") to derive "*gāo zhě*" (高者), meaning "*that which is tall.*" Similarly, the structure "*kě shĭ bào Qín zhě*" in (23) previously can be paraphrased as "*those who can serve as an envoy to report to the Qin.*"

The second type of nominalization is formed with the word *suǒ* 所, which is also classified as a pronoun, or rather a nominalizer whose function is to turn a verbal structure into the noun phrase referring to the object of the verb. Thus, its function is the opposite of that of *zhě*, if we consider the subject and object positions opposites. For example, from "*zhī*" (知, "to know"), we can derive "*suǒ zhī*" (所知), which refers to "*that which is known*" or "*what is known.*"

Both *zhě* and *suǒ* are still quite commonly used in Modern Standard Chinese. For example, *zhě* can be used as an agentive suffix comparable to the English -*er*. Words like "*xué zhě*" (學者, "study + *zhě*" → "scholar"), "*dú zhě*" (讀者, "read + *zhě*" → "reader"), and "*zuò zhě*" (作者, "write + *zhě*" → "writer") are just a few examples. *Suǒ* is often used in more formal or idiomatic expressions, such as in "*suǒ jiàn suǒ wén*" (所見所聞 "suǒ see suǒ hear" → "what is seen and what is heard").

The third type of nominalization is *zhī* 之, which is used between the subject and the predicate of a sentence to turn it into a subordinate clause. In this case, the verbal structure is complete with its subject and object, in contrast to the verbal structures in the *zhě* nominalization, which do not have a subject, and the verbal structures in the *suǒ* nominalization, which do not have an object.

(24) *Zé   wú   wàng   mín   zhī   duō   yú   lín      guó   yě*   (*The Mencius*)
     則   無   望     民    之    多    於   鄰      國    也。
     then not  hope   people NOM many than neighbor state PAR
     "Then you should not hope that the people in your state will become more than your neighboring states."

In (24), the part "*mín zhī duō yú lín guó yě*" after the verb "*wàng*" is the object of the verb. If the word *zhī* is taken out of the object clause, then we get a full stand-alone sentence "*mín duō yú lín guó*" ("the people are more than the neighboring state"). The function of "*zhī*" here is to turn this stand-alone sentence into a nominal component that can be the object of the verb "*wàng*." To some extent, this can be compared to structures such as the English sentence "*I appreciate your taking time to discuss this with me*" in which the original sentence "*you take time to discuss this with me*" is turned into a nominal phrase with the subject in the possessive case, that is, "*your taking time to discuss this with me*." Interestingly, the word *zhī* 之 in (24) is actually also the most common marker in possessive phrases in Classical Chinese, such as shown in (25).

(25) *Yǐ   zǐ   zhī   máo   xiàn   zǐ   zhī   dùn*            (*The Hánfēizǐ*)
     以   子   之   矛   陷   子   之   楯。
     with you POSS spear sink  you POSS shield
     "(What if we try to) break your shield with your spear?"

Here "*zǐ*" 子 is the polite form of addressing a person, and "*zhī*" 之 is similar to a possessive particle, such as the "*s*" in "*Jane's book*" in English. Thus, "*zǐ zhī máo*" can be translated as "*your spear*." The use of "*zhī*" to turn a sentence into a subordinate clause, as shown in (24), can be considered an extension of the possessive *zhī*, similarly to how the subject of an object clause can be in the possessive case in English.

Next let's discuss a special type of sentence called the equative, which has more or less the same function as a modern copula structure, although there is no copula verb used in the equative sentence of Classical Chinese. The equative pattern is ". . . (*zhě* 者) . . . *yě* 也." The word *zhě* 者 is the same as the nominalizer *zhě* 者 mentioned previously. But its function is now a subject marker, although it can be omitted in the equative sentence pattern. The particle *yě* 也 is one of many sentence-final particles in Classical Chinese to express various types of sentential meanings or modalities, such as the interrogative, the factual, surprise, and so on. In (26), there are two equative sentences. The word "*yě*" expresses a factual meaning. It is where the "*copula*" sense comes from in this pattern. The subject marker *zhě* is used in both clauses of (26), but in (27), the *zhě* is omitted.

(26)  *Jūn  zhě  zhōu  yě,    shùrén     zhě  shuǐ  yě*                (*The Xúnzǐ*)
　　　君　者，舟　也；庶人　　　者，水　　也。
　　　ruler SUBJ boat　PAR　commoner SUBJ water PAR
　　　"The ruler is the boat; the people are the water."

(27)  *Dǒng Hú  gǔ    zhī  liáng  shǐ      yě*                        (*Shǐ Jì*)
　　　董狐，　　古　之　良　史　　也。
　　　Dong Hu　ancient POSS good　historian PAR
　　　"Dong Hu was a great historian in ancient time."

A similar way of expressing the copula sentence is by employing the verb *wéi* 爲, as in (28). The negative counterpart of the equative sentence is formed with the negator *fēi* 非 in the pattern "...*fēi* 非 ... (*yě* 也)," as shown in (29). The interrogative form of the equative sentence is constructed via the question particle *yú* 歟, as in (30), which is different from the general question particle *hū* 乎 from example (18) previously.

(28)  *zǐ     wéi   shuí*                                            (*The Analects*)
　　　子　爲　誰？
　　　you　be　who
　　　"Who are you, sir?"

(29)  *Fēi   wú    tú     yě*                                       (*The Analects*)
　　　非　吾　徒　也。
　　　NEG　my　disciple PAR
　　　"(He) is not my disciple."

(30)  *Fūzǐ      shèngzhě  yú*                                     (*Bái Hǔ Tōng*)
　　　夫子　　聖者　　歟？
　　　Confucius sage　　QUES
　　　"Is Confucius a sage?"

As for passive constructions, there are many different ways of expressing passivity in Classical Chinese. In some cases, a verb can be used in the passive sense without any help of passive markers, and the passive meaning has to be deduced from the context, for example, in (31), where the verb "*zhū*" 誅 is used as a passive, since according to the context of the discussion, it refers to a punishment for a petty crime as contrasted to situations where people who stole the whole country were awarded with noble titles. Note the use of *zhě* with a verbal structure is a typical example of nominalization.

(31)  *Qiè   gōu   zhě   zhū*                              (*The Zhuāngzǐ*)
      竊     鉤     者     誅。
      steal hook NOM kill
      "One who steals a hook is to be killed."

Alternatively, the word "*wéi*" 爲 can be used as the agentive marker, similar to the preposition "*by*" in English, for example, in (32).

(32)  *Wéi   tiānxià   xiào*                              (*Shǐ Jì*)
      爲     天下       笑。
      by     world      laugh
      "He was laughed at by the whole world."

Actually, the more typical passive construction in Classical Chinese is "(subject) + *wéi* 爲 + agent + *suǒ* 所 + verb," in which the subject is often the patient, while the noun after *wéi* 爲 is usually the agent, as in (33).

(33)  *Wéi   rén   suǒ   yí*                              (*The Xúnzǐ*)
      為     人     所     疑。
      by     people NOM doubt
      "He is doubted by people."

Additionally, two other words, that is, *jiàn* 見 and *bèi* 被, can also be used in front of a verb to signal a passive reading, for example, in (34). The word *jiàn* is a passive marker, and if the agent is needed, it can be introduced by the preposition *yú* following the verb, for example, in (35). The word *bèi* is originally a noun, meaning "*sleep cover, quilt*." In the structure in (34), it is followed by a verb. In this case, it can be interpreted metaphorically to mean "*to experience, to undergo*." Let's call this the BEI-construction in Classical Chinese. The verbs used in this construction normally would have a negative connotation, for example, the verb "*slander*" in (34).

(34)  *Xìn   ér   jiàn yí,   zhōng ér   bèi   bàng*         (*Shǐ Jì*)
      信     而   見   疑,   忠     而   被     謗。
      sincere and PASS doubt loyal   and suffer slander
      "He was sincere but was doubted, and loyal but was slandered."

(35)  *Wú   cháng   jiàn   xiào   yú   dàfāngzhījiā*        (*The Zhuāngzǐ*)
      吾     長       見     笑     於   大方之家。
      I     long     PASS   laugh by   wise people
      "I would have been laughed at for long by those wise people."

In summary, this chapter provides a brief sketch of Classical Chinese grammar, with its morphological devices and sentence patterns based upon the usual classes of words, such as nouns, verbs, adjectives, prepositions, and so on. There might have been more morphological devices in pre-classical times, and, more interestingly, the basic word order could have been SOV in much earlier times, which would then be in line with the Proto-Sino-Tibetan word order, as still retained in modern Tibeto-Burman languages. In the next chapter, we discuss how the grammar of Classical Chinese changed in the post-classical times.

## Notes

1   When example sentences are cited, the first line is the *pīnyīn*. The second line is the corresponding characters. A word-for-word gloss is given on the third line. Then a translation is provided on the fourth line.
2   This is my own translation. All the other translations like this without a note on the translator are my translations.
3   The translations of Classical Chinese examples in this chapter are often those by James Legge (1815–1897), as indicated here. Although his translations are nowadays considered not entirely accurate, and for research purposes in Chinese philosophy and literature, the quality of the translations is one of the most important considerations for valid conclusions, such issues with translations do not actually matter for our purposes, because grammatical analyses are based on the original examples and the glosses and do not hinge upon any particular translation.
4   The *N-* represents the positional allophones of either *n-* or *ŋ-*.
5   The word 折 *shé* had the initial 禪. In Li's (1980) system, the initial 禪 is reconstructed as *z-*, and thus in Li's (1980) reconstruction, 折 *shé* should be *zjet*. But as mentioned in footnote 4 of Chapter 4, according to Baxter (1992: 52–54), the reconstructed sound of the initial 禪 should be *dz-*. Thus, the word 折 *shé* should be *dzjet*. We use this reconstruction here because it corresponds better to the initial *tɕ-* of the word 折 *zhé*.
6   Norman (1988: 85) translated 清濁別義 as "*derivation by manner of articulation.*"
7   The French sinologist Jean-Pierre Abel-Rémusat (1788–1832) published a book in 1822 titled *Élémens de la grammaire chinoise, ou, Principes généraux du kou-wen ou style antique, et du kouan-hoa, c'est-à-dire, de la langue commune généralement usitée dans l'Empire chinois* [*Elements of Chinese grammar, or General principles of Gǔwén or ancient style, and of Guānhuà, that is, of the common language generally used in the Chinese Empire*] (Paris: Impremerie Royale), in which he discussed Chinese characters, spoken Chinese, and Literary Chinese grammar. He classified Literary Chinese words in categories such as nouns, adjectives, verbs, and so on.
8   This is my own translation.
9   This example is similar to example (50) from Norman (1988: 104).

# 7 Vernacular writing

According to Jiang (2005: 1–6), the grammatical development of Chinese can be divided into three stages: Ancient Chinese (12th century BC to 10th century AD), Early Modern Chinese (10th to mid-18th centuries), and Modern Chinese (mid-18th century to present).[1] This chapter discusses how Classical Chinese grammar developed in the post-classical period, especially since the 10th century, as attested in vernacular writing from Early Modern Chinese in Jiang's (2005) terminology.

## 7.1 Diglossia

Classical Chinese, in the form of Literary Chinese, continued to function as the official written language of Chinese after the Han dynasty, but the actual spoken varieties of Chinese increasingly diverged from Literary Chinese, resulting in a system of historical bilingualism referred to as diglossia by Ferguson (1959). In many linguistic communities, a superimposed prestigious language is used alongside vernacular varieties, for example, in the Arabic-speaking countries, where Classical Arabic is the prestigious formal language used in settings such as news broadcast, while, in contrast, different modern varieties like Egyptian Arabic are mostly used informally, such as during conversations with family, friends, and colleagues. In this sense, the linguistic situation in pre-modern China is comparable, as Table 7.1 indicates.

On the two sides in Table 7.1, that is, during the eras of Classical Chinese and Modern Standard Chinese, there is one language with its spoken and written forms. Note here some scholars would object to the view that Classical Chinese was based on the spoken language of Old Chinese, as Mair (1994) argues. See Chapter 6 for more discussion on issues with the nature of Classical Chinese.

In Table 7.1, the long period in the middle shows the use of Literary Chinese alongside vernacular writing. The official written language, that is, Literary Chinese, was modeled on Classical Chinese, while the vernacular writing would contain more elements from the spoken language, although instances of classicism have always been present, even in Modern Standard Chinese. Literary Chinese was used in formal settings, such as in government documents and formal literary genres, including poetry and prose writings of Confucian philosophy. It was considered the prestigious language. In contrast, the actual spoken varieties may

*Table 7.1* Diglossia in Chinese

| *5th century BC to AD 200* | *AD 200 to 9th century* | *10th to mid-18th centuries* | *Mid-18th to early 20th centuries* | *Early 20th century to now* |
|---|---|---|---|---|
| Spoken Old Chinese, with written records in Classical Chinese | Literary Chinese modeled on Classical Chinese | | | Modern Standard Chinese in both spoken and written forms |
| | Sporadic vernacular writing | Continued development of vernacular writing into a full-fledged system | | |

be substantially different from the literary language, and correspondingly vernacular writings developed based on spoken varieties for informal uses, such as folk literature (Snow 2013).

Despite the similarity between the types of diglossia in Arabic and Chinese, there is one key distinction that makes the notion of diglossia quite problematic in Chinese. The prestigious form of Arabic is a true spoken language, for example, used on TV in news broadcasts, but as Mair (1994) points out correctly, during the medieval period in China, Literary Chinese was not a real spoken language but strictly used as a written language. In Mair's (1994) term, Literary Chinese is "*unsayable*," because it was not possible to know how to pronounce Chinese characters using authentic pronunciations of that classical language. This is an important difference between Literary Chinese and other classical languages written in phonetic scripts, such as Classical Arabic and Latin. Thus, the prestigious language in the diglossia situation in Chinese is more of a written system but not a spoken one, differing from the typical examples of diglossia.

One other clarification is that even though Literary Chinese is based on Classical Chinese, writers after the Tang dynasty could only imitate Classical Chinese to the extent that they mastered the grammar and vocabulary of Classical Chinese and also as much as their attitudes toward classicism allowed. Therefore, Literary Chinese texts have to be examined carefully if they are used as records to study the grammatical development of Chinese. In many cases, the authors of Literary Chinese used their own spoken language grammar and vocabulary. Such instances can actually help us glimpse the actual spoken language of those ancient times. But systematic studies of the grammar of the spoken language in the post-classical period rely on real vernacular writing.

## 7.2    Sources of vernacular writing

The origins of vernacular writing of Mandarin can be traced to a time period well before the Tang dynasty. There are sporadic records of the spoken language, such as in early Buddhist works from the Eastern Han dynasty onward, and also folk songs, verses, and stories. More systematic vernacular writing would be found during and after the Tang dynasty.

Arguably the most important type of vernacular writing in Chinese is the *biàn-wén* 變文 ("transformation text"), the discovery of which is quite remarkable. In 1900, at the ancient Buddhist site at Dunhuang in northwestern China on the ancient Silk Road, *Wáng Yuánlù* 王圓籙, a Daoist priest, while cleaning up a deserted and dilapidated section of the Mogao Caves, discovered a hidden room full of ancient manuscripts and reported this discovery to the authority immediately. The government showed only lukewarm interest in such a seemingly trivial matter. However, the news of the hidden room caught the attention of Aurel Stein, a Hungarian-British archaeologist, who traveled to Dunhuang in 1907 and bought manuscripts from *Wáng Yuánlù*. Then, in 1908, Paul Pelliot, a French sinologist, followed Aurel Stein's steps to Dunhuang and bought a large number of manuscripts. Eventually Chinese scholars took notice of these ancient texts, and the government ordered the manuscripts to be transported to Beijing in 1910. The room discovered by *Wáng Yuánlù* was later named the Library Cave. The manuscripts in the Library Cave, dated between the 5th and 11th centuries AD, are now dispersed around the world, mostly in Beijing, London, and Paris. These ancient written records proved to be extremely valuable materials for the study of Chinese history and culture. Of special importance to linguistic research is a type of Buddhist text called *biànwén*, which had its origins in the Tang dynasty, when stories from Buddhist scriptures and Chinese folklore were adapted to be accessible to the common people. Naturally, these texts were written in a language that was close to the actual spoken language of the audience. These vernacular writings are valuable records of the Chinese language during the Tang dynasty and Five Dynasties period.

The *biànwén* texts are the most systematic early records of vernacular writing, and they influenced subsequent development of other types of vernacular writing in Chinese, especially drama and fiction works since the Yuan dynasty. In addition to folk literature, vernacular writing can also be found in a genre called *yǔlù* 語錄 (literally "records of spoken words"), which are dialogues between Chan Buddhist masters and their students during the Tang and Song dynasties. There are also records of dialogues between Neo-Confucian scholars from the Song dynasty, such as *Zhū Xī* 朱熹 (1130–1200), and their students. Moreover, sporadic records of the spoken language may be identified in texts that are primarily in Literary Chinese, such as history books and poetry.

It is important to point out that purely vernacular writing is very rare in Chinese, because in most of the types of texts mentioned previously, including the *biànwén*, the language contains both Literary Chinese and vernacular elements.

Texts in vernacular writing are the main basis for the study of grammatical change. The research method primarily relies on comparisons of written records from different periods in order to discover changes in the grammar pertaining to the lexicon, word order, syntactic structures, and semantic interpretations. Thus, how much we can conclude about a certain grammatical feature depends on the availability of written records and how extensive the research is. Sometimes earlier records are discovered, so that our hypothesis about when certain grammatical phenomena first appeared can be pushed back in time.

## 7.3 Morphological developments

As in Chapter 6 on Classical Chinese grammar, we discuss the morphology and syntax of vernacular writing in this chapter, often in comparison with Classical Chinese to show the changes and new developments. Let's take a look at the morphology of vernacular writing first. In terms of morphological processes, that is, affixing, reduplication, and compounding, these all became more common in vernacular writing.

For example, the prefix *ā* 阿, introduced in Chapter 6, is attested first in the *Shǐjì* dated between the 2nd and 1st centuries BC. It can be attached to names to indicate a sense of familiarity and affection. This prefix became more commonly used in the post-Han era. One famous example is the infant name "*Ā Dǒu*"[2] (阿斗) of emperor *Liú Shàn* 劉禪 of the State of *Shǔ* 蜀 in the Three Kingdoms period. Because of *Liú Shàn*'s lack of leadership ability or ambition, the name *Ā Dǒu* has become a trope for a person who does not live up to expectations. The prefix *ā-* can also be attached to kinship terms. The following words are all attested in texts from the end of the Han dynasty to the Northern and Southern dynasties: *ā-fù* (阿父, *ā* + "father" → "dad"), *ā-shū* (阿叔, *ā* + "uncle" → "uncle"), *ā-nǚ* (阿女, *ā* + "daughter" → "daughter"), and so on. This prefix is still quite common in modern times, especially in southern Chinese dialects. Interestingly, *ā-* could also be attached to pronouns in vernacular writing, such as *shuí* (誰, "who") and *nǐ* (你, "you"), to form *ā-shuí* 阿誰 and *ā-nǐ* 阿你. But in Modern Standard Chinese, *ā-* cannot be used with pronouns anymore.

Many new prefixes developed in the post-classical era, for example, the word "*lǎo*" 老 originally meant "*old*," but after the Northern and Southern dynasties, "*lǎo-*" gradually became a prefix of familiarity used in front of names of persons or animals. The Tang poet *Yuán Zhěn* 元稹 was called "*Lǎo Yuán* 老元" by another famous poet, *Bái Jūyì* 白居易 in one of his poems. The modern nouns of "*lǎoshǔ*" (老鼠, "mouse") and "*lǎohǔ*" (老虎, "tiger") can be found in texts from the Tang and Song dynasties.

As for suffixes, "*ér*" (兒) originally meant "*son*" but developed into a diminutive suffix, mostly of nouns of animals as early as the Tang dynasty, for example, *yú'ér* (魚兒, "fish" + *ér* → "small fish"), *yàn'ér* (雁兒, "wild goose" + *ér* → "small wild goose"). In Modern Standard Chinese, the suffix -*ér* 兒 is often unstressed or incorporated into the preceding syllable. But many of such -*ér* examples from the Tang dynasty are found in poems, and judging by the poetic rules, these suffixes were still full syllables with full tones in Tang poetry. By the Song dynasty, it became more common after other types of nouns, such as objects or things, for example, *dié'ér* (碟兒, "plate" + *ér* → "saucer"), *guàn'ér* (罐兒, "jar" + *ér* → "a smaller jar").

Reduplication continued to be a major morphological process. Besides the reduplication of adjectives and sound imitations, kinship terms could also take such forms, for example, *gēge* (哥哥, "brother"), attested in Tang dynasty (Pan 1989: 57). In Modern Standard Chinese, most kinship terms can have such reduplicated forms.

Although in Classical Chinese, words were predominantly monosyllabic, there were already many compound words. In later times in the post-classical period, compounding became a major morphological device of creating new words, especially disyllabic ones. This trend to have more words with two syllables is called disyllabification. One of the reasons for disyllabification is due to simplification of the phonological system, causing formerly distinct syllables to become homophones. For example, the Classical Chinese word for "*arrow*" is 箭 *\*[tsʲ]en-s* in Old Chinese and *tsjɛn* with the *qù* tone in Middle Chinese, and the word for "*sword*" is 劍 *\*s.kr[a]m-s* in Old Chinese and *kjɐm* with the *qù* tone in Middle Chinese, but both of them are pronounced as *jiàn* in Modern Standard Chinese. Similar simplifications created more homophonous words that were not homophones before. But according to Pan (1989), the proliferation of compounding and especially disyllabic words in the post-classical era cannot merely be attributed to the simplification of the phonological system. He lists three counterarguments. First, the phonological reconstructions of Middle Chinese are actually more complex than Old Chinese. Many categories of sounds in Old Chinese diverged into different sounds in Middle Chinese. Actually, in Old Chinese, there were already a lot of homophones. If it is partially due to the simplification of sounds that more words became disyllabic after Middle Chinese, we cannot maintain the same explanation of such a trend before Middle Chinese. The reason for disyllabification might lie in the generalized use of the *shuāngshēng* and *diéyùn* method in the post-classical era, for example, in the formation of compound words. In Classical Chinese, according to Pan (1989), compounding may have already been related to *shuāngshēng* and *diéyùn*, for example, *qīnqi* (親戚, "relatives") and *sīsuǒ* (思索, "ponder") in the *shuāngshēng* category and *pānyuán* (攀援, "climb") in the *diéyùn* category. By analogy, this type of compounding may be generalized to combine monosyllabic words, for example, *kǒngjù* (恐懼, "fear"), *jǐnshèn* (謹慎, "cautious"), *biànhuà* (變化, "change"), and so on. Pan's (1989) third reason is that many phrases, for example, *rìshí* (日蝕, "solar eclipse") and *yuèshí* (月蝕, "lunar eclipse"), became compound words due to conventional use. Such a process can be considered a type of lexicalization, in which a former unit of language larger than the word became fixed as a lexical item. On a related note, affixing and reduplication, as discussed previously, also contributed to the growth of disyllabic words, besides compounding.

## 7.4 Word classes in the vernacular

In Classical Chinese, there are two main words for the first-person pronoun, that is, *wǒ* 我 and *wú* 吾. In the post-classical era, *wǒ* gradually became the predominant form in the spoken language, while *wú* still lingered on in writing. The division of labor between *wǒ* and *wú* in Classical Chinese disappeared both in writing and in the spoken language. In Classical Chinese, the pronoun *wǒ* originally tended to function as the object of a verb, but we find examples where *wú* can be used in such a position after the Han dynasty. Sentence (1) is from the 3rd century.

(1)  *Jīn    rén    guī    wú*                              (*Sānguó Zhì*)
今    人    歸    吾。
now   people  affiliate  me
"Now these people are coming to me."

It should be noted that even though *wú* 吾 was used in vernacular writing in the post-classical era, it is not definite proof that the word still existed in the spoken language. It might have been preserved as an instance of classicism, since writing in many ways is more conservative. Actually, the word *wú* 吾 may have gradually become obsolete in the spoken language by the Tang dynasty (Norman 1988: 118). In addition to *wǒ* 我 and *wú* 吾, a new word for the first-person pronoun, *nóng* 儂, appeared as early as the Eastern Jin dynasty. It was mostly a dialect form used in the *Wu* 吳 and *Chu* 楚 regions, which are roughly the present-day Jiangsu-Zhejiang area and the Hunan-Hubei area, respectively. In modern *Wu* 吳 dialects, the second-person pronoun form is also 儂, but the connection between the early vernacular form of 儂 as a first-person pronoun and the current Wu 吳 dialect word 儂 as second-person pronoun is not clear.

The second-person pronouns in Classical Chinese, that is, *ěr* 爾 and *rǔ* 汝, were simplified. *Ěr* (Middle Chinese: *ȵzjě* with the *shǎng* tone) developed into *nǐ* 你 (Middle Chinese: *nǐ* with the *shǎng* tone) in the colloquial form, although *rǔ* was also widely used in vernacular writing until the Song dynasty. But according to Xiang (1993: 233), in vernacular writing such as the *biànwén* from the Tang dynasty, *nǐ* was predominantly used already. The second-person pronoun in Modern Standard Chinese is still *nǐ* 你.

The third-person pronouns in Classical Chinese, that is, *qí* 其 and *zhī* 之, had a division of labor, with *qí* being used as a possessive and *zhī* as the object of a verb. But in post-classical times, a new form, *qú* 渠, appeared in the 3rd century. Two other third-person pronouns also developed, that is, *tā* 他 and *yī* 伊, both of which can be used as the subject and the object. The word *tā* 他 in Classical Chinese means "*other*," and its pronominal use is widely attested in texts from as early as the Tang dynasty. The word *yī* 伊 is a demonstrative pronoun meaning "*that*" in Classical Chinese. Its use as a third-person pronoun is attested in texts from the Northern and Southern dynasties, and it is used widely in subsequent written sources. But the distribution of these three new forms of pronouns in modern Chinese dialects is different. The pronoun *tā* 他 is used mostly in Mandarin dialects; *yī* 伊 is used in some Wu and Min dialects; and *qú* 渠 is used mostly in the Yue, Kejia, and some Min dialects.

In Classical Chinese, there was no distinction between singular and plural pronouns such as that between "*I*" and "*we*." The word *wú* 吾 can mean either "*I*" or "*we*." If a distinction is needed, then a word that refers to a group of people such as *chái* 儕 can be attached to a pronoun, for example, *wúchái* 吾儕 ("we"). In the post-classical era, forms such as *wǒbèi* 我輩, in which the word *bèi* 輩 refers to a group of people, appeared in the Northern and Southern dynasties. According to Lü (1984), the word *bèi* 輩 developed into *mí* 弭 in the Tang dynasty, for example, *wǒmí* 我弭 ("we"), which could be regarded as the early form of the plural suffix

-*men* 們 in Modern Standard Chinese, such as in *wǒmen* 我們 ("we"), *nǐmen* 你們 ("you" plural), and *tāmen* 他們 ("they"). The word *mí* 弭 further developed into *mèn* 懣 and some other related forms in the Song dynasty. In the Yuan dynasty, it was written as *měi* 每 in northern vernacular writings. But by the Ming dynasty, the morpheme -*men* 們 with a form and function similar to its Modern Standard Chinese counterpart was already commonly used.

In Modern Standard Chinese, there is a polite form of the second-person pronoun, that is, *nín* 您, which is comparable to the French polite form of "*vous*," Spanish "*usted*," or German "*Sie*." The word *nín* is attested in texts from as early as the Song dynasty, as a contracted form of *nǐmen* 你們 ("you" plural). But in its early use, *nín* 您 could be used for both the singular and plural forms of the second-person pronoun, and it did not have a polite connotation. In Modern Standard Chinese, *nín* 您 is used as polite form of the second-person pronoun, both singular and plural. Therefore, if addressed to more than one person in a polite form, *nín* 您 is still considered a more correct form than *nínmen* 您們, although *nínmen* 您們 is used by some speakers.

The pronouns for "*this*" and "*that*" are *cǐ* 此 and *bǐ* 彼 in Classical Chinese. But these words were replaced by new forms in the post-classical period. The word *zhè* 這 and its variant forms are attested in texts from the Tang dynasty. Wang (1958) proposed that *zhè* came from the Classical Chinese word *zhī* 之, which, apart from being an object third-person pronoun, could also be used as a demonstrative pronoun meaning "*this*." Thus, to some extent, both in terms of meaning and pronunciation, *zhī* 之 is a possible source for *zhè* 這. The word for "*that*" is *nà* 那, which appeared as early as in the Tang dynasty. The character 那 was originally used for the word *nǎ*, meaning "*how*" during the late Han and Three Kingdoms period. But subsequently, a new character, 哪, was created for this interrogative meaning, while the character 那 was reserved for the demonstrative pronoun "*that*." The origin of "*nà*" is not quite clear yet.

As for the interrogative pronouns such as "*who*" and "*what*," the word *shuí* 誰 ("who") has not changed much since Classical Chinese. In Modern Standard Chinese, it is still the standard form for "*who*." In Classical Chinese, the word *hé* 何 can be used as "*what*," "*how*," "*where*," and "*why*." However, the modern word *shénme* 什麼 for "*what*" came from *shíwù* 什物 or *shìwù* 是物, attested in its original meaning, "*miscellaneous utensils*," as early as in the Northern and Southern dynasties (Zhang 1982; Norman 1988). The word *shénme* 什麼, with the meaning "*what*," is attested in texts from the Tang dynasty. The Middle Chinese initial of *wù* 物 is *m-*. Thus, phonologically speaking, the Modern Standard Chinese "*shénme*" could be a reduced form of *shíwù*.

Another major development in post-classical times is the proliferation of measure words. In Modern Standard Chinese, a noun phrase such as "*three people*" generally requires a measure word between the number and the noun, for example, *sān gè rén* ("three + measure-word + person"). Measure words could already be found in the oracle bone script in the Shang dynasty, and the number of measure words continued to grow ever since. In Classical Chinese, however, measure words were not used between numbers and nouns, as shown in the phrase "*sānrén xíng*

三人行" ("three people walk") from the *Analects*. If a measure word is needed, the number and measure word combination follows the noun, for example, *chē sì shèng* 車四乘 ("chariot" + "four" + "measure word") → "four chariots"). Thus, let's call the structure "number + measure word" a Classifier Phrase, since the more general term for "*measure word*" is "*classifier*." To some extent, these post-nominal classifier phrases in Classical Chinese can be regarded as either a post-nominal modifier or some kind of predicate. One of the most common measure words is *gè* 個, attested in Classical Chinese already as a measure for arrows, as shown in (2).

(2)  *Fù    fú      shǐ    wǔshí   gè*                    (*The Xúnzǐ*)
     負     服      矢      五十    個。
     carry  quiver  arrow  fifty   CL
     "(Ask them to) carry quivers of fifty arrows."

In (2), "*gè*" is the measure word, labeled as CL in the gloss, which is an abbreviation of "*classifier*." The classifier phrase "*wǔshí gè*" follows the noun that it modifies. Although in terms of the original meaning of "*gè*," it actually refers to bamboo stalks, and the majority of examples of *gè* in Classical Chinese are used as the measure word for arrows made of bamboo, the measure word *gè* could be used for animals and people in Classical Chinese sometimes as well. In post-classical period, *gè* could be more generally applied to people, animals, and abstract nouns by the Tang dynasty. At the same time, with the increase in the number of measure words, the classifier phrase also moved to the front of the modified noun. At least by the Northern and Southern dynasties, examples such as (3) emerged:

(3)  *Jiàn rén   dú    shù    shí juǎn shū,   biàn zì    gāo  dà* (*Yánshì Jiāxùn*)
     見 人      讀     數      十 卷 書,      便 自      高   大。
     see people read several ten CL  book then self tall   big
     "We see that some people became self-conceited just after reading several volumes of books."

In example (3), the phrase "*shù shí juàn shū*" has the structure of "number + measure-word + noun," which contrasts with the phrase "*fú shǐ wǔshí gè*" in example (2), which has the structure "noun + number + measure-word." Therefore, by this time, the position of the classifier phrase had changed to prenominal, consistent with other types of modifiers in Chinese in general. This leads the discussion to word order change in the post-classical period.

## 7.5  Word order in the post-classical era

In Classical Chinese, a pronoun as the object of the verb in a negative sentence is usually placed before the verb rather than after the verb, as is the case for normal objects. But we do find examples where the object pronoun of a verb in a negative sentence appears after the verb in Classical Chinese and the pre-classical period. For example:

(4) *Ěr    bù    xǔ    wǒ*                                    (*Shàngshū*)
    爾    不    許    我。
    you   not   allow   me
    "If you don't allow me, . . ."

(5) *Yǒu    shì    ér    bú    gào    wǒ*                    (*Zuǒ Zhuàn*)
    有      事     而    不    告     我。
    there-is   affair   and   not   tell   me
    "If there is an affair and you don't tell me, . . ."

Sentence (4) is an example from the pre-classical period, where the object pronoun *wǒ* follows the verb; sentence (5) is from Classical Chinese, where *wǒ* also follows the verb. Thus, it seems that in the pre-classical period, the transition from the preverbal position to the post-verbal position in the case of the object pronoun in a negative sentence was still incomplete. According to Wang (1958), the postverbal position for such pronouns tends to be attested more often from the Han dynasty on, for example:

(6) *Shì    guǒ    bù    zhī    wǒ    yě*                    (*Shuō Yuàn*)
    是      果     不    知     我    也。
    this   indeed   not   know   me   PAR
    "This is indeed an example of not knowing me."

A search within written records from the Han dynasty yields many examples of postverbal pronouns in negative sentences, especially in direct quotations of dialogues contained in passages written in Classical Chinese. Sentence (6) is an example from the Western Han dynasty. The pronoun *wǒ* here follows the verb. The example in (7) is from the Northern and Southern dynasties, which shows the same word order.

(7) *Dìng    bù    rú    wǒ*                                (*Shì Shuō Xīn Yǔ*)
    定       不    如    我。
    definitely   not   compare   me
    "You are definitely not as good as I."

Besides personal pronouns in negative sentences, interrogative pronouns are also placed before the verb as a general rule in Classical Chinese, as mentioned in Chapter 6. To a lesser extent, there are indeed examples where the interrogative pronoun appears after a verb in Classical Chinese, for example:

(8) *Zǐ    xià    yún    hé*                                (*The Analects*)
    子     夏     云     何。
    Zǐ    Xià    say    what
    "What does Zi Xia say?"

In example (8), the interrogative pronoun *hé* is post-verbal. Starting from the Han dynasty, more examples of such post-verbal interrogative pronouns emerged, such as the example in (9), possibly from the late Eastern Han dynasty, although actually the book was compiled during the Northern and Southern dynasties.

(9)  *Chóu    sī       dāng    gào    shuí*            (*Gǔ Shī Shíjiǔ Shǒu*)
    愁      思      當      告    誰?
    sad    thought  should  tell  who
    "To whom should I talk about my sad thoughts?"

Wang (1958) concluded that the transition from the pre-verbal position to the post-verbal position of personal pronouns in negative sentences and interrogative pronouns was evident in Classical Chinese and completed by the Northern and Southern dynasties, when both types of pronouns would be placed after the verb in the spoken language, although in writing, the pre-verbal uses were still existent due to influences from Classical Chinese.

Next, in terms of the change of word order concerning locative phrases with *yú*, originally in Classical Chinese, such locative *yú* phrases would almost always occur after the verb, but by the Han dynasty, pre-verbal locative *yú* phrases could be found. In the following example from the Han dynasty, the locative phrase "*yú dào*" is pre-verbal.

(10)  *Bāo    yú      dào     bìng     sǐ*              (*Hàn Shū*)
     褒     於     道     病     死。
     Bao   at    road  get-sick  die
     "Bao got sick and died on the road."

However, there are examples of both pre-verbal and post-verbal positions of locative phrases with *yú* in the Han dynasty and afterwards. Wang (1958) pointed out that it was not until the appearance of a pre-verbal locative phrase with the preposition *zài* 在, which replaced *yú*, that the locative phrase became predominantly pre-verbal. In Modern Standard Chinese, the typical position of locative phrases with *zài* is still pre-verbal. See Chapter 9 for a more detailed discussion on the semantic differences between pre-verbal *zài* and post-verbal *zài*.

Thus, by the Northern and Southern dynasties, major adjustments of word order in Chinese had already taken place, with all objects occurring after the verb and locative phrases before the verb.

## 7.6  Syntactic changes

This section focuses on some special grammatical constructions and their changes in the post-classical period. Our analysis here is couched in the theory of grammaticalization, or *xūhuà* 虛化 and *yǔfǎhuà* 語法化 in Chinese. Grammaticalization typically refers to the process by which a lexical item develops into a functional grammatical word. In general, a regular lexical item has concrete semantic content, while grammatical words tend to lack such concrete meanings, and, instead, they have functions of various sorts. Another distinction between a lexical item and a grammatical item is that the latter is usually phonologically unstressed and reduced. Thus, the process of grammaticalization is often accompanied by semantic bleaching and phonological weakening. Grammaticalization often proceeds in stages. A lexical item can grammaticalize but retain some of its original meaning, and then it may further grammaticalize until it becomes a purely grammatical word. Campbell (1999) provides an example with the English future modal "*will*." Originally, "*will*" meant "*want*," as still can be seen in such idiomatic expressions as "*if you will*." But now "*will*" is generally used as a future marker, as in "*John will go to China this summer*." Such uses of "*will*" can be contracted, for example, "*I'll*," "*you'll*," and so on, showing phonological reduction. In addition to grammaticalization as a general mechanism, there are three related mechanisms of change, that is, reanalysis, extension, and borrowing.[3]

Reanalysis refers to the change of the underlying structure or semantic relations in a string of words without affecting the surface form of words. Reanalysis depends on the possibility of multiple interpretations. Let's use an example similar to Campbell's (1999) to illustrate how reanalysis happens. The verb "*to go*" as used in (11) can be interpreted in two ways: as a motion verb or involving a purposive reading.

(11)   John is going to study in China this summer.

For the interpretation as a motion verb, (11) means that John will travel to China and study there. But traveling also implies a purpose in doing so. Thus, we have the purposive reading that John will travel to China in order to study there. Since the purposive reading is about what one plans to do in the future, it can be reinterpreted as a future marker to mean that John will study in China this summer.

A typical example of reanalysis can be readily found in the grammaticalization in the post-classical period in Chinese with the development of the copula sentence, comparable to sentences with the verb "*to be*" in English such as "*John is a linguist*." In Classical Chinese, the equative sentence in the pattern ". . . (*zhě* 者), . . . *yě* 也" is used to express the meaning of a copula sentence in Modern Standard Chinese. Since the modern copula verb is *shì* 是 as in "*wǒ shì xuéshēng* 我是學生" ("I am a student"), we may trace the use of the word *shì* in written records of Classical Chinese and post-classical literary and vernacular writings to see how it grammaticalized into the current use. *Shì* 是 originally was a pronoun for "*this*." For example, in (12), the word *shì* is attached to a noun, and it is used exactly as a demonstrative pronoun.

(12)   *Shì niǎo yě,  hǎi yùn   zé    jiāng xǐ     yú nán   míng* (*The Zhuāngzǐ*)
       是   鳥   也，海   運   則   將   徙   於   南   冥。
       this bird PAR sea move then will   move to south ocean
       "When the sea is moved, this bird will migrate to the Southern Ocean."

Another meaning of *shì* 是 in Classical Chinese can be glossed as "*that which is right*," as contrasting with the word *fēi* 非, which means "*that which is wrong*," such as in example (13). The word "*shì*" and "*fēi*" can be considered antonyms.

(13) *Lì      shì     fēi      fēi*                                    (*The Huáinánzǐ*)
　　立 　  是 　  廢 　   非。
　　establish  right   abolish  wrong
　　"(A person of virtue) should establish what is correct and terminate what is wrong."

Oftentimes multiple interpretations are possible for the same structure with the pronoun *shì* 是, especially when it occurs in the middle of a compound sentence, as in example (14).

(14) *Zhī   zhī wéi zhī   zhī,   bù zhī    wéi bù zhī,    shì zhī    yě* (*The Analects*)
　　知 　之 爲 知 　之，不 知 　爲 不 知， 是 知 也。
　　know it  is   know it,  not know  is   not know,  this know PAR
　　"When you know a thing, to hold that you know it; and when you do not know a thing, to allow that you do not know it; – this is knowledge."
　　(Trans. James Legge)

The compound sentence in (14) comprises three clauses: (i) "*zhī zhī wéi zhī zhī* 知之爲知之," (ii) "*bù zhī wéi bù zhī* 不知爲不知," (iii) "*shì zhī yě* 是知也." The third clause, "*shì zhī yě* 是知也," is an equative sentence in the ". . . (*zhě*), . . . *yě*" pattern, with the *zhě* omitted here. The word *shì* 是 here should be interpreted as the pronoun "*this*." Thus, the third clause means "*this is knowing*." Note here the copula verb "*is*" in the translation is derived from the factual particle *yě* but not from the pronoun *shì* 是 itself. The referent of the pronoun *shì* 是 is the first and second clauses. Such is the typical semantic and syntactic structure of this type of sentences in Classical Chinese.

However, the position of the pronoun *shì* 是 makes it possible to interpret the whole structure as a subject-verb-object construction, with the word *shì* 是 functioning as the verb. Let's use a more literal but stilted translation to show the original structure in Chinese more clearly, that is, "<u>*Knowing is knowing and not-knowing is not-knowing*</u>. *This* <u>*knowing is*</u>." In some sense, the first underlined part, that is, "*Knowing is knowing and not-knowing is not-knowing*" can be reanalyzed as the subject; the pronoun *shì* 是 is simply a reiteration of the subject, while the second underlined part, that is, "*knowing is*," which corresponds to "*zhī yě*" in the original Chinese sentence, is the predicate, as explained by Norman (1988: 125). This alternative interpretation would eventually lead to reanalysis of the word *shì* 是 being the copular verb, taking over the equative meaning conveyed originally by "*yě*."

One other motivation that can facilitate the reanalysis of *shì* 是 as a verb is by comparison to its negative form *fēi* 非, which typically functions as the verb in an SVO structure, as Norman (1988) argued, such as shown in (15).

(15) *Zĭ    fēi    wŏ*                                          (*The Zhuāngzĭ*)
　　 子　　非　　我。
　　 you　 NEG　 me
　　 "You are not I."

Therefore, by analogy to such SVO structures with the verb "*fēi*," the reitera-
tive use of the pronoun "*shì*" in (14) can be further reanalyzed as the copula "*to
be*," that is, the opposite of "*fēi*." According to Wang (1958), the copula use of
"*shì*" emerged as early as in the Han dynasty around the 1st century BC, that is,
toward the end of the Western Han and at around the beginning of the Eastern
Han, although Xiang (1993: 326) argues that the copula verb *shì* appeared even
earlier, toward the end of the Warring States period. In the example in (16)
from the Han dynasty, the subject is just a pronoun *qí* 其 ("he"), and it does
not need to be reiterated like in (14) previously. Moreover, the sentence in (16)
does not contain any grammatical particle such as the *yě* used in the equative
pattern. Clearly, the word *shì* in example (16) is the real copula verb "*to be*."

(16) *Qí    shì    wú    dì    yú*                              (*Shĭjì*)
　　 其　　是　　吾　　弟　　與?
　　 he　　is　　 my　　brother　 QUES
　　 "Is he my younger brother?"

Many more similar examples can be found in texts after the Han dynasty. The following two examples are from vernacular writings in the Northern and Southern
dynasties.

(17) *Wèn    jīn    shì    hé    shì*                           (*Táohuāyuán Jì*)
　　 問　　 今　　是　　何　　世。
　　 ask　　now　　is　　 what　 era
　　 "They asked what era it is now."

(18) *Ěr    shì    hé    rén*                                   (*Băi Yù Jīng*)
　　 爾　　是　　何　　人?
　　 you　 are　　what　 person
　　 "Who are you?"

In both (17) and (18), *shì* is situated between two nominal elements, and there is no
particle *yě* at the end of the sentences. As for the negation of the copula sentence,
there are examples from the Northern and Southern dynasties using *fēi* 非 or *fēishì*
非是, as shown in (19) and (20).

(19) *Zhŭ    fēi    Yáo    Shùn*                                (*Shì Shuō Xīn Yǔ*)
　　 主　　 非　　尧　　 舜。
　　 master　 NEG　 Yao　　Shun
　　 "The master is not Yao or Shun (legendary ancient rulers)"

(20) *Chén　　kǒng　cǐ　yào　　　fēi　shì　zhēn　yào* (*Dūnhuáng biànwén jí*)
　　臣　　　恐　　此　药　　　非　是　真　　药。
　　minister afraid this medicine NEG is real medicine
　　"I am afraid that this is not the real medicine."

But as early as the Northern and Southern dynasties, *búshì* 不是 as the negative form of the copula sentence appeared. Example (21) is from the Northern and Southern dynasties. Example (22) is from the Tang dynasty.

(21) *Fù　　bú　　shì　Fú　　Jiān*　　　　　　　　　(*Sòng Shū*)
　　複　　不　　是　苻　　堅。
　　again NEG is Fú Jiān
　　"Moreover I am not *Fú Jiān*."

(22) *Yìng　　dé　　fúróng　bú　shì　huā*　　(from a poem by *Bái Jūyì*)
　　映　　　得　　芙蓉　　不　是　花。
　　reflect COMP hibiscus not be flower
　　"In comparison the hibiscus isn't even a flower."

In both sentences (21) and (22), *búshì* 不是 is used as the negation of *shì* 是. The negative form for the copula is still *búshì* 不是 in Modern Standard Chinese.

According to Xiang (1993), the copula verb *shì* in the Han dynasty tended to be used in conjunction with the sentence-final particle *yě* 也, although such copula sentences did not appear very often in the Han dynasty. But starting from the Northern and Southern dynasties, copula sentences with *shì* 是 became much more common in text with more vernacular elements. For example, Xiang (1993) shows that in the *Shì Shuō Xīn Yǔ* 世說新語 ("*A New Account of the Tales of the World*") compiled during AD 420–479, the number of copula sentences with *shì* 是 is equal to that of the Classical Chinese equative sentences. In the slightly later text *Bǎi Yù Jīng* 百喻經 ("*One Hundred Buddhist Parables*"), the ratio of copula *shì* 是 sentences reaches 90%. Further, in later vernacular writings such at the *biànwén*, the copula verb *shì* 是 is used more frequently, and the sentence-final particle *yě* 也 disappeared as well.

The development of the copula verb *shì* 是 in Modern Standard Chinese is a typical example of reanalysis. Originally, *shì* 是 was used as a reiteration of the subject, which allows for an alternative interpretation of *shì* 是 as the copula verb. Then it became a real copula verb in sentences without the particle *yě* 也. This process was also facilitated in comparison to the use of *fēi* 非 as the negative form of the equative sentence in Classical Chinese. The analogy between *fēi* 非 and *shì* 是 served as a further contributing factor in the reanalysis of the word *shì* 是. On the other hand, the negative form of the copula sentence had variant forms including *fēi* 非, *fēishì* 非是, and *búshì* 不是, but the form *búshì* 不是 finally won out, probably due to the use of *bù* 不 as a general negative word in Chinese. In this case, it may be argued that the function of *bù* 不 was extended to replace *fēi* 非, which is an instance of extension in grammatical changes.

Extension often follows reanalysis. First, a new structure based on multiple possibilities of interpretation is derived via reanalysis. The new structure can then be generalized or extended to other similar situations. In line with Campbell's (1999) arguments, we may identify two types of changes associated with example (11) mentioned previously. First, reanalysis results in the future structure "*be going to*," but initially it was only used with people as the subject because of the purposive connection. But then such a future structure can undergo development on its own further away from the original restriction to only subjects of people. In sentences like "*It is going to rain*," the subject is extended to dummy subjects such as "*it*," which is required by verbs of natural phenomena. Additionally the structure "*be going to*" can even be applied to the verb "*go*" itself, for example, "*I am going to go to France.*" Therefore, the initial reanalysis brought about extensions in various directions.

Such explanations in terms of reanalysis followed by extension can also be made for the development of the typical passive construction formed with the word *bèi* 被, that is, the BEI-construction, in Modern Standard Chinese. For example:

(23) *Yuēhàn*  *bèi*  *lǎoshī*  *pīpíng*  *le*
     約翰    被    老師    批評    了。
     John   PASS  teacher  scold   PAR
     "John was scolded by the teacher."

In such sentences, the passive marker *bèi* 被 can be optionally followed by the agent of the action. In Classical Chinese, there were various equivalent ways of expressing passivity, as mentioned in Chapter 6, for example, by using the passive marker *jiàn* 見. In Classical Chinese, the word *bèi* 被 originally refers to "*sleep cover, quilt.*"[4] It can be used as a verb in Classical Chinese to signify that the event denoted by the verb is experienced by the subject. This verbal use of *bèi* in Classical Chinese is often interpreted as the verb "*to suffer from,*" with a negative connotation. At this stage, the verb *bèi* 被 can only be followed by the verb but not the agent of the verb, like in its typical use in Modern Standard Chinese, as shown in example (23). Toward the end of the Eastern Han dynasty, examples like (24) appeared, where the word *bèi* 被 is followed by the agent.

(24) *Chén*  *bèi*  *Shàngshū*  *zhào*  *wèn*  (*Cài Zhōngláng Jí*)
     臣     被    尚書      召     問 。
     minister PASS  Shàngshū  summon  ask
     "I was summoned by the *Shàngshū* (title of a government official) to answer some questions."

This is a key example in the development of *bèi* 被 as a passive marker. At this point, there are two possible interpretations. If "*Shàngshū zhào wèn* 尚書召問" is considered an event of "*the Shàngshū summoning and questioning someone*," then the word *bèi* 被 can still be understood in a similar way as in earlier Classical Chinese examples. But alternatively, a syntactic unit with "*bèi Shàngshū* 被尚書"

can be formed first where the word "*Shàngshū*" refers to the agent of the event of "*summoning.*" Therefore, although the surface string of words is the same, the underlying structure of the sentence may be different. Obviously in examples like (24), the word that follows *bèi* 被 does have an agentive meaning, but the following example from the Tang dynasty is quite different, since the noun *huā* ("flower") is an inanimate object, which does not have any agentive meaning in its typical sense.

(25) Bèi     huā      nǎo                              (from a poem by *Dù Fǔ*)
     被      花       恼。
     PASS    flowers  annoy
     "(I was) annoyed by the flowers."

Arguably, there is an extension of the semantic role of the noun that follows *bèi* from the agent role associated with people to inanimate objects such as "*flowers.*"

A common semantic property in examples (23)–(25) is that there is a negative connotation in the typical uses of the BEI-construction in both vernacular writing and Modern Standard Chinese, which can be related to the original meaning of the word *bèi* as a verb to denote an event that affects the subject negatively. However, we can find examples from the Ming and Qing dynasties where such a restriction was relaxed and the BEI-construction had neutral connotations. A further extension to cases with appreciative meanings is not uncommon in Modern Standard Chinese, such as shown in (26).

(26) Yuēhàn   bèi    lǎoshī    biǎoyáng   le
     約翰      被     老師      表揚        了。
     John      PASS   teacher   praise      PAR
     "John was praised by the teacher."

The verb in (26) has an appreciative connotation, in contrast to the verb "*scold*" in (23). Although such uses of *bèi* with appreciative verbs are still quite limited in Modern Standard Chinese, they are nonetheless further extensions of the passive construction. This newer type of BEI-construction may also have been influenced by the passive construction in European languages via syntactic borrowing.

Grammatical structures are actually quite easily borrowed between languages. Campbell (1999) gives an example from Pipil, an Uto-Aztecan language in El Salvador, in which the pattern of comparison is definitely borrowed from the Spanish "*mas . . . que . . .,*" as shown in (27), a typical comparison construction from Pipil.

(27) Ne     siwa:t    mas     gála:na    ke      taha    (Campbell 1999: 288)
     the    woman     more    pretty     than    you.
     "That woman is prettier than you are."

It is obvious that in (27) the Pipil "*mas . . . ke . . .*" is the same as the Spanish "*mas . . . que . . .*" both functionally and phonologically. Similarly, since the early 20th century, Modern Standard Chinese has borrowed certain uses or structures from European languages. Such new uses are called Europeanized Chinese (*Ōuhuà Jùfǎ* 歐化句法). The BEI-construction is used more and more often nowadays, thus becoming increasingly comparable to how the passive voice is used in English.

Therefore, to sum up the development of the BEI-construction in Modern Standard Chinese, the word *bèi* originally refers to "*sleep cover*" or "*quilt*" in Classical Chinese. It can be used as a verb to mean that the subject experiences a certain event, but it was not followed by the agent noun. The verbal meaning of *bèi* in Classical Chinese is associated with events with negative connotations. As early as the Eastern Han dynasty, examples of *bèi* followed by the agent noun emerged. At this stage, the word *bèi* was reanalyzed as a passive marker. Then the newly formed passive construction was extended to include inanimate objects as the element that follows *bèi*. In terms of the semantic properties associated with the BEI-construction, originally there was a tendency to use verbs that had a negative connotation. But in more recent times, verbs with appreciative meanings are also possible in certain contexts in the BEI-construction, albeit still limited. Under the influence of European languages, *bèi* is used to translate passive constructions in languages such as English, leading to further extension of the functions and uses of the BEI-construction. Such new developments are partially due to syntactic borrowing.

The BEI-construction is one of two key grammatical constructions in Modern Standard Chinese, with the other being the BA-construction, named after the structural word *bǎ* 把 in such constructions. The function of *bǎ* is to extract the object of a verb to the pre-verbal position and place the focus of the sentence on the verbal structure but not on the pre-verbal object. For example, in (28), the sentence is in the normal SVO order, where the object *fàn* 飯 is in its post-verbal position. The focus of the sentence can be the whole verbal structure "*chī wán fàn le*," and "*finish eating the food*" is the new information of the sentence. In comparison, in example (29), the object *fàn* is extracted by using *bǎ*. Now the focus is only the "*chī wán le*" part, meaning that the reference to the noun *fàn* is already made in prior contexts, and what is conveyed by the sentence as new information is that of the completion of consumption of the food, as is clear from how it is translated via the topic marker "*as for . . .*" in English. In some sense, the Chinese word *bǎ* can be considered a topic marker, as indicated by the label TOP in the gloss.

(28) *Wǒ    chī    wán    fàn    le*
    我    吃    完    飯    了。
    I    eat    finish    food    PAR
    "I have finished eating the food."

(29) *Wǒ    bǎ    fàn    chī    wán    le*
    我    把    飯    吃    完    了。
    I    TOP    food    eat    finish    PAR
    "As for the food, I have finished eating it."

Originally, *bǎ* 把 is a verb meaning "*to grasp, to take*," attested in texts from the Tang dynasty. For example, Wang (1958) cited the following lines from poems by *Dù Fǔ* 杜甫 (AD 712–770):

(30)  *Zuì*     *bǎ*      *qīng*    *hé*      *yè*
     醉      把      青      荷      葉。
     drunk  grasp  green  lotus  leaf
     "I grasped a green leaf of lotus while being drunk."

(31)  *Zuì*     *bǎ*      *zhūyú*    *zǐxì*     *kàn*
     醉      把      茱萸     仔细     看。
     drunk  grasp  silverberry  carefully  look
     "Grasping a branch of silverberry while being drunk, I looked at it carefully."

In (30), the word *bǎ* is the only word that could be the verb of the sentence. In (31), there are two verbs, that is, *bǎ* and *kàn*, and there are multiple possibilities of interpretation. The focus of the sentence can be on the second verb, while the verb *bǎ* functions as some kind of adverbial, as is done in the translation. Since both sentences are from the same poet, the two uses of the word *bǎ* must both be verbs. But shifting the focus in sentences like (31) may lead to a further development of the word *bǎ* being reanalyzed as simply a marker of the noun as being the topic of the sentence, thus resulting in the development of the BA-construction. Its origin is generally argued to be the Tang dynasty, since there were no equivalent constructions to the BA-construction before Tang.

Now let's shift our discussion to the verb-resultative structure in Modern Standard Chinese, such as the phrase "*chī-wán* 吃完" mentioned in (28) and (29), in which the second component *wán* 完 is the result of the preceding verb. According to Xiang (1993), such verbal structures originated as early as the Warring States period but became more common in the Han dynasty. Examples such as *dǎhuài* 打壞 ("hit" + "broke" → "break"), *kànjìng* 看竟 ("look" + "finish" → "finish looking") are from this period. Xiang (1993) further points out that if an object is needed, there are two possible combinations, which developed from different sources.

One was originally a coordinate structure, for example, "*jī ér shā zhī*" (擊而殺之, "hit and kill him") from the *Zuǒ Zhuàn*. The words "*jī* 擊" and "*shā* 殺" are verbs connected by "*ér* 而" ("and"). The word "*zhī* 之" is the object pronoun. This is a coordinate structure, but the "*ér*" could be omitted, and "*jī ér shā zhī*" became "*jīshā zhī*," which was further reanalyzed as a verb-resultative structure, that is, the result of the hitting is that the person was killed.

The other type of verb-resultative with an object was originally called a "*pivot structure*" such as "*chāi lóng pò*" (拆籠破, "tear cage break" → "tore the cage and the cage broke"), from a poem by *Bái Jūyì* 白居易 (AD 772–846), in which the noun *lóng* ("cage") is both the object of the preceding verb "*chāi*" ("tear") and the subject of the following verb "*pò*" ("break"). The noun *lóng* ("cage") is thus metaphorically the pivot of the sentence. In such structures, if the second verb, that is, *pò*, switches positions with the noun, that is, *lóng* here, then a verb-resultative structure with a nominal object is derived, that is, *chāipò lóng* ("tear down the cage").

Related to the verb-resultatives is the perfective aspect marker *-le* 了 in Modern Standard Chinese. The basic function of *-le* is to indicate that the event denoted by the verb is complete, hence the term "*perfective aspect marker.*" An example in Modern Standard Chinese is as follows in (32).

(32)   *Wǒ*    *kàn*     *le*     *liǎng*   *gè*    *diànyǐng*
      我     看      了      兩     個     電影。
      I      watch   PERF   two    CL    movie
      "I watched two movies."

Note that the word *-le* is not a past tense marker, since it can be used in a future context in the sense of completion by a future reference time point. In Classical Chinese and early vernacular writing, the meaning of completion was expressed either by adverbs or verbs that had a meaning of completion. According to Xiang (1993), the verb of completion *liǎo* 了, among a few others, is attested in texts from the Han dynasty, for example, *shí liǎo* 食了 ("eat" + "complete"). But it is during the Tang dynasty that *liǎo* 了 became more common in vernacular writings such as the *biànwén*. At first the *liǎo* 了 appeared after the object, for example, *chī fàn liǎo* 吃飯了 ("eat" + "food" + "complete"). Mei (1981) argues that the *liǎo* 了 then gradually switched positions with the object, for example, *chī fàn liǎo* → *chī liǎo fàn*, as an analogical change comparable to the movement of the resultative from after the object to right next to the verb, as shown previously in the discussion of the verb-resultative structure. By the Song dynasty, the word *liǎo* 了 had clearly moved to a position after the verb, thus becoming a perfective aspect marker, just as in Modern Standard Chinese. The development of the verb *liǎo* to a grammatical perfective aspect marker is a typical process of grammaticalization. As pointed out earlier, along with the grammaticalization process, there is often semantic bleaching and phonological weakening. Semantic bleaching of the verb *liǎo* 了 is from its original verbal meaning "*to complete*" to the purely grammatical meaning of the perfective aspect. In terms of phonological weakening, the pronunciation of the word in Modern Standard Chinese has been reduced from *liǎo* to *-le*. This *-le* is attached to the verb as an unstressed syllable.

In addition to its use as a perfective aspect marker, the word *-le* 了 can also be used as a sentence-final particle. Actually, most such particles in Chinese can be accounted for via grammaticalization, for example, the contrastive topic marker *-ne* 呢 and the question particle *-ma* 嗎, as discussed by Dong (2018, 2019). Thus, grammaticalization is a useful theoretical framework of research in the grammatical changes in Chinese.

This chapter has sketched the development of grammar in the post-classical period of Chinese via descriptions of some representative structures. In the next chapter, we turn to lexical and semantic changes.

## Notes

1 The Chinese terms for these three stages are *Gǔdài Hànyǔ* 古代漢語 ("Ancient Chinese"), *Jìndài Hànyǔ* 近代漢語 ("Early Modern Chinese"), and *Xiàndài Hànyǔ* 現代漢語 ("Modern Chinese"). There is no accurate translation for *jìndài* 近代, which literally means "*recent time*." The usual translation is "*Early Modern*," but the 10th century would be too early to be "*Early Modern*." Lü (1984) originally grouped *Jìndài Hànyǔ* and *Xiàndài Hànyǔ* together in one stage, contrasting with *Gǔdài Hànyǔ*. Thus, Lü (1984) only proposed two stages of grammatical development in Chinese. But Jiang (2005) considers *Jìndài Hànyǔ* and *Xiàndài Hànyǔ* separate stages.

2 It is also alternatively pronounced as "*ē dǒu.*"

3 According to Campbell (1999: 296), the relation between grammaticalization and these other types of mechanisms is still somewhat debated. Most scholars do not regard grammaticalization as a stand-alone mechanism independent from reanalysis, extension, and borrowing. Typically, grammaticalization relies on these other mechanisms. It is reasonable, thus, to consider reanalysis, extension, and borrowing three specific mechanisms of grammaticalization. One objection to this view is that certain reanalysis cases do not involve grammaticalization, such as word-order changes. Campbell's (1999: 297) conclusion is that there is an overlap between grammaticalization and reanalysis in that grammaticalization often involves reanalysis, but the mechanism of reanalysis is more general, often beyond mere grammar changes. For some, the notion of grammaticalization may not be needed at all in the analysis of grammatical changes.

4 The *Shuō Wén Jiě Zì* 說文解字 provides the following entry: 被: 寢衣，長一身有半。从衣皮聲。平義切。

# 8 Lexical and semantic changes

When we read ancient texts, the words might have different meanings, and the interpretation of these texts is full of uncertainties. This chapter discusses lexical and semantic changes. While many words remain more or less the same in meaning throughout time, for example, *fēng* (風, "wind"), *yǔ* (雨, "rain"), *jī* (雞, "chicken"), *mǎ* (馬, "horse") in Chinese, major and subtle semantic changes are more of the norm. Generally speaking, the meaning of a word can be extended, narrowed, or shifted. In traditional Chinese linguistics, the concept called *yǐnshēn* (引申, "to extend") is used as a general way of meaning change.

## 8.1 Extension

Let's see a few examples of extension. In Chapter 2, it is mentioned that the words *jiāng* 江 and *hé* 河 originally were proper names for the Yangtze River in the south and the Yellow River in the north, respectively. But they were also used as general terms for "*river*" in early texts, for example, *sān jiāng* (三江, "three rivers") and *jiǔ hé* (九河, "nine rivers") from the pre-classical era such as the *Shàngshū*. In Modern Standard Chinese, both terms are still used primarily as general words for "*river*." Interestingly, the names of rivers in the south are often called ". . . *jiāng*," while the rivers in the north tend to be called ". . . *hé*," although there are some major exceptions, for example, the *Hēilóng Jiāng* ("the Amur river") in northeastern China. The original meanings of these words can still be seen in set phrases such as *jiāngnán* 江南 ("south of the Yangtze River"), and *Hénán* 河南, that is, the name of Henan province, which is mostly located to the south of the Yellow River.

Location words such as *shàng* (上, "top"), *xià* (下, "bottom"), *qián* (前, "front"), and *hòu* (後, "back") can be extended to temporal senses. For example, *shàng* and *qián* can refer to time in the past, such as in *shàng xīngqī* (上星期, "last week") and *qiántiān* (前天, "the day before yesterday"), while *xià* and *hòu* can refer to time in the future, such as *xià xīngqī* (下星期, "next week") and *hòutiān* (後天, "the day after tomorrow").

The word for "*the sun*" is *rì* 日 in Classical Chinese. It is naturally extended to the notion of "*day*," although both words were further replaced in Modern Standard Chinese, that is, *tàiyang* 太陽 for "*the sun*" and *tiān* 天 for "*day*," while the word *rì* 日 is preserved mostly in compound words, for example, *jiàrì* (假日,

"holiday, vacation"), *xīngqīrì* (星期日, "Sunday") and so on.[1] Similarly, *yuè* 月 ("the moon") was also extended to the notion of "*month*," since the traditional Chinese calendar is based upon cycles of the lunar phase.

Here are some further examples such as the words *chì* 赤 and *hóng* 紅, both of which are related to the color "*red*." Originally, the word *chì*, which was considered the color of fire, was the general term for the color "*red*." Different shades of red could all be called *chì*, with *zhū* 朱 being the brightest shade and *hóng* referring to the very light, pinkish red color of silk. Later on, *hóng* became a general term for all shades of red, and we find compound words such as *dàhóng* (大紅, "big red"), *fěnhóng* (粉紅, "pinkish red"), *qiǎnhóng* (淺紅, "light red"), and *shēnhóng* (深紅, "dark red") in Modern Standard Chinese. The words *chì* and *zhū* are still retained as bound morphemes such as in *chìzì* (赤字, "deficit") and *zhūhóng* (朱紅, "bright red"). Besides the meaning of "*red*," *chì* was also extended to refer to the color of newborns, thus the term *chìzi* (赤子, "newborn"), which is further extended metaphorically to the people of a country. The idiom *chìzi zhī xīn* (赤子之心, "a newborn's mind") is attested in the *Mencius*. The word *chì* is also used in adjectives such as *chìchéng* (赤誠, "very loyal"). Another route of extension of this word has a connection with the meaning of "*exposing all*," such as in *chìshēn* (赤身, "bare" + "body" → "nude"), *chìjiǎo* (赤腳, "bare" + "foot" → "barefoot"), *chìshǒu* (赤手, "bare" + "hand" →" barehanded), *chìdì* (赤地, "bare" + "land" → "barren land"), and so on.

The word *bǐ* 筆, according to the dictionary *Shuō Wén Jiě Zì* (early 2nd century), originally meant "*that which is used to write*."[2] Thus, it was used as a general term for writing tools in Classical Chinese. However because ink brushes were the only writing instruments in ancient China, the word *bǐ* merely referred to such brushes in pre-modern times. Nowadays in Modern Standard Chinese, the word *bǐ* can refer to all kinds of writing tools, such as pens, pencils, and brushes. Is there a semantic change here? If by "*semantic change*," we strictly refer to the dictionary definition, then the meaning of the word *bǐ* has not changed, because from Classical Chinese to Modern Standard Chinese, it always refers to "*writing tools*." But intuitively, there seem to be some semantic differences between the ancient word *bǐ* and its modern counterpart. If the objects that a word refers to are extended to a larger set, usually because of technological advances, then the meaning of the word does change. Although such a semantic change in terms of the set of entities that a word refers to seems to be less noticeable, it is very important for the correct interpretation of ancient texts. Even when the same word is used with the same meaning, the word may have referred to quite different things in ancient times.

To further theorize on such semantic changes, as shown in the discussion of the word *bǐ*, we need to distinguish two sides of the meaning of a word. The kind of meaning as defined in a dictionary is called the *intension* (*nèihán* 內涵) of a word, while the set of things that the word picks out in the real world is called the *extension* (*wàiyán* 外延) of the word.[3] Note here the term "*extension*" (*wàiyán* 外延) is part of the meaning of a word, and it should be distinguished from "*extension*" (*yǐnshēn* 引申) as a general semantic change process discussed in this section. Obviously, in semantic developments, it is usually the intension of a word that changes, and consequently the extension would be different as a result of intensional changes. But it is also possible for the intension of a word to stay the same while the extension changes to a different set of entities. Such extensional semantic changes are not commonly discussed in books on historical linguistics, but a theory of meaning that deals with intension and extension calls for a distinction in these two types of semantic changes.

## 8.2   Narrowing

Word meaning can be narrowed as well. Wang (1958) gives a few such examples. The word *chóng* 蟲 originally was a general term for animals. But nowadays it can only refer to certain insects, worms, and bugs. In vernacular writing from the Early Modern Chinese period, one of the words for "*tiger*" is "*dàchóng*" (大蟲), in which *dà* means "*big*," and clearly here the word *chóng* means "*animal*" but not "*insects*" like in modern uses. Interestingly, there is a parallel development in English with the word "*deer*," which originally referred to all kinds of animals in Old English with the spelling "*dēor*."

The word *tāng* 湯 originally meant "*hot water*" or "*a hot type of liquid food*," for example, "*soup*," in Classical Chinese. But in Modern Standard Chinese, only the second meaning is still retained. Interestingly, the meaning "*hot water*" of the word *tāng* is actually retained in Japanese.

## 8.3   Shift of word meaning

The word *zǒu* 走 means "*to walk*" or "*to leave*" in Modern Standard Chinese, but in Classical Chinese, it means "*to run*." Apparently, the modern meaning should have been derived from the original meaning "*to run*," although it is neither a case of extension or narrowing, but the meaning has been shifted to a related one. According to Pan (1989), the meaning of "*to leave*" associated with 走 was used as early as the Warring States period, while the new meaning of "*to walk*" associated with 走 did not appear until the Northern and Southern dynasties. The original word *xíng* 行 for "to walk" in Classical Chinese is obsolete in Modern Standard Chinese, but is still retained in many southern dialects now, such as Cantonese. In the north, the meaning "*to run*," originally associated with 走, is now taken over by a new word, *pǎo* 跑.

The word for "*lower leg*" in Classical Chinese is *jiǎo* 腳, and the word for "*upper leg, thigh*" is *gǔ* 股. But the meaning of the word *jiǎo* later shifted to refer to "*foot*," replacing the original Classical Chinese word *zú* 足 for "*foot*." With such changes, a new word, *tuǐ* 腿, was created as early as in the Northern and Southern dynasties to refer to the lower leg, the original meaning of the word *jiǎo*. The new word, *tuǐ*, later was extended to refer to the whole leg. In Modern Standard Chinese, the compound words *dàtuǐ* 大腿 and *xiǎotuǐ* 小腿 can refer to the upper leg and the lower leg, respectively. The original words *gǔ* and *zú* are used in Modern Standard Chinese mostly as morphemes in compound words or idioms such as *gǔgǔ* (股骨, "thigh bone"), *zúqiú* (足球, "soccer") and so on.

## 8.4    Substitution of lexical items

Besides word meaning changes through extension, narrowing, and shift, new words can be created and eventually replace older terms. After the substitution, older terms can nonetheless be preserved in compound words, idioms, or simply as obsolete terms used in special contexts. Let's see a few interesting examples.

According to Wang (1958), in Classical Chinese, the word for "*face*" is *miàn* 面. In late Northern and Southern dynasties, a new word, *liǎn* 臉, appeared to refer primarily to the cheeks until it replaced the earlier word, *miàn*, to refer to "*face*" in the Tang dynasty. In Modern Standard Chinese, *liǎn* is still the primary word for "*face*," while "*miàn*" is preserved in compound words such as *miànzi* (面子, "face"), which is used in a metaphorical way. Mao (1994) and Sun (2006) point out the difference between the connotations of *liǎn* and *miànzi* in Chinese culture. *Liǎn* emphasizes the respect that one receives in the community in terms of one's conformity to social and moral norms. *Miànzi* emphasizes the public recognition of one's social prestige, influence, or reputation. The term "*yǒu miànzi*" (有面子, "have" + miànzi) is usually used to mean that one is well respected and somehow treated preferentially due to one's social prestige or rank. In this case, the word "*liǎn*" cannot be substituted for "*miànzi*." Conversely, the common phrase "*diū liǎn*" (丟臉, "lose face") is often used when one has done something that is not approved by social and moral norms. Similarly in this phrase, the word "*miànzi*" would not be used. Apparently the cultural importance of the metaphor of "*face*" is so important in the Chinese culture that it was borrowed by the English-speaking expat communities in China, and eventually similar phrases such as "*lose face*," "*save face*," and so on became widely used in general by English speakers.

In addition to the words for "*face*" in Chinese, words for facial features also changed. For example, the word for "*eye*" was *mù* 目 in Classical Chinese, and now the word is *yǎnjing* 眼睛 in Modern Standard Chinese. The word for "*mouth*" was *kǒu* 口, but has changed to *zuǐ* 嘴. The terms for "*eyebrows*" (*méi*, 眉), "*nose*" (*bí*, 鼻), and "*ears*" (*ěr*, 耳) have not changed much. The Classical Chinese words *méi* 眉, *bí* 鼻, and *ěr* 耳 were monosyllabic words, but in Modern Standard Chinese, they are morphemes in disyllabic words, that is, *méimao* 眉毛, *bízi* 鼻子, and *ěrduo* 耳朵.

Another rather amusing example is the word for "*chopsticks*." The modern word is *kuàizi* 筷子, although the original word is *zhù* 箸. Norman (1988: 76) cited a written record in the Ming dynasty that says the word *zhù* 箸 sounded the same as the word for "*to stop, to stay*," and therefore for people who made a living on boats, it was not a welcome association in meaning. However the word for "*fast*" is *kuài* 快, which was considered a great connotation by the these people. Consequently, the word *kuàizi* 筷子 was created to replace the word *zhù* 箸. This new word, *kuàizi* 筷子, eventually spread to most dialectal areas in modern China.

## 8.5    Hybrid changes

We have discussed extension, narrowing, shift, and substitution in semantic changes. But in many cases, it is not just one type of change that took place but rather a combination of these four different types. For example, in the semantic changes of the words for "*foot*" and "*leg*," it is actually both shift and substitution.

As an example of narrowing and shift, the development of color terms related to the color "*blue*" is also quite interesting. The Classical Chinese word *qīng* 青 is a general term for "*blue*," but the actual reference ranges from bordering the color "*black*" to the color "*green*." There are words like "*qīngyī*" (青衣, "black" + "clothes" → "clothes in black"), "*qīngtiān*" (青天, "blue sky") and "*tàqīng*" (踏青, "tread" + "green" → "a short excursion out of town in spring"). In Modern Standard Chinese, *qīng* primarily refers to a type of blue similar to indigo. The modern general term for "*blue*" is *lán* 藍, originally referring to a type of grass used as a dye that can produce colors from green to blue.

The modern term for "*green*" is *lǜ* 綠, which originally refers to the color of certain fabric, considered a mixture of blue and yellow. Another term, *bì* 碧, originally referring to green jade stones, was also used as a color term for "*green*" in Classical Chinese but is not used as the modern term for "*green*" anymore.

Since we are discussing the words for the color "*blue*," there is another related color, *zǐ* (紫, "purple"), which has not changed much in its basic meaning. The color *zǐ* was used in the past as the color of clothing of emperors and government officials of high ranks. Therefore, it was extended to refer to things related to the emperor, such as in the name of the Forbidden City, which is *Zǐ Jìn Chéng* 紫禁城, literally meaning "*Purple Forbidden City*." The color purple was also a preferred color in the Daoist religion. Thus, by its association with royalty and Daoism, the color *zǐ* was further extended to mean "*auspicious*," such as *zǐqì* (紫氣, "auspicious signs").

Therefore, the meaning changes here involve extension of *lán* and *lǜ* to take over the meanings of "*blue*" and "*green*," narrowing of *qīng* from a general term for "*blue*" to a subtype of blue, substitution of *lǜ* for *bì* as "*green*," and also extension of "*zǐ*" to mean "*royal*" and "*auspicious*." Note that the occasional use of *qīng* to refer to the color black has also been taken over by the word *hēi* 黑, which has not changed much from its original meaning as the color "*black*."

The other basic color terms, such as *bái* (白, "white") and *huáng* (黄, "yellow") have not changed much either. The extension and substitution of the color *hóng* for *chì* have been discussed already.

## 8.6   Euphemism and taboos in lexical changes

There are other types of changes in the vocabulary. Lexical changes can be results of euphemism. For government officials to retire from their imperial positions in the past, the word *guītián* 歸田 (literally "return to the fields") was commonly used.

A type of taboo called *bìhuì* 避諱 (literally "avoid") was a unique way of creating new words in imperial China to avoid using specific words out of respect for certain people, such as the emperor, superiors, seniors, and the deceased. For example, if the emperor's name contained a certain character, to use that character would be considered disrespectful, comparable to calling the emperor by his name.

Thus, that same character used in words in the language needed to be replaced. Since the emperor was the highest ruler, to whom everyone had to pay the highest respect, changes made to words out of respect for the emperor would often affect the lexicon in the language. The word *zhìjī* (雉雞, "pheasant") was changed to *yějī* (野雞, literally "wild chicken") during the Han dynasty, because Empress Lü's given name was *zhì* 雉. Although the original word could be reinstated after the fall of the relevant ruler or dynasty, the newly coined word would have already gained currency in the language. Nowadays, the formal term for *"pheasant"* is still *zhìjī* 雉雞, although in colloquial usage, the word *yějī* 野雞 is used more often.

Pan (1989) gives another interesting example. The lunar goddess *Cháng'é* 嫦娥 in Chinese mythology was originally called *Héng'é* 姮娥, but because the Emperor Wen of the Han dynasty had a similar character, *huán* 桓, in his name, the character *héng* 姮 in 姮娥 was changed to *cháng* 嫦. In modern times, the name *Cháng'é* is still the standard name of the lunar goddess instead of the original *Héng'é*.

In some cases of *bìhuì*, characters used in standard versions of books such as the Confucian classics would have to be replaced to avoid using a character in the emperor's name. Such changes would lead to different versions of the same text in later stages. For scholars in later times, it would be necessary to know why the original character was changed in order to understand the real meaning of the relevant text.

## 8.7   Loanwords and calques

All of the previously mentioned changes in the vocabulary would give rise to new words in many cases. But the major source of new words is borrowing. Chapter 2 discusses a few words such as *jiāng* (江, "river"), *gǒu* (狗, "dog"), and *hé* (禾, "rice plant"), which were borrowed into Chinese from Austroasiatic, Miao-Yao, and Kam-Tai languages in ancient times. If in pre-classical times, the major borrowing was between Chinese and the *Bǎiyuè* 百越 languages in the south, then by the Han dynasty, the main source of borrowing had shifted to the north and to the west.

Pan (1989) shows that the word *luòtuo* 駱駝 for *"camel"* in its current written form appeared in the Tang dynasty. But actually it was borrowed into Chinese in different forms as early as the classical period from languages of non-*Hàn* peoples to the north. According to Luo (2003) the word *pútao* (葡萄, "grape") was borrowed from the Proto-Iranian word *\*budāwa* or *\*buðawa*. The Persian word for *"wine"* is still *"bade,"* which might be related to the ancient root morpheme for *"grape."* According to historical records, the Emperor Wu of Han sent *Zhāng Qiān* 張騫 as an envoy to countries to the west of the Han Empire in the 2nd century BC. *Zhāng Qiān* brought grapes and alfalfa back to China from a country called *Dà Yuān* 大宛 in Central Asia. The Chinese word for alfalfa is *mùxū* 苜蓿, which is related to the proto-Iranian word *\*buksuk*, *\*buxsux*, or *\*buxsuk*.

But sometimes words can be borrowed back and forth between two languages. A famous example is the word *bóshì* 博士, which originally was used in Chinese for certain government positions and also referred to an erudite person. The use of *bóshì* in such senses can be traced back to Classical Chinese. Much later, it was borrowed into Mongolian to mean "*teacher*." During the Yuan dynasty, this word was borrowed back into Chinese in a different form, *bǎshi* 把式, to refer to people with certain manual skills. The same Mongolian word was also borrowed back as *bǎxi* 把戲 to mean "*small tricks*." In Modern Standard Chinese, *bóshi* is used primarily to refer to an academic degree equivalent to the doctorate, while *bǎshì* is still used to refer to a skilled person of certain profession, and *bǎxi* means "*small tricks*." In Chapter 2, we have also mentioned Mongolian loanwords in Chinese, such as the word for "*station*," that is, *zhàn* 站.

Since Buddhism was introduced into China during the Eastern Han dynasty, many Sanskrit terms were successively borrowed into Chinese directly or indirectly through other ancient languages such as Tocharian. To borrow a word from another language, the original word can be used with some phonological adaptations. Let's call such borrowed words loanwords. The earliest loanword for "*Buddha*" was *fútú* 浮屠 from the Eastern Han dynasty. As a side note here, loanwords from Sanskrit to Chinese can be very useful to the studies of the sounds of Chinese of the time when these terms were borrowed. Here we see that the modern pronunciation of the word *fútú* has the initial sound *f-*, which corresponds to the original sound *b-* in Sanskrit. This reminds us of *Qián Dàxīn*'s claim that there was no labiodental sound in Old Chinese. Thus, it is further confirmed by this correspondence between *f-* in Modern Standard Chinese and *b-* in Sanskrit, because at the time of the borrowing, this Chinese word should have had the initial *b-* as well. Furthermore, the initial consonant of the second syllable in the word *fútú* is *t-*, but it corresponds to the Sanskrit voiced stop *dh-*. Therefore, we may infer that there must have been voiced stops in Late Old Chinese as well. In the Northern and Southern dynasties, the word for "*Buddha*" was also written as *fótuó* 佛陀, or simply *fó* 佛. The correspondence between the final of the second syllable of the word *fótuó*, that is, *-uo*, in Modern Standard Chinese pronunciation and the Sanskrit vowel *-a* can be evidence that the final of the word 陀 in Middle Chinese must have been more like the "*a*" in "*Buddha*."

According to Pan (1989), the very common colloquial word *chànà* 剎那, meaning "*an instant*," or "*a very short time*," came from the Sanskrit word "*kṣaṇa*" of the same meaning. Even the name of the jasmine flower, *mòlì* 茉莉, was borrowed from Sanskrit "*mallikā*." Such examples are abundant in the Chinese language.

But this type of borrowing based on sounds is not the preferred method, since each Chinese character has a meaning, and native speakers want to understand how the meaning of the whole word is related to those of the characters used. Thus, another type of borrowing called loan translation or calque is used quite often in Chinese. A calque is a new word coined by using a word-for-word translation. Thus, the meaning is borrowed, but the shape of the word is not. For example, in many languages, the word for railway is based on the same meaning, such as the French "*chemin de fer*" ("road of iron") and the Chinese *tiělù* 鐵路 ("iron" +" road"). To translate concepts from Sanskrit to Chinese, many such calque words were created, such as *shìjiè* (世界, "world"), *xiànzài* (現在, "now"), *píngděng* (平等, "equality"), *xìnyǎng* (信仰, "belief"), and so on.

Since calques may not always be the easiest method of borrowing words, oftentimes a combination of phonological and semantic borrowings would be the best option. Pan (1989) provides such an example. The word *píngguǒ* 蘋果 for "*apple*" was based on the Sanskrit word "*bimba*." The first syllable in the Chinese word, that is, *píng*, corresponds to the "*bim*" in the Sanskrit word, and then the Chinese word for "*fruit*," that is, *guǒ* 果, is added.

## 8.8   Clues to meaning change in Chinese characters

Since Chinese characters encode semantic information, a study of the composition of a character can point toward the original meaning of a word. Take *xí* 習, as used in words like *xuéxí* (學習, "to study") and *liànxí* (練習, "to practice"), for example. There is actually a component of "*wings*" as the top part of the character, that is, the 羽 component. It seems quite unrelated to the meaning of "*study*" or "*practice*." But originally the word *xí* 習 did mean "*(of young birds) to flap wings in order to learn how to fly*." In the *Book of Rites*, we find the following text "*yīng nǎi xué xí* (鷹乃學習)" meaning "*the young hawks then learn to flap their wings*." The modern word for "*study*" is also *xuéxí* 學習, but it probably is a compound verb that consists of *xué* (學, "to study") and *xí* (習, "to practice, to review." The word *xuéxí* 學習 in the sense of "*to study*" is attested in texts as early as in the Han dynasty.

This chapter discusses various patterns and sources of semantic and lexical changes. As of this chapter, we have covered topics related to the sounds, grammar, and vocabulary in the Chinese language up to early modern times.

## Notes

1 The notion of extension used here is more general than that used by Campbell (1999: 254). He considers different metaphorical devices of semantic change separately from extension. For example the semantic change from "*sun*" to "*day*" is common in many languages because of synecdoche as a common cognitive process.
2 The original text from the *Shuō Wén Jiě Zì* 說文解字 is: 聿，所以書也。楚謂之聿，吳謂之不律，燕謂之弗。筆，秦謂之筆。从聿从竹。
3 Note the term "*intension*" is different from "*intention*." Here "*intension*" may be better defined as the internal counterpart to the "*extension*" of the meaning of a word. The extension is external, that is, a set of entities in the world, while the intension is the "*internal*" meaning of a word. This explanation is only an informal one. The notions "*intension*" and "*extension*" have technical definitions in logic and philosophy.

# 9 Formation of Modern Standard Chinese

In the preceding chapters, the phonology, grammar, and lexicon of Old Chinese, Middle Chinese, and Old Mandarin are described. Now, in this chapter, we discuss how Modern Standard Chinese, that is, *Pǔtōnghuà* 普通話 (literally "Common Speech"), was created, what linguistic features it has, and how it is related to earlier stages of the language.

## 9.1 Origin of the national language

Toward the end of the 19th century, Chinese scholars and politicians began to work on a series of modernizing reforms. Linguistic issues were heatedly discussed and debated in relation to concerns with literacy, education, and national identity. It was widely believed that a more effective language could help to eliminate the then-rampant problems of illiteracy and to facilitate education, which in turn would lead to a unified modern society. The linguistic reforms fall into three related categories: (1) the vernacular writing movement; (2) creation of the national language, that is, the *Guóyǔ* 國語; and (3) script reform. We discuss each of these three aspects here.

First, the vernacular writing movement addressed the issue of diglossia. As has been discussed in Chapters 6 and 7, for nearly 2000 years since the end of the Han dynasty, Literary Chinese, based upon Classical Chinese, functioned as the prestigious official written language for all formal uses, including education and writing government documents. For Chinese speakers in the Qing dynasty, no matter what variety of Chinese they spoke, Literary Chinese represented an entirely different stage of the language that required extensive training to master. It was probably not difficult for the early reformers to make a connection between Literary Chinese and the low literacy rate of the country at that time, although Literary Chinese alone could not have been the cause of illiteracy. Another disadvantage of using Literary Chinese is that it is modeled on an obsolete language, the grammar of which could not be fully grasped and imitated by modern speakers. Therefore, writings in Literary Chinese tend to have more problems when it comes to lucidity and clarity. Unsurprisingly, Literary Chinese was viewed with hostility among progressive scholars of the time, and it was regarded as a major obstacle to the advancement of modern education.

In the early 20th century, drastic political changes took place in China with the overturn of the Qing dynasty and the establishment of a new republic. Building on such political momentum, scholars during the New Culture Movement advocated for the abolishment of Literary Chinese. Vernacular writing was proposed to be the new official written language because it corresponded better to the spoken language. One of the foremost proponents of vernacular writing was Hu Shih (1981–1962), who, like many educated people of his time, received a typical classical education during his younger years but felt that it was time for new learning. In 1910, at 19 years of age, he went to the United States to study agriculture at Cornell University on a special scholarship. He subsequently changed his major to philosophy and literature and went on to do a doctoral degree in philosophy with John Dewey (1859–1952) at Columbia University in 1915. At the beginning of 1917, Hu Shih published an essay in the Chinese magazine *La Jeunesse* (*Xīn Qīngnián* 新青年, "New Youth"), which was the literary bastion of the New Culture Movement, to call for reforms in the literary language by liberating the written language from the restricting and impractical rules of unnecessary archaisms prevalent in Literary Chinese writings. Upon returning to China later that same year, Hu Shih not only advocated for the use of vernacular writing but also composed literary pieces to set examples for others. Although traditionalists opposed the movement, it gained support from the new government, and consequently Literary Chinese was officially abolished in 1920. The standard written form of *Pǔtōnghuà* evolved from such early reform measures to elevate vernacular writing to its official status.

The second linguistic issue is about the standard of the national language. As we have described in this book, there was always a common spoken language from Old Chinese based on Luoyang to the *Guānhuà* 官話 ("*language of the official-dom*") or Mandarin of the Ming and Qing dynasties. There is debate on what the standard of Mandarin as the *Guānhuà* was during the Ming dynasty. One influential view, for example, by Lu (1985), is that the Nanjing dialect was the base of Mandarin of the Ming. One important type of evidence is that Jesuit missionaries during the Ming dynasty described how the Nanjing dialect was considered by the Chinese to be the prestigious standard form of Mandarin. However, Mai and Zhu (2012) argue that Nanjing Mandarin[1] was never a nationally recognized standard, although it may have enjoyed a prestigious status as a regional standard. Detailed phonological comparisons between Mandarin records in the Ming dynasty and modern dialects from Beijing, Nanjing, and Luoyang show that the Luoyang dialect is closer to the system of Mandarin in the Ming dynasty than the other two modern dialects are. Therefore, Mai and Zhu (2012) conclude that the dialect of Henan, that is, where Luoyang is, should be the base of Mandarin in Ming dynasty and possibly the early Qing dynasty as well. Additionally, Wang (1958) suggested that Beijing Mandarin was the standard in the Yuan, Ming, and Qing dynasties.[2] Despite such debates and uncertainties with the standard spoken language of the Ming and early Qing, there is more consensus that starting from the mid-Qing dynasty, the standard had shifted to the Beijing dialect. Thus, at the turn of the 20th century, Beijing Mandarin would be the basis of the common spoken language. However, the actual language use was more complicated.

As Chen (1999) points out, Mandarin as the *Guānhuà* was rather a vague, attitudinal, and unofficial language used in polite society or for cross-dialectal communication. This view is similar to Geng's (2007) argument that Mandarin in Ming and Qing may have been broadly based on northern Chinese dialects with no clear unified pronunciation standard, although in the second half of the Qing dynasty, Beijing Mandarin became the most prestigious variety of Mandarin. In fact, speakers of different dialects could pick up a Mandarin dialect out of practical needs instead of learning it systematically in schools. This can be partially confirmed by the Mandarin campaign initiated by Yongzheng Emperor of the Qing dynasty in 1728, when he complained that officials from Guangdong and Fujian in southern China could not speak Beijing Mandarin well enough and decreed that spoken Beijing Mandarin be taught in schools in those provinces. Historical records show that even with such an imperial edict, local officials did not care much about teaching the spoken language of Beijing. After it was reported that the campaign was mostly a waste of money, the official policy to teach Beijing Mandarin in schools in Guangdong and Fujian was abolished by 1775.

Therefore, even though there was a common spoken language in the Qing dynasty, it may have lacked a clear standard. Beijing Mandarin was the prestigious form during the late Qing dynasty, but speakers of various Chinese dialects may not have been able to speak Beijing Mandarin well enough to communicate effectively. Thus, there was a need to create a national language to be taught uniformly across the country.

In 1911, the Ministry of Education of the Qing dynasty passed an act with guidelines for the national language, and it was decided that Beijing Mandarin should be the basis for the new standard, which could incorporate linguistic elements from old stages of the language and from other dialects.

After the founding of the new Republic of China in 1912, the base dialect of the national language became a thorny issue in the 1910s. Since the imperial power of the Qing dynasty was abolished, Beijing Mandarin suddenly became just one of the possible candidates for the national language, alongside such prestigious dialects as Shanghai and Nanjing. In 1913, the Republic of China government called for a national conference with representatives from various provinces led by a committee of linguistic experts to set the standard for the national language. After extensive debating and voting, a compromise was made to include some major archaic and dialectal features in the phonological system based on Beijing Mandarin to create a mixed standard, the pronunciations of around 6500 commonly used Chinese characters were determined, and, after a few years of political turmoil, this mixed system was published as the Old National Pronunciation (*Lǎo Guóyīn* 老國音) in a standard dictionary in 1919 and further promulgated in 1920 by the government in schools.

The overall phonological property of this version of the national language is similar to that of Beijing, with added modifications based on important features in various dialects, mostly those in the Jiang-Huai Mandarin and Wu areas, that is, in the lower Yangtze River region. For example, the Old National Pronunciation included a voiced labiodental initial [ v ] common in the Wu dialects but largely disappeared in Mandarin.

One major addition is that a separate *rù* tone category was retained in this mixed system, in addition to the four tones in Beijing Mandarin. As introduced in Chapter 4, the *rù* tone, or the entering tone, in Middle Chinese was originally associated with syllables ending in a consonant like -*p*, -*t*, or -*k*, but these consonantal codas disappeared in Beijing, while they merged to a glottal stop in Jiang-Huai Mandarin, for example, in the Nanjing dialect. Thus, considering the *rù* tone both as an archaic feature and a dialectal one, some words were listed as having the *rù* tone in the mixed standard of 1913, although a native speaker of Beijing, and most other Mandarin dialects, did not have such a tone in their linguistic systems. Supposedly, for speakers whose dialects did not have the *rù* tone anymore, they could simply pronounce the *rù* tone with a short flat pitch shape to imitate how they were pronounced in the Nanjing dialect.

Another major addition is the distinction between syllables such as [ tsiŋ ] 精 and [ tɕiŋ ] 經, in which a contrast exists between alveolar sibilant initials like [ ts- ] and palatal ones like [ tɕ- ] before high front vowels, for example, [ i ]. Such a distinction, to be discussed in more detail in Section 9.2, may have existed in Mandarin of the Ming dynasty, but in most Mandarin dialects now, syllables like [ tsiŋ ] have merged into syllables such as [ tɕiŋ ], although in Jiang-Huai Mandarin, such as Nanjing, and in the Wu dialects, this distinction is retained. Again, considering such a contrast both as an archaic feature and a dialectal one, it is incorporated in the Old National Pronunciation. For a native speaker of Beijing Mandarin, the characters 精 and 經 are homophones pronounced as [ tɕiŋ ], and consequently to learn this mixed standard, these speakers would have to memorize that 精 should be pronounced as [ tsiŋ ] instead.

With these added dialectal features, the actual Old National Pronunciation sounds like a stilted version of Beijing Mandarin. It is easily intelligible to speakers of Beijing Mandarin and possibly other Mandarin dialects as well.

It is interesting to note here the Old National Pronunciation may be compared to the *Qièyùn* system described in Chapter 4. Both standards were determined after discussions among scholars, and both of these systems incorporated certain archaic and dialectal features from the lower Yangtze River region, although the main base dialect was that of the old capital, that is, Luoyang in the *Qièyùn* era, according to some scholars,[3] and Beijing in the Republican era of China. Furthermore, both systems were meant for cross-dialectal uses. However, there is one major difference. The *Qièyùn* standard was only a literary pronunciation system, which was not intended for spoken purposes, while the Old National Pronunciation was a spoken standard that needed to be learned and used in daily communication. Due to the artificial nature of the mixed standard of 1913, it became very impractical, thus leading to further discussions among scholars. Some preferred a system completely based on the real pronunciation of Beijing Mandarin, while others still argued for a hybrid system, until in 1926, a consensus to use Beijing Mandarin exclusively as the basis for the national standard was reached among the members of the committee in charge of the unification of the national language under the Ministry of Education of the Republic of China. This new system of pronunciation is called the New National Pronunciation (*Xīn Guóyīn* 新國音) and was eventually officially adopted as the phonological basis of the national language in 1932, when the Ministry of Education published a new edition of the standard dictionary from 1919. The New National Pronunciation of the national language, that is, the *Guóyǔ*, evolved into the standard phonology of *Pǔtōnghuà* of contemporary China.

One clarification here is that even though Beijing Mandarin is the sole basis of *Pǔtōnghuà*, they are not synonymous, because dialect features that have a strong Beijing flavor are only selectively adopted in the codification of *Pǔtōnghuà*. For example, Beijing Mandarin is characterized by its rhotacized syllables such as *huār* 花兒 ("flower"), in which the *-r* sound is added to the word *huā*. In contrast, *Pǔtōnghuà* only adopts a subset of these rhotacized syllables. Peculiar Beijing words are generally not admitted into the national standard, such as the local Beijing word *cèi* ("to break"), pronounced as [ tsʰei⁵¹ ].

According to Chen (1999), the adoption of vernacular Beijing Mandarin pronunciation exclusively as the official phonological system of the national language is especially significant in that for the first time in the history of the Chinese language, vernacular pronunciations gained prestige over literary pronunciations. Thus, with both Literary Chinese and its literary pronunciations demoted, diglossia was eventually eliminated entirely, thus paving the way for modern literacy and education policies.

The third issue in the linguistic reforms of the early 20th century is about the Chinese script. From the beginning of written records of Chinese, characters have always been used as the only official writing system in China. The most important feature of Chinese characters, in comparison to phonetic writing systems such as the Latin alphabet, is that Chinese characters do not directly represent, or are not directly associated with, any particular fixed sounds. Although the majority of Chinese characters contain phonetic components, the whole system by and large cannot be called a phonetic writing system. In the early 20th century, it was believed that a phonetic script was more efficient in writing down a language and consequently more effective in literacy and education. Therefore, scholars embarked on script reform measures in two different directions, including the invention of phonetic writing systems for Chinese and the simplification of Chinese characters.

There are generally two types of phonetic writing systems for Chinese. Some would use symbols based on obsolete and simple Chinese characters, while others would use the Latin alphabet. The character-based phonetic writing system is represented by the *Zhùyīn Zìmǔ* 注音字母 ("*Letters for Annotating Sounds*"), as shown in Table 9.1 with their *pīnyīn* correspondences.

The *Zhùyīn Zìmǔ* was actually based on previous versions in the earlier years of the 20th century. The *Zhùyīn Zìmǔ* was associated with the Old National Pronunciation, because it was used as the official phonetic script to annotate the sounds

*Table 9.1* Examples of *Zhùyīn Zìmǔ*

| Zhùyīn Zìmǔ | ㄅ | ㄆ | ㄇ | ㄈ | ㄚ | ㄠ | ㄨ | ㄡ |
|---|---|---|---|---|---|---|---|---|
| Pīnyīn | b | p | m | f | a | ao | o | ou |

of characters in the dictionary of 1919. In this system, each of these symbols corresponds to one sound or one fixed combination of sounds, and each sound or combination is represented by one symbol. Although similar in appearance to Chinese characters, these symbols in the *Zhùyīn Zìmǔ* are fixed phonetic symbols.[4]

Since the Old National Pronunciation was a mixed system, some of the phonetic symbols in the *Zhùyīn Zìmǔ* represented sounds that were not used in Beijing Mandarin. Subsequently, in the New National Pronunciation, only those symbols which represented Beijing Mandarin sounds were retained, and the new edited version was renamed *Zhùyīn Fúhào* 注音符號 ("*Symbols for Annotating Sounds*") in 1930. The *Zhùyīn Fúhào* was used alongside a Romanized script called *Gwoyeu Romatzyh* (國語羅馬字, *Guóyǔ Luómǎzì*, "*Romanized Symbols for the National Language*") in the dictionary published by the Ministry of Education in 1932.

The *Gwoyeu Romatzyh*, as spelt in the script itself, is a representative system of Latin-based script, designed in 1925–1926 by a group of linguists, including *Qián Xuántóng* 錢玄同 (1887–1939), a renowned philologist who was well versed in the classics of traditional Chinese culture but was definitely not a staunch conservative. In an article published in 1923 in the National Language Monthly (*Guóyǔ Yuèkān* 國語月刊), *Qián Xuántóng* called for a "revolution of the Chinese writing system" to replace Chinese characters by a phonetic script such as those used in Western countries, because he believed that Chinese characters represented an old era and were not suitable for a modern Chinese society. Such views, albeit not justifiable, were held by many progressive scholars of that time as arguments for the need of a phonetic script for Chinese.

Initially used together with the *Zhùyīn Fúhào* in the dictionary of 1932 to annotate the pronunciations of characters, the *Gwoyeu Romatzyh* was designed to be a fully functional writing system, which, according to its original designers, would ultimately replace Chinese characters. However, the *Gwoyeu Romatzyh* was not widely adopted, partly because it was too complicated to learn and was thus considered somewhat impractical.

In contrast, the *Latinxua sin wenz* (拉丁化新文字, *Lādīnghuà Xīn Wénzì*, "*Latinized New Script*") was more successful, in that it was the only Romanized script that has ever been implemented in practical literacy movements on a large scale. The *Latinxua sin wenz* was designed by Chinese communist scholars together with Soviet linguists in the Soviet Union during 1928–1931 and was employed in literacy programs for the 100,000 Chinese workers in the Soviet Far East. Later, in the early 1940s, it was introduced to the Communist-controlled areas in China.

After the founding of the People's Republic of China in 1949, the government created a new Romanized script called *pīnyīn* 拼音 ("spell sounds"), with diacritic marks for tones, in 1958. Currently, the *pīnyīn* system is the standard annotation system for Chinese characters.

As mentioned earlier, script reform entails two areas of tasks: creating a phonetic writing system for Chinese and simplifying Chinese characters. Admittedly, it takes a long time for anyone to acquire proficiency in reading and writing Chinese characters. In *Qián Xuántóng*'s view, Chinese characters should eventually be replaced by a Romanized script, but he acknowledged that such a radical reform needed to proceed in stages, first by simplification of characters. In the early 1920s, *Qián Xuántóng* proposed a set of methods to simply Chinese characters, which led to a movement among linguistic reformers to create simplified Chinese characters, but it was only after 1949 that more systematic work to simplify Chinese characters across the board was carried out in batches, in the 1950s and then in the late 1970s, although further simplifications proposed in the late 1970s were officially revoked in 1986 because there was real concern that the writing system had been oversimplified, and it had caused confusion and other practical issues. Currently, the system of simplified Chinese characters used in China is mostly that of the 1950s. Traditional Chinese characters are still used in limited settings. Most educated speakers of Chinese can read both traditional and simplified characters.

Note that the original idea of designing a phonetic script for Chinese is to replace Chinese characters. But at present, transitioning from a character-based system to a Romanized one is no longer supported by scholars or the government, partially because it has been proven that the literacy rate could be improved without resorting to a radical change to a phonetic script. Furthermore, especially when issues with displaying and typing Chinese characters during the early years of computers have been successfully resolved now, using Chinese characters seems to have become easier and more fun, as the Internet age ushered in new interesting developments in the writing system. Nowadays young people read and type characters more often than they write. Therefore, writing Chinese characters has become increasingly challenging for many. On the other hand, since typing Chinese characters requires selection of the correct character from a long list of homophones, people often fail to select the correct character or just do not bother to do so, thus leading to creative uses of homophones on the Internet. For the younger generations, who are usually familiar with English or other Western languages, they tend to mix Chinese characters and foreign words or even make new inventions using materials from both Chinese and Western languages. No wonder such innovative and sometimes sloppy uses of the written language are called "*Martian writings*," because it is very hard for people who do not follow the latest trends on the Internet to understand them.

Now we have provided a sketch of the three areas of linguistic reforms that created Modern Standard Chinese, or *Pǔtōnghuà*, which was officially established in 1956. According to the definition of *Pǔtōnghuà*, the pronunciation is based on that of Beijing, the grammar is based on exemplary vernacular literary works such as those written by *Lǎo Shě* 老舍 (1899–1966) and other writers of the 20th century, and the vocabulary is based on words with generality within the Mandarin dialect group.

The *Guóyǔ* of the Republic of China era was brought to Taiwan in 1949 and continues to function as the standard language there. The *Pǔtōnghuà* and the *Guóyǔ* essentially share the same base dialect and grammatical norms, but there are notable differences. The *Guóyǔ* has more of a southern flavor, with vocabulary influences from Taiwanese, the Min dialect spoken in Taiwan. The pronunciations of certain characters may differ from *Pǔtōnghuà* as well. For example, 夕 ("sunset") is pronounced as *xī* in *Pǔtōnghuà* but as *xì* in *Guóyǔ*, and 艘 (measure word for ships) is *sōu* in *Pǔtōnghuà* but *sāo* in *Guóyǔ*. Of course the most obvious differences lie in the use of traditional Chinese characters and the *Zhùyīn Fúhào* in the *Guóyǔ*.

In the next sections of this chapter, we discuss the sounds, grammar, and vocabulary of Modern Standard Chinese and how they are connected to earlier stages of the Chinese language, especially Old Mandarin.

## 9.2    The modern phonological system

First, let's compare the initials of Modern Standard Chinese, as shown in Table 9.2, with those of Old Mandarin in Table 5.1 from Chapter 5. The system of initials in Table 9.2 is based on Chen (1999: 35).

The initial [ ʋ ] of Old Mandarin disappeared at around the beginning of the Qing dynasty. Words with a [ ʋ ] initial are pronounced with a zero-initial in Modern Standard Chinese. For example, the word *wēi* 微 ("tiny") was pronounced as [ ʋui⁴⁵ ] in Old Mandarin but as [ uei⁵⁵ ] now. The initial [ ŋ ] also disappeared during the 15th century. For example, the word *wǒ* 我 ("I") was pronounced as [ ŋɔ²¹⁵ ] in Old Mandarin, but as [ uo²¹⁴ ] now with a zero initial. Note that although the [ ŋ ] initial disappeared, the sound [ ŋ ] itself is still existent in Modern Standard Chinese as a syllable coda, for example, in the word for soup, 湯 *tāng* [ tʰaŋ⁵⁵ ].

A major change in the initials is the appearance of the set of palatal sibilant consonants in Modern Standard Chinese, that is, [ tɕ, tɕʰ, ɕ ]. These sounds are results of palatalization of the alveolar sibilants [ ts, tsʰ, s ] and the velar stop and fricative sounds [ k, kʰ, x ] before a high, front vowel such as [ i ] or [ y ]. Note that the IPA symbol [ y ] is the rounded high front vowel such as the *ü* (umlaut) in the German word *über*. There are two successive waves of palatalization involved here. First, as early as in the 16th century during the Ming dynasty, the velar stop and fricative initials began to change to their corresponding palatals. For example:

[ ki ] > [ tɕi ]    [ kʰi ] > [ tɕʰi ]    [ xi ] > [ ɕi ]
[ ky ] > [ tɕy ]    [ kʰy ] > [ tɕʰy ]    [ xy ] > [ ɕy ]

At this point, the alveolar sibilants had not changed to palatals yet. Thus, there would be a contrast between the following syllables in each pair.

[ tsi̅ ] vs [ tɕi ]    [ tsʰi ] vs [ tɕʰi ]    [ si ] vs. [ ɕi ]
[ tsy ] vs [ tɕy ]    [ tsʰy ] vs [ tɕʰy ]    [ sy ] vs. [ ɕy ]

*Table 9.2* Modern Standard Chinese initials

| Bilabial | Labiodental | Alveolar | | Retroflex | Palatal | Velar | Zero |
|---|---|---|---|---|---|---|---|
| p | f | t | ts | tʂ | tɕ | k | ø |
| pʰ | | tʰ | tsʰ | tʂʰ | tɕʰ | kʰ | |
| m | | n | s | ʂ | ɕ | x | |
| | | l | | ɻ | | | |

The contrast is essentially between the alveolar and palatal sibilant initials in each pair. The alveolar initials [ ts, tsʰ, s ] in these syllables with the vowels [ i ] and [ y ] are called "*sharp sounds*" (尖音, *jiānyīn*) due to their auditory perception of sharpness, while the palatal initials [ tɕ, tɕʰ, ɕ ] are called "*round sounds*" (團音, *tuányīn*) because of their auditory perception of smoothness. This contrast between round sounds and sharp sounds is still maintained in the Peking Opera, although the contrast disappeared in Beijing Mandarin during the Qing dynasty, resulting in homophones such as the following: 劍 *jiàn* ("sword") vs. 箭 *jiàn* ("arrow"). However, in Old Mandarin, the word for "*sword*" 劍 was [ kiɛm⁵¹ ], while the word for "*arrow*" 箭 was [ tsiɛm⁵¹ ]. Then, in the Ming dynasty, 劍 [ kiɛm⁵¹ ] palatalized to [ tɕiɛn⁵¹ ], contrasting with 箭 [ tsiɛn⁵¹ ]. In the Qing dynasty, 箭 [ tsiɛn⁵¹ ] also palatalized to [ tɕiɛn⁵¹ ], becoming homophones with 劍. As mentioned earlier in this chapter, the Old National Pronunciation included the distinction between "*sharp*" and "*round*" sounds, because in the Nanjing dialect and Wu dialects, such a contrast still existed. But for Beijing Mandarin speakers, it would not be possible to tell these syllables apart by their native pronunciations unless artificial distinctions were learned for such words. This was one of the major reasons the mixed standard in the Old National Pronunciation was eventually abandoned when the New National Pronunciation based solely on the phonological system of Beijing Mandarin was adopted.

Now let's look at the finals of Modern Standard Chinese, as shown in Table 9.3, in comparison with the finals of Old Mandarin in Table 5.2 from Chapter 5. The system of finals in Table 9.3 is based on Chen (1999: 35).

*Table 9.3* Modern Standard Chinese finals

| *No Medial*<br>開口呼 | *[ i ] series*<br>齊齒呼 | *[ u ] series*<br>合口呼 | *[ y ] series*<br>撮口呼 |
|---|---|---|---|
| ɿ<br>ʅ | i | u | y |
| a | ia | ua | |
| o | | uo | |
| ɤ | iɛ | | yɛ |
| ɚ | | | |
| ai | | uai | |
| ei | | uei | |
| au | iau | | |
| ou | iou | | |
| an | ian | uan | yan |
| ɔn | in | un | yn |
| aŋ | iaŋ | uaŋ | |
| ɔŋ | iŋ | uɔŋ | yŋ |
| | | uŋ | |

The major change in the system of finals is the formation of the four vocalizations, or *sìhū* 四呼. In Modern Standard Chinese, finals without a medial are called *kāikǒuhū* 開口呼 (literally *"open-mouth sound"*), finals with an [ i ] medial or main vowel are called *qíchǐhū* 齊齒呼 (*"even-teeth sound"*), finals with an [ u ] medial or main vowel are called *hékǒuhū* 合口呼 (*"closed-mouth sound"*), and finals with an [ y ] medial or main vowel are called *cuōkǒuhū* 撮口呼 (*"round-mouth sound"*). In Old Mandarin, these four types of finals were almost formed, with the exception of the *cuōkǒuhū*, which at that time had the [ iu ] medial or main vowel. Later the [ iu ] fused into [ y ], making the development of the four vocalizations complete.

Furthermore, there is the development of the Modern Standard Chinese rhotic final "er," or [ ɚ ] from the Old Mandarin syllable [ ɻï ] that included words like *ér* 兒 ("son"), *ér* 而 ("and, but"), *ěr* 爾 ("you"), *ěr* 耳 ("ear"), and *èr* 二 ("two"). The *ɻï* > ɚ change took place sometime during the Ming dynasty. Because the word *ér* 兒 is also a suffix, the [ ɚ ] syllable can merge with the preceding syllable in various ways to create rhotacized syllables. Such rhotacized syllables appeared as early as in the 17th century. In Modern Standard Chinese, one of the functions of the suffix -*ér* is a diminutive suffix. For example, *lánzi* 籃子 is a basket, while *lán'ér* 藍兒 is a small basket. The pronunciation of *lán'ér* is by deleting the nasal coda -*n* in the first syllable and adding the retroflex -*ɻ* as the coda, that is, *láɻ*, although still written as 籃兒. Syllables like *láɻ* are called rhotacized syllables, which are a major feature of Modern Standard Chinese. But note that the rhotic final "er" is a regular phoneme of Modern Standard Chinese, while the rhotacized syllables are results of the morphological process of suffixing the -*er* to other words. These two notions are related but nonetheless belong to different realms of the linguistic system.

Another change is that the nasal coda -*m* merged into the nasal coda -*n* during the Ming dynasty. Thus, formerly different syllables such as [ tʰam⁴⁵ ] 談 ("talk") and [ tʰan⁴⁵ ] 壇 ("altar") in Old Mandarin are not distinguishable in Modern Standard Chinese anymore. Both words are pronounced as *tán* now. We have actually seen one example of this merger previously, when the distinction between the "*sharp*" and "*round*" sounds is discussed. The word for "*sword*" 劍 changed from [ kiɛm⁵¹ ] in Old Mandarin to [ tɕiɛn⁵¹ ] in the Ming dynasty.

Additionally, there are some other simplifications in the system of finals, such as the merger of the Old Mandarin [ uɔn ] into [ uan ].

In terms of tonal development, the basic system is the same as in Old Mandarin, although there are some minor differences among the actual tonal shapes, that is, *yīnpíng* 55, *yángpíng* 35, *shǎngshēng* 214, and *qùshēng* 51.

As discussed in Chapter 5, a register distinction developed in Late Middle Chinese in each of the *píng*, *shǎng*, *qù*, and *rù* tones. The split in the *píng* tone has been retained from Old Mandarin up to now in Modern Standard Chinese. Specifically, if a *píng*-tone character had a voiceless initial in Middle Chinese, it is generally in the *yīnpíng* tonal category in Modern Standard Chinese. If a *píng*-tone character had a voiced initial in Middle Chinese, it is generally in the *yángpíng* tonal category.

In terms of the *shǎng* tone, part of the *yángshǎng* characters merged with the *qù* tone in Modern Standard Chinese. The phonological condition is that if a Middle Chinese *shǎng*-tone character had a voiced obstruent initial, such as a voiced stop, affricate, or fricative, then it would merge into the *qù* tone category in Old Mandarin and consequently in Modern Standard Chinese as well. The remaining *yángshǎng* characters, that is, those with sonorant initials, merged with the *yīnshǎng*. Thus, there is only one *shǎng* tone category in Old Mandarin and Modern Standard Chinese.

The *yīnqù* and *yángqù* tones merged back together in Old Mandarin, and that merge is retained up to the present time. Note here the *qù* tone also includes some of the *yángshǎng* characters, as mentioned previously.

The *rù* tone characters are also distributed into the four tonal categories in Modern Standard Chinese according to the voicing qualities of the initials. For example, if a character in the *rù* tone category had a voiced obstruent initial in Middle Chinese, its modern tonal category is generally *yángpíng*, while characters with other types of voiced consonants, such as nasal consonants, became *qù* tone characters. The characters in the *rù* tone category with voiceless initials are distributed into the other four tonal categories without clear rules. Although the *rù*-tone characters were distributed into the other tones in Old Mandarin as well, the actual distribution in Modern Standard Chinese is quite different from that in Old Mandarin.

One new development in the tonal system is tone sandhi, that is, tone changes in connected speech. There may or may not be tone sandhi in earlier stages of Chinese, for example, Middle Chinese and Old Mandarin, but we really do not have any data or evidence to make a conclusion there. However, tone sandhi is a main feature of modern tones. For example, two consecutive third tones, that is, 214–214, in Modern Standard Chinese are actualized as 35–214. The first 214 tone should be changed to a 35. This is the case in the most common phrase for "*hello*," that is, *nǐ hǎo* 你好, which should be pronounced rather as *ní hǎo*. The third-tone sandhi is the most common type in Modern Standard Chinese, although there are some other minor types of tone sandhi. In general, tone changes in connected speech are relatively simple and straightforward in Mandarin Chinese, while many southern dialects have highly complex systems of tone sandhi.

Also typical of Modern Standard Chinese is the development of unstressed syllables called *qīngshēng* 輕聲 ("light tone"), in which the original tones are neutralized. For example, the pronunciation of the word *tàiyáng* 太陽 ("sun") is quite often *tàiyang* in actual speech. In the actual pronunciation, the first syllable has the main stress with the full tonal shape, and the second syllable is unstressed, with the loss of its tonal shape, as shown by the lack of its original tone mark. Such unstressed neutral tones are not as common in southern dialects.

In summary, the overall phonological system of Modern Standard Chinese is quite similar to that of Old Mandarin, with some minor adjustments. Now let's turn to the grammar of Modern Standard Chinese by discussing its morphology first.

## 9.3   Morphological properties

The majority of Modern Standard Chinese morphemes are still monosyllabic, with a small number of disyllabic morphemes, such as *húdié* (蝴蝶, "butterfly"), *pútao* (葡萄, "grape"), and *zhīzhū* (蜘蛛, "spider"). Both of these two types of morphemes have been common throughout the history of the language. With the translation of ideas and concepts from Western cultures, there are also many multisyllabic morphemes in Modern Standard Chinese, for example, *màikèfēng* (麥克風, "microphone") and so on.

In terms of morphological processes, affixing, reduplication, and compounding are all quite common, with compounding being the major device for creating new words in Chinese. For example, the prefix *lǎo* 老 is still a common way of indicating familiarity, such as in *Lǎo Zhāng* (老張, "Old Zhang"), in which the prefix *lǎo* is attached to a family name, usually of an older person. Similarly, the prefix *xiǎo* 小 can be attached to surnames of younger people to show familiarity as well, such as in *Xiǎo Zhāng* (小張, "Little Zhang"). The prefix *dì* 第 can be attached to cardinal numbers to form ordinal numbers, such as *dìyī* (第一, "first"), *dìwǔ* (第五, "fifth"), and so on.

As for suffixes, the diminutive *-ér* 兒 is attested in texts as early as from the Tang dynasty, as mentioned in Chapter 7. In Modern Standard Chinese, the *-ér* suffix is both a phonological phenomenon, with its function of rhotacizing the preceding syllable, and a morphological phenomenon, typically with its diminutive meaning. More examples of this *-ér* suffix include: *píng'ér* (瓶兒, "small bottle"), *qǔ'ér* (曲兒, "a tune"), and so on. But in many cases, the *-ér* morpheme is purely stylistic. For example, the word for "movie" is *diànyǐng* 電影, but it is often pronounced as *diànyǐng'ér* 電影, without the diminutive meaning. Another type of *-ér* morpheme serves to distinguish between different words. For example, *gài* 蓋 is the verb "*to cover*," while *gài'ér* 蓋兒 is the noun for "*lid, cover*." Also, *xìn* 信 means "*letter, correspondence*," while *xìn'ér* 信兒 is a short message. The word *huǒxīng* 火星 is the planet Mars, while *huǒxīng'ér* 火星兒 is a spark, such as from a fire.

There are a number of new suffixes as well. For example, *huà* 化 is similar to the English "*-ize*" such as in "*modernize.*" The word for "*modern*" in Chinese is *xiàndài* 現代, from which *xiàndài-huà* 現代化 ("modernize, modernization") can be derived. The suffix *xué* 學 is similar to the English "*-ology*," such as in "*geology*" and "*phonology*." Many words of such fields of studies have this *xué* suffix, for example, *dìzhì-xué* (地質學, "geology"), *yīnxì-xué* (音系學, "phonology"), *shù-xué* (數學, "mathematics").

The plural morpheme *-men* 們, originally used in pronouns, such as in *wǒmen* (我們, "we"), can now be attached to nouns of people, for example, *háizi* (孩子, "child") → *háizi-men* (孩子們, "children"), *xuéshēng* (學生, "student") → *xuéshēng-men* (學生們, "students"). Thus, it seems that the morpheme *-men* could be an inflectional morpheme similar to the English plural morpheme *-s*. However, *-men* is not compatible with number words, for example, "*sān-ge háizi*" ("three CL child") for "*three children*," but not "*sān-ge háizi-men*." Thus, some scholars argue that -*men* is not an inflectional morpheme at all but rather a morpheme denoting a group, which seems to be quite reasonable judging from the origin of -*men* being the word for a group of people, that is, *bèi* 輩, in Classical Chinese.

Reduplication is quite common in Modern Standard Chinese as well. Nouns, adjectives, verbs, and measure words can all be reduplicated. For example, kinship terms are normally in a reduplicated form, such as *bàba* (爸爸, "dad"), *māma* (媽媽, "mom"), *shūshu* (叔叔, "father's younger brother, uncle"), *dìdi* (弟弟, "younger brother"). Note that in these terms, the second syllable is always unstressed with a neutral tone. Adjectives can be reduplicated to be more descriptive and vivid. For example, from "*lán*" (藍, "blue") is constructed the vivid form "*lánlán-de* 藍藍的." The semantic difference may be illustrated by the following examples where the noun *tiān* 天 ("sky") is modified by the adjective "*blue*" in the two forms: "*lán tiān*" 藍天 ("blue sky") and "*lánlán-de tiān*" 藍藍的天 ("sky that is really blue"). Adjectives with two syllables of type AB, can be reduplicated either as AABB, for example, *jiǎndān* (簡單, "easy") → *jiǎnjiǎndāndān* 簡簡單單, or as ABAB, for example, *bīngliáng* (冰涼, "icy cold") → *bīngliángbīngliáng* 冰涼冰涼. Verbs can be reduplicated to derive a tentative or a delimitative aspect meaning, that is, "*do something a little bit*" (Li and Thompson 1981: 232). For example, from the verb *kàn* (看, "to look at"), we can form *kànkan* 看看,[5] meaning "*take a look*," and it can often be used in a suggestion as in "*nǐ kànkan*" 你看看 ("you" + "look-look") to mean "*please take a look*." Some disyllabic verbs can be reduplicated as ABAB, for example, *tǎolùn* (討論, "to discuss") → *tǎolùntǎolùn* 討論討論. Measure words can be reduplicated to mean "*every*," for example, *tiáo* (條, the measure word for *xīnwén* 新聞 "news") → *tiáotiáo xīnwén* (條條新聞, "every piece of news").

As a result of the general trend of disyllabification in Chinese, more words are being created by compounding. In terms of the internal structures of compound nouns and verbs, according to Packard (2000: 127), about 90% of compound nouns in Chinese have the main nominal morpheme on the right, and about 85% of compound verbs have the main verbal morpheme on the left. For example, the word for "*volcano*" is *huǒshān* 火山 ("fire" + "mountain"). The main nominal element, that is, *shān* 山, is on the right. The word for "*to put on a demonstration*" is *shìwēi* 示威 ("show" + "power"). The main verbal element, that is, *shì* 示, is on the left. However, the boundary between a compound word and a phrase is not always easy to draw, because the verbal and the nominal elements in compound verbs do not form a tight unit but rather can be separated by other words and phrases. For example, from the compound verb *shìwēi*, we can get a phrase "*shì-le yícì wēi*" 示了一次威 ("show-PERF one-CL power" → carried out demonstration once).

## 9.4 Word classes and cross-category flexibility

The major word classes are still the same as before, including nouns, verbs, adjectives, measure words, conjunctions, interjections, pronouns, prepositions, helping words, and so on. There is still a certain degree of flexibility across the major word classes. Specifically, nouns, verbs, and adjectives share many common grammatical properties. For example, nouns can take the sentence-final particle *-le*, which often occurs in a sentence with a verb or an adjective, as shown in (1), (2), and (3).

(1) *Wǒ    huì    huábīng    le*
    我    會    滑冰    了。
    I    can    skate    PAR
    "I can skate now [for example, in contrast to the past when I didn't know how]."

(2) *Jīntian    tiānqi    rè    le*
    今天    天氣    熱    了。
    today    weather    hot    PAR
    "It is becoming hot today [for example, compared to yesterday]."

(3) *Xīngqītiān    le*
    星期天    了。
    Sunday    PAR
    "It is Sunday now."

This word *-le*, which appears at the end of a sentence, is different from the perfective aspect marker *-le*, first mentioned in Chapter 7. The grammatical meaning of this sentence-final particle *-le* is still debated among linguists. According to Li and Thompson (1981), the basic communicative function of this sentence-final *-le* is to signal a "*currently relevant state*," such as a change of state. In (1), the *-le* indicates that there has been a change in the state of one's knowing how to skate. In (2), there is a contrast between today's being hot and another time. In (3), it is the change of time that is expressed. Since sentence-final particles are normally attached to a sentence, it can be argued that Chinese nouns can function as the predicate of a sentence, as in (3). This shows one of the common properties of nouns shared with verbs and adjectives. As discussed in Chapter 6, Chinese adjectives are more like verbs; thus, an alternative term for Chinese "adjective" is "stative verb." In Modern Standard Chinese, adjectives can be predicates without a linking verb, as shown in (2). The linking verb *shì* 是 can be used with adjectives only in certain emphatic contexts but not in a neutral one.

    In terms of the pronoun system, the first-person, second-person, and third-person pronouns are *wǒ* 我, *nǐ* 你, and *tā* 他 in the singular form, respectively. The plural versions of these pronouns are formed by adding *-men*, such as *tāmen* (他們, "they"). One recent development is that a gender distinction is now made in the written forms of "*tā*." Although the spoken form is one and the same "*tā*," it is written as "他" if it refers to a male person, as "她" if it refers to a female person, and the character 它 is a gender-neutral pronoun like "*it*." Similarly for the plural forms, the distinction is also maintained in writing as 他們 ("they" masculine), 她們 ("they" feminine), and 它們 ("they" animals and things), although all three forms are pronounced exactly the same as "*tāmen*." This feature of gender distinction in the written forms of pronouns was a result of linguistic reforms in the early 20th century, when European grammars were considered clearer and more systematic by progressive Chinese scholars and linguists.

Similarly to Classical Chinese, prepositions can be used as verbs. For example:

(4) *Qǐng    gěi    wǒ    dǎ    diànhuà*
　　請　　給　　我　　打　　電話。
　　please　to　　me　　make　phone
　　"Please make a phone call to me."

(5) *Qǐng    gěi    wǒ    yì    běn    shū*
　　請　　給　　我　　一　　本　　書。
　　please　give　me　　one　CL　　book
　　"Please give me a book."

In (4), the main verb is "*dǎ*," while the word "*gěi*" is used as a preposition. In (5), the only verb is "*gěi*." Most prepositions can be used as verbs, such as *gēn* 跟 (the preposition "together with" and the verb "to follow"), *yòng* 用 (instrumental "with" and the verb "to use"), *zài* 在 (the preposition "at" and the verb "to be present, to be located"). Thus, prepositions in Chinese are also referred to as coverbs.

## 9.5   Typical word order

The basic word order of Modern Standard Chinese is SVO, although there is quite a degree of flexibility. For example, the object can be relatively freely fronted as a topic of the conversation, such as in (6):

(6) *Měi    ge    rén,    wǒ    dōu    xǐhuan*
　　每　　個　　人，　我　　都　　喜歡。
　　every　CL　　person　I　　all　　like
　　"I like everyone."

The phrase "*měi ge rén*" is the object of the verb "*xǐhuan*," but here it is fronted as the topic of the sentence. The fronting is also required by the adverb "*dōu*," because phrases formed with "*měi*" need to appear to the left of "*dōu*." Another way of fronting the object is by using the BA-construction, as in (7).

(7) *Qǐng    bǎ    shū    gěi    wǒ*
　　請　　把　　書　　給　　我。
　　please　TOP　book　give　me
　　"Please give me the book."

In (7), the direct object of the verb is "*shū*," and it is fronted by using the word *bǎ*, which functions as a topic marker. Such sentences are usually uttered in a context where the noun denoted by the object of the verb is already known, hence being the topic of the conversation.

Prepositional phrases generally precede the verb. But for locative phrases, they have some special properties. Pre-verbal locative prepositional phrases indicate the location where an event takes place, while, in general, post-verbal prepositional phrases indicate the location as the result of the action denoted by the verb. Sentences (8) and (9) show such a contrast.

(8)  *Bié      zài     zhuōzi   shang    tiào*
     别       在      桌子      上       跳。
     don't    at      desk     top      jump
     "Don't jump on top of the desk."

(9)  *Tā      tiào     zài     zhuōzi   shàng*
     他       跳       在      桌子      上。
     he       jump    at      desk     top
     "He jumped onto the desk."

In (8), the locative phrase "*zài zhuōzi shang*" is where the "*jumping*" takes place; in (9), the result of the "*jumping*" is that "*he landed on the desk.*"

## 9.6   Aspect markers

Modern Standard Chinese does not have a grammatical device for tense. But there are systematic ways of indicating the aspect of verbs. The concept "*tense*" concerns the temporal relations between an eventuality and the speech time. Here, the term "*eventuality*" includes both events such as "*jumping*" and states like "*knowing.*" The concept "*aspect*" concerns the perspective from which the internal makeup of an event or a state is viewed. Theoretically speaking, a certain language may encode either tense or aspect or both in its grammar. If a language encodes both tense and aspect grammatically, it may use different morphemes or morphemes that fuse the functions of these two different dimensions. For example:

(10)   I was reading a book at 2:00 pm yesterday.

In (10), the event of reading happened before the speech time, as indicated by the use of the past tense form "*was*" of the verb "*to be.*" The event is viewed as ongoing, as indicated by the use of the present participle form "*reading.*" Both tense and aspect are encoded in the verbs. However, in Chinese, only the concept of aspect is specified but not tense. For example:

(11)  *Wǒ     zài      kànshū*
      我       在       看書。
      I        PROG    read
      "I am/was reading."

The morpheme *zài-* is a progressive aspect marker, which together with a verb phrase forms a construction similar to the English "*be Verb-ing.*" However in (11), there is no specification of time, and actually the sentence can be used as a past ongoing event, or a current ongoing event, as seen in the translation given. To further specify these readings, time words can be added, for example:

(12)  *Wǒ   xiànzài   zài    kànshū*
      我     現在      在     看書。
      I     now      PROG    read
      "I am reading now."

We have discussed the perfective aspect maker -*le*. Here is one more example, where it is used in a future context, thus showing that the word -*le* is not past tense.

(13)  *Wǒ   míngtiān   xià   le   kè     jiù    huí     jiā*
      我     明天       下    了   課     就     回      家。
      I     tomorrow   off   PERF  class   then   return   home
      "I will go home right after class is over tomorrow."

There are two other aspect markers: the durative -*zhe* 著 and the experiential -*guo* 過. For example:

(14)  *Bié    kàn    zhe    diànshì   chī   fàn*
      別      看     著     電視      吃    飯。
      don't   watch   DUR    TV       eat   food
      "Don't eat food while watching TV."

(15)  *Wǒ   qù    guo    Zhōngguó*
      我     去    過     中國。
      I     go    EXP    China
      "I have been to China."

The durative aspect marker -*zhe* is often used as a background state for some other ongoing event, as shown in (14), while the experiential aspect marker -*guo* is typically employed to talk about a past experience which has current relevancy. As mentioned in Chapter 7, the perfective aspect marker -*le* was originally a verb of completion. It has undergone grammaticalization and switched positions with the object of the verb, and consequently now the perfective marker -*le* is attached to the verb directly. Similarly, all three other aspect markers, that is, *zai*-, -*zhe*, and -*guo*, were originally verbs as well and have been grammaticalized into aspect markers that are attached to verbs.

## 9.7   Current uses of special grammatical constructions

In terms of the passive construction, there have been further developments after it was established in the Tang dynasty. A new type of BEI-construction where the verb is followed by an object appeared already during the Tang. A modern example is given in (16).

(16)  *Yuēhàn   bèi    xiǎotōu'ér   tōu    le     qiánbāo*
      約翰      被     小偷兒       偷     了     錢包。
      John     PASS    thief       steal   PERF   wallet
      "John's wallet was stolen by a thief."

In (16), the object "*qiánbāo*" has a semantic relation with the subject "*Yuēhàn*," that is, the subject being the possessor of the object, hence the translation "*John's wallet*" in English. Although it is possible to use "*John's wallet*" as the subject, as in (17), the meanings of (16) and (17) are not quite the same. Example (16) says that what happened to John is the event of "*wallet-being-stolen*," while (17) has a different perspective on the event, and it says what happened to the wallet is the event of "*being-stolen*." Although they amount to more or less the same actual happenings in the actual world, the contexts of use are slightly different for these two examples.

(17)  *Yuēhàn*   *de*    *qiánbāo*   *bèi*   *xiǎotōu'ér*   *tōu*   *le*
　　　約翰　　　的　　　錢包　　　被　　　小偷兒　　　偷　　　了。
　　　John       POSS    wallet      PASS    thief          steal   PERF
　　　"John's wallet was stolen by a thief."

Besides *bèi*, other new passive markers appeared. Two of the most often-used ones in the spoken language now are *jiào* 叫, attested as early as during the late Yuan dynasty, and *gěi* 給, attested quite late during the Qing dynasty. These morphemes are used in a similar fashion as the word *bèi* in the BEI-construction. For example:

(18)  *Yuēhàn*   *de*    *qiánbāo*   *jiào/gěi*   *xiǎotōu'ér*   *tōu*   *le*
　　　約翰　　　的　　　錢包　　　叫/給　　　小偷兒　　　偷　　　了。
　　　John       POSS    wallet      PASS        thief          steal   PERF
　　　"John's wallet was stolen by a thief."

There have been new developments in the BA-construction as well. For example, a type of BA-construction without a verb is attested in texts from as early as the Yuan dynasty. The following is a modern example.

(19)  *Wǒ*   *bǎ*   *nǐ*   *ge*   *méi*       *liángxīn*   *de*
　　　我　　把　　你　　個　　沒　　　　良心　　　的。
　　　I       TOP   you   CL    not-have   morals       NOM
　　　"You are such a person without morals!"

Such BA-constructions are often used to express certain strong feelings where the verb can be considered omitted but vaguely implied in the context of use.

In the typical use of the BA-construction, the focus of the sentence is what is done to the object of the word *bǎ*. For example in (20), the meaning of the sentence focuses on what has been done to the book, that is, "*it has been returned*," or in a more general sense, how the object has been affected.

(20)  *Wǒ*   *bǎ*   *shū*   *huán*    *le*
　　　我　　把　　書　　還　　　了。
　　　I       TOP   book   return   PERF
　　　"As for the book, I have returned it."

Another type of BA-construction, without the connotation of *"what is done to the object,"* appeared in the late Yuan dynasty. The following is a modern example.

(21) | *Kàn* | *bǎ* | *nǐ* | *gāoxìng* | *de* | *zuǐ* | *dōu* | *hé* | *bù* | *lǒng* | *le* |
|---|---|---|---|---|---|---|---|---|---|---|
| 看 | 把 | 你 | 高興 | 得 | 嘴 | 都 | 合 | 不 | 攏 | 了。 |
| look | TOP | you | happy | COMP | mouth | even | close | not | touch | PAR |

"Look, you are so happy that your mouth cannot close (since you are smiling)!"

In (21), the object *"nǐ"* is an experiencer of the stative verb *"gāoxìng."* Thus, there is no real sense of *"what is done to the object"* here, because there is no object at all. It is rather a general notion of *"being affected"* that is the focus in such a new type of BA-construction.

New grammatical features can be borrowed from other languages or dialects. For example, Europeanized grammatical structures have been quite common since the early 20th century during the linguistic reforms. More recently, influences from English can commonly be seen in the grammar of Modern Standard Chinese. The passive construction is more widely used in translation, although the typical use of the passive construction in Chinese was confined to negative contexts not that long ago. Furthermore, sentence structures may become more and more complex, modeling on long sentences in English and other European languages, although traditional Chinese sentences were mostly shorter.

On the other hand, Chinese dialects other than Beijing Mandarin have also exerted their influences on the standard language. Often it is the case that a popular expression or grammatical structure would become widely used even when it is not admitted into the national standard. For example, the usual way of saying *"haven't done something"* is by using the structure *"méiyǒu + verb,"* such as in *"méiyǒu hēshuǐ* 沒有喝水" ("have not drunk water," "did not drink water"). The corresponding affirmative structure uses the perfective marker *-le*, as in *"hē le shuǐ* 喝了水" ("have drunk water," "drank water"). But in the *Pǔtōnghuà* spoken in certain southern dialectal regions, the affirmative form is simply *"yǒu + verb,"* such as *"yǒu hēshuǐ* 有喝水" ("have drunk water," "drank water"), since the word *méiyǒu* 沒有 is the negation of the word *yǒu* 有. This might have been an influence from southern dialects where the affirmative structure of *"méiyǒu + verb"* is indeed formed by using *"yǒu"* as in *"yǒu + verb"* Although such a new usage of the verb *"yǒu"* has not been approved by the government agency in charge of the standardization of the national language, it is nonetheless quite popular among many speakers, even in the north. Therefore, there is always a certain degree of variation between regulations and speakers' actual linguistic practice. Even for speakers of Beijing Mandarin, some of the typical Beijing Mandarin features are not adopted by Modern Standard Chinese either, as has been briefly mentioned earlier in this chapter. The influence from Modern Standard Chinese on dialects probably is stronger in many ways. Dialects that have always had more contact with Mandarin dialects have absorbed many features from the national language in recent years.

In summary, this section discusses the grammar of Modern Standard Chinese with respect to its connections with earlier stages of the language. Next, we provide a brief account of some lexical changes in Modern Standard Chinese.

## 9.8   Changes in the modern lexicon

Vocabulary is a reflection of the cultural aspects of a linguistic community. Compared to earlier stages of the language, Modern Standard Chinese has a large lexicon of modern science and technology. In the Ming dynasty, Jesuit missionaries started to carry out proselytizing activities in China. These missionaries, such as Matteo Ricci (1552–1610), were among the first to translate or help to translate texts of Western science and technology into Chinese, thus creating the first batch of such new words in recent history. The following words were created in the Ming dynasty but are still standard terms in the modern language: *zìxíngchē* (自行車, "bicycle"), *bǐlì* (比例, "ratio"), *dìpíngxiàn* (地平線, "horizon"), *huǒchē* (火車, "train"), *gōngsī* (公司, "company").

In the Qing dynasty, quite a few Manchu words were borrowed into Chinese, for example, *mǎmǎhūhū* (馬馬虎虎, "in a careless way"), *lāta* (邋遢, "unkempt," "messy"), *luōsuo* (囉嗦, "wordy," "nagging"), *hēhù* (呵護, "to take care of"). Toward the end of the Qing dynasty, scholars translated further concepts from Western languages into Chinese, thus giving rise to the second batch of new words from Western languages, such as *zhǔzhāng* (主張, "proposal"), *jiàoyù* (教育, "education"), *jīchǔ* (基礎, "foundation"), *yínháng* (銀行, "bank"), *rìbào* (日報, "daily newspaper"), *jīqì* (機器, "machine"), and so on.

Some words related to modern society were borrowed into Chinese from Japanese, since many words were created in Japan when new concepts were translated into Japanese using *kanji* characters as a result of the Meiji Restoration that started in 1868. There are three types of such words, and only one type would generally be considered true loanwords. First, some of these words used in Japanese to translate Western concepts are actually Classical Chinese words, but they were afforded new meanings, for example, *zhǔyì* (主義, "doctrine"), *lǐxìng* (理性, "reason"), *lèguān* (樂觀, "optimistic"), *bǎoxiǎn* (保險, "insurance"), and so on. This type of loanword from Japanese is generally not considered real borrowings. The second type includes new words in Japanese that were created by using *kanji* characters with roughly the same meanings as those used in Chinese, for example, *chōuxiàng* (抽象, "abstract"), *biāoběn* (標本, "specimen"), *zhèngdǎng* (政黨, "political party"), *zhéxué* (哲學, "philosophy"), and so on. The meanings of these characters are more or less the same in both languages, and therefore these compound words can be readily understood in Chinese as well. For this reason, some scholars argue that this type of loanword should be distinguished from true borrowings too. The third type of Japanese words cannot be readily interpreted in Chinese, for example, *jījí* (積極, "active"), *chǎnghé* (場合, "occasion"), *shǒuxù* (手續, "procedures"). Such words in Chinese are considered genuine loandwords by most scholars.

With the introduction of Marxism and communism into China in the 1910s, many new words related to communism were created, for example, *zīběn zhǔyì*

(資本主義, "capitalism"), *shēngchǎnlì* (生產力, "productive force"), *zhímíndì* (殖民地, "colony"), *dìguózhǔyì* (帝國主義, "imperialism"), *jīhuì zhǔyì* (機會主義, "opportunism"), *sīwéi* (思維, "thought"), *wéiwù zhǔyì* (唯物主義, "materialism").

In more recent years, new concepts were created again to reflect new developments in science and technology, forming the third batch of such new words, such as *hùliánwǎng* (互聯網, "Internet"), *shǒujī* (手機, "cellphone"), *dǎyìnjī* (打印機, "printer"), *shǔbiāo* (鼠標, "mouse, used with a computer").

As pointed out in Chapter 8, purely phonetic loanwords are generally not well received in Chinese. Therefore, calques, or loan translations, are preferred, and in many cases, mixed borrowings are even better. For example, "*telephone*" was once "*délǜfēng*" 德律風, which was a purely phonetic loan, but it was replaced by the semantic loanword "*diànhuà*" 電話 ("electricity" + "speech"). The word "*democracy*" was once "*démòkèlāxī*" 德謨克拉西, a phonetic loanword, but was replaced by the calque "*mínzhǔ*" 民主 ("people" + "rule"). Here are two examples of mixed borrowings. The word "*píjiǔ*" 啤酒 ("beer") contains the syllable "*pí*" as the phonetic part corresponding to "*beer*," followed by "*jiǔ*," the Chinese term for "alcoholic drinks in general." The word "*bǐsàbǐng*" 比薩餅 consists of the phonetic part "*bǐsà*" for "pizza," followed by the Chinese word "*bǐng*" for "*pancake*." But, of course, there are indeed quite a number of purely phonetic loanwords, for example, *màikèfēng* (麥克風, "microphone") and *gāo'ěrfū* (高爾夫, "golf").

In addition to this layer of foreign words in Modern Standard Chinese, there are layers of formal expressions derived from Literary Chinese, such as the four-character idioms. These set expressions are highly condensed and often based on stories from ancient texts or well-known literary allusions. Many words from Literary Chinese are still often used in formal writings. For example, the Literary Chinese *zhī* 之 as a marker of nominal modifier can often replace the Modern Standard Chinese *de* 的 in academic essays. Instead of saying "*Hànyǔ de yǎnbiàn*" (漢語的演變, "Chinese language" + *de* + "development" → "development of the Chinese language"), one could use "*Hànyǔ zhī yǎnbiàn*" (漢語之演變) in formal writings and speeches. Literary Chinese knowledge is also needed to understand the morphemic composition in many modern words and phrases. Therefore, it is often not easy to demarcate the boundaries between modern and classical elements in the modern standard language.

With this, we conclude the discussion on Modern Standard Chinese. The next chapter focuses on modern Chinese dialects.

## Notes

1 According to Mai and Zhu (2012), Nanjing Mandarin of the Ming dynasty should be distinguished from the Nanjing dialect per se. It is only the Nanjing Mandarin that was a regional prestigious form of spoken language.
2 But if Li (1983) is right in arguing that Beijing Mandarin of the Yuan dynasty was actually that of Henan, then what was referred to as Beijing Mandarin during the Ming and early Qing may still be close to the Henan dialect. In this sense, Wang's (1958) view can be grouped with Mai and Zhu's (2012).

3  As discussed in Chapter 4, the base dialect of the *Qièyùn* is still debated, and no agreement has been reached. Pan (2000) argues that the Luoyang dialect was the basis of the *Qièyùn*.
4  The 36 initials of Late Middle Chinese in Table 4.2 may be considered an early prototype of a phonetic writing system by using fixed Chinese characters conventionally to represent sounds.
5  For monosyllabic verbs, the reduplicated form may have the number *yī* 一 in the middle, for example, *kàn yí kàn* 看一看.

# 10 Modern Chinese dialects

This chapter focuses on linguistic diversity in China by discussing the classification of Chinese dialects and their linguistic features in relation to earlier stages of the Chinese language such as Old Chinese and Middle Chinese.

## 10.1 Formation of Chinese dialects

The main factor in the formation of Chinese dialects is the migration of the Sinitic people from the north to the south.

In Chapter 2, we show that archaeological and genetic studies provide evidence that the Sino-Tibetan language family originated in the upper and middle Yellow River basin area. The Sinitic people migrated eastward and then southward, and in the first millennium BC, the territory of the Zhou dynasty extended from the Yellow River in the north to the Yangtze River in the south, including the State of Chu in the middle Yangtze River area and the State of Wu in the lower Yangtze River area. According to historical records, the languages in these southern regions of the Zhou dynasty differed greatly from the northern language. Mencius called a person from the State of Chu a "*shrike-tongued barbarian.*" He also argued that if a person from the State of Chu wanted to learn the dialect of the State of Qi in the eastern part of the north, they would have to live in the State of Qi and hear the local language around them, while it would be otherwise impossible to learn the language of Qi if they stayed in the State of Chu. We cannot draw any direct connection between the languages of the Wu and Chu with any modern Chinese dialects, although the Wu dialect group gets its designation because the area around Suzhou and Shanghai is traditionally called Wu after the ancient State of Wu. Although the origin of the modern Wu dialects may be traced back to the ancient State of Wu (Sun 2006: 30), some of the languages in these ancient southern states of the Zhou dynasty were definitely not Sinitic (Chamberlain 2016).

In the northern territory of the Zhou dynasty, the language may have been more uniform. In Chapter 3, we have used the *Shījīng* as one of the main texts upon which Old Chinese is reconstructed. According to the *Analects*, the language used in the *Shījīng* and by Confucius himself in his teaching was called the *yǎyán* (雅言, "elegant speech"), based on the dialect of the Zhou dynasty's capital city, which, during Confucius' time, was located in present-day Luoyang of Henan province. The name "*elegant speech*" itself suggests that the speech varieties in other regions or states may be different from the language of the capital city. The folk songs in the *Shījīng* are categorized by where they were collected from. For example, there are songs from the states of Qin 秦 and Bin 豳 in the western part of the country and from Chen 陳 and Qi 齊 in the eastern part of the country, just to name a few. Some records indicate that there were as many as 3000 songs at one time, but they were narrowed down to 305 as a result of selection and, possibly, editing by Confucius. Therefore, it is not surprising that the language of the *Shījīng* is still mostly based on the *yǎyán* (Wang 1985: 11). But since the folk songs were collected from different regions, it is possible that there were more dialectal elements in the *Shījīng* originally, although in its standard version, there is very little evidence for such dialectal variations.

In the Qin dynasty, the territory of the empire was extended further south to present-day Guangdong and Guangxi provinces. The origin of the modern Yue dialects may be traced back to Chinese-speaking people first brought to these areas during this time (Sun 2006: 31).

In the Han dynasty, *Yáng Xióng* 揚雄 (53 BC–AD 18) compiled a dictionary titled *Fāngyán* 方言 ("regional speech"), which is the origin of the modern Chinese term *fāngyán* for "*dialect*." *Yáng Xióng*'s dictionary provides an extensive list of lexical items from different regions of the country, thus being a valuable source for studying the sounds in Late Old Chinese and tracing origins of certain words in modern Chinese dialects.

In the Western and Eastern Jin 晉, when the north experienced constant wars between the *Hàn* Chinese and non-*Hàn* peoples, waves of immigration from the north brought northern dialects to the Yangtze River area such as the southern capital located in the present-day Nanjing. *Hàn* Chinese also moved into the Fujian area during this period, bringing their language further south, and this language may be the origin of the modern Min dialects (Sun 2006: 32). According to the Hakka people's own account, their ancestors moved from the north to southern Anhui and northern Jiangxi during this period as well (Norman 1988: 222).[1]

In the Northern and Southern dynasties, the dialects differed considerably in pronunciation. According to the preface of the *Qièyùn*, in the Wu and Chu areas in the south, the speech sounded light and shallow; in the Yan and Zhao areas in the north, the pronunciation was heavy and muddy, while people in the north-western part of the country pronounced the departing tone similarly to the entering tone, and in the southwest, their even tone sounded like the departing tone. These descriptions are clearly based on the auditory perceptions of these dialects, although the exact phonetic nature of such differences is not easy to pinpoint.

Toward the end of the Tang dynasty in the late 9th century, the country was again war-tone, especially in the north, which resulted in waves of immigration from the north to the south, bringing the northern dialects into various southern areas. It is also during this time that a group of Hakka speakers moved to southwestern Fujian and northern Guangdong (Luo 1958; Norman 1988: 222).

In the Southern Song dynasty (AD 1127–1279), the northern part of China was again ruled by non-*Hàn* peoples, and consequently many northerners moved to the south, bringing their northern dialects. Such southward migrations continued in the Yuan dynasty. The Mandarin dialects in southwestern China and northeastern China are related to migrations after the Yuan dynasty, when Mandarin speakers brought their dialects to the southwest in the Ming dynasty in the late 14th century and to the northeast during the Qing dynasty.

We have described the historical context of the formation of Chinese dialects in terms of migrations of the Sinitic people from the north to various regions of present-day China. Although a direct connection between such population movements and specific modern dialects would often be difficult to establish, especially when we talk about migrations in ancient times, such a context can nonetheless help to explain certain major themes in Chinese dialectology. For example, the lexicon and pronunciations in many Chinese dialects are differentiated into different strates. In southern dialects, there is often a substratum of lexical items that were borrowed from non-Sinitic languages when the Sinitic people migrated to the south, coming into contact with peoples who spoke languages that may very well be ancestors of languages in the Austroasiatic, Kra-Dai, Miao-Yao, or Austronesian families. Norman (1988: 18–19) argued that a common word meaning "*shaman*" or "*spirit healer*" in the Min dialects is evidence of an Austroasiatic substratum in the Min. The reconstructed Proto-Min pronunciation of this word is *$dəŋ$ or *$duŋ$, based on modern reflexes such as $tøiŋ^2$ in Fuzhou and $taŋ^2$ in Xiamen,[2] and these words are quite likely cognates with words that have similar sounds and meanings in Austroasiatic languages, for example, $ʔdoŋ^2$ in Vietnamese. In addition to a substratum, there are layers of literary pronunciations in Chinese dialects, as opposed to colloquial pronunciations. For example, the word for the adjective "*long*" in Chaozhou, a Southern Min dialect, is $tuŋ^2$ in colloquial pronunciation or $tsʰiaŋ^2$ in literary pronunciation, which is closer to the Mandarin pronunciation *cháng*. Literary pronunciations were borrowed from the linguistic standards at different times, for example, the *Guǎngyùn* system in Middle Chinese or Mandarin pronunciations since the Yuan dynasty. Southern dialects have more systematic literary pronunciations because these dialects split off from the north quite early via migrations to the south at different times but maintained contacts with the linguistic standards in the north. Colloquial pronunciations form the core layer in each of these southern dialects, which borrowed lexical items and pronunciations both from earlier non-Sinitic languages in their substrates and from later linguistic standards from the north in their literary pronunciations as superstrates. Such stratified systems can be nicely explained in terms of the historical context of the formation of Chinese dialects. Another example to show the usefulness of the historical context is that many dialects in the lower Yangtze River area are Mandarin, due to the multiple dynasties and their ruling classes that moved from the north to the south and established their capitals in those areas.

The second major factor in the formation of Chinese dialects is geography. The reason the mutually intelligible Mandarin dialects span the vast area in the north while the smaller area in the south is divided into six major groups of mutually unintelligible dialects is partially due to the different geographical features. The terrain in the north in general is quite flat, which contributed to a higher degree of communication and interactions between different areas. The south, by contrast, is quite hilly, which creates a higher degree of isolation among the different groups of people. In the southern dialectal regions, different geographical features may have contributed to the different extents to which they interacted with the north. Ramsey (1987: 96) argues that the Gan River in Jiangxi is an important route into the more remote southern provinces, and consequently, the dialects along the Gan River have been influenced more by Mandarin than the Min dialects because not only is the Fujian region very mountainous, it also lacks a major river that connects the region to the north. The time-depth of the Min dialects and their isolation from the north and from each other result in the most conservative or archaic forms of dialects with the least internal homogeneity (Norman 1988: 228).

The third contributing factor to the sharp contrast between the more innovative Mandarin dialects and the more conservative or archaic southern dialects can be stated in sociopolitical terms. As van Driem (1999: 54) points out, languages usually change more rapidly in societies that are rapidly evolving. Northern China has generally been the political and cultural center in Chinese history, where changes in social norms and political systems would often first take place and then diffuse to the south later.

As we have discussed in Chapter 1, the term "*fāngyán*" does not readily translate into "*dialect*" in English (Mair 1991). The major groups of Chinese dialects are not mutually intelligible, and even within the same group, speakers from different places do not necessarily understand each other either. Therefore, strictly speaking, the major groups of Chinese dialects are actually different Sinitic languages. This terminological choice, that is, "*Sinitic language*", is preferred by many scholars. But since the more widely used term is still "*Chinese dialect*," we continue to adopt this traditional term here in this chapter, as long as readers are aware of the fact that major groups of Chinese are more comparable to a group of different languages such German, English, Swedish, and so on.

## 10.2   Classification of Chinese dialects

Let's recall the seven major groups of modern Chinese dialects introduced in Chapter 1, that is, Mandarin, Wu, Xiang, Gan, Kejia (Hakka), Min, and Yue. The first question we have to ask here is: What are the criteria for the classification? The most useful criterion is the development of Middle Chinese voiced stops into the modern dialects. For example, the Middle Chinese voiced stop [ d ] may develop in three directions, that is, developing into [ d ], [ t ], or[ tʰ ]. A dialect may preserve the Middle Chinese [ d ] as [ d ], while another dialect may have devoiced versions of [ d ] in a number of possibilities: (1) only the voiceless unaspirated version [ t ], (2) only the voiceless aspirated version [ tʰ ], or (3) both versions [ t ] and [ tʰ ] depending on tonal distinctions. While this criterion works well in distinguishing among most of the major groups of Chinese dialects, it cannot separate the Gan dialects from the Hakka dialects, because the voiced stops all developed into voiceless aspirated stops in both groups. Therefore, we need to look at additional criteria. Li (1989: 245) used the development of the entering tone to separate the

Jin dialects from the Mandarin group. This is, however, not completely satisfactory, because both the Gan and the Hakka dialects preserve the entering tone, and even among the Mandarin dialects, the entering tone is preserved in the lower Yangtze River areas, similarly to the Jin dialects.

Norman (1988: 182) proposed a new set of ten diagnostic features that include certain lexical items and grammatical particles, in addition to a few phonological features. These criteria refer to the third-person pronoun; the subordinative particle; negation; gender marker for animals; words for "*to stand*," "*to walk*," "*son*," and "*house*"; plus the phonological features of the split of the even tone and the palatalization of velar stops.

The primary distinction among the seven major groups of dialects is between Mandarin and the other six southern dialects. Norman (1988) used the ten diagnostic features to reevaluate the major groupings among Chinese dialects and arrived at three major divisions. Mandarin is still a major division by itself. Southern dialects now only include Hakka, Min, and Yue, while the remaining three groups, that is, Wu, Xiang, and Gan, form a central division. This new classification system is based on an ancient distinction between northern Chinese and what Norman (1988: 210) called Old Southern Chinese that goes back at least to the late Han dynasty. In terms of the ten diagnostic features, Hakka, Min, and Yue are all conservative, while Mandarin shows innovations in all of them. By contrast, the Wu, Xiang, and Gan dialects have been influenced by Mandarin, being innovative in some of the features but conservative in some other features.

This new system proposed by Norman (1988) offers an interesting perspective on the formation and classification of Chinese dialects. It gets further support by more recent studies based on lexical features of Chinese dialects. For example, Wang (1994) uses data on shared basic lexical items among major urban dialects of Chinese, including Xiamen, Meixian, Guangzhou, Nanchang, Changsha, Suzhou, and Beijing. The higher the percentage shared between two dialects, the more recently they became different dialects. For example, the highest percentage is that between Changsha and Nanchang. These two dialects share 88% of their basic lexicon, while Xiamen and Beijing only share 56%, which is the lowest number in the dataset. Thus, the percentage numbers are inversely related to distances between dialects. The higher the percentage, the closer the distance. The data show that Xiamen is the most distant from all the other dialects. Then Meixian is the second most distant, and Guangzhou is the third most distant. To some extent, Xiamen, Meixian, and Guangzhou seem to have split off from the main group rather early. If we take them as representing their dialect groups, then Min, Hakka, and Yue may indeed be in one southern archaic division. Sagart (2011) points out that Norman's (1988) southern division is not based on shared innovation but instead on shared retention. Therefore, to better classify Chinese dialects, shared innovations in basic lexicon and morphology should be used uniformly as the criteria. Sagart (2011) proposes a different set of lexical and morphological diagnostics to determine the time depth of each dialect group. For example, the Min dialects branched off early with lexical innovations such as 戍 *shù* ("a frontier outpost") as the Min word for "*house*," for example, Xiamen $ts^hu^5$ and Fuzhou $ts^hio^5$ (Norman 1988: 232), while in contrast, the word for "*house*" in Mandarin is related to 房 *fáng*, and that in Cantonese is related to 屋 *wū*. In Sagart's (2011) classification, after the Min dialects branched off, the Yue and Hakka separated from the main Sinitic group next. Thus, Sagart's (2011) new criteria also confirmed Norman's (1988) three-division system, where Min, Hakka, and Yue are considered the most archaic.

What is noteworthy in Sagart's (2011) data is that he includes two new varieties of Sinitic within the Old Chinese tree, that is, Waxiang 瓦鄉話 in Hunan and Caijia 蔡家話 in Guizhou. He argues that these two Sinitic languages represent an even older branch than the Min dialects. Since the exact classification of Waxiang and Caijia is still debated, we do not include them in the major groups of Chinese dialects here.

In addition to the traditional seven groups of Chinese dialects, Li (1989) identified three more groups: Jin dialects 晉語, Hui dialects 徽語 and Pinghua 平話, thus making the total number of dialect groups ten instead of the traditional seven.

The Jin dialects are spoken in Shanxi province and its surrounding areas in Hebei, Henan, Shaanxi, and Inner Mongolia, in cities such as Taiyuan, Zhangjiakou, and Hohhot. One of the differentiating features of the Jin dialects is the existence of the *rù* tone and its consonantal coda. Yuan et al. (2001) reports that there are four tones in the Taiyuan dialect spoken by the younger generation, that is, *píng* 11, *shǎng* 53, *qù* 55, and *rù* 21. The -*p*, -*t*, -*k* codas have merged into a glottal stop -ʔ. For example, the word "*eight*," that is, *bā* 八 (Middle Chinese: *pat*) is pronounced as [ paʔ²¹ ] in Taiyuan. Moreover, in the Jin dialects, there is a unique morphological device called -*l*- infixing. For example, from 蹦 [ pəŋ⁵⁵ ] ("to jump") we can derive [ pəʔ ²¹ ləŋ⁵⁵ ], and from 巷 [ xɤ̃⁵⁵ ] ("alleyway") we can derive [ xəʔ²¹ lɤ̃⁵⁵ ]. This type of -*l*- infixing is actually used as supporting evidence for the existence of consonant clusters in Old Chinese in Chapter 3. Therefore, Li (1989) proposed to list Jin as a separate group from Mandarin.

The Hui dialects, also called Huizhou dialects, or *Huīzhōu huà* 徽州話, spoken in southern Anhui province and its surrounding areas share certain phonological features with Lower Yangtze Mandarin, Gan, and Wu dialects. It has been difficult to clearly classify Huizhou dialects. It is common now to list Huizhou as a separate group. Pinghua spoken mostly in Guangxi and southern Hunan province is considered a separate group due to its unique phonological features that are also difficult to classify clearly.

Recent research in these three groups of dialects provides new data to help us better understand these varieties of Chinese. In the following sections, we provide an overview of each of the traditional seven groups of dialects.

## 10.3  Mandarin dialects

Mandarin dialects are generally spoken in the area north of the Yangtze River, including the northern, northeastern, northwestern, and southwestern regions of China. Besides the *Hàn* people, minority peoples such as the Hui and the Manchu have long adopted Mandarin as their native language. According to Yuan et al. (2001), Mandarin is spoken in about three quarters of all areas of Chinese dialects, and the number of speakers of Mandarin is about 70% of speakers of all seven groups of dialects. It is the largest group of dialects both in terms of geographical distribution and number of speakers.

The general features of Mandarin dialects are quite similar to the Beijing dialect, on which Modern Standard Chinese is based. Some of the commonly shared phonological characteristics of Mandarin dialects include:

1  The voiced stops and affricates in Middle Chinese became voiceless aspirated in the *píng* tone and voiceless unaspirated in the other tones.
2  The stop codas *-p*, *-t*, *-k* have generally been dropped in most Mandarin dialects or merged to a glottal stop in some areas, such as the lower Yangtze River region.
3  Nasal coda *-m* merged with *-n*.
4  Typically, there are four tones, that is, *yīnpíng*, *yángpíng*, *shǎng*, and *qù* tones, in most varieties of Mandarin. The phonological condition of the split of the Middle Chinese *píng* tone is the same as in Beijing, that is, the voicing quality of the initial. Moreover, the Middle Chinese *shǎng* tone characters with voiced obstruent initials merged with the *qù* tone. Note that in areas where there is still the *rù* tone, the total number of tones is more than four.

The grammar and vocabulary of Mandarin dialects also show a high degree of internal uniformity. Among others, the diminutive morpheme *-er* 兒 is a common suffix as a morphological device, and phonologically it is attached to the preceding syllable, although the exact phonetic value of the *-er* can vary in different dialects. The pronoun systems in Mandarin dialects are mostly based on the same 你 *nǐ*, 我 *wǒ*, 他 *tā* distinction found in Modern Standard Chinese. The plural forms take the *-men* 們 suffix. In general, the vocabulary of Mandarin shows more innovation compared to the southern dialects, in which many archaic words are still used in colloquial speech. Let's use one of the ten diagnostic features from Norman (1988), that is, the word for "*to walk*," to illustrate this point. In Chapter 8, we have given a detailed description of the distinctions between *zǒu* 走 and *xíng* 行 in Classical Chinese, with the former meaning "*to run*," while the latter means "*to walk*." In Mandarin dialects, *xíng* 行 has generally become obsolete in its meaning "*to walk*," *zǒu* 走 is most commonly the word for "*to walk*," and a relatively new word, *pǎo* 跑, is used for the meaning "*to run*."

As mentioned previously, one of the main criteria for separating the Jin dialects from Mandarin is the *rù* tone in the Jin dialects. However in Lower Yangtze Mandarin, or equivalently, Jiang-Huai Mandarin, spoken in parts of the Jiangsu, Anhui, Hubei, and Jiangxi provinces along the lower Yangtze River in cities such as Yangzhou and Nanjing, there are also separate tones derived from the *rù* tone. The Nanjing dialect has five tones: *yīnpíng* 32, *yángpíng* 14, *shǎng* 22, *qù* 44, and *rù* 5. The *-p*, *-t*, *-k* endings have merged into a glottal stop. For example, the word for "*eight*" is [ pa$^5$ ] in Nanjing.

Geographically speaking, the Jiang-Huai Mandarin area borders southern dialectal regions such as the Wu and Gan dialects. As has been sketched previously in the formation of Chinese dialects, Mandarin dialects in this area were brought to the south from the north when the capitals of different dynasties in the north were moved to this southern region. As early as the Three Kingdoms period, *Jiànyè* 建業, that is, present-day Nanjing, was already the capital city of the Wu Kingdom (229–280). During the Eastern Jin dynasty (317–420), the capital was moved to *Jiànkāng* 建康, that is, the former *Jiànyè*, and therefore the Luoyang dialect of the previous Western Jin dynasty was brought to the southern area. Nanjing served as the capital of the subsequent four dynasties in the south during the Northern and Southern dynasties.

In the Southern Song dynasty (1127–1279), the capital city of the Northern Song was moved from *Biànjīng* 汴京 in the north, located in present-day Kaifeng in Henan province, to *Lín'ān* 臨安, that is, present-day Hangzhou in the Zhejiang province. The Hangzhou dialect is a Wu dialect in terms of its phonology, but there are considerable Mandarin characteristics in its lexicon and grammar. For example, in the Hangzhou dialect, the third person pronoun is related to 他 *tā*, the plural morpheme is related to 們 -*men*, and the diminutive 兒 -*ér* is quite productively used.

In the early Ming dynasty, the capital was set primarily in Nanjing, then called *Yìngtiānfǔ* 應天府, from 1368 to 1421, before Beijing, then called *Shùntiānfǔ* 順天府, became the primary capital. Thus, Nanjing dialect was considered by many one of the most prestigious dialects in the Ming dynasty.

Besides these Mandarin dialects within China, there is also a Mandarin dialect called the Dungan language spoken by the Dungan people, mostly in Kyrgyzstan and Kazakhstan. They are descendants of the Hui people who migrated to these regions in the late 19th century. Between 1862 and 1877 during the late Qing dynasty, the Hui Muslims in northwestern China, including Shaanxi, Gansu, Ningxia, and Xinjiang, launched a series of military actions against the Qing government. But such revolts were suppressed by the government, and as a consequence, many ethnic Hui people in northwestern China fled across Xinjiang to Central Asia, thus bringing their Northwestern Mandarin to Central Asia. The Dungan language is actually still intelligible to speakers of other Mandarin dialects. Although there have been many loanwords from Russian and Arabic in the Dungan language, the major part of the vocabulary is still Chinese. A speaker from Beijing is able to carry a conversation with a Dungan speaker.

## 10.4    The Wu dialects

Currently, the Wu dialects are spoken in the part of Jiangsu south of the Yangtze River, generally to the east of Jiang-Huai Mandarin, and also in the Zhejiang province. The southern part of the Wu dialects, for example, Wenzhou in southern Zhejiang, are considerably more archaic than the northern Wu, for example, Shanghainese. The Wu area was inhabited by the Sinitic people as early as the Zhou dynasty. Thus, the archaic features of southern Wu may be related to archaic features in Old Chinese. On the other hand, northern Wu has been more influenced by Mandarin due to geographical adjacency. The traditional prestigious variety of Wu is that of Suzhou, the cultural center of the region in much of its history. However, Shanghainese has become the new eminent form of Wu in more recent times. Common phonological features of Wu include:

1   There are voiced obstruents, such as [ b, d, g, v, z, dʑ ], which are important evidence for the existence of such sounds in Middle Chinese. For example, the Middle Chinese initial of the word 群 *qún* ("group") is *g-*, and it is pronounced as [ dzyn²⁴ ] in Suzhou. Although the Middle Chinese velar *g-* is palatalized in Suzhou, the initial [ dʑ ] is nonetheless still voiced. However, the voiced obstruents in Wu are not typical. Instead, a voiced consonant in Wu starts out as a voiceless consonant, and voicing sets in rather late and is associated with a "*breathy*" quality of the vowel, thus giving rise to the auditory impression of the voiced consonant being "*aspirated*." Ramsey (1987: 91) hypothesizes that such "*voiced aspirates*" may be what the traditional terminology *zhuóyīn* 濁音 "*muddy sound*" in Chinese originally referred to.

2   The Middle Chinese -*m*, -*n*, and -*ŋ* codas have generally merged into -*ŋ*.

3   The -*p*, -*t*, -k endings associated with the *rù* tone have merged into a glottal stop.

4   The four tones in Middle Chinese have generally split into two categories each.[3] Thus, many Wu dialects have seven to eight tones. For example, Suzhou has seven tones: *yīnpíng* 44, *yángpíng* 24, *shǎng* 52, *yīnqù* 412, *yángqù* 31, *yīnrù* 4, and *yángrù* 23. By contrast, Wenzhou has eight tones: *yīnpíng* 44, *yángpíng* 31, *yīnshǎng* 45, *yángshǎng* 34, *yīnqù* 42, *yángqù* 22, *yīnrù* 323, and *yángrù* 212.

5   The distinction between literary and colloquial pronunciations is common. For example, the word *yú* 魚 ("fish") in Suzhou is [ jy²⁴ ] in literary pronunciation and [ ŋ²⁴ ] in colloquial pronunciation. The literary pronunciation is practically the same as Mandarin, while the colloquial pronunciation differs greatly from Mandarin.

In terms of grammar and vocabulary, influences from Mandarin can be seen in many Wu dialects, especially in the north. For example, there were three words for the third-person pronouns, *qú* 渠, *yī* 伊, and *tā* 他, in early vernacular writing from the late Han to Tang dynasties. All three forms can be found in different Wu dialects. But 他 *tā* should be considered a Mandarin influence. The first-person pronoun in Wu dialects is generally a cognate of *wǒ* 我. The second-person pronoun is a cognate of *nǐ* 你 or *nóng* 儂. In terms of the plural forms of pronouns, various forms are used, but in general, -*men* 們 is not the original Wu dialect morpheme and can only be found in dialects with more Mandarin influences, such as in Hangzhou. Some words from the Wu dialects have also been adopted in Modern Standard Chinese, such as *gāngà* 尷尬 ("embarrassed"). A few compound words in the Wu dialects have different morpheme orders from Modern Standard Chinese, for example, 亮月 instead of 月亮 *yuèliang* ("the moon"), as in Mandarin, 歡喜 instead of 喜歡 *xǐhuan* ("happy"), 道地 instead of 地道 *dìdao* ("authentic").

The Wu dialect region has been a cultural center in China for hundreds of years. A written form based on the Suzhou dialect using Chinese characters appeared in the Ming dynasty (Snow 2013: 600). In the late Qing dynasty from the 1890s to 1910s, written Wu based on Shanghainese was already quite developed. In general, written Wu is used mostly in less formal genres of writing, for example, folk songs, Kun opera scripts, popular novels, and so on.

## 10.5   The Xiang dialects

The Xiang dialects are spoken mostly in Hunan province, where the main river is the Xiang River. The Sinitic people migrated to this area as early as the Warring States period. The more conservative dialects in the mountainous areas of Hunan retain certain archaic features of Chinese, while the dialects in major cities such as the provincial capital Changsha are becoming more Mandarin-like due to geographic adjacency with Mandarin dialects. Therefore, the Xiang dialects are usually distinguished between the Old Xiang, for example, in Shuangfeng, and the New Xiang, for example, in Changsha. The mutual intelligibility between these two forms of Xiang is quite low, while by contrast, the New Xiang is partially intelligible to Mandarin speakers, especially southwestern Mandarin speakers (Ramsey 1987: 97). Here we list some main features of New Xiang and Old Xiang. The phonological features of New Xiang in Changsha include:

1   The voiced obstruents in Middle Chinese became voiceless unaspirated. For example, the Middle Chinese initial of the word 同 for "*same*" is *d-*. The word is pronounced as [ tən¹³ ] with a voiceless unaspirated initial in Changsha, and by contrast, it is *tóng* with a voiceless aspirated [ tʰ ] initial in Beijing Mandarin, because it is a *píng*-tone word. The word 動 for "*to move*" had *d-* in Middle Chinese. It is pronounced as [ tən²¹ ] in Changsha and *dòng* in Beijing, with a voiceless unaspirated [ t ], because it is a non-*píng* tone. Therefore, the Middle Chinese voiced obstruents became voiceless unaspirated regardless of tones in Changsha.

2   The *-p*, *-t*, *-k* codas associated with the Middle Chinese entering tone, that is, the *rù* tone, disappeared, but the entering tone itself is retained as a separate tonal category.

3   There are six tones: *yīnpíng* 33, *yángpíng* 13, *shǎng* 41, *yīnqù* 55, *yángqù* 21, *rù* 24.

In contrast, the more conservative Old Xiang as represented by Shuangfeng has the following phonological features:

1   There are voiced obstruents. For example, the Middle Chinese initial of the word 旗 for "*flag*" is a voiced velar *g-*. The word is pronounced as [ dʑi²³ ] in Shuangfeng, with a voiced palatal initial dʑ-, and by contrast, it is pronounced as [ tɕi¹³ ] in Changsha, which is similar to its pronunciation *qí*, that is, [ tɕʰi³⁵ ], in Beijing Mandarin, minus the aspiration. The voiced

consonants in Old Xiang are typical voiced sounds, which are different from the "*breathy*" voiced consonants in the Wu dialects.

2    There are no labiodental initials such as *f-*. Most words with an *f-* initial in Modern Standard Chinese have a velar fricative in Shuangfeng, for example, [ x ]. The word 飛 for "*to fly*" is pronounced as [ xui⁵⁵ ], as opposed to *fēi* in Beijing Mandarin.

3    Some words with retroflex initials such as [ tʂ ] in Mandarin are pronounced as alveolars in Shuangfeng, such as [ t ]. For example, the word 豬 for "*pig*" is [ ty⁵⁵ ], as opposed to *zhū* in Beijing Mandarin, with the retroflex initial [ tʂ ].

4    The *-p*, *-t*, *-k* codas disappeared, and the *rù* tone merged with *yángpíng* or *yīnqù*.

5    There are five tones: *yīnpíng* 55, *yángpíng* 23, *shǎng* 21, *yīnqù* 35, *yángqù* 33.

The New Xiang and the Old Xiang do share some similar phonological features. For example, in both varieties of Xiang, the Middle Chinese consonantal codas *-p*, *-t*, and *-k* are all dropped. The tonal systems are also quite similar in that a register distinction is present in both the *píng* and the *qù* tones. There is no register distinction in the *shǎng* tone. The actual contour 24 of the *rù* tone in Changsha is similar to the tonal contours of Shuangfeng *yángpíng* and *yīnqù* tones, that is, 23 and 35, respectively. Interestingly, the Middle Chinese *rù* tone merged with *yángpíng* and *yīnqù* in Shuangfeng.

However, there are far more differences between the New Xiang and Old Xiang. Features 1, 2, and 3 in Shuangfeng are all archaic. Shuangfeng has a three-way distinction in its stop initials, for example, [ p, pʰ, b ], which is the same as the three-way contrast in Middle Chinese.

The lack of labiodental initials in Shuangfeng reminds us of *Qián Dàxīn*'s claim that *qīngchúnyīn* ("light-lip sounds") did not exist in ancient times, as discussed in Chapter 3, while the pronunciations of retroflex initials as alveolars in Old Xiang remind us of *Qián Dàxīn*'s other claim that *shéshàngyīn* ("laminal sounds")⁴ did not exist in ancient times. These two features of Old Xiang are also present in the Min, which is the most archaic group among all Chinese dialects. However, we should also note that Old Xiang does have retroflex initials, similar to Beijing Mandarin, for example, the word 池 for "*pond*" is *chí*, that is, [ tʂʰ˩˧⁵ ] in Beijing, [ dʐ˩²³ ] in Shuangfeng, [ tsɿ¹³ ] in Changsha, but [ ti²⁴ ] in Xiamen. Therefore, although Old Xiang is more archaic than the New Xiang, it nonetheless shows more innovation than the Min dialects.

In terms of grammar and vocabulary, there are some typical southern features in Xiang. Gender markers follow nouns of animals in both New and Old Xiang dialects, while in Mandarin dialects, gender morphemes for animals, that is, "male" and "female," are pre-nominal, meaning that they precede the nouns of animals. For example, Xiang 雞公 ("chicken" + "male") corresponds to Mandarin 公雞 *gōngjī* ("male" + "chicken" → "rooster") and Xiang 雞婆 ("chicken" + "female") to Mandarin 母雞 *mǔjī* ("female" + "chicken" → "hen"). Elsewhere in the grammar and lexicon of Xiang, Mandarin influences can be spotted commonly. For example, all of the personal pronoun forms, including the plural forms, in Changsha are cognates with Mandarin. Even Shuangfeng's personal pronouns are also quite similar to Mandarin, except for the first-person singular, which is cognate with 卬 *áng*, an archaic pronoun attested occasionally in the *Shījīng* and the *Shàngshū* (Xiang 1993). In some Old Xiang dialects, the third-person pronoun can be related to 渠 *qú* or 其 *qí* in earlier vernacular writings. The plural morpheme may also be different from 們 *-men*. Thus, Xiang dialects, in the central division in Norman's (1988) classification, show a mixture of Mandarin and southern features. The New Xiang has absorbed more Mandarin features compared to the Old Xiang, which retains some archaic features, to different extents depending on the locations.

## 10.6   The Gan dialects

To the east of Hunan is Jiangxi province, where the Gan River, a tributary of the Yangtze River, is the main waterway connecting the north with the south. The Gan dialects are spoken in the central and northern part of Jiangxi. Geographically speaking, Jiangxi is located south of the Yangtze River, thus being a southern region. But due to its easy access to the Yangtze River where Jiang-Huai Mandarin is spoken, the Gan dialects have been influenced by Mandarin. Moreover, the Gan dialect group has contacts with the Hakka dialects to its south and Xiang dialects to its west. All these influences from Mandarin, Hakka, and Xiang have made Gan less distinct as a separate group of dialects. The traditional representative variety of Gan is that of Nanchang, the provincial capital. In terms of phonology, the Nanchang dialect has the following features:

1   The voiced obstruents in Middle Chinese have become voiceless aspirated. For example, the words for "*to handle*" 辦 and "*plate*" 盤 both had the voiced bilabial stop *b-* initial in Middle Chinese. The pronunciations in Nanchang are [ p$^h$an$^{21}$ ] and [ p$^h$ɔn$^{24}$ ], while in Beijing, the pronunciations are [ pan$^{51}$ ] and [ p$^h$an$^{35}$ ]. The devoiced versions are all aspirated in Nanchang but either aspirated or unaspirated in Beijing, depending on the tones.
2   The stop coda *-p* merged into *-t*, while the *-k* coda is still preserved. For example, the word "*ten*" 十 had a *-p* coda in Middle Chinese, but it is pronounced as [ sət$^{21}$ ] with a *-t* coda in Nanchang now. Compare with the Cantonese pronunciation of "*ten*" in Guangzhou: [ ʃɐp$^2$ ], retaining the original *-p* coda. However Nanchang is located in the northern part of Jiangxi, closer to the Mandarin area. In more conservative Gan dialects, for example, Linchuan and the southernmost parts of Gan, all three stop codas, that is, *-p, -t, -k*, are distinguished (Luo 1958; Ramsey 1987: 96).
3   There are seven tones: *yīnpíng* 42, *yángpíng* 24, *shǎng* 213, *yīnqù* 45, *yángqù* 21, *yīnrù* 5, and *yángrù* 21.
4   The equivalent to the Mandarin labiodental *f-* varies between *f-* and a bilabial fricative [ ɸ ]. For example, the word 飛 for "*to fly*" can be pronounced as [ ɸui$^{42}$ ], according to Yuan et al. (2001), while the Beijing Mandarin pronunciation is fēi.

In terms of the grammar and vocabulary, Nanchang shows a mixture of both southern and Mandarin features. For example, the third-person pronoun in Nanchang is cognate with 渠 *qú*, different from the Mandarin *tā*; the plural morpheme is *-tən*, while the Mandarin 們 *-men* is also an alternative form. The gender markers in words for animals follow the nouns they modify, for example, 雞公 ("chicken" + "male" → "rooster") and 雞婆 ("chicken" + "female" → "hen"), the same as in Xiang.

Therefore, the Wu, Xiang, and Gan dialects in Norman's (1988) central division all have features from both Mandarin and southern dialects. The northern varieties in each of these three groups have absorbed more Mandarin features compared to their southern counterparts within each group, obviously due to geographical reasons. In the next three sections, we discuss the three southern dialects per se, as in Norman's (1988) southern division, that is, Kejia (Hakka), Yue, and Min.

## 10.7   The Kejia dialects

The Kejia dialects, or the Hakka dialects, are spoken mostly in the area consisting of southern Jiangxi, northeastern Guangdong, and southwestern Fujian. The Hakka dialects can also be found in Taiwan, Guangxi, and Sichuan. There are Hakka diasporas worldwide, especially in Southeast Asian countries like Singapore, Malaysian, Thailand, and so on.

The name Hakka is originally a Cantonese word that literally means "*guest people.*" The same word in Mandarin is Kejia. According to the Hakka people's account, their ancestors migrated from the central plains in the north to the south as early as the Eastern Jin dynasty. There were subsequent waves of migration in later dynasties. The designation 客家 *Kèjiā* could be traced to the Song dynasty, when the new immigrants from the north were considered non-natives in those southern areas by other groups of *Hàn* Chinese. The Hakka people lived in the Jiangxi, Fujian, and Guangdong areas for centuries until, in the mid-Qing dynasty in the 18th century, they further dispersed to a larger area, including Sichuan and Taiwan. The Hakka people and their dialects are rather homogeneous compared to other *Hàn* Chinese groups and dialects. The historical account of Hakka people's origin is well documented. However, the linguistic features of Hakka may not correspond directly to the migration scenario, because the Hakka dialects are definitely southern and archaic on a par with the Yue and Min dialects, although their immigration into the southern regions may be later than the Yue and Min, as the historical account and the name "*guest people*" suggest. Therefore, we focus on the linguistic features of Hakka by listing typical phonological properties of the Hakka dialects, as represented by the Meixian variety, spoken in Meizhou City in Guangdong province.

1   The voiced obstruents became voiceless aspirated. Let's use the same words as in the discussion of the Gan dialects previously to illustrate this point. The words for "*to handle*" 辦 and "*plate*" 盤 both had the voiced bilabial stop *b*- initial in Middle Chinese. The pronunciations in Meixian are [ $p^han^{21}$ ] and [ $p^han^{24}$ ], while in Beijing, the pronunciations are [ $pan^{51}$ ] and [ $p^han^{35}$ ].

2   All three stop codas in Middle Chinese, that is, *-p, -t, -k*, are preserved, for example, the numbers [ səp⁵ ] ("ten"), [ tsʰit¹ ] ("seven"), [ liuk⁵ ] ("six").

3   All three nasal codas in Middle Chinese, that is, *-m, -n, -ŋ*, are retained, for example, the numbers [ sam⁴⁴ ] ("three"), [ tsʰiɛn⁴⁴ ] ("thousand"), [ laŋ¹¹ ] ("zero").

4   There are six tones: *yīnpíng* 44, *yángpíng* 11, *shǎng* 31, *qù* 52, *yīnrù* 1, and *yángrù* 5.

5   The three sets of sibilant initials in Modern Standard Chinese, that is, the palatal *j/q/x*, alveolar *z/c/s*, and retroflex *zh/ch/sh*, are merged into the alveolar series, that is, [ ts, tsʰ, s ].

6   Some words with bilabial initials such as [ p, pʰ, b ] in Middle Chinese now have the initial *f-*, while the original bilabials are retained in many other cases. For example, the word 敷 for "*to apply, to spread*" had a bilabial initial in Middle Chinese, and it is pronounced as [ fu⁴⁴ ] in Meixian, while the word 斧 for "*axe*" is [ pu³¹ ], still having a bilabial initial. The bilabial initial tends to be preserved more commonly in colloquial pronunciations. Moreover, the distinction between literary and colloquial pronunciations is common in Hakka.

Obviously, feature 1 concerning the devoicing of Middle Chinese voiced obstruents is quite similar to Gan. Thus, some scholars, for example, Luo (2003), propose that Gan and Hakka should form one single group, especially considering that the devoicing criterion is the most important standard in classifying Chinese dialects. However, when we take other phonological characteristics into consideration, Hakka differs from Gan considerably.

First, Hakka retains all of the six consonantal codas in Middle Chinese, that is, *-p, -t, -k, -m, -n, -ŋ*. This is only true for some conservative varieties of Gan dialects, while in the Nanchang dialect, *-m* merged into *-n* similarly to Mandarin, and *-p* merged into *-t*. In fact, the retention of the six consonantal codas in Hakka resembles Yue, which we discuss next. Moreover, the merger of the three sets of sibilants in Hakka is also similar to the Yue dialects. In terms of feature 6, for some of the words that have the labiodental initial *f-* in Mandarin, the original bilabial place of articulation of Middle Chinese is retained in Meixian, especially in colloquial pronunciations. For example, the word 複 for "*complex*" is pronounced as [ puk¹ ] in colloquial pronunciation and [ fuk¹ ] in literary pronunciation, similar to the Mandarin pronunciation *fù*. This partial retention of the original bilabial initials can be considered an archaic southern feature shared with Cantonese and Min.

The grammar and vocabulary of Hakka are generally quite different from Mandarin. The third-person singular pronoun is [ ki¹¹ ], related to 渠 *qú* in early vernacular writing. The plural morpheme is also very different from Mandarin. For example, in Meixian, it is [ teu⁴⁴ ] or [ teu⁴⁴ ŋin¹¹ ], such as in [ ki¹¹ teu⁴⁴ ŋin¹¹ ] ("they"). In terms of the order between nouns and their modifiers, there are more post-nominal modifiers in addition to the more commonly seen post-nominal gender markers in nouns of animals like in Gan and Xiang. For example, in addition to 雞公 ("chicken" + "male" → "rooster"), there are forms like 菜乾 ("vegetable"

+ "dry" → "dried bok choy"), the corresponding word order of which in Mandarin would be 乾菜 *gāncài*. In this aspect, Hakka resembles Yue as well. Also in terms of morpheme orders, in some compound words, the two morphemes are in the opposite order from those in Mandarin. For example, 歡喜 for the Mandarin 喜歡 *xǐhuan* ("like") and 鬧熱 for the Mandarin 熱鬧 *rènao* ("bustling with activity"). This Hakka feature is similar to the Wu dialects.

## 10.8　The Yue dialects

Cantonese, for many people, is arguably the most familiar variety of Chinese after Mandarin. Technically speaking, the terms *Cantonese* and *Yue* are different, even though, for practical purposes, they are interchangeable. Yue dialects are spoken widely in Guangdong, Guangxi, and Hong Kong. There are Yue diasporas worldwide, especially in North America and Europe. The prestigious form of Yue is that of Guangzhou, called Cantonese. The internal uniformity among the different varieties of Yue is quite high compared to the Wu and Min dialects. Historically speaking, the Guangdong and Guangxi area was inhabited by the ancient Yue people in the Zhou dynasty, hence the name of this region and its dialects. But there are two different characters for Yue. One is 越, reserved for reference to the ancient Yue people and language, while the character 粵 is used for the Yue dialects of Chinese.

Although in ancient times, the Yue area was considered rather remote from the perspective of the *Hàn* people, starting from the Song dynasty, the region gradually became a cultural and economic center in South China, especially when trade between China and the outside world began to be conducted by sea in the Ming and Qing dynasties. In the past few decades, Guangdong, together with Hong Kong, has become one of the wealthiest regions of China. Since the cultural and economic influences of Hong Kong and Guangdong are not only confined to South China, the Yue dialects, especially Cantonese, have also become very popular in other dialect regions. Especially in the 1990s, words and phrases from Cantonese were commonly used in the north, and young people picked up Cantonese by listening to Cantonese pop songs and watching Cantonese movies. There was even a Cantonese-style Mandarin that was imitated by many non-Cantonese speakers to construct a chic or hip identity, especially among pop singers. Given its cultural influences, Yue is among the most researched of Chinese dialects. Here we list some common features of Yue. All of the examples are Guangzhou pronunciations.

1　The voiced obstruents have become voiceless. But whether they became aspirated or unaspirated varies in different Yue dialects. For example, in Guangzhou, the voiced obstruents became aspirated in the *píng* tone and unaspirated otherwise. To illustrate this, we can take a look at the words *píng* 瓶 ("bottle") and *bìng* 病 ("illness"), both of which had the voiced initial *b-* in Middle Chinese. The first word had a *píng* tone, and the second word had a *qù* tone. The Guangzhou pronunciations are [ pʰɪŋ²¹ ] and [ pɛŋ²² ], with an aspirated [ pʰ ] and an unaspirated [ p ], respectively. But some words with a voiced stop and the *shǎng* tone in Middle Chinese devoiced to an aspirated stop; for example, the word *bàng* 棒 ("stick") is pronounced as [ pʰaŋ²³ ] in Guangzhou.

2    All of the Middle Chinese consonantal codas, that is, *-p*, *-t*, *-k*, *-m*, *-n*, *-ŋ*, are preserved, for example, the numbers [ sɐp² ] ("ten"), [ tsʰɐt⁵ ] ("seven"), [ lʊk² ] ("six"), [ sam⁵⁵ ] ("three"), [ tsʰin⁵⁵ ] ("thousand"), [ lɪŋ²¹ ] ("zero").

3    There is a distinction between long and short vowels, for example, [ sɐm⁵⁵ ] ("heart") vs. [ sam⁵⁵ ] ("three"), where [ a ] is a long vowel and [ ɐ ] is short.

4    In most places, the *píng*, *shǎng*, and *qù* tones have each split into two registers. The *rù* tone commonly splits into *yīnrù* and *yángrù* first, and then the *yīnrù* further splits into *shàng-yīnrù* if the vowel is short and *xià-yīnrù* is the vowel is long. In some places, the *yángrù* tone also further splits into two according to the length of the vowel. The number of tones ranges from six to ten. Guangzhou dialect has nine tones:[5] *yīnpíng* 53 or 55, *yángpíng* 21, *yīnshǎng* 35, *yángshǎng* 23, *yīnqù* 33, *yángqù* 22, *shàng-yīnrù* 5, *xià-yīnrù* 33, and *yángrù* 22 or 2. The *yīnpíng* tonal contour may vary between 53 and 55. The *yángrù* tone is either 22 or 2 depending on the vowel length.

5    The three sets of sibilant initials in Modern Standard Chinese, that is, the palatal *j/q/x*, alveolar *z/c/s*, and retroflex *zh/ch/sh*, are merged into one set. This set varies between the alveolar series [ ts, tsʰ, s ] and the palatal series [ tʃ, tʃʰ, ʃ ].

6    Some words with bilabial initials such as [ p, pʰ, b ] in Middle Chinese now have the initial *f-*, while the original bilabials are retained in many other cases. For example, the word 敷 for "*to apply, to spread*" had a bilabial initial in Middle Chinese, and it is pronounced as [ fu⁵⁵ ] in Guangzhou, while the word 浮 for "*to flow*" still has a bilabial initial, as in [ pʰou²¹ ] in its colloquial pronunciation. Both words have the labiodental initial *f-* in Beijing Mandarin. In general, in Yue dialects, the bilabial initials are usually more common in colloquial pronunciations. The distinction between literary and colloquial pronunciations in the Yue dialects is quite common.

The Yue dialects are important for reconstructing the six consonantal codas in Middle Chinese. Tang poetry read in Cantonese often sounds more melodious and harmonious due to the rich tonal distinctions. Therefore, some people jokingly say that the *Guǎngyùn* 廣韻, on which Middle Chinese was reconstructed, is the sounds of Cantonese, because *Guǎngdōng-huà* 廣東話, that is, the name of Cantonese in Chinese, shares the same character 廣 *guǎng* with the *Guǎngyùn* 廣韻. Despite the joking nature of this claim, the Yue dialects indeed preserve many Middle Chinese features quite well. Based on the features listed previously, Yue and Hakka share many characteristics, for example, the six consonantal codas, merger of the three sets of sibilants, and retention of the bilabial place of articulation of initials in some of the words that in Mandarin have the labiodental initial *f-*.

In terms of grammar and vocabulary, Yue also shares many similarities with Hakka. For example, the third-person singular pronoun is cognate with 渠 *qú*, and the plural morpheme is not *-men*. In general, the plural morpheme in Yue is [ tei$^{22}$ ]. The use of post-nominal modifiers is common in Yue, for example, 雞公 ("chicken" + "male" → "rooster") and 菜乾 ("vegetable" + "dry" → "dried bok choy"), both of which are mentioned previously in the discussion on Hakka. Regarding vocabulary, Yue has more monosyllabic words than Mandarin. Archaic lexical items are often preserved, such as the use of [ haŋ$^{21}$ ] 行 (Mandarin *xíng*) for "*to walk*," instead of the Mandarin word 走 *zǒu*. Other examples include the use of [ jɐm$^{35}$ ] 飲 (Mandarin *yǐn*) for "*to drink*" instead of the Mandarin word 喝 *hē*, and the use of [ mou$^{21}$ ] 無 (Mandarin *wú*) for "*not have*," instead of the Mandarin 沒有 *méiyǒu*. Some words have different orders of morphemes from Mandarin, for example, 歡喜 for Mandarin 喜歡 *xǐhuan* ("to like") and 齊整 for Mandarin 整齊 *zhěngqí* ("tidy"). There have been many loanwords from Western languages like English in the Yue dialect, for example, [ pɔ$^{55}$ ] for "*ball*," [ pʰaŋ$^{55}$ ] for "*pan*," and [ si$^{22}$ tik$^{5}$ ] for "*stick*." But Western languages might also have borrowed a few words from the Yue dialects as well. Among theories of the origin of the word "*ketchup*" in English, it is possible that it was ultimately borrowed from the Yue dialects. The Cantonese word [ kʰɛ$^{35}$ tsɐp$^{5}$ ] (茄汁, "tomato" + "sauce" → "ketchup") seems to be a pretty good candidate.

The Yue dialects possess some unique grammatical features and constructions not found in other dialects. For example, the common way of saying "*I go first*" in Yue is [ ŋɔ$^{23}$ haŋ$^{21}$ sin$^{55}$ ] 我行先 ("I go first"), while in Mandarin, it is "*wǒ xiān zǒu*" 我先走 ("I first go"). Such a contrast shows that in Yue, some adverbs such as "*first*" follow the verb, while in Mandarin, adverbs usually precede verbs. Another example is regarding ditransitive, or double-object, constructions. To say "*He gives me three books*," the Yue version is [ kʰœy$^{23}$ pei$^{35}$ sam$^{55}$ pun$^{35}$ sy$^{55}$ ŋɔ$^{23}$ ] 佢畀三本書我 (word-for-word gloss: "he give three CL book me"), in which the indirect object, that is, the person "*ŋɔ$^{23}$*," follows the direct object "*sam$^{55}$ pun$^{35}$ sy$^{55}$*," while in Mandarin, they should be switched, as in "*tā gěi wǒ sān běn shū*" 他給我三本書 ("he give me three CL book").

Among all Chinese dialects, Yue has the most developed written language, which can be traced back to at least the Ming dynasty (Snow 2013: 601). Earlier genres include the southern songs (南音, *nányīn*), wooden fish songs (木魚歌, *mùyú-gē*), Cantonese love songs (粵謳 *yuè'ōu*), and Cantonese opera scripts, which were all informal popular genres. The use of written Cantonese was later expanded to include more types of writing, such as newspaper and magazine articles. Especially in Hong Kong, written Cantonese has been standardized and can be used as an independent written language to write down spoken Cantonese. Although Cantonese and Mandarin share a large number of lexical items, including up to 74% of basic vocabulary (Xu 1991: 422; Wang 1994: 1448), new characters have been created to write Cantonese-specific words. With such a long tradition of writing, Cantonese is one of the most prominent varieties of Chinese.

Although Cantonese is quite different from Mandarin, it is actually not difficult for Mandarin speakers to learn Cantonese, especially in terms of listening comprehension. The most difficulty type of Chinese dialects is no doubt the Min.

## 10.9   The Min dialects

The Min dialects are spoken in Fujian, Taiwan, Guangdong, Hainan, and southern Zhejiang. Various Min dialects are also widely spoken in Southeast Asia and North America among the Chinese diasporas. Min is the name of Fujian, a mountainous region in southeastern China, where *Hàn* immigrants arrived as early as the Western and Eastern Jin. Due to geographical obstacles, the Min dialects not only differ from all other groups of Chinese dialects greatly but also are the most heterogeneous internally as well. Thus, some scholars propose to further divide the Min dialects into smaller, more homogeneous groups. Traditionally, a primary division is made between a northern group and a southern group among the Min dialects. According to Yuan et al. (2001), the Min dialects consist of as many as five subgroups, including the Eastern Min, with Fuzhou as the representative variety, and Southern Min, with Xiamen as the representative. Taiwanese is the Southern Min variety spoken in Taiwan. Norman (1988: 233), based on an earlier similar proposal and his own extensive fieldwork, divided the Min dialects primarily into an eastern group and a western group, as opposed to the traditional north-south division just mentioned. Both Fuzhou and Xiamen are in the eastern group along the Fujian coastline. The western group are from the inland areas of Fujian, parallel to the coastal eastern division. Since the internal differences among the varieties of the Min dialects are quite great, it is not possible to provide an outline of all the subtle differences and features among different Min dialects. Instead, we focus on the Southern Min, mostly that of Xiamen, here to discuss representative features of the Min dialects. Some of these characteristics may not apply to all Min dialects.

The phonological features of Southern Min include:

1   The voiced obstruents have become voiceless. For example, the words *píng* 瓶 ("bottle") with a *píng* tone and *bìng* 病 ("illness") with a *qù* tone both had the voiced initial *b*- originally. The Xiamen pronunciation of 瓶 ("bottle") is [ pɪŋ²⁴ ] (literary pronunciation) or [ pan²⁴ ] (colloquial pronunciation), while 病 ("illness") is pronounced as [ pɪŋ³³ ] (literary) or [ pĩ³³ ] (colloquial). The tilde "~" above the vowel indicates nasalization. However, we cannot readily say that all voiced obstruents devoiced to unaspirated ones, because some words have aspirated versions. For example, the word *táng* 糖 ("sugar") had a *píng* tone and the voiced initial *d*- but is pronounced as [ tʰɔŋ²⁴ ] (literary) and [ tʰŋ̩²⁴ ] (colloquial) in Xiamen. Norman (1988: 228) argued that the devoicing of obstruents in Min cannot be described with the same phonological condition based on tonal distinctions as in other Chinese dialects, but instead the situation in Min reflects phonological properties of a stage earlier than Middle Chinese, but the detailed explanation of such an earlier phonological distinction lies beyond the scope of this book.

2   In some words, nasal initials [ m-, n-, ŋ- ] are pronounced as voiced stops such as [ b-, d-, g- ]. In Xiamen, there are voiced *b*- and *g*- as developments from earlier nasal initials. For example, the word 陌 *mò* ("path") had the initial *m*- originally but is now pronounced as [ bɪk⁵ ], and the word

牛 *niú* ("ox") originally had *ŋ-* as its initial but is now [ gu²⁴ ] in colloquial pronunciation and [ giu²⁴ ] in literary pronunciation. Note that we are talking about nasal initials here, although the same nasal consonants can be syllable codas as well, as show in the next point.

3 Nasal codas *-m*, *-n*, *-ŋ* are present in Xiamen, for example, the literary pronunciations of these numbers: [ sam⁵⁵ ] ("three"), [ tsʰiɛn⁵⁵ ] ("thousand"), [ lɪŋ²⁴ ] ("zero"). However, their colloquial pronunciations are [ sã⁵⁵ ] ("three"), [ tsʰɪŋ⁵⁵ ] ("thousand"), [ laŋ²⁴ ] ("zero"). In the word for "*three*," the final *-am* is nasalized, as indicated by the tilde ~ on top of the vowel. In the word for "*thousand*," the nasal *-n* is merged with the *-ŋ*. Thus, the three nasal codas are retained to different extents in Xiamen. It is the same in other Southern Min dialects.

4 The *-p*, *-t*, *-k* codas are preserved to different extents in different places. Some have *-p*, *-k* but no *-t*, while some have *-t*, *-k* but no *-p*, while some merged all three to a glottal stop. But Xiamen has all three stop codas, for example, the numbers [ tsap⁵ ] ("ten"), [ tsʰit³² ] ("seven"), [ lak⁵ ] ("six"). But in some words in Xiamen, the stop codas have turned into glottal stops, for example, the colloquial pronunciation of the word for "*eight*" in Xiamen is [ pueʔ³² ], although the literary version [ pat³² ] retains the original *-t*.

5 There are seven to nine tones, with seven being more common. For example Xiamen has the following seven tones: *yīnpíng* 55, *yángpíng* 24, *shǎng* 51, *yīnqù* 11, *yángqù* 33, *yīnrù* 32, *yángrù* 5. There is a register distinction in each of the *píng*, *qù*, and *rù* tones, while the *shǎng* tone is one category.

6 There is no labiodental *f-*. The corresponding initial in Southern Min is often [ h ]. For example, Mandarin *fù* 附 ("attach") is pronounced as [ hu³³ ] in Xiamen. But in the colloquial pronunciation, the original bilabial initials are more common. For example, the word 斧 ("axe") is pronounced as [ pɔ⁵¹ ] in its colloquial pronunciation in Xiamen, retaining the original bilabial place of articulation, while its literary pronunciation is [ hu⁵¹ ], more similar to the Mandarin pronunciation *fǔ*.

7 Many words with retroflex initials in Mandarin are pronounced with alveolar initials. For example in Xiamen, the Mandarin word *zhū* 豬 ("pig") is pronounced as [ ti⁵⁵ ]; *zhī* 知 ("to know") is also [ ti⁵⁵ ], and *zhāng* 張 (a surname) is [ tĩũ⁵⁵ ].

8 As shown by examples previously, in the Southern Min, and also more broadly in Min dialects in general, there are nasalized finals and also a more systematic distinction between literary and colloquial pronunciations.

The most striking features of Southern Min are 6 and 7, corresponding to the two claims by *Qián Dàxīn* introduced in Chapter 3, that is, that *qīngchúnyīn* ("light-lip sounds") did not exist in ancient times and that *shéshàngyīn* ("laminal sounds") did not exist in ancient times. We have mentioned previously that in the Old Xiang, there are also similar characteristics as those in Min. However, Min retains the older bilabial and alveolar initials more systematically than Old Xiang. Min dialects are important for reconstructing Old Chinese phonology exactly due to these archaic features. The original alveolar initials, such as in the words mentioned in 7, had developed into retroflex stops in Middle Chinese under the influence of the -*r*- medial. Thus, Min dialects should be older than Middle Chinese, because they bypassed the development from alveolar initials with the -*r*- medial into retroflex sounds. If we consider the complex situation with devoicing in Min, as mentioned in feature 1, it adds further support to Min being older than Middle Chinese.

Min, Yue, and Hakka together form the southern division in Norman's (1988) classification of Chinese dialects. They are all more archaic or conservative than the other dialect groups. However, within the southern division, Min is obviously the most archaic, having split off from Old Chinese first. But, of course, not everything is archaic in Min. For example, the earlier voiced obstruents, which are still retained in Wu, have become voiceless in Min, and the -*p*, -*t*, -*k* endings are not preserved completely as in the Yue dialects.

In terms of the grammar and vocabulary, the first-person pronoun in Southern Min is cognate with *wǒ* 我, while the second-person pronoun is cognate with *rǔ* 汝, which is one of the Classical Chinese terms. The third-person singular pronoun forms are related to *yī* 伊 in Southern Min, but in other Min dialects, cognates of *qú* 渠 can also be found. The plural morpheme in Southern Min is generally by adding -*n*, which is, however, not related to the Mandarin -*men*.

One interesting morphological feature in Southern Min is that reduplication of adjectives can be up to three syllables, although reduplication in other Chinese dialects is often limited to a doubling of the root morpheme. For example [ sui$^{51}$ ] 水 means "*pretty*," [ sui$^{55}$ sui$^{51}$ ] 水水 means "*very pretty*," and [ sui$^{55}$ sui$^{55}$ sui$^{51}$ ] means "*extremely pretty*." Such a use of reduplication is quite unique to the Min dialects.

In Southern Min, the verb "*to have*" can be used to express verbal aspect similar to the perfective aspect marker -*le* in Mandarin. For example, [ i$^{55}$ u$^{55}$ kʰũã$^{11}$ ] (伊有看, "he have see" → "he saw"). This use of the verb "*to have*" is sometimes used by speakers of the Min dialects when they speak Modern Standard Chinese, although the verb "*to have*" in Modern Standard Chinese cannot be used this way.

In terms of vocabulary, there are more archaisms in the Min dialects compared to other Chinese dialects. For example, in Xiamen the word for "*to walk*" is [ kĩã$^{24}$ ] 行 (Mandarin *xíng*) instead of the Mandarin word *zǒu* 走, and the word for "*cooking vessel*" is [ tĩã$^{51}$ ] 鼎 (Mandarin *dǐng*) instead of *guō* 鍋. Some of these archaic lexical items, for example, 行 as the word for "*to walk*," are shared by other southern dialects such as Yue and Hakka. But many archaic words in Min are unique, for example, 鼎 for "*cooking vessel*." Additionally, gender markers for animals follow nouns in Min, similar to Yue and Hakka. For example, 雞母 ("chicken + female" → "hen") and 牛公 ("ox + male" → "ox").

Probably the most famous Min dialect word that everybody knows is the word "*tea*," which originally came from the dialect of Xiamen, once a major point of contact with Western traders. The word for "*tea*" in Xiamen is [ te$^{24}$ ] in colloquial pronunciation, which is the origin of the word "*tea*" in English and many other European languages, for example, French *thé* and Italian *tè*. The origin of the word "*chaĩ*" in English, many languages in India, and also in Japanese and Korean, is the Mandarin pronunciation of the same word, that is, *chá*. Note that the literary pronunciation of the word "*tea*" in Xiamen is [ ta²⁴ ]. We see that the retroflex initial *ch* in Mandarin corresponds to the alveolar *t* in Min, which represents the older pronunciation. Also, the vowel in the literary pronunciation of this word in Xiamen, that is, "*a*," is more similar to the vowel in Mandarin. In general, the literary pronunciation would be more recent and more similar to Mandarin compared to the colloquial pronunciation.

In terms of vernacular writing, Southern Min also enjoys a long tradition of written culture as well, going back at least to the Qing dynasty, in genres such as songs and opera texts (Snow 2013: 601). Written Southern Min may even be traced back to an opera script titled *The Tale of the Lychee Mirror* (*Lì Jìng Jì* 荔鏡記), dated to 1566 in the Ming dynasty (Dong 2017: 472). In addition to a Chinese character-based writing system for Southern Min, the Church Romanization system, or the POJ system (*Pėh-ōe-jī* 白話字), created in the 19th century by the Presbyterian Church, has also been widely used. One major difference between written Southern Min and other types of written vernacular in Chinese dialects is that written Southern Min has been used in formal writings such as academic essays in Taiwan (Snow 2013: 601). Similarly to how Cantonese is standardized and promoted in Hong Kong, Southern Min has also been standardized and promoted in Taiwan.

## 10.10   Influences of the national language on dialects

In terms of linguistic diversity, China's situation is probably quite comparable to that of Europe. However, as Blum (2005) points out, the linguistic form of nationalism, termed "*linguism*," does not seem to be prominent in China, in that issues with boundaries among different languages and dialects have historically been less contentious in China. Although this is largely true, the promotion of one unified spoken language in ancient China was never effectively carried out, compared to how Modern Standard Chinese has been successfully promoted in all aspects of life in every corner of the country nowadays with the facility of modern technology of communication and travel. For all of the Chinese dialects, there has been a gradual shift of language use among younger generations (Dong 2017: 464). This can be shown in two different but related phenomena.

First, because young people learn the national language at school and use the national language more often, their versions of dialects are noticeably absorbing Mandarin words, grammar, and pronunciations more rapidly than the older generations' dialects. Researchers of Chinese dialects have often pointed out the generational variations in most Chinese dialects, for example, in Taiyuan, Shanghai, and Xiamen, that is, from the north to the south. Although qualitatively, this new wave of Mandarin influence is no different from how non-Mandarin dialects have always adopted certain Mandarin features, for example, as shown in the central division in Norman's (1988) classification, and in the literary pronunciations in southern dialects, the recent Mandarin influence is significant quantitatively.

Second, more and more young people are becoming less fluent in their parents' native dialects. Most young people understand their parents' dialects but would be reluctant to use dialects, due to a combination of their limited proficiency in local varieties of Chinese and a less favorable attitude toward dialects.

To some extent, the diversity of dialects in China is being replaced by convergence toward Modern Standard Chinese. The gradual loss of dialects has led to debates on the current status of dialects, especially those that have historically enjoyed a long tradition of written culture or a regional prestige, such as Shanghainese, Cantonese, and Southern Min. More people are beginning to realize the importance of regional cultural products such as traditional operas, folksongs, pop culture, and films and their connections to regional dialects.

In addition to the official use of the national standard language, there have been new unofficial, informal channels to promote Chinese dialects (Liu 2013; Dong 2017). Therefore, a new kind of balance between the national language and regional varieties of Chinese may need to be established so that linguistic diversity can be maintained at a reasonable level.

## Notes

1 Note that such historical accounts may not be accurate linguistically. As Norman (1988: 222) argued, the linguistic features of Hakka go back to at least the Han and Three Kingdoms period (1st–3rd centuries AD), which is earlier than the Western and Eastern Jin.

2 When dialect pronunciations are given in IPA without brackets, the tone numbers 1–8 represent the register distinctions in the four tones of Middle Chinese, that is, 1 for *yīnpíng*, 2 for *yángpíng*, 3 for *yīnshǎng*, 4 for *yángshǎng*, 5 for *yīnqù*, 6 for *yángqù*, 7 for *yīnrù*, and 8 for *yángrù*. By contrast, when dialect pronunciations are given in IPA with brackets, the tonal numerals indicate the tonal contours.

3 The tonal numerals for dialects described in this chapter are mostly based on the descriptions from *Hànyǔ fāngyīn zì huì* 汉语方音字汇 [*A collection of dialect pronunciations of Chinese characters*], edited by the Department of Chinese Language and Literature, Peking University (北京大学中国语言文学系语言学教研室编). Beijing, China: Wénzì Gǎigé Chūbǎnshè 文字改革出版社 [Script Reform Press], 1962.

4 This is the term used by Norman (1988: 44) to translate "*shéshàngyīn.*"

5 The three *rù* tones are associated with *-p*, *-t*, *-k* codas. Thus, the *rù* tone is not solely a tonal property. Some linguists treat Guangzhou Cantonese as having six tones. The same treatment of the *rù* tone can be done for other dialects that preserve the stop codas, including the glottal stop.

# 11 The Chinese writing system

The study of writing systems, *Wénzìxué* 文字學, is fascinating field of research. In reconstructing the sounds of Old Chinese, we have relied on the phonetic information encoded in Chinese characters in addition to rhyming in the *Shījīng*. This chapter provides a more detailed look at various aspects of the Chinese writing system.

## 11.1  Origin of Chinese characters

The invention of Chinese characters is often attributed to the legendary person *Cāngjié* 倉頡, who lived more than 4000 years ago. Chinese records describe *Cāngjié* as a gifted person with great intelligence and physical features. By observing footmarks left by birds and animals and astronomical signs in the sky, he came up with the idea of writing with distinctive shapes and created many characters as written symbols to distinguish meaning. This story about *Cāngjié* is just a legend in its details, although it is possible that there was indeed a person who was instrumental in systemizing the written symbols invented in a long period of time.

The earliest known system of Chinese characters is the oracle bone script, that is, *jiǎgǔwén* 甲骨文. Its discovery is quite an interesting story as well. There is a type of medicinal ingredient in traditional Chinese medicine called "*dragon bones*," which are fossils of animal bones. They are believed to have calming and sedating functions. In the late 1890s, farmers in Xiaotun Village of Anyang in the Henan province often dug at the site of the ancient capital city of the Shang dynasty from about 3000 years ago. They found animal bones with markings on them. These were sold as medicinal dragon bones. In 1899, a scholar called *Wáng Yìróng* 王懿榮 saw some of these dragon bones in a drugstore and was intrigued by the markings on them. He immediately recognized the connection between these markings and the ancient Chinese characters from the Zhou dynasty that he had been studying. These "*dragon bones*" turned out to be ox bones and turtle shells. The Shang dynasty rulers believed in pyromancy. When there was an important event, the rulers would often order the people in charge of divination to carve the characters of the possible outcomes of the event on a piece of animal bone and heat it over fire. The direction of the cracks on the bone would be used to tell the outcome of the event. After the Shang dynasty, divination by means of fire fell out of practice, and such oracle bones were soon forgotten, although people had probably known the existence of such animal bones from the ancient cite of the Shang capital for a long time before the recognition of the markings as writing. This system of written symbols discovered in 1899 is called the *oracle bone script*, which dates back to around 1200 BC. It is a well-developed system of writing. Thus, it is reasonable to assume that the oracle bone script was the result of a long period of inventing and accumulating written symbols. Archaeology may help us connect the oracle bone script to even earlier systems of writing.

## 11.2 Development of the writing system

The oracle bone script is characterized by sharp and square lines and by shapes that bear a certain degree of resemblance to objects. At about the same time during the Shang dynasty and afterwards, there was the bronze script, that is, *jīnwén* 金文, thus named because characters were inscribed on bronzeware. The bronze script from the early Zhou dynasty and the Spring and Autumn period resembles the oracle bone script in the style of the written lines and their shapes, probably due to the tools and materials used in writing both types of scripts. There may have been more writing done in these early times, but only the oracle bone script and the bronze script have been well preserved to present time thanks to the endurance of the materials used. There are relics of writings on bamboo and wooden slips and occasionally on silk from the Warring States period. The lines and shapes on these materials are smoother and more stylized.

After *Qín Shǐ Huáng* 秦始皇 united China in 221 BC, a series of standardizing measures were taken, and unification of the writing system was one important aspect. Eventually the official script of the Qin Empire was determined to be the small seal script, that is, *xiǎozhuàn* 小篆, based on the earlier large seal script, that is, *dàzhuàn* 大篆. Consequently all the other types of scripts that had been used in different states were abolished. The small seal script has smooth curved lines, and the shapes became more regularized and conventionalized. At about the same time of the appearance of the small seal script, the clerical script, that is, *lìshū* 隸書, was gradually developed to facilitate faster writing, especially for government record-keeping purposes. The clerical script became increasingly popular for general purposes in the Han dynasty, while the small seal script started to be used mostly for more formal types of writing. The clerical script is also characterized by its smooth lines and is much simplified compared to the small seal script.

During the Han dynasty, the cursive script, that is, *cǎoshū* 草書 (literally "grass writing"), gradually developed into a separate style from earlier forms used in faster writing. The cursive script was confined mostly to personal uses such as jotting down something or writing a personal letter. The lines and strokes in the cursive script are more simplified and connected compared to the clerical script. Toward the end of the Eastern Han dynasty, the semi-cursive or running script, that is, *xíngshū* 行書, began to appear based on the styles and shapes of both the clerical script and the cursive script. In terms of the writing style, what we know as the running script today is somewhere between the cursive script and the regular

*Table 11.1* Historical development of Chinese characters

| Word | quǎn "dog" | mù "eye" | zǐ "child" | shuǐ "water" |
|---|---|---|---|---|
| Oracle bone | 犬 | 目 | 子 | 水 |
| Bronze | 犬 | 目 | 子 | 水 |
| Small seal | 犬 | 目 | 子 | 水 |
| Clerical | 犬 | 目 | 子 | 水 |
| Regular | 犬 | 目 | 子 | 水 |
| Running | 犬 | 目 | 子 | 水 |
| Cursive | 犬 | 目 | 子 | 水 |

script, that is, *kǎishū* 楷書, which appeared between the end of the Eastern Han and Three Kingdoms period, but it was not considered a distinctive type of script until the Northern and Southern dynasties (Qiu 2001: 96). The regular script has straight lines and square shapes compared to other types of scripts. In the Tang dynasty, the regular script flourished and since then has been used as the standard script in formal writings, printed books, and so on.

Nowadays the regular script is still the official script by default, but most people use the running script for common writing tasks, such as note taking, personal communication, and writing drafts. The seal script is still widely used on seals and in calligraphy as a form of art. The clerical script is not used in common writing tasks anymore, while the cursive writing is practiced more often as an art form as well.

Table 11.1 shows a few example characters in each script style. By comparing the shape changes vertically, readers can get some general idea of the development of Chinese characters.

## 11.3   Six types of characters in the *liùshū* system

Now let's turn to the topic of the traditional six types of characters, that is, *liùshū* 六書, proposed and discussed in a dictionary called the *Shuō Wén Jiě Zì* (說文解字), composed by *Xǔ Shèn* 許慎 in AD 100 during the Han dynasty. It is the first character dictionary that systematically explained the structures and origins of about 9353 characters.[1] According to the *Shuō Wén Jiě Zì*, Chinese characters can be classified primarily into two categories, that is, the *wén* 文 and the *zì* 字. If a character is a single graphic element which cannot be further analyzed into smaller contributing components, for example, 山 (shān, "mountain"), then it is a *wén*; if a character is composed of multiple elements that contribute to the meaning and pronunciation of the whole character in different ways, then it is a *zì*, for example, 好 (hǎo, "good"). This is why the dictionary itself is titled "*Shuō Wén Jiě Zì*," which literally means "*to talk about the wén and analyze the zì*." Correspondingly, the word for "*writing*" in Chinese is *wénzì* 文字.

In the *Shuō Wén Jiě Zì*, Chinese characters are further classified into six different types: pictograms, ideograms, ideogrammic compounds, rebus, phono-semantic compounds, and derivative cognates, each of which is explained in detail next.

The notion of pictograms, that is, *xiàngxíng* 象形, is self-explanatory. Some examples of pictograms are: 日 (rì, "sun"), 月 (yuè, "moon"), 山 (shān, "mountain"), 人 (rén, "person"), 木 (mù, "tree"), and 田 (tián, "field"). Originally in the oracle bone script, pictogram characters resembled the objects that they represented. But in the regular script, the original shapes could not be readily recognized to make an association between the characters and their meanings. For example, by looking at the character "木," no one without having learned it would be able to guess that it is meant to be a tree. Therefore, although the name of this type is pictogram, such characters are nonetheless not pictures but rather abstract presentations based on original pictorial shapes. Pictograms only account for a small percentage of all Chinese characters.

Ideograms, that is, *zhǐshì* 指事 ("indication"), are typically based on pictograms with extra strokes added to indicate the focus of the meaning. For example, from the character 木, we can derive two characters by adding one line to the top as in 末 (mò, "top of a tree") and to the bottom as in 本 (běn, "root of tree"). The connection between these two characters with the original 木 (mù, "tree") is quite clear. This type of character also accounts for a very small percentage of all Chinese characters.

Ideogrammic compounds, that is, *huìyì* 會意, are best explained via some representative examples. By putting two instances of the character 木 together, we get 林 (lín, "woods"), and by adding one more 木, we get 森 (sēn, "full of trees"). Another commonly used example is 休 (xiū, "rest"), which is composed of the characters 人 (rén, "person") on the left and 木 on the right. A person leaning against a tree is supposed to represent the idea of taking a rest. Note here the character 人 is stylized as 亻 when used as a radical. Thus, an ideogrammic compound character represents a new meaning by combining two characters, each of which contributes to the semantic composition of the compound character.[2] Therefore, such characters are also referred to as semantic-semantic compounds. Characters in this type are comparable to pictograms in terms of their percentage in the inventory of Chinese characters.

Rebus, or borrowing of homophones, that is, *jiǎjiè* 假借, is the most important type of Chinese character, according to DeFrancis (1984). This is the use of a graph for its phonetic value only without regard to the meaning. For example, a series of pictures that correspond to a soda can, a ewe, a sea, and a well in that order, can represent the English sentence "*can you see well?*" The picture of the soda can is used to stand for the sound "*can*" but not the meaning of "*can.*" Similarly in Chinese, the character 又 (yòu, "again") originally was a pictogram that represents the right hand. But the word for "*right hand*" and the word for "*again*" were, and still are, homophones. Therefore, the graph 又 was borrowed for its phonetic value to write the word "*again.*" In many cases, after the original graph was borrowed to write a homophone, a new different graph would be used for the original meaning. In this case, 右 (yòu, "right" as opposed to "left") is used now to write the word for "*right.*" If we know that two characters are related by the concept of rebus, we can deduce that their pronunciations must have been more or less the same originally, even if they are not homophones anymore. For example, the character 來 (lái, "come") was originally a pictogram of the wheat plant. But it was borrowed to write the homophonous word "*to come.*" Then a new character 麥 (mài, "wheat") was created for the original meaning. The pronunciations of these two words are not the same in Modern Standard Chinese, because one has the initial *l*-, the other has the initial *m*-, and they have different tones. If they were homophones, one possibility is that in Old Chinese or even earlier, both the word "*to come*" and the word "*wheat*" were pronounced with a consonant cluster similar to *ml*-. The Old Chinese form of these two words in Baxter-Sagart's system is *\*məˑrˤək*. If the minor syllable "*mə*-" was later dropped, it would eventually develop into *lái*. If the *rˤ*- was deleted, it would eventually develop into *mài*. Although the rebus type of Chinese characters only accounts for about 1% of all Chinese characters, they are the most productive type of written symbols, because the rebus principle is key to the invention of phono-semantic compounds, the most common type of Chinese characters.

A phono-semantic or *xíngshēng* 形聲 character has two primary components: one that indicates the meaning of the whole character, and one which indicates the pronunciation of the whole character. The function of the phonetic component is based on the method of rebus as just discussed. Note that both the semantic and the phonetic connections between the two components and the whole character should be closer at the time the character was created, but in the modern language, there may be problems with both the semantic and the phonetic connections. Let's see two examples that still retain the meaning and sound relations in their modern pronunciations.

The character 清 is composed of 氵 and 青. The water radical 氵 indicates that the whole character 清 is semantically related to water. The graph 青 is used for its phonetic value, which is *qīng* in modern pronunciation, and it indicates that the pronunciation of the whole character should be similar to *qīng*. In this case, the compound character 清 means "*(of water) clear,*" and the pronunciation is *qīng*. But the pronunciation of the phonetic component does not have to be exactly the same as the whole character. This was the original design principle of such characters. For example the character 室 is composed of the semantic part 宀, which is a roof, and a phonetic part 至, which is pronounced as *zhì*. The whole character 室 means "*room*" and is pronounced as "*shì.*" The pronunciations *zhì* and *shì* are similar enough although not the same.

But how similar were they meant to be originally in Old Chinese and earlier times? Chapter 3 discusses phonetic series in terms of *xiéshēngzì* 諧聲字, which is essentially the same as phono-semantic characters, or *xíngshēngzì* 形聲字. When a phonetic series is used to derive the categories of initials and rhymes in Old Chinese, the relevant characters should share certain similarities in terms of their Old Chinese pronunciations. First, characters in a phonetic series should be in the same rhyme group in Old Chinese. Second, their initials should have the same place of articulation. For the character 室 and its phonetic component 至, their phonetic relations in Old Chinese are still retained in Modern Standard Chinese, since they have the same rhyme and their initial consonants have the same place of articulation, that is, retroflex in modern pronunciation, although their Old Chinese forms, that is, *s.ti[t]* for 室 and *ti[t]-s* for 至, were quite different. Thus, sound change has not affected the usefulness of the phonetic cue 至, and it was originally not completely accurate in providing the pronunciation of 室. But it is often the case that in modern pronunciation, the original phonetic connections have not been preserved due to sound change, such as in the character 英 (yīng, "flower"), which is composed of the radical 艹 (meaning "grass") as the semantic component, and 央 *yāng* as the phonetic part. The rhymes of *yīng* and *yāng* have become very different now, although they both have the zero initial. Their Old Chinese pronunciations, *ʔ<r>aŋ* for 英 and *ʔaŋ* 央, were more similar.

Despite the problems with the accuracy of the phonetic cues, the phono-semantic method of creating new characters has been very productive. The percentage of phono-semantic characters in the entire inventory increased from around 30% in Early Old Chinese to 90% in the Tang dynasty (Li 2020: 49). However, among commonly used characters, the percentage is lower (Qiu 2001: 32). Of the 2000 common characters on a list published in 1952, phono-semantic compounds account for 74% (Chen 1999: 135).

There is one more type of Chinese character: derivative cognates, that is, *zhuǎnzhù* 轉注. There are very few such cases. The most often cited example is 老 *lǎo* and 考 *kǎo*. These two characters were originally the same graph, with the same meaning of "*old*" and the same pronunciation.[3] The reconstructed Old Chinese form is *k-rˤuʔ*. Later the character developed in different directions. Their meanings, shapes, and pronunciations all changed until they are hardly recognized as having descended from the same word. The character 老 *lǎo* still means "*old*," while 考 *kǎo* nowadays mostly just mean "*to examine*," although in certain archaic expressions, it retains the original meaning of "*old*."

Clearly, not all of these six types of Chinese characters were derived from original methods of creating new characters. The derivative cognates of the *zhuǎnzhù* type are meant to explain later developments in the writing system. The phono-semantic compounds of the *xíngshēng* type are based on pictograms and the rebus principle. The ideogrammic compounds of the *huìyì* type are based on other characters as well, and the ideographic characters of the *zhǐshì* type often modify a pictogram to indicate a new idea. The rebus uses of characters in the *jiǎjiè* type are not new characters but rather new functions assigned to existing characters. Therefore, strictly speaking, only the pictograms represent the ultimate original method of creating new characters, while extensions based on the functions and forms of these original pictograms can be made in different directions (Li 2020: 46–49). The most important extension is the rebus principle (DeFrancis 1984: 136–140).

In the *Shuō Wén Jiě Zì*, there were 9353 characters and 1163 variant forms. But new characters kept being added, mostly by using the phono-semantic method. For example, in the dictionary called *Jí Yùn* 集韻 from the Northern Song dynasty, there are 53,525 characters, although many of them are variant forms, unofficial popular forms, or rare characters. The total inventory of Chinese characters is so large that no human being can master all of them or keep them in their active vocabulary. But fortunately, in order to read and write, only a much smaller number of Chinese characters are needed. For a Modern Standard Chinese speaker, it is enough to know between 2000 and 3000 characters for most common tasks. For specialized purposes such as the study of ancient texts or history, generally, one needs to know many more characters.

## 11.4   Characters in vernacular writing and dialects

With the development of vernacular writing in the post-classical era, new words needed to be written down with characters.

First, a character can be borrowed to write a new meaning. For example, the Classical Chinese word for "*to eat*" is 食 (Old Chinese: *mə-lək*. Modern Standard Chinese: *shí*), which is still used in many southern dialects, such as Yue and Min. The Modern Standard Chinese word for "*to eat*" is 吃 *chī*. According to the *Shuō Wén Jiě Zì*, "吃" originally means "*to stutter*." This meaning is still preserved in Modern Standard Chinese words such as "*kǒuchī*" (口吃, "to stutter"). In vernacular writing, this character 吃 was borrowed to write the new word for "*to eat*," and consequently the character 吃 is used primarily in its new meaning of "*to eat*," while its original meaning became less commonly used. Sometimes a new character would be created to write down a new word. For example, Chapter 8 mentions the new character 筷 that was created in vernacular writing for the word "*chopsticks*."

Besides the vernacular writing based broadly on Mandarin dialects, various southern dialects developed their own vernacular writing and created new functions for characters or new characters altogether. For the cognate words across different dialects, they are usually written down with the same characters, as long as there is enough etymological evidence thereof. But in many cases, a word in a certain dialect may not have a clear etymological source that can be confirmed by consulting ancient texts and dictionaries. Therefore, a homophone character can be borrowed. For example, the Suzhou Wu word for "*he, she*" is [ li⁴⁴ ] and is written with 俚 (Norman 1988: 77), but the character 俚 was mostly used in the sense of "*vulgar*" in Classical Chinese, as is also shown in the Modern Standard Chinese word *lǐyǔ* (俚語, "slang"). More often for major dialects with a literary tradition such as the Wu and Yue dialects, new dialect characters were created to write down special words in these dialects. For example, the Cantonese word for "*not have*" [ mou²³ ] is written with "冇," contrasting with the word for "*have*"

[ jau²³ ], which is written the etymologically correct character "有." Taking out the two lines inside the character 有 yields the character for "*not have*." But such completely new characters created in certain dialects are relatively few, while most dialectal words can be written down either by borrowing other homophone characters or by using etymologically correct characters.

## 11.5   Simplification of Chinese characters

Chinese characters are often considered the most difficult writing system to learn because of how complex the structures of characters are, especially in the traditional forms, and there are so many of them, too. It seems easy enough to write characters like 一, 人, 山, which have very few strokes and very simple structures, but 龜 has 16 strokes and a very complex structure, while the character 鬱 has 29 strokes, although its structure is actually very simple and clear. Therefore, simplification of Chinese characters has always been a trend in the history of the development of the Chinese writing system. From the oracle bone script and bronze script to clerical script, simplification was already at work. According to the preface of the *Shuō Wén Jiě Zì*, the reason for simplification in the clerical script was due to the increasing need of writing a large number of documents in the imperial governments of the Qin and Han dynasties. Although this view of the appearance of the clerical script is not supported by historical facts, as Qiu (2001) argues, the trend toward simplification is nonetheless a major theme. In the running script and the cursive script, the details of characters were often omitted. Also, for popular uses, some unofficial forms were created during different time periods. But in general, the regular script had not changed or been simplified much ever since its debut in the Northern and Southern dynasties. Note that in addition to simplifying the structural complexity of characters, the total number of characters may also be reduced so that the whole system is further simplified.

Chapter 9 mentions the simplification scheme proposed by *Qián Xuántóng* in the 1920s. The government eventually promulgated a list of 324 simplified characters in 1935, but the policy was repealed after six months (Chen 1999: 153). After the founding of the People's Republic of China, the government took further measures to simplify Chinese characters, adopting *Qián Xuántóng*'s scheme while adding further methods of simplification. In 1956, the *Scheme of Simplifying Chinese Characters* was promulgated in which there were 54 simplified radicals and 515 simplified characters. We describe the main methods of simplification here.

Homophone characters are ubiquitous in the Chinese writing system. Some of these characters in a homophone group are simpler, while others may be more complex. Thus, by adopting the simpler version in a group of homophones, the structural complexity and number of characters can be straightforwardly reduced. For example, the characters 後 and 后 in Classical Chinese are homophones. The character 後 means "*after*," while 后 is the word for "*queen*." In Modern Standard Chinese, these two words are still homophones, both pronounced as *hòu*. Thus, the simpler 后 can be used for both meanings.

Beside homophones, there are also variant forms for many characters, such as 群 and 羣 (qún, "group, herd"). The two components 君 and 羊 are arranged differently in the two versions. Similarly, in the pair 峰 and 峯 (fēng, "mount, peak"), the two components 山 and 夆 are also structured differently. In traditional Chinese texts, the writing order is usually top-down, with characters written in columns. Thus, it is easier to write the version with the vertical arrangement of the components, such as 羣 and 峯. But in Modern Standard Chinese, the writing direction is the same as in English, in left-to-right rows. Thus, 群 and 峰 are more convenient for writing. In the simplified Chinese character system now, 群 and 峰 are used. Other groups of variant forms can be studied, and the options are narrowed down to the most practical versions. This method can reduce the number of characters in use very effectively.

One method that is historically correct is the restoration of original graphs. For example, the character of the word for "*vital energy*," that is, *qì* in Modern Standard Chinese, might have been 气 originally instead of the standard traditional form 氣 with the "*rice*" component 米. In such cases, the earlier simpler form, that is, 气, is selected to replace 氣. In the dictionary *Shuō Wén Jiě Zì*, there are many examples of older simpler forms that were replaced later by more complex characters. The word for "*rites*," that is, *lǐ* in Modern Standard Chinese, is written as 禮 in the traditional form, but the original character is the much simpler 礼, which is now used as a simplified character. Thus, by restoring older simpler forms, we can reduce the number of strokes of certain characters.

Another slightly different example is 云. Originally, this was the correct character for "*cloud*." But later by using the phono-semantic method, the "*rain*" radical 雨 was added to form the standard traditional character 雲 for "*cloud*," because the character 云 was borrowed to write the Classical Chinese word "*to say*," which is "*yún*," as in the phrase "*zǐ yuē shī yún*" (子曰詩云) mentioned at the beginning of Chapter 3. The words "*cloud*" and "*to say*" were homophones, and they still are. But in Modern Standard Chinese, the word "*yún*" as the verb "*to say*" has become obsolete and is only preserved in certain archaic or set expressions. Therefore, the character 云 is restored to write the word "*yún*" for "*cloud*" in the simplified Chinese system, because the verb "*yún*" meaning "*to say*" is not a colloquial word in Modern Standard Chinese anymore.

Alongside traditional characters used as official forms, there have always been simpler unofficial forms that were popular for informal uses. For example, the character 声 *shēng* for the word "*sound*" was originally such an unofficial form, contrasting with the official traditional character 聲. In such cases, the unofficial simpler forms such as 声 can be selected to replace the more complex ones, such as 聲.

Furthermore, since many characters are simplified in the semi-cursive script, the shape in the semi-cursive script can be regularized to derive a simpler character. For example, the character 書 (shū, "book") is written in a simple form in the semi-cursive script with more curved lines and linked strokes, which resembles the simplified character 书, because the simplified form is based on the semi-cursive writing. The radical 言 ("speech"), as in the character 語 (yǔ, "language"), is often written in semi-cursive writing with a form similar to 讠, and by adopting this semi-cursive version in its regularized form 讠 to replace the standard 言, we can batch-convert characters that contain the same radical. For example, 請 → 请 (qǐng, "invite"), 諒 → 谅 (liàng, "forgive"), 記 → 记 (jì, "to write down, to record"). This method is probably the most efficient one for simplifying the structures of Chinese characters.

As mentioned earlier, phono-semantic characters are the largest type in all Chinese characters, and therefore in addition to simplifying the radicals, we may also focus on the phonetic component and choose simpler forms. For example in the character 讓 *ràng*, the right part 襄 *xiāng* is the phonetic component, but it is quite complex. In the simplified character system, the character 上 *shàng* is substituted. Moreover, the radical 言 on the left is also simplified accordingly via regularizing the semi-cursive version of it. Consequently, the character 讓 is simplified to 让. But note that such replacements of the phonetic components are not generalizable in the same fashion as the simplified radicals are. Many characters that share the same phonetic component are not simplified uniformly. The character 嚷 (rǎng, "quarrel") shares the same phonetic component as 讓, but the phonetic component in 嚷 is not replaced by 上. Thus, the character 嚷 is kept unchanged in the simplified system. Another example of replacing the phonetic component in a phono-semantic compound is the character 燈 (dēng, "lamp"), which has 登 *dēng* as its phonetic component. By replacing 登 with 丁 *dīng*, the simplified form 灯 is derived. However, in many other characters, such as 蹬 (dēng, "to step on"), the phonetic component is not replaced by 丁.

In some cases, different phonetic components are replaced by the same placeholder symbol, which does not have any phonetic connection with the pronunciations of the whole characters. For example the character 又 *yòu* replaces the phonetic component 蒦 *guàn* in 歡 *huān* ("happy") to form the simplified 欢 and also the completely different phonetic component 登 *dēng* in 鄧 *dèng* (a surname) to form the simplified 邓. The traditional characters 歡 and 鄧 are both phono-semantic compounds, but because of the non-phonetic placeholder 又, their simplified versions 欢 and 邓 are not phono-semantic compounds anymore.

Additionally, a smaller number of completely new forms were created, for example, the simplified 卫 to replace 衛 (wèi, "defend"), 灶 to replace 竈 (zào, "stove").

Thus, by applying the methods mentioned previously, traditional Chinese characters can be simplified. The initial idea to simplify characters was related to the eradication of illiteracy and to the advancement of modern education, in addition to the ultimate goal of transitioning to a Romanized script such as *pīnyīn* as the primary writing system. The simplification proceeded in stages. The first batch of simplified characters in 1956 was followed by a second batch in 1977 with further simplifications. For example, in the first batch of simplified characters from 1956, the character 嚷 was left unchanged, although the character 讓 was simplified as 让, while in the second batch from 1977, 嚷 was also simplified to 吐.[4] But such further simplified forms as 吐 are not currently in use.

The radically simplified second batch led to various practical, cultural, and aesthetical issues. Due to the oversimplification, many characters became even more similar and created problems for identifying or distinguishing them. Further reducing homophones caused semantic problems with written words. The structures of traditional Chinese characters have been optimized over the thousands of years of development, and consequently simplifying these characters too much would interfere with the aesthetic principles of the writing system. In practical use, the further simplifications in 1977 created a certain degree of chaos when multiple forms of different degrees of simplification were in use, and the conventionalized nature of writing suddenly became quite fluid, which hindered the effectiveness of communication and caused confusion. It was felt that one could even simplify a character according to practical needs, regardless of whether it was standard. Actually, scholars were already against the simplification of Chinese characters of the first batch back in 1956, out of concern for cultural identity and continuity. The further simplification in 1977 was regarded as going too far, and thus it received stronger opposition. In 1986, the second batch of simplified Chinese characters was revoked, and the plan to use a Romanized script to replace Chinese characters was also indefinitely tabled, although *pīnyīn* is still used as a way to annotate the pronunciation of Chinese characters in addition to being a standard system to transcribe Chinese characters for use in other languages. The overly simplified Chinese characters in the second batch are no longer officially supported by the government, but they were in wide circulation and use for almost ten years, and some of these simplified Chinese characters in the second batch are still seen in unofficial uses nowadays.

Meanwhile, traditional Chinese characters have continued to be in use in Taiwan, Hong Kong, and many overseas Chinese communities, although in recent years, Singapore has adopted simplified Chinese characters. Thus, for Chinese speakers, it is practically necessary to be able to read both versions, which actually complicates the situation rather than making it simpler as the original linguistic reformers envisaged. For learners of the Chinese language, the two systems of Chinese characters make it an even more daunting task to study the writing system of Chinese. Currently there are still some debates about the pros and cons of simplifying Chinese characters.

## 11.6   Debates about the nature of Chinese writing

The first question that needs to be answered is how language works in general and how writing is associated with language.

Intuitively, a language is a system of linguistic signs that comprise the signifier and the signified, as in the theory of de Saussure (1983). The signifier is the mental representation of the sound of a word, while the signified is the mental representation of the object denoted by the word, thus corresponding to the meaning of a word in its ordinary sense. The association between the signifier and the signified is largely arbitrary. There is no particular reason the sound "*water*" has to be associated with the meaning of "*water*." Although some words may have a non-arbitrary association between the signifier and the signified, such as onomatopoeic words, these words are very few in the lexicon of any language. By using morphological

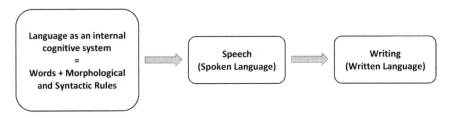

*Figure 11.1* The relation between speech and writing

and syntactic rules, sentences can be constructed out of words. When a speaker utters a word or a sentence, it is the externalization of the internal linguistic system. Such utterances can be written down using written symbols. To some extent, speech is the externalization of language, and writing is the materialization of speech. Historically speaking, language was first only spoken. Writing is a later development. Thus, for linguists, language is primary, and writing is secondary and derivative. In linguistics research, the term "*language*" refers to the spoken language or speech primarily. But in everyday talk, the term "*language*" is used to refer to either "*speech*" or "*writing*." Often people do not even distinguish speech from writing. Figure 11.1 shows the relationship between speech and writing.

But apparently, this view does not quite apply to Chinese straightforwardly, because Chinese characters do not simply record speech sounds. As we have shown in this chapter, there are semantic components in Chinese characters, and the phonetic components are not always accurate or used in a more conventionalized fashion as a fixed set of symbols.

Then what is the nature of Chinese writing? This question turns out to be quite difficult to answer. Debates among scholars can be rather heated. But it is easier to say what Chinese character are not. Obviously, Chinese characters are not silent little pictures of objects. A more sophisticated, albeit incorrect, view is that Chinese writing is ideographic, conveying ideas without regard to speech sounds. This kind of view is called the Ideographic Myth by DeFrancis (1984).

The Ideographic Myth can be traced back to early missionary accounts of Chinese in the 16th century. Many such accounts were not based on linguistic knowledge or facts about the Chinese language. DeFrancis (1984) argued that no fully functional writing system can be ideographic, because ideographic symbols are limited in number and too cumbersome to be used to express anything beyond immediate and concrete ideas. According to DeFrancis (1984), ancient writing systems in the world started with pictograms. The crucial step toward real writing is the use of a symbol exclusively for its phonetic value, that is, the rebus principle. The difference between Chinese characters and other types of writing systems in the world today is that the rebus principle is not used to create fixed symbols to represent fixed sounds in Chinese, because in the phono-semantic compound characters, the phonetic component can vary, and it does not indicate the exact pronunciation of the whole character either. Moreover, according to the fundamental assumption in modern linguistics, all writing is necessarily phonographic, and ideographic writing is impossible. Therefore, DeFrancis (1984) concludes that Chinese writing is basically a phonetic system, although it is not as efficient as a truly phonetic one such as alphabetic writing systems.

To debunk the Ideographic Myth is necessary. For one thing, the ideographic myth of Chinese writing instills the wrong idea about the Chinese language. People would try to look for meaning where there is none. More specifically, the phonetic components in phono-semantic characters usually have nothing to do with the meaning of the whole characters.[5] But if someone assumes that all the components in a Chinese character contribute to its meaning, then incorrect analyses would often ensue. Take the character 洋 (yáng, "ocean") for example. The semantic component is the water radical 氵, and the phonetic component is 羊 (yáng, "sheep"), which clearly does not contribute to the meaning of the word 洋.

But is Chinese writing really just simply a phonetic system? The answer is no. In the *liùshū* system, there are definitely characters that do not fit into any phonetic design, for example, the pictograms, the indication type, and the ideogrammic compounds, although they account for a small number of all Chinese characters. But even in the absolute majority of Chinese characters of the phono-semantic type, at least half of the information is about the meaning of the whole character. Such semantic information is considered very important cues for reading Chinese texts. Thus, there is indeed reason for the claim that Chinese characters are ideographic or logographic.

No consensus has been reached on the nature of the Chinese writing system. But it seems accurate to say that there are both phonetic and ideographic elements in Chinese characters as a hybrid writing system. Together with the previous ten chapters, this chapter concludes our very brief introduction to the history of the Chinese language.

## Notes

1 The earliest dictionary of Chinese characters is the *Ěryǎ* 爾雅, dating to a time period before the 3rd century BC. This dictionary, however, only focuses on the meaning of characters rather than their structural compositions.
2 Some authors dispute the notion of ideogrammic compound characters. See Li (2020: 48) for more discussion and references.
3 Since 老 *lǎo* and 考 *kǎo* were originally the same word, and they have different initials now, that is, "*l-*" and "*k-*," their original pronunciations could have had a consonant cluster similar to "*kl-*." This is also evidence for the existence of consonant clusters in Old Chinese and earlier stages.
4 Note that according to the *Kāngxī Zìdiǎn* 康熙字典, there was an older character, 吐 *màng* or *mǎng*, meaning 問而不答, that is, "to not answer a question." But this older character 吐 probably is not related to the simplified character used for 嚷 in the second batch of 1977.
5 In some instances, the phonetic component doubly functions as an extra semantic component as well.

# References

Baxter, William H. 1992. *A Handbook of Old Chinese Phonology*. Berlin: Mouton de Gruyter.

Baxter, William H. and Sagart, Laurent. 2014. *Old Chinese: A New Reconstruction*. Oxford: Oxford University Press.

Benedict, Paul K. 1972. Sino-Tibetan: A conspectus. In James A. Matisoff (Contributing Ed.), *Princeton-Cambridge Studies in Chinese Linguistics*. Cambridge: Cambridge University Press.

Blum, Susan D. 2005. Nationalism without linguism: Tolerating Chinese variants. In W. Martin Bloomer (Ed.), *The Contest of Language: Before and Beyond Nationalism* (pp. 134–164). Notre Dame, IN: University of Notre Dame Press.

Brindley, Erica F. 2015. *Ancient China and the Yue: Perceptions and Identities on the Southern Frontier, c. 400 BCE–50 CE*. Cambridge: Cambridge University Press.

Campbell, Lyle. 1999. *Historical Linguistics: An Introduction*. Cambridge, MA: The MIT Press.

Chamberlain, James R. 2016. Kra-Dai and the proto-history of South China and Vietnam. *The Journal of the Siam Society* 104: 27–77.

Chang, Kwang-chih. 1986. *The Archeology of Ancient China*. 4th edition. New Haven, CT: Yale University Press.

Chang, Will, Cathcart, Chundra, Hall, David and Garrett, Andrew. 2015. Ancestry-constrained phylogenetic analysis supports the Indo-European steppe hypothesis. *Language* 91(1): 194–244.

Chen, Baoya (陈保亚). 1993. Qiāng Xià – Ào Yuè yǔyán wénhuà liánméng lùn 羌夏–澳越语言文化联盟论 [On the linguistic and cultural area of Qiang-Xia and Austro-Viet]. *Kunming, China: Yúnnán Mínzú Xuéyuàn Xuébào (Zhéxué Shèhuì Kēxué Bǎn)* 云南民族学院学报(哲学社会科学版) [*The Journal of Yunnan Nationalities College (Edition on Philosophy and Social Sciences)*] 3: 75–80.

Chen, Baoya (陈保亚). 1996. *Lùn yǔyán jiēchù yǔ yǔyán liánméng* 论语言接触与语言联盟 [*On Language Contacts and Language Areas*]. Beijing, China: Yǔwén Chūbǎnshè 语文出版社 [Language and Culture Press].

Chen, Ping. 1999. *Modern Chinese: History and Sociolinguistics*. Cambridge: Cambridge University Press.

Chen, Renqiu (陈壬秋). 1995. *Hànyǔ yīnyùnxué gàiyào* 汉语音韵学概要 [*An Overview of Traditional Chinese Phonology*]. Chengdu, China: Sìchuān Dàxué Chūbǎnshè 四川大学出版社 [Sichuan University Press].

Coblin, South W. 1986. *A Sinologist's Handlist of Sino-Tibetan Lexical Comparisons*. Monumenta Serica monograph series 18. Nettetal, West Germany: Steyler Verlag.

DeFrancis, John. 1984. *The Chinese Language: Fact and Fantasy*. Honolulu, HI: The University of Hawai'i Press.

Department of Chinese Language and Literature, Peking University (北京大学中国语言文学系语言学教研室编) (Eds.). 1962. *Hànyǔ fāngyīn zì huì* 汉语方音字汇 [*A Collection of Dialect Pronunciations of Chinese Characters*]. Beijing, China: Wénzì Gǎigé Chūbǎnshè 文字改革出版社 [Script Reform Press].

de Saussure, Ferdinand. 1983. *Course in General Linguistics*. Eds. Charles Bally and Albert Sechehaye. Trans. Roy Harris. La Salle, IL: Open Court.

Dong, Hongyuan. 2017. Language policy, dialect writing and linguistic diversity. In *Proceedings of the 29th North American Conference on Chinese Linguistics* (NACCL 29), Vol. 2 (pp. 463–480). Memphis, TN: University of Memphis.

Dong, Hongyuan. 2018. A semantic analysis of -ne as a topic marker: A grammaticalization perspective. In *Proceedings of the 30th North American Conference on Chinese Linguistics* (NACCL 30), Vol. 2 (pp. 472–489). Columbus, OH: The Ohio State University.

Dong, Hongyuan. 2019. *Semantics of Chinese Questions: An Interface Approach*. The Routledge Studies of Chinese Linguistics Series. New York, NY and Abingdon: Routledge.

Duanmu, San. 2007. *The Phonology of Standard Chinese*. 2nd edition. In *Phonology of the World's Languages*. Oxford: Oxford University Press.

Edmondson, Jerold A. and Solnit, David B. (Eds.). 1988. *Comparative Kadai: Linguistic Studies Beyond Tai*. Summer Institute of Linguistics Publications in Linguistics, no. 86. Arlington, TX: Summer Institute of Linguistics.

Ferguson, Charles A. 1959. Diglossia. *Word* 15(2): 325–340. https://doi.org/10.1080/0043 7956.1959.11659702

Fromkin, Victoria, Rodman, Robert and Hyams, Nina. 2013. *An Introduction to Language*. 10th edition. Boston, MA: Wadsworth, Cengage Learning.

Geng, Zhensheng (耿振生). 2007. Zài tán jìndài guānhuà de "biāozhǔn yīn" 再谈近代官话的标准音 [More on the standard pronunciation of Mandarin in early modern times]. *Gǔ Hànyǔ Yánjiū* 古汉语研究 [*Research in Ancient Chinese Language*] 1: 16–22.

Greenberg, Joseph H. 1963. Some universals of grammar with particular reference to the order of meaningful elements. In Joseph H. Greenberg (Ed.), *Universals of Language* (pp. 40–70). Cambridge, MA: MIT Press.

Haudricourt, André. 1954. De l'origine des tons en viêtnamien [On the origin of tones in Vietnamese]. *Journal Asiatique* 242: 68–82.

Ho, Dah-an. 2016. Such errors could have been avoided – Review of "Old Chinese: A new reconstruction" by William H Baxter and Laurent Sagart. *Journal of Chinese Linguistics* 44(1): 175–230.

Howie, John Marshall. 1974. On the domain of tone in Mandarin. *Phonetica* 30: 129–148.

Hu, Tan (胡坦). 1980. Zàngyǔ (Lāsà huà) de shēngdiào yánjiū 藏语（拉萨话）的声调研究 [Studies on tones in Lhasa Tibetan]. *Mínzú Yǔwén* 民族语文 [*Minority Languages of China*] 1: 22–36.

Huang, Bufan. 1996. Contemporary traces of the verb suffix *-s of Proto-Tibeto-Burman. *Linguistics of the Tibeto-Burman Area* 19(1): 29–42.

Jacques, Guillaume. 2006. *Introduction to Chinese Historical Phonology*. Leiden, The Netherlands: Manuscript.

Jiang, Shaoyu (蒋绍愚). 2005. *Jìndài Hànyǔ gàiyào* 近代汉语概要 [*Outline of Early Modern Chinese*]. Beijing, China: Běijīng Dàxué Chūbǎnshè 北京大学出版 [Peking University Press].

Karlgren, Bernhard. 1915–1926. *Études sur la phonologie chinoise* [*Studies on Chinese Phonology*]. Archives d'études orientales, Vol. 15 (in 4 parts). Leiden: E. J. Brill; Uppsala: K. W. Appelberg.

Karlgren, Bernhard. 1923. *Analytic dictionary of Chinese and Sino-Japanese.* Paris, France: Librairie Orientaliste Paul Geunthner.

Karlgren, Bernhard. 1954. Compendium of phonetics in ancient and archaic Chinese. *Bulletin of the Museum of Far Eastern Antiquities* 26: 211–367.

Li, Charles and Thompson, Sandra. 1981. *Mandarin Chinese: A Functional Reference Grammar.* Berkeley, CA: University of California Press.

Li, Fang-Kuei (李方桂). 1971. Shànggǔyīn yánjiū 上古音研究 [Studies in Old Chinese phonology]. *Qīng Huá Xuébào* 清華學報 [*Tsing Hua Journal of Chinese Studies*], New Series 9: 1–61.

Li, Fang-Kuei (李方桂). 1973. Language and dialects in China. *Journal of Chinese Linguistics* 1(1): 1–13.

Li, Fang-Kuei (李方桂). 1980. *Shànggǔyīn yánjiū* 上古音研究 [*Studies in Old Chinese phonology*]. Beijing, China: Shāngwù Yìnshūguǎn 商务印书馆 [The Commercial Press].

Li, Paul Jen-kuei. 2015. The discovery of Liangdao Man and its implications for the pre-Austronesian homeland. *Journal of Chinese Linguistics* 43(1): 224–231.

Li, Rong (李荣). 1989. Hànyǔ fāngyán de fēnqū 汉语方言的分区 [Classification of Chinese dialects]. *Fāngyán* 方言 [*Dialects* (Journal)] 4: 241–259.

Li, Xinkui (李新魁). 1983. *Zhōngyuán Yīnyùn yīnxì yánjiū* 《中原音韵》音系研究 [*Studies on the Phonological System in the Zhōngyuán Yīnyùn*]. Zhengzhou, China: Zhōngzhōu Shūhuà Shè 中州书画社 [Zhongzhou Press of Calligraphy and Paintings].

Li, Yu. 2020. *The Chinese Writing System in Asia: An Interdisciplinary Approach.* Abingdon, UK: Routledge.

Liu, Jin. 2013. *Signifying the Local: Media Productions Rendered in Local Languages in Mainland China in the New Millennium.* Leiden, The Netherlands: Brill.

Lu, Guoyao (鲁国尧). 1985. Míngdài guānhuà jí qí jīchǔ fāngyán wèntí – Dú "Lì Mǎdòu Zhōngguó zhájì" 明代官话及其基础方言问题 – 读《利玛窦中国札记》[Mandarin of the Ming dynasty and issues with its base dialect: Reading Matteo Ricci's De Christiana expeditione apud Sinas]. *Nánjīng Dàxué Xuébào* 南京大学学报 [*Journal of Nanjing University*] 4: 292–304.

Lü, Shuxiang (吕叔湘). 1984. *Jìndài hànyǔ zhǐdài cí* 近代汉语指代词 [*Pronouns and Demonstratives in Early Modern Chinese*]. Shanghai, China: Xuélín Chūbǎnshè 学林出版社 [Xuelin Press].

Lu, Zhiwei (陆志伟). 1946. *Shì Zhōngyuán Yīnyùn* 释《中原音韻》[An account of the Zhōngyuán Yīnyùn]. *Yānjīng Xuébào* 燕京学報 [*Yenching Journal of Chinese Studies*] 31: 35–70.

Luo, Changpei (罗常培). 1932. Zhōngyuán Yīnyùn shēnglèi kǎo 中原音韻聲類考 [On the initial categories in the Phonology of the Central Plains]. *Guólì Zhōngyāng Yánjiūyuàn Lìshǐ Yǔyán Yánjiūsuǒ Jíkān* 國立中央研究院歷史語言研究所集刊 [*Bulletin of the Institute of History and Philology, Academia Sinica*] 2(4): 423–440.

Luo, Changpei (罗常培). 1958. *Línchuān yīnxì* 临川音系 [*The Phonology of Linchuan Dialect*]. Beijing, China: Kēxué Chūbǎnshè 科学出版社 [Science Publishing House].

Luo, Changpei (罗常培). 2003. *Yǔyán yǔ wénhuà* 语言与文化 [*Language and Culture*]. Beijing, China: Běijīng Chūbǎnshè 北京出版社 [Beijing Publishing House].

Mai, Yun (麦耘) and Zhu, Xiaonong (朱晓农). 2012. Nánjīng fāngyán búshì Míngdài Guānhuà de jīchǔ 南京方言不是明代官话的基础 [The Nanjing dialect was not the base dialect of Ming dynasty Mandarin]. *Yǔyán Kēxué* 语言科学 [*Linguistic Sciences*] 11(4): 337–358.

Mair, Victor. 1991. What Is a Chinese "Dialect/Topolect"? Reflections on Some Key Sino-English Linguistic Terms. *Sino-Platonic Papers*, No. 29.

Mair, Victor. 1994. Buddhism and the rise of the written vernacular in East Asia: The making of national languages. *The Journal of Asian Studies* 53(3): 707–751.

Mao, LuMing Robert. 1994. Beyond politeness theory: "Face" revisited and renewed. *Journal of Pragmatics* 21: 451–486.

Maspero, Henri. 1912. Étude sur la phonétique historique de la langue annamite: les initiales [Studies on the historical phonetics of Annamese: The initials]. *Bulletin de l'École Française d'Extrême-Orient* 12: 1–26.

Mei, Tsu-Lin (梅祖麟). 1970. Tones and prosody in Middle Chinese and the origin of the rising tone. *Harvard Journal of Asiatic Studies* 30: 86–110.

Mei, Tsu-Lin (梅祖麟). 1980. Sìshēng biéyì zhōng de shíjiān céngcì 四声别义中的时间层次 [On the different strata in derivation by tone-change]. *Zhōngguó Yǔwén* 中国语文 [*Studies of the Chinese Language*] 6: 427–433.

Mei, Tsu-Lin (梅祖麟). 1981. Xiàndài Hànyǔ wánchéngmào jùshì hé cíwěi "le" de láiyuán 现代汉语完成貌句式和词尾 "了" 的来源 [On the origin of the perfective construction and the sentence-final particle -le in Modern Chinese]. *Yǔyán Yánjiū* 语言研究 [*Studies in Language and Linguistics*] 1: 65–77.

Mei, Tsu-Lin (梅祖麟). 1989. The causative and denominative functions of the *s- prefix in Old Chinese. In *Proceedings of 2nd International Conference on Sinology: Section on Linguistics and Paleography* (pp. 33–51). Taipei: Academia Sinica.

Mei, Tsu-Lin (梅祖麟). 2012. The causative* s- and nominalizing *-s in Old Chinese and related matters in Proto-Sino-Tibetan. *Language and Linguistics* 13(1): 1–28.

Mihalicek, Vedrana and Wilson, Christin (Eds.). 2011. *Language Files: Materials for an Introduction to Language and Linguistics*. 11th edition. Columbus, OH: The Ohio State University Press.

Ning, Jifu (宁继福). 1985. *Zhōngyuán Yīnyùn biǎo gǎo* 中原音韵表稿 [*A Manuscript of Tables of the Phonology of the Central Plains*]. Changchun, China: Jílín Wénshǐ Chūbǎnshè 吉林文史出版社 [Literature and History Press of Jilin].

Norman, Jerry. 1988. *Chinese*. Cambridge Language Survey series. Cambridge, UK: Cambridge University Press.

Norman, Jerry. 1994. Pharyngealization in early Chinese. *Journal of the American Oriental Society* 114: 397–408.

Ostapirat, Weera. 2000. Proto-Kra. *Linguistics of the Tibeto-Burman Area* 23(1): 1–251.

Ostapirat, Weera. 2005. Kra–Dai and Austronesian: Notes on phonological correspondences and vocabulary distribution. In Laurent Sagart, Roger Blench and Alicia Sanchez-Mazas (Eds.), *The Peopling of East Asia: Putting Together Archaeology, Linguistics and Genetics* (pp. 107–131). London and New York: Routledge-Curzon.

Packard, Jerome. 2000. *The Morphology of Chinese*. Cambridge, UK: Cambridge University Press.

Pan, Wuyuan (潘悟云). 1997. Hóuyīn kǎo 喉音考 [On the origins of guttural sounds]. *Mínzú Yǔwén* 民族语文 [*Minority Languages of China*] 5: 10–24.

Pan, Wuyuan (潘悟云). 2000. *Hànyǔ lìshǐ yīnyùnxué* 汉语历史音韵学 [*Chinese Historical Phonology*]. Shanghai, China: Shànghǎi Jiàoyù Chūbǎnshè 上海教育出版社 [Shanghai Education Press].

Pan, Yunzhong (潘允中). 1989. *Hànyǔ cíhuì shǐ gàiyào* 汉语词汇史概要 [*Outline of the History of the Vocabulary of Chinese*]. Shanghai, China: Shànghǎi Gǔjí Chūbǎnshè 上海古籍出版社 [Ancient Books Press of Shanghai].

Pulleyblank, Edwin G. 1970. Late Middle Chinese, Part I. *Asia Major* 15: 197–239.

Pulleyblank, Edwin G. 1971. Late Middle Chinese, Part II. *Asia Major* 16: 121–166.

Pulleyblank, Edwin G. 1984. *Middle Chinese: A Study in Historical Phonology*. Vancouver, Canada: University of British Columbia Press.

Pulleyblank, Edwin G. 1995. *Outline of Classical Chinese Grammar*. Vancouver, Canada: University of British Columbia Press.

Purnell, Herbert C. 1970. *Toward a Reconstruction of Proto-Miao-Yao*. PhD dissertation, Cornell University, Ithaca, NY.

Qiu, Xigui (裘錫圭). 2001. *Wénzìxué gàiyào* 文字學概要 [*Outline of Studies on Writing Systems*]. Beijing, China: Shāngwù Yìnshūguǎn 商务印书馆 [The Commercial Press].

Ramsey, S. Robert. 1987. *The Languages of China*. Princeton, NJ: Princeton University Press.

Sagart, Laurent. 1993. Chinese and Austronesian: Evidence for a genetic relationship. *Journal of Chinese Linguistics* 21: 1–64.

Sagart, Laurent. 2011. Classifying Chinese dialects/Sinitic languages on shared innovations. Ms. of paper presented at the *Séminaire Sino-Tibétain du CRLAO*, 28 mars 2011.

Sagart, Laurent and Baxter, William H. 2012. Reconstructing the *s- prefix in Old Chinese. *Language and Linguistics* 13: 29–59.

Sagart, Laurent, Jacques, Guillaume, Lai, Yunfan, Ryder, Robin J., Thouzeau, Valentin, Greenhill, Simon J. and List, Johann-Mattis. 2019. Dated language phylogenies shed light on the ancestry of Sino-Tibetan. *Proceedings of the National Academy of Sciences* 116(21): 10317–10322.

Schuessler, Axel. 2007. *ABC Etymological Dictionary of Old Chinese*. Honolulu, HI: University of Hawai'i Press.

Shen, Zhongwei. 2020. *A Phonological History of Chinese*. Cambridge, UK: Cambridge University Press.

Shi, Cunzhi (史存直). 1985. *Hànyǔ yīnyùnxué gāngyào* 汉语音韵学纲要 [*Outline of Chinese Historical Phonology*]. Hefei, China: Ānhuī Jiàoyù Chūbǎnshè 安徽教育出版社 [Anhui Education Publishing House].

Shi, Jianguo (时建国). 2002. Shànggǔ Hànyǔ fùshēngmǔ yánjiū zhōng de cáiliào wèntí 上古汉语复声母研究中的材料问题 [The defects of materials in the study of Ancient Chinese consonant clusters]. *Gǔ Hànyǔ Yánjiū* 古汉语研究 [*Research in Ancient Chinese Language*] 57(2): 8–13.

Snow, Don. 2013. Towards a theory of vernacularisation: Insights from written Chinese vernaculars. *Journal of Multilingual and Multicultural Development* 34(6): 597–610.

Su, Bing, Xiao, Chunjie, Deka, Ranjan, Seielstad, Mark T., Kangwanpong, Daoroong, Xiao, Junhua, Lu, Daru, Underhill, Peter, Cavalli-Sforza, Luca, Chakraborty Ranjit and Jin, Li. 2000. Y chromosome haplotypes reveal prehistorical migrations to the Himalayas. *Human Genetics* 107: 582–590.

Sun, Chaofen. 2006. *Chinese: A Linguistic Introduction*. Cambridge, UK: Cambridge University Press.

Sun, Yuwen (孙玉文). 2002. Hànyǔ lìshǐ yīnyùnxué shànggǔ piān zhǐ wù《汉语历史音韵学上古篇》指误 [Errors in Chinese historical phonology ("The chapter of archaic Chinese")]. *Gǔ Hànyǔ Yánjiū* 古汉语研究 [*Research in Ancient Chinese Language*] 57(4): 13–24.

Swadesh, Morris. 1971. *The Origin and Diversification of Language*. Ed. Joel Sherzer. Chicago: Aldine.

Tang, Zuofan (唐作藩). 2013. *Yīnyùnxué jiàochéng* 音韻學教程 [*A Course in Traditional Chinese Phonology*]. 4th edition. Beijing, China: Běijīng Dàxué Chūbǎnshè 北京大学出版社 [Peking University Press].

Thurgood, Graham. 2002. Vietnamese and tonogenesis: Revising the model and the analysis. *Diachronica* 19(2): 333–363.

van Driem, George. 1999. A new theory on the origin of Chinese. *Bulletin of the Indo-Pacific Prehistory Association* 18: 43–58.

Wang, Li (王力). 1937. Shànggǔ yùnmǔ xìtǒng yánjiū 上古韻母系統研究 [Studies in the system of Old Chinese finals]. *Qīng Huá Xuébào* 清華學報 [*Tsing Hua Journal of Chinese Studies*] 3: 474–539.

Wang, Li (王力). 1958. *Hànyǔ shǐ gǎo* 汉语史稿 [*A Manuscript of the History of the Chinese Language*]. Beijing, China: Kēxué Chūbǎnshè 科学出版社 [Science Publishing House].

Wang, Li. (王力). 1985. *Hànyǔ yǔyīn shǐ* 汉语语音史 [*A History of the Phonology of the Chinese Language*]. Beijing, China: Zhōngguó Shèhuì Kēxué Chūbǎnshè 中国社会科学出版社 [China Social Sciences Press].

Wang, William S.-Y. 1994. Glottochronology, lexicostatistics, and other numerical methods. In *The Encyclopedia of Language and Linguistics*, Vol. 3 (pp. 1445–1450). Oxford, UK: Pergamon.

Wang, William S.-Y. 1998. Three windows on the past. In V. H. Mair (Ed.), *The Bronze Age and Early Iron Age Peoples of Eastern Central Asia* (pp. 508–534). Philadelphia, PA: University of Pennsylvania Museum Publications.

Xiang, Xi (向熹). 1993. *Jiǎnmíng Hànyǔ shǐ* 简明汉语史 [*A Brief History of the Chinese Language*]. Beijing, China: Gāoděng Jiàoyù Chūbǎnshè 高等教育出版社 [Higher Education Press].

Xu, Tongqiang (徐通锵). 1991. *Lìshǐ yǔyánxué* 历史语言学 [*Historical Linguistic*]. Beijing, China: Shāngwù Yìnshūguǎn 商务印书馆 [The Commercial Press].

Yuan, Jiahua (袁家骅) et al. 2001. *Hànyǔ fāngyán gàiyào* 汉语方言概要 [*An Overview of Chinese Dialects*]. 2nd edition. Beijing, China: Yǔwén Chūbǎnshè 语文出版社 [Language and Culture Press].

Zhang, Huiying (张惠英). 1982. Shì "shénme" 释什么 [An explanation on "shénme"]. *Zhōngguó Yǔwén* 中国语文 [*Studies of the Chinese Language*] 4: 302–305.

Zhang, Menghan, Yan, Shi, Pan, Wuyun and Jin, Li. 2019. Phylogenetic evidence for Sino-Tibetan origin in northern China in the Late Neolithic. *Nature* 569(7754): 112–115.

Zhengzhang, Shangfang (郑张尚芳). 1987. Shànggǔ yùnmǔ xìtǒng hé sìděng, jièyīn, shēngdiào de fāyuán wèntí 上古韵母系统和四等、介音、声调的发源问题 [The system of finals in Old Chinese and issues with the origins of the four divisions, medials and tones]. *Wēnzhōu Shīfàn Xuéyuàn Xuébào* 温州师范学院学报 [*The Journal of Wenzhou Normal College*] 4: 67–90.

Zhengzhang, Shangfang (郑张尚芳). 2003. *Shànggǔ yīnxì* 上古音系 [*The Phonological System of Old Chinese*]. Shanghai, China: Shànghǎi Jiàoyù Chūbǎnshè 上海教育出版社 [Shanghai Education Press].

Zhou, Zumo (周祖谟). 1966. Qièyùn de xìngzhì hé tā de yīnxì jīchǔ 切韵的性质和它的音系基础 [On the nature of the Qièyùn and its phonological basis]. In *Wènxué jí* 问学集 [*Collection of Research Explorations*]. Beijing, China: Zhōnghuá Shūjú 中华书局 [Zhonghua Book Company].

# Appendix I

## Major chronological divisions of Chinese history

| | | |
|---|---|---|
| 夏 | Xia dynasty | 21st–16th centuries BC |
| 商 | Shang dynasty | 16th–11th centuries BC |
| 西周 | Western Zhou dynasty | 11th century–771 BC |
| 春秋 | Spring and Autumn period | 770–476 BC |
| 戰國 | Warring States period | 475–221 BC |
| 秦 | Qin dynasty | 221–207 BC |
| 西漢 | Western Han dynasty | 206 BC–AD 24 |
| 東漢 | Eastern Han dynasty | AD 25–220 |
| 三國 | Three Kingdoms | AD 220–265 |
| 西晉 | Western Jin dynasty | AD 265–316 |
| 東晉 | Eastern Jin dynasty | AD 317–420 |
| 南北朝 | Northern and Southern dynasties | AD 420–589 |
| 隋 | Sui dynasty | AD 581–618 |
| 唐 | Tang dynasty | AD 618–907 |
| 五代 | Five Dynasties period | AD 907–960 |
| 北宋 | Northern Song dynasty | AD 960–1127 |
| 南宋 | Southern Song dynasty | AD 1127–1279 |
| 遼 | Liao dynasty | AD 916–1125 |
| 金 | Jin dynasty | AD 1115–1234 |
| 元 | Yuan dynasty | AD 1271–1368 |
| 明 | Ming dynasty | AD 1368–1644 |
| 清 | Qing dynasty | AD 1644–1911 |

Notes:
1 The Eastern Zhou dynasty (770–256 BC) is generally divided into two periods: the Spring and Autumn period and the Warring States period.
2 The Western Zhou dynasty and the Eastern Zhou dynasty together are referred to as the Zhou dynasty (11th century–256 BC).
3 The Western Han dynasty and the Eastern Han dynasty together are referred to as the Han dynasty (206 BC–AD 220).
4 The Western Jin dynasty and the Eastern Jin dynasty together are referred to as the Jin dynasty (AD 265–420), that is, Jìn 晉. This Jin dynasty is not to be confused with the later Jīn dynasty (AD 1115–1234), that is, Jīn 金. These are written with two different characters with different tones.
5 The Northern Song dynasty and the Southern Song dynasty together are referred to as the Song dynasty (AD 960–1279).

# Appendix II

## Articulatory phonetics and International Phonetic Alphabet

Phonetics studies the properties of linguistic sounds. Specifically, articulatory phonetics describes how sounds are uttered in the vocal tract using different configurations of articulators that participate in the utterance of linguistic sounds. Correspondingly, each sound can be represented by a symbol from the International Phonetic Alphabet (IPA for short). Using IPA symbols, we can describe and compare sounds in any human language. Some symbols look familiar, for example, [ b ], [ d ], [ g ]; some are not common. Here we provide a brief introduction to articulatory phonetics and IPA. Only the minimum that is required for a better understanding of chapters in this book is introduced here.

Sounds in human languages can be primarily classified into consonants and vowels. If there is a complete or partial obstruction of air when a sound is uttered, it is considered a consonant. If the vocal tract is open with no or little obstruction of air, the sound can be regarded as a vowel. The most typical consonants include stop or plosive sounds, such as the "*b*" in "*bay*." Typical vowels include sounds like the "*a*" in "*spa*," and so on. Let's discuss the articulatory phonetics of consonants first.

There are four major dimensions in the description of consonants: place of articulation, manner of articulation, voicing, and aspiration. The first two dimensions are the most basic ones.

*Table A2.1* Places of articulation

| Places of articulation | Description | Examples |
|---|---|---|
| bilabial | Uttered with lower and upper lips | *b* "*bay*"<br>*p* "*pay*"<br>*m* "*may*" |
| Labiodental | Uttered with lower lip against upper teeth | *f* "*face*"<br>*v* "*vase*" |
| Dental | Tongue against teeth | *th* "*thigh*"<br>*th* "*thy*" |
| Alveolar | Tongue against the gum area right above the upper teeth | *t* "*too*"<br>*d* "*do*"<br>*n* "*no*"<br>*l* "*low*"<br>*r* "*right*"<br>*s* "*sip*"<br>*z* "*zip*" |

(*Continued*)

*Table A2.1* (Continued)

| Places of articulation | Description | Examples |
|---|---|---|
| Post-alveolar or palatal | Tongue a little further back than alveolar sounds | *sh "show"* *s "measure"* |
| Retroflex | Roll the tip of tongue up against the palatal area | Chinese *"sh"* as in *"shéi"* *("who")* |
| Velar | The back of the tongue raised against the back of palate | *k "kite"* *g "gate"* *ng "sing"* |
| Uvular | The back of the tongue raised against the uvula | Hebrew *q "qol"* for *"voice"* The French *r* as in *"rouge"* |
| Glottal | Uttered at the vocal folds | *h "hide"* For some English speakers: *"tt"* in *"button"* |

*Table A2.2* Manners of articulation

| Manner of articulation | Description | Examples |
|---|---|---|
| Stop or plosive | Total obstruction of air | *p "pie"* *t "tie"* *g "guy"* |
| Nasal | Total obstruction of air in the mouth, but air comes out of the nose | *m "may"* *n "nay"* *ng "sing"* |
| Trill | Relevant articulators, such as the tip of tongue and so on, flap quickly | The Spanish *r "carro"* |
| Tap or flap | A quick tap on the back of the upper gum area or immediately above it | *"dd"* in *"ladder"* *"t"* in *"later"* |
| Fricative | Narrowing of air passage, causing friction | *f "fin"* *th "thin"* *sh "shin"* |
| Affricate | A combination of a stop and a fricative | *ch "chat"* [t+sh] *ts "cats"* [t+s] |
| Approximant | Narrowing of air passage but not causing frication | *r "right"* *j "yes"* |
| Lateral | The center of air passage is blocked, but air can flow out of the sides of the tongue | *l "like"* |

The place of articulation refers to where the obstruction of air occurs. For example, when you say the *b* in *"bay,"* you use your lips to block the airflow first. The major places of articulation are shown in Table A2.1.

The manner of articulation refers to what kind of obstruction of air there is when you utter a consonant. For example, when you pronounce the *b* in *"bay,"* there is a total obstruction of air flow in the vocal tract. But when you pronounce the *f* in *"face,"* there is a narrowing of the vocal tract but air can still pass through. The manners of articulation are shown in Table A2.2.

Now we are ready to combine these two dimensions into one table. The horizontal dimension listed on top of Table A2.3 shows the places of articulation.

Table A2.3 IPA consonant symbols

| | Bilabial | Labio-dental | Dental | Alveolar | Palato-alveolar | Alveolo-palatal | Retroflex | Palatal | Velar | Uvular | Pharyngeal | Glottal |
|---|---|---|---|---|---|---|---|---|---|---|---|---|
| Plosive | p b | | t d | | | t̠ ɖ | ʈ ɖ | c ɟ | k ɡ | q ɢ | | ʔ |
| Nasal | m | ɱ | n | | | ɳ | ɳ | ɲ | ŋ | ɴ | | |
| Trill | ʙ | | r | | | | | | | ʀ | | |
| Tap or flap | | ⱱ | ɾ | | | | ɽ | | | | | |
| Fricative | ɸ β | f v | θ ð | s z | ʃ ʒ | ɕ ʑ | ʂ ʐ | ç ʝ | x ɣ | χ ʁ | ħ ʕ | h ɦ |
| Affricate | | | ts dz | | tʃ dʒ | tɕ dʑ | tʂ dʐ | | | | | |
| Lateral fricative | | | ɬ ɮ | | | | | | | | | |
| Approximant | w | ʋ | ɹ | | | | ɻ | j | ɥ | | | |
| Lateral | | | l | | | | ɭ | ʎ | ʟ | | | |

*Table A2.4* American English consonants[1]

|  | Bilabial | Labio-dental | Inter-dental | Alveolar | Post-alveolar | Palatal | Velar | Glottal |
|---|---|---|---|---|---|---|---|---|
| Plosive | p  b<br>*pay bay* |  |  | t  d<br>*too do* |  |  | k  g<br>*king guy* | ʔ<br>*button* |
| Tap or flap |  |  |  | ɾ<br>*ladder* |  |  |  |  |
| Fricative |  | f  v<br>*face vase* | θ  ð<br>*thigh thy* | s  z<br>*sue zoo* | ʃ  ʒ<br>*shy azure* |  |  | h<br>*how* |
| Affricate |  |  |  |  | tʃ  dʒ<br>*chin gin* |  |  |  |
| Nasal | m<br>*may* |  |  | n<br>*no* |  |  | ŋ<br>*sing* |  |
| Lateral |  |  |  | l<br>*low* |  |  |  |  |
| Approximant | w<br>*water* |  |  | ɹ<br>*right* |  | j<br>*yes* |  |  |

The vertical dimension listed in the first column is the manner of articulation. The combinations are shown in the cells. All the symbols are IPA symbols. Readers can try to figure out how to utter these sounds based on the two dimensions.

In each of the cells, the IPA symbols are aligned either on the left or on the right. Actually, that's the third dimension: voicing. The vocal cords are two thin strips of membrane in the throat. If they vibrate as a sound is produced, the sound is voiced, for example, [ b, d, g, z, v, m, n, l, w, j ] and so on. If the vocal cords do not vibrate as a sound is produced, it is voiceless, for example, [ p, t, k, s, f ] and so on. American English consonants are shown in Table A2.4, using the IPA symbols. Each sound is provided with an example word.

The fourth dimension is aspiration. If a puff of air follows the release of an obstruction, then the consonant is aspirated. Otherwise, it is unaspirated. This can be represented by a superscripted *h*. In fact, we can find such pairs of sounds in English, for example:

| [ pʰ ] vs. [ p ] | as in | *pit* vs. *spit* |
|---|---|---|
| [ tʰ ] vs. [ t ] | as in | *take* vs. *stake* |
| [ kʰ ] vs. [ k ] | as in | *Kate* vs. *skate* |

But since the distinction between aspirated and unaspirated sounds in English is not contrastive, meaning that there is no pair of words that are distinguished only by the difference in aspiration, we can just use one symbol, say "*p*," to represent these two different sounds in English. Then, whether it is aspirated or unaspirated is conditioned on the phonological context. For example, if the letter *p* occurs at the beginning of a monosyllabic word, such as "*pit*," it is aspirated. If the letter *p* occurs after *s*, such as in "*spit*," it is unaspirated. Therefore, we say there is a phoneme / p / in English that has two allophones, [ pʰ ] and [ p ].

In contrast, Modern Standard Chinese uses such a distinction of aspiration as a primary feature that distinguishes between words in a minimal pair such as "*pā*" and "*bā*." Note that the Modern Standard Chinese *pīnyīn* "*b*" is actually a voiceless [ p ]. Thus, the "*p*" in "*pā*" is [ pʰ ] and the "*b*" in "*bā*" is [ p ]. The only distinction between these two words is the aspiration. Therefore, we say that / pʰ / and / p / are two different phonemes in Chinese. Note that generally, IPA symbols are in square brackets, for example, [ p ], but if we need to indicate that a certain sound is a phoneme, we use a pair of slashes, for example, / p /.

Thus, consonants can be described in the four dimensions, for example:

[ s ]    is a voiceless alveolar fricative.
[ b ]    is a voiced bilabial stop.
[ tʃ ]    is a voiceless palato-alveolar affricate.
[ pʰ ]    is an aspirated voiceless bilabial stop.

Consonants are also further grouped into major phonetic classes. Some of the classes of sounds used in this book are listed as follows.[2]

**Obstruents** include non-nasal stops, fricatives, and affricates.
**Sonorants** include nasal stops, laterals, glides, and other approximants. Basically, sonorants are non-obstruents.
**Sibilants** are sounds that have some kind of hissing quality, including fricatives such as [ s, z, ʃ, ʒ, ʂ, ʐ, ɕ, ʑ ], and their corresponding affricates, such as [ ts, dz, tʃ, dʒ, tʂ, dʐ, tɕ, dʑ ].

Consonantal sound change patterns can be described by which feature in the four dimensions has changed. In this book, we focus mostly on how Chinese consonants have changed. Some of the patterns we discuss include:[3]

**Palatalization**: a non-palatal consonant, usually alveolar or velar, changes to a palatal consonant when it is preceded or followed, typically, by a high front vowel such as [ i ] or by a semivowel such as [ j ]. For example: "*I bet you*" > "*I betcha*," where *t* > *tʃ* before the semi-vowel [ j ].
**Affrication**: a stop or a fricative changes to an affricate. This often co-occurs with palatalization, as in the previous example of "*I betcha*," where *t* > *tʃ*.
**Fricativization**: usually an affricate or a stop could change to a fricative. For example, Latin "*pedis*" vs. English "*foot*," in which \*p > f, as in Grimm's Law. This change is also called "**spirantization**."
**Weakening**: this is a general type of change where a stronger sound becomes weaker in various different ways. For example, Sanskrit "*bhrātr̥*" vs. English "*brother*," in which \*bʰ > b, as in Grimm's Law. The voiced aspirates like *bʰ* are stronger than a regular unaspirated voiced *b* in terms of the extra aspiration. This type of change is also called "**lenition**." The change *fricativization* or *spirantization* just mentioned is a typical type of *weakening* or *lenition*.

**Devoicing**: a voiced consonant, usually of the obstruent type, changes to a voiceless one. This often happens word-finally or syllable-finally. For example, the German word "*Tag*," pronounced as "[ ta:k ]," where *-g* > *-t*.

**Intervocalic voicing**: a voiceless sound becomes voiced between vowels. For examples, Latin "*lupus*" vs. Spanish "*lobo*" ("wolf"), where *p* > *b* between vowels. Note that the intervocalic "*b*" in Spanish has further spirantized into [ β ].

Now let's see how vowels can be described. By definition, if there is no obstruction of air stream or very little constriction of the vocal tract, the sound produced is a vowel.

Vowels can be described according to the following three dimensions: vertical position of the tongue, horizontal position of the tongue, and lip-rounding. The four vowels [ i, u, a, ɑ ] as described next and represented in Figure A2.1, can be used as reference points to define all other vowels.

[ i ]   tongue position at highest and frontmost
[ u ]   tongue position at highest and backmost
[ a ]   tongue position at lowest and frontmost
[ ɑ ]   tongue position at lowest and backmost

Front vowels are usually unrounded, meaning that when you utter these vowels, your lips are not rounded. Suppose you are trying to pronounce [ i ] as in the English word "*feet*," but round your lips first without moving your tongue position at all; then you get the rounded version of [ i ], that is, [ y ], which is the *ü* (umlaut) in the German word "*über*," or the French "*u*" in the word "*tu*."

Back vowels are normally rounded, such as [ u ], but if you try to spread your lips when saying [ u ], you get the unrounded version [ ɯ ].

Now if we divide the vertical space into four equidistant levels, that is, high, mid-high, mid-low, and low, and the horizontal space into front, central, and back, then we get a full specification of all possible vowels. Some of the more common ones are represented here in Figure A2.2.

In this figure, there are two sounds at each point in the front and at the back. The first one of each pair is the unrounded version, while the second one of each pair is the rounded version. Table A2.5 shows the vowels in American English, with examples.

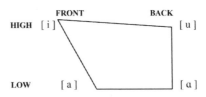

*Figure A2.1* Space of vowels

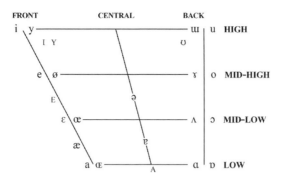

*Figure A2.2*  Vowels in IPA symbols

*Table A2.5*  American English vowels[4]

| | Monophthongs | | | Diphthongs |
|---|---|---|---|---|
| | *Front* | *Central* | *Back* | |
| **High** | [ i ] *feet*<br>[ ɪ ] *fit* | | [ u ] *tool*<br>[ ʊ ] *good* | [ aɪ ] *my*<br>[ aʊ ] *how*<br>[ eɪ ] *day*<br>[ oʊ ] *boat*<br>[ ɔɪ ] *boy* |
| **Mid** | [ ɛ ] *bed* | [ ə ] *about*<br>[ ʌ ] *but* | [ ɔ ] *paw* | |
| **Low** | [ æ ] *tap* | | [ ɑ ] *hot* | |

Now we can use all three dimensions to describe vowels, for example:

[ i ]    is a high front unrounded vowel.
[ y ]    is a high front rounded vowel.
[ o ]    is a mid-high back rounded vowel.
[ ɑ ]    is low back unrounded vowel.

Nasalized vowels are indicated via a tilde on top of the vowel, for example, the French word "*bon*" ("*good*") pronounced as [ bõ ].

## Notes

1  This system is based on Mihalicek and Wilson (2011).
2  These definitions are based on Fromkin et al. (2013: 209–210).
3  These definitions are based on Campbell (1999: 40–46).
4  This system is based on Mihalicek and Wilson (2011).

# Appendix III
## Chinese *pīnyīn* pronunciation guide

The following guide describes the pronunciations of *pīnyīn* letters and combinations in Modern Standard Chinese in comparison to similar sounds in English. Although such comparisons cannot be totally accurate in their exact phonetic values, they can still be useful for readers who wish to know how to pronounce the *pīnyīn* symbols used in this book.

The comparable sounds in English are underlined. Notes are added to address common tendencies to pronounce those letters otherwise. Except for the first table, the other three tables have a column called "extension to other *pīnyīn*." These are combinations that use the listed *pīnyīn* letters as components.

### Initial consonants

The following are similar to English:

> *b* as in "*boy*," *p* as in "*pie*," *m* as in "*my*," *f* as in "*five*."
> *d* as in "*day*," *t* as in "*tea*," *n* as in "*no*," *l* as in "*love*."
> *g* ALWAYS as in "*guy*," *k* as in "*kite*."
> *h* is similar to the "*wh*" in "*who*," but more precisely, the Chinese *h* is a
>   velar fricative like the "*ch*" in the German pronunciation of "*Bach*."
> *s* ALWAYS as in "*say*," *sh* as in "*shy*," *ch* ALWAYS as in "*chat*."

The following consonants are quite different from English:

| Pīnyīn | Approximation | Note |
|---|---|---|
| *j* | *jeep* | Never as the *s* in *measure* |
| *q* | *cheese* | Never as *k* |
| *x* | *sheep* | Not pronounced as *k*-, *z*-, or *ks*- |
| *z* | *cards* | Not the same as *zoo* |
| *c* | *cats* | Never as *k* |
| *zh* | *jar* | Never as *zoo* or *measure* |
| *r* | *measure* | Less strong than the *s* in *measure*; acceptable if pronounced as the English *r* |

## Simple vowels

In the extension to other *pīnyīn*, different spellings of the same sounds are indicated via a slash. For example, "*ia / ya*" means that "*ia*" is spelt as "*ya*" word-initially. Thus, "*ia*" is spelled as such in the syllable "*jia*," but as "*ya*" if there is no initial consonant in front.

| *Pīnyīn* | *Approximation* | *Note* | *Extension to other* pīnyīn |
|---|---|---|---|
| *a* | <u>*ah*</u> | Never as *b<u>a</u>ck* or *b<u>ay</u>* | *ia / ya, ua / wa* |
| *o* | *p<u>aw</u>* | Never as *kn<u>ow</u>* | *uo / wo* |
| *e* | *<u>ugh</u>, <u>uh</u>, d<u>uh</u>* | More tense, never as in *b<u>ay</u>, b<u>e</u>d*, and so on | *ie / ye*, but pronounced as in "*y<u>e</u>s*" |
| | | | *üe*, but the *e* is pronounced as "*y<u>e</u>s*" |
| | | | *ue / yue*, but the *e* is as in "*y<u>e</u>s*" |
| | | | The letters *ü, u, yu* in these combinations are all pronounced as *ü* (umlaut) |
| *i* | *L<u>ee</u>* | More tense, never as in *<u>i</u>t* | *ui / wei*, but pronounced as in "*w<u>ai</u>t*" |
| *u* | *t<u>oo</u>l* | More tense, never as *p<u>u</u>t* | *iu / you*, but as "*ee-oh*" |
| *ü* or *u* after *j/q/x/y* | No English equivalent. Same as German *<u>übe</u>r* and French *t<u>u</u>* | Never as "*y<u>ou</u>*" | *üe*, but the *e* is pronounced as "*y<u>e</u>s*" |
| | | | *ue / yue*, but the *e* is as in "*y<u>e</u>s*" |
| *i* after *z/c/s* | The *i* sounds like a prolonged *z*, that is, *zzzzz* | Never as "*ee*" | To pronounce the syllables *zi, ci*, and *si*, just prolong the initial consonants *z, c*, and *s*. Do not add any vowel after them |
| *i* after *zh/ch/ sh/r* | The *i* sounds like a prolonged "*zh*" sound such as the *s* in "*mea<u>s</u>ure*" | Never as "*ee*" | To pronounce the syllables *zhi, chi, shi*, and *ri*, just prolong the initial consonants *zh, ch, sh*, and *r*. Do not add any vowel after them |

## Compound vowels

| *Pīnyīn* | *Approximation* | *Extension to other* pīnyīn |
|---|---|---|
| *ai* | *<u>I</u>* | *uai / wai* |
| *ei* | *h<u>ay</u>* | *wei* |
| *ao* | *<u>ou</u>ch* | *iao / yao* |
| *ou* | *<u>oh</u>* | *pīnyīn "you"* sounds like *"ee-oh"* |

## Rhotic and nasal finals

| Pīnyīn | Approximation | Note | Extension to other pīnyīn |
|---|---|---|---|
| er | *are* | Sometimes pronounced as "err" | |
| an | *ah-n* | Never as in *ant* | *uan / wan*<br>*ian / yan*<br>*üan*, spelled as "*uan*" after *j/q/x/y*<br>Also, the *ü* and *u* in these spellings are pronounced like the German *ü* |
| ang | *ah-ng* | Never as in *sang* | *uang / wang*<br>*iang / yang* |
| en | *uh-n, deepen* | Never as *enter* | |
| eng | *uh-ng* | Never as *ginseng* | *weng* |
| in | *been* | More tense, never as *in* | |
| ing | *ee-ng* | More tense, never as *bing* | |
| un | *oo-n* | More tense than *tool* | *wen* is pronounced as *oo-uh-n*, but NOT as "*when*" |
| un after *j/q/x/y* | *ee-oo-n* | The letter *u* here is actually the *ü* | *yun* |
| ong | *oo-ng* | The *o* is never as in *hot* | |
| iong | *ee-oo-ng* | The letters "*io*" should be pronounced as the *ü* | *yong* |

## Tones

1st tone: high flat. Sing the note G and prolong it.

2nd tone: rising, as if asking a question, as in "*yes?*"

3rd tone: low dip and rise. Lower your voice as much as you can, and keep the shape relatively flat. Do not emphasize the contour, especially the rising part.

4th tone: high falling, as if confirming something, for example, "*yes!*"

# Appendix IV
## Correspondence charts of *pīnyīn* and International Phonetic Alphabet symbols

The correspondences here are based on Chen (1999: 35) with modifications.

**Modern Standard Chinese Initials**

| Pīnyīn | IPA | Pīnyīn | IPA |
|--------|-----|--------|-----|
| b | [ p ] | j | [ tɕ ] |
| p | [ pʰ ] | q | [ tɕʰ ] |
| m | [ m ] | x | [ ɕ ] |
| f | [ f ] | z | [ ts ] |
| d | [ t ] | c | [ tsʰ ] |
| t | [ tʰ ] | s | [ s ] |
| n | [ n ] | zh | [ tʂ ] |
| l | [ l ] | ch | [ tʂʰ ] |
| g | [ k ] | sh | [ ʂ ] |
| k | [ kʰ ] | r | [ ɻ ] |
| h | [ x ] | zero initial | |

**Modern Standard Chinese Finals**

| No Medial 開口呼 | [ i ] series 齊齒呼 | [ u ] series 合口呼 | [ y ] series 撮口呼 |
|------------------|---------------------|---------------------|---------------------|
| i [ ɿ ]¹ or [ ʅ ]² | i [ i ] | u [ u ] | ü [ y ]³ |
| a [ a ] | ia [ ia ] | ua [ ua ] | |
| o [ o ] | | uo [ uo ] | |
| e [ ɤ ] | ie [ iɛ ] | | üe [ yɛ ] |
| er [ ɚ ] | | | |
| ai [ ai ] | | uai [ uai ] | |
| ei [ ei ] | | ui [ uei ] | |
| ao [ au ] | iao [ iau ] | | |
| ou [ ou ] | iu [ iou ] | | |
| an [ an ] | ian [ ian ] | uan [ uan ] | üan [ yan ]⁴ |
| en [ ən ] | in [ in ] | un [ un ] | ün [ yn ]⁵ |
| ang [ aŋ ] | iang [ iaŋ ] | uang [ uaŋ ] | |
| eng [ əŋ ] | ing [ iŋ ] | ueng [ uəŋ ]⁶ | iong [ yŋ ] |
| | | ong [ uŋ ] | |

## Notes

1 This is the apical vowel after alveolar sibilants in syllables like *zi*, *ci*, and *si*.
2 This is the apical vowel after retroflex initials in syllables like *zhi*, *chi*, *shi*, and *ri*.
3 In general, the two dots in this letter are omitted whenever it is preceded by *j-*, *q-*, *x-*, or *y-*, for example, *ju*, *jue*, *jun*, *juan*.
4 This final is used in syllables such as *juan*, *quan*, *xuan*, *yuan* with the two dots omitted.
5 This final is used in syllables such as *jun*, *qun*, *xun*, *yun* with the two dots omitted.
6 This final is always a syllable by itself. Thus, it is always written as "*weng*" in actual spelling.

# Index

Note: page numbers in **bold** indicate tables on the corresponding pages.

Printed in Great Britain
by Amazon

56302006R10137